**Stripe
Press**

Ideas for progress
South San Francisco, California
press.stripe.com

Scaling People

Tactics for Management and Company Building

Claire Hughes Johnson

For my family.

Scaling People: Tactics for Management and
Company Building
© 2022 Claire Hughes Johnson

Published in the United States of America
by Stripe Press / Stripe Matter Inc.

Stripe Press
Ideas for progress
South San Francisco, California
press.stripe.com

Printed by Hemlock in Canada

ISBN: 978-1-953953-21-6
Library of Congress Control Number: 2022944483
First Edition

Table of Contents

Introduction

In July 2004, I found myself in a windowless—but somehow still coveted—office at Google, standing in front of a whiteboard with a green dry-erase marker in one hand and a blue marker in the other. In front of me were the two categories I was using to list the members and start dates of the Gmail user support team, which I managed: ANS (accepted not started) and BIS (butts in seats). Yes, these are actual standard company recruiting terms. At that time, I had no support from finance, and the only people-related function that was humming along was recruiting. But even in recruiting, no one could agree on how many people I should have on my team. It wasn't a very big team, but we still dithered over how many slots I had open for new hires. Was it two? Three?

Truth be told, I didn't mind the challenge all that much. In fact, I'd chosen it. When I joined Google, I was given two options: Be one of the many managers for the AdWords online sales team, or take on the fledgling Gmail product support team. In my mind, AdWords was already a big operation—a laughable assessment in retrospect, since it was just a few hundred people at the time. Today, it's tens of thousands of people strong. So I chose Gmail. Better to be the only one doing that job and chart my own course, I thought. Plus, as a user, I loved Gmail.

It turned out that managing Gmail's growth from its beta phase to a generally available product was rocky, both technically and in terms of customer experience. Internally, Google was growing and changing so quickly that it was hard to get data about basically anything other than product usage. That's how I ended up at the whiteboard, scribbling names in two colors. Then I'd copy the numbers into an email that I'd send to finance and HR in order to account for all of my people and make sure I didn't lose access to recruiting resources. It was a messy, jerry-rigged process, but I loved the chaos and ambiguity, and I knew enough to focus on organizing my little corner of the company instead of trying to organize everyone else's, too.

But I also worried. "These are *people*," I thought as I copied the numbers and sent them off, "and we can't even track about 15 of them." My job was to scale the operation, which involved technology, of course, but also the people—these people!—who were building it. I firmly believed that doing so should not come at the cost of knowing the humans behind the product and fostering their careers—their personal scaling—alongside Google's. Almost 20 years later, I believe that even more strongly. That's why I wrote this book.

The path that led me to that windowless office at Google began not in Silicon Valley but with a state gubernatorial campaign in Massachusetts. It was 1994 and the candidate was widely known to be unlikely to win, which meant that I, a 21-year-old fresh out of college, didn't have much trouble working my way into the deputy communications director role. I think I made about 5¢ an hour and worked 70 hours a week. Following side forays into publishing and magazine writing, I was recruited to run a state senate campaign in 1996. It was a seven-days-a-week job that involved coordinating hundreds of volunteers and personally delivering lawn signs across several towns. Although we lost, my reputation for hard work and versatility—you have to play every role when you're the only full-time employee—earned me a spot as a deputy campaign manager for yet another gubernatorial campaign. And this time, the candidate stood a chance of winning.

When I first joined the campaign, I wrote a memo on campaign strategy that made its way to the candidate, who circulated it to his team and promptly invited me to a key planning meeting. At that meeting, the candidate's pollster, a well-known Massachusetts institution unto himself, walked in and thundered, "Who's the asshole who wrote that memo?" It was an interesting start for my ambitious self. We worked 18-hour days, except some Sundays, for well over a year. I was 26 and managing three or four different teams with the help of about five other people, and I coordinated hundreds of volunteers who showed up—or didn't!—on nights and weekends. We lost a very close election, but I left with a whole lot of practice in management.

After being accepted to law school and deciding not to attend for three years in a row—read one's own signals much?—I instead applied to and attended business school. After graduating, I cut my teeth in management basics while working for a business and technical consulting firm in New York City. Thanks and no thanks to the economic downturn of the early 2000s, I ended up being one of the only people remaining after a company layoff and found myself as the project leader for a massive customer relationship and data strategy project for Dow Jones. When the project ended, I realized it was time to leave consulting and find my career. Since I've consistently been a bit of a risk-taker on the career front, in 2004 I moved with my then boyfriend, now husband, to California. Neither of us had a job. I loved Google's products, and through a business school friend's connection, I interviewed and received an offer to join the company. It had fewer than 2,000 people at the time, but it proceeded to grow at an incredible pace—as did my responsibilities.

By the time I left, almost 11 years later, Google had over 50,000 employees. I had been promoted five times by my seventh year. I had managed various groups in support, sales, engineering, product, and even industrial design across as many as 16 countries. I had led divisions ranging from a few hundred to over 2,000 employees. The variety and the speed at which things changed meant I worked with a lot of different teams and managed a lot of different people. At one time, I was selected to integrate operations when Google acquired YouTube. At another, I held an $11 billion sales quota. Still, I was often solving similar problems across the varying personalities, functions, and divisions I dealt with. I tested out new methods, made mistakes, learned from them, and tried again.

Among the roles I took on was VP and business lead of Google's self-driving car project. In early 2013, Chris Urmson, its head, gave me a call to ask if I would consider joining the group to help run the business and product side. I had no experience building hardware, I didn't have a background in machine learning, and I didn't know much about cars. But Chris kept pushing, and it became clear to me that there was something I could bring to the table. The group was filled with brilliant engineers whose lunch conversations sounded like they were straight out of *2001: A Space Odyssey*, but the team also needed to manage supply chains, perform complex operational testing, coordinate across teams building hardware and software, run planning processes, and motivate team members. Plus, they had to work with Google's leadership to set the vision for both the team and the ultimate business that might emerge from what was then primarily an R&D project. In short, what Chris needed was an experienced operator and manager—a COO, in today's parlance. I joined the team and spent the next 10 months setting up the structures, teams, and direction to help move Google's self-driving division forward. Unfortunately, this story does not end with all of us zipping around in our own autonomous, AI-powered vehicles, but that's a tale for another book.

This experience did, however, underscore two important lessons for me. First, I got the job because I had built a reputation as a great manager, and being a great manager can be a significant career differentiator. Second, no matter how brilliant a company is, it will not get far, let alone have an impact at scale, without strong management and sound operating systems—what you might call core processes. Over time, my experience made me a person many founders consult on the combination of these two elements.

A few years ago, I was giving a talk at a 40-person startup. During the Q&A, someone asked what processes I thought the company should put in place. My answer was "I'm not going to tell you which processes you should put in place. But I will tell you that you need them, and you need them sooner than you realize." When the person asked why, I said, "You know why playing a game is fun? Because it has rules, and you have a way to win. Picture a bunch of people showing up at an athletic field with random equipment and no rules. Someone is going to get hurt. You don't know how to play, you don't know how to score, and you don't know how to win." It's critical for companies and teams to establish the playing field on which everyone participates and marks progress.

When I joined Gmail, I inherited a talented associate manager as a direct report. After working together for several months, she remarked to me, "What I think you've taught me most is how important it is to state the obvious." Yes, it felt like a backhanded compliment. But what I think she meant is that I strive to make implicit structures and beliefs explicit. Making those elements clear to everyone allows a group of people to become a true team and a company to scale. Perhaps because of those abilities, and certainly due to Google's success, in the second half of my career there I wound up on a kind of underground list of COO candidates for growth-stage startups. I came quite close several times to leaving for such a role, but each time it felt more like I was running away from frustrations at Google after a long tenure than like I was running toward the right opportunity for my combination of skills, mission orientation, and desire to find the mix of founders and business model that I felt could match or exceed the very high impact bar Google had had in its first decade.

Then came the self-driving car position. It was an excellent chance to try a COO-like role, but after making a few operational hires and setting up the mechanisms to run the team and manage the roadmap, I realized I missed having a live product and, most of all, customers. I had also become enamored with a small company called Stripe. The company's mission and founders attracted me, but most of all, it offered the chance to build again, and to scale the type of product that I thought could positively impact millions of businesses—and, in doing so, potentially create millions of jobs. This has been a motivation of mine since I first worked in politics, where I saw how economic opportunity is the real engine that levels the proverbial playing field.

I left Google in late 2014 to join Stripe as chief operating officer. At the time, Stripe had tens of millions in revenue and about 160 employees, of whom only 20 were managers, most of them newly promoted. Today, Stripe has billions in revenue and is growing quickly beyond 7,000 employees.

People often ask me what surprised me when I joined Stripe. It wasn't the people or the product—both the founders and I had done our mutual due diligence, and I felt very much steeped in Stripe's product, business, and priorities. It was that management appeared to be a new concept to the company. When we sent out our first StripeSat—our internal employee engagement survey—in May 2015, satisfaction with team-level management was among our lowest-scoring areas. We had promoted a lot of people into management internally, which is an effective way to reward high performers and build company scaffolding, but we hadn't invested enough in giving people the resources and the support they needed to be the most effective managers they could be. After that, we worked hard to help managers improve their skills. Just a few years later, satisfaction with team-level management became one of the top three highest-scoring categories on the survey. It's stayed in that position ever since.

When you hire senior leaders into a young company, they can have a disproportionate impact, positive or negative, on your organization. (This book aims for the positive!) I would venture that one of my most positive impacts was my strong belief in good management.

I also think of joining Stripe as the point in my career when I finally grew from being a strong manager into a true leader—a distinction I'll cover later in this book—while helping to build a great company. I'm proud to say that I avoided some of the mistakes I think we made at Google, but I'll also admit that I'm sure I made new ones. That's the reality of working at a fast pace. There's much I'm proud of, and much I would have done differently if only I could bend the space-time continuum.

I'm still lucky enough to be sought out for advice by founders and leaders who are scaling companies—even more so now thanks to Stripe's success. In fact, my 2021 transition from Stripe's COO to a downshifted, part-time role as a corporate officer and adviser (an appropriately amorphous title!) was in part so that I could spend more time providing advice to founders of companies beyond Stripe, many of them Stripe customers. This book is designed to share some of that advice with anyone and everyone who might be interested in it—to help ensure others can manage growth without having to stare at numbers in spreadsheets or at whiteboards that stand in for relationships with the people they represent. It covers how to create and embed the systems that help build a company you can be proud of—and, more importantly, how to do so in ways that inspire just as much pride in the people who work there. Done right, the company and the culture will evolve, but the center will always hold.

Setting your metronome

I've seen what great management can accomplish, particularly when a company is growing rapidly. On a practical level, teams with strong management will deliver more—and better—work, which any scaling company needs. On a more personal level, a great manager can change someone's trajectory. They can push employees to make career choices that leave them much more fulfilled. They can coach their people through balancing a tough personal situation with work commitments. By doing this, a great manager can help their people make a more meaningful impact, integrating all that personal development with the development of the company as a whole. The role is both operational and managerial. To have a job that focuses on just one of these elements—delivering business results or producing personal impact—is already a big task. But to work in a job that does both? There's a lot riding on those responsibilities, and meaningful rewards when they're done right.

You can always spot a great manager by the strength of their team. A top-level manager builds a fanatical followership. When they move to a new company, old reports will leave their jobs to join the manager there. Their organization delivers results, their teams perform better, and employees perform better on their teams.

The hardest parts of company building and management are done in private: designing your planning process, deciding who gets promoted, planning a reorganization, reducing the scope of a person's role. But how can you develop your own building and management techniques when you haven't experienced enough similar scenarios to build pattern recognition? How can you test new approaches when each conversation has such high stakes? You can't sit in on another manager's 1:1s. You don't get to observe how your colleague handled that termination conversation. You're not privy to how your peers give their reports difficult feedback. You're asked to fly a very complicated aircraft, but you never get time in the practice simulator.

What you can begin with is some fundamental structure. The concept of management structure has existed for thousands of years, and—aside from some industry forays into a decentralized approach called holacracy[1]—I believe it's because management structures work. They create connections that encourage individual accountability for outcomes and allow for scale. But how do you get really good at that work?

In the 1960s, two psychologists, Paul Fitts and Michael Posner, set out to understand human performance, especially the acquisition of new skills. One of their best-known frameworks came from their examination of a series of studies of

[1]

holacracy.org.

people learning to touch-type.[2] At first, typists' skills improved quickly as they graduated from single-finger pecking to using two hands, and eventually to gliding across the keyboard without even looking at it. But then they hit a wall. No matter how many more hours they practiced, most typists didn't get faster beyond a certain point. This was surprising, because Fitts and Posner expected the typists' skills to continue improving the more they practiced.

Fitts and Posner described their skills acquisition observations in three stages. The first is the "cognitive" phase, in which a person starts off slowly and clumsily as they familiarize themselves with a task and discover new ways to accomplish it. The second is the "associative" phase, in which the person becomes more efficient and makes fewer errors. The last is the "autonomous" phase, in which they complete the task reasonably well without thinking about it. The typists were all plateauing in this last phase, unable to make further progress.

Building on this work years later, psychology professors K. Anders Ericsson and Nina Keith conducted a study of intermediate-level typists in which they found that the ones who improved the most were those who dedicated themselves to a frequent practice of typing quickly.[3] I first read about this insight in Joshua Foer's book *Moonwalking with Einstein*, where it serves as a supporting story for Foer's own work with Ericsson to improve his memorization skills.[4] He recounts that Ericsson advised him to buy a metronome and then set it 10–20 percent faster than his current memorization limit. This led to more errors, but Ericsson advised him to forge ahead. Soon enough, Foer had pushed through the memorization plateau he had hit.

psycnet.apa.org

Additional research has found that people who outperform in their fields employ strategies that move them past the autonomous stage of learning, like athletes who use speed workouts to improve their performance.[5] In other words, to make a breakthrough performance improvement during the autonomous stage, you need to set an uncomfortable pace for yourself. Kind of sounds like the pace of a company that's growing rapidly, building its support systems as it goes, right? By taking a series of jobs at high-growth companies that needed to establish both management practices and operational structures, that's exactly what I've done. It's led me to a set of essential structures that I believe are a great starting point for anyone looking to become

journalofexpertise.com

not just a good manager but a great one, and to help build a high-impact company in the process.

The core frameworks

Company-wide frameworks are indicators of your company's priorities. Think of them as the set of actions or processes that everyone must perform or follow in concert and in the same way. The Mandalorian mantra "This is the way" comes to mind. It's my belief that the most successful and enduring companies foster strong internal adherence to their core frameworks. This was recently reinforced when I read *Working Backwards* by Colin Bryar and Bill Carr.[6] The book discusses the combination of core frameworks, such as hiring and planning practices, and underlying leadership principles, like customer obsession, that the authors view—rightly, I think—as key to Amazon's success: the Amazon Way. Taken together, a company's core frameworks form an architecture that keeps systems consistent and running smoothly so that people can do their best work.

Unless you're running a process- and production-oriented business, like a manufacturing company, there are only a small number of frameworks that I think should apply to everyone. There are massive coordination costs to company-wide processes, and if you impose too many, chances are your employees and managers will devote their time and headspace to following your processes instead of developing new ideas and getting work done. The benefits of uniformity must also outweigh the benefits of variability, and there aren't too many structures that, when standardized, benefit the entire company.

I believe core, company-wide frameworks should apply in the following areas, each of which has its own chapter in the pages to come:

1. Foundations and planning for goals and resources
2. A comprehensive hiring approach
3. Intentional team development
4. Feedback and performance mechanisms

Depending on your business, there is also likely a set of cross-company or cross-team day-to-day activities that should be standardized. At Stripe, for example, we have a standard approach for product launches because they require coordination across many different teams. These launches are incredibly important, and we want to make sure we get them right. But, again, these standardized processes should be limited, and leaders should take a critical eye toward what they mandate across their company.

However, processes—and by now I think you can tell how much I believe in them—can't do all the work. You need people for that. And for people to do their best work, you need a management style that encourages them to show up as fully as possible. I believe that most people don't neatly compartmentalize their home and work lives. In the right environment, they are open and trusting enough to share the celebrations and challenges in all aspects of their lives. I always like to know what's going on with people personally, their hopes and ambitions for their whole existence, not just their work. That way I can see the entire picture, and how that picture fits into a team, a division, and the company as a whole. If something good happens, taking time to celebrate it reinforces the value of remembering that each of us has a life that we're equally devoted to outside of the office and that the experience we gain there is a part of who we are. If something difficult is going on, I like to know so that I can be there to support the person, and the team too.

This multidimensional knowledge also helps when you need to assess whether the people you're managing have the potential to keep scaling. I once worked with an HR partner who described a talent evaluation approach he learned when working at Dell, which he called "scaling to the call"—meaning that as a company grows, the individuals within it are called to lead in larger and more complex roles. Even if a person's job hasn't changed, the scope of it has, and the individual must "scale to the call" to maintain their performance and produce results. I like the idea of being called to action and rising to the challenge. As I think about each person behind the work the company requires, I ask myself: Can they scale to the call? Developing an intuition for whether they can, and for how you might help the person rise to the next level, is as critical to scale as the company frameworks themselves.

In 2013, I joined the board of Hallmark, which mystified many of my friends and colleagues in tech. I asked them to name a few companies that had been around for over 100 years. Not many could name more than one. Hallmark was founded in 1910. Most people know it as a greeting card company, but it's also a media company (Crown Media) and a manufacturing company (in addition to making cards and ornaments, it owns Crayola). Beyond all that, though, it has consistently been one of the most progressive companies in the world when it comes to programs that care for its people not just as employees but as human beings. Why would I *not* want to join the board of a company that embodies all of the elements I believe create an enduring business: a strong mission, clear structures, execution-focused leaders, and people-centric practices? What else is company building for if not to create an organization that lasts?

Who is this book for?

This book is for company builders who value creating a long-term legacy and share a people-oriented viewpoint on the work they're doing. It's a guide to managing well while you build, particularly for practitioners whose management lives are becoming more complicated. Perhaps you've started managing multiple teams or coaching managers of managers. You may be leading employees in a geographic region that's different from your own. Or you're at a fast-growing company where change is happening rapidly and you don't have the time to develop some of the harder management skills, like adding a new leader and layering a team, or asking someone to leave who helped you get from point A to point B but doesn't have the skills to help you get to point C. I also hope this book is useful for founders and founding teams of new companies. Founders have the most difficult management jobs, especially because many of them learn the job for the first time while their companies are growing at breakneck pace.

For the most part, I won't be covering the basics of management. There isn't a section on making sure you have regular 1:1s with your direct reports (but you should!). There *are* sections on how to have difficult conversations in those 1:1s. The basics are, obviously, still very important, so while I won't go into detail on the requirements, I've included a checklist of management work at the end of this chapter to help you ensure you have those bases covered. If you can tick off all the items on this checklist, you're ready to start this book.

How to read this book

Scaling People provides you with tools to help you build solid company structures and navigate all kinds of management situations. It's based on years of practicing management at an accelerated pace, talking to other practitioners, and learning from many great managers, including peers, direct reports, and my direct managers, plus a few leadership coaches. I've structured the writing so that when you're confronted with a hard management situation, you can look up the topic at hand and find practitioners' advice and real-life stories. This is not a book that's meant to be read once from beginning to end. Instead, I hope you'll pick it up multiple times and flip to the page that covers the question on your mind at that moment. I hope it can help you set the metronome a little bit faster, accelerating both your company's growth and your impact on that growth.

What follows are six chapters. The first covers what I think of as the four essential principles of good management. The following four chapters each tackle one of the core operating frameworks in detail, including how to adopt a holistic approach to the people on your team and all the human conditions they bring along with them. The last, the conclusion, addresses the key person in all of this: you. At the end of each chapter, you'll find useful exercises and templates related to the chapter's topic. Nearly all of this material was created within Stripe. In some cases, I've credited a specific author, but the majority of these documents were written by me in collaboration with colleagues, or by a team of people within a function, such as the Stripe recruiting team. Taken as a whole, these sections cover what I consider to be the most essential aspects of both company building and management.

Chapter 1
Essential Operating Principles
In work, as in life, you usually have a set of mental models that help guide your decisions. I refer to these mental models as operating principles. In this chapter, I introduce four overarching principles that will help guide you as you build your core structures. These are the touchstones I've come back to often as I've navigated my management career, and they're recurring themes in my management advice:

1. Build self-awareness to build mutual awareness.
2. Say the thing you think you cannot say.
3. Distinguish between management and leadership.
4. Come back to your operating system.

These principles are threaded throughout the rest of the book.

Chapter 2
Core Framework 1: Foundations and Planning for Goals and Resources
This chapter is all about how to build your operating system. It covers how to establish frameworks for goals, starting with your highest aspirations as a company, including values and long-term objectives. It also covers shorter-term goals, as well as metrics to measure your progress toward those goals. It then covers resource allocation tactics and review and accountability systems that will help you reach your goals at both the company and team levels.

Chapter 3
Core Framework 2: A Comprehensive Hiring Approach
Yes—people are, in fact, a company's most valuable resource. This chapter covers a variety of issues that come up in the recruiting and hiring processes at all levels. It's broken into sections on leadership and employee roles and covers assessing your needs, interviewing, selecting candidates, onboarding, promoting from within versus hiring externally, and working with new hires.

Chapter 4
Core Framework 3: Intentional Team Development
This chapter covers how to turn a group of individuals into a team that is greater than the sum of its parts. It starts with a focus on setting up and structuring new teams, then moves on to daily teamwork, from communicating and decision-making to running meetings and offsites to handling reorganizations and managing distributed teams. It also discusses diversity, equity, and inclusion, which are critical to building high-functioning teams, and ends

and inclusion, which are critical to building high-functioning teams, and ends with some advice for setting your team up for success when you're gone.

Chapter 5
Core Framework 4:
Feedback and Performance Mechanisms

All companies, regardless of stage or size, need to orient their culture around and provide a framework for giving feedback that fosters improvement. This doesn't need to be complicated, especially at the beginning. It's far better to start with a basic system and build on it as you go than to try to run a company with nothing in place. This chapter covers how to build those structures, including why it's important to ensure no one is ever surprised by the feedback they receive; how to manage both high and low performers, as well as other managers; how to approach performance reviews, coaching, compensation, firing, and layoffs; and what to do when something bad happens to an employee.

Conclusion
You

I end the book with the most important person in the management journey: you. This chapter contains some of the advice I've given managers on managing their own careers and finding happiness and fulfillment, including building relationships that will foster both professional and personal growth. After all, you have to put your own proverbial oxygen mask on first before you can help others. I also touch on time and energy, managing up and managing sideways, assessing potential, and more.

Everything I share here has been tried and tested by me and by many people I've coached and mentored. (And, as a quick disclaimer, the views and advice I share here are my own, and don't represent the official positions of Stripe or Google.) Of course, this is just one way to approach structuring and managing a company, and it's heavily weighted toward my experience in politics, consulting, and technology. Yet I'm a firm believer that human behavior is universal, and because of that, so is management. With that in mind, I've asked experts in other fields to share their own experiences and learnings. You'll find some of their thoughts throughout the text. You can read full interviews with Zanny Minton Beddoes, editor in chief of *The Economist*; Reid Hoffman, investor and founder of LinkedIn; Eric Yuan, CEO and founder of Zoom; and many more at press.stripe.com/scaling-people/interviews. I think the resulting advice will surprise you in its consistency and broad applicability. As a bonus, these amazing people share some fascinating stories from their careers and companies.

There's a Pablo Picasso quote we like to repeat at Stripe: "When art crit_ ics get together, they talk about Form and Structure and Meaning. When painters get together, they talk about where you can buy cheap turpentine."[7] Sometimes you want to read a book about Picasso's life, and sometimes you just want to know where to buy the cheapest turpentine. Consider this the latter: an insider's guide to management turpentine.

—

Introduction

Scan the QR code to access printer-friendly versions of these worksheets.

Management Prerequisites Checklist

O **You are aware of your legal responsibilities as a manager in the jurisdiction in which you operate.**

O **You and individual reports:**

☐ Hold regular 1:1s on a weekly or biweekly cadence, and they are rarely rescheduled.

☐ Create agendas for your 1:1s that include contributions from both sides, notes, and agreed-upon actions.

☐ Have quarterly goals that you track together.

☐ Hold bidirectional feedback sessions with your reports every three to six months.

☐ Hold more formal performance conversations every 3, 6, or 12 months (the more rapidly your company is changing, the more often these should occur) that emphasize both the results the person achieved (or didn't) and *how* the person did or did not achieve those results.

O **You and your teams:**

☐ Hold weekly or biweekly meetings.

☐ Show up on time for meetings and avoid rescheduling them.

☐ Benefit from time together, whether aligning on plans, making decisions, or workshopping challenges to aid one another in getting the work done.

O **You and your division:**

☐ Have job descriptions and an interview rubric for the roles you're hiring for.

☐ Have job ladders and levels that are clearly communicated with employees.

☐ Have a compensation philosophy and a clear framework for compensation that employees understand.

O **You:**

☐ Understand your own job description and the function of your team.

☐ Have quarterly goals that you've agreed on with your own manager.

☐ Have 1:1s on a regular cadence with your own manager.

☐ Can access information from your manager or leaders in your organization that provides regular context on overall company priorities and goals.

Essential Operating Principles

There are thousands of ways to run an organization and make decisions, so why do you do it the way you do? Maybe you strongly believe that management is a practice of leading by example, so you try to emulate the most important behaviors for your teams' success, like preparing thoroughly for a customer meeting or leaving detailed comments in a design review. Maybe you believe that no decision should be made without data, so you require all of your teams to conduct experiments with measurable results before they make major decisions. Or maybe you're a master delegator, so you spend most of your time matching the right talent with the right problems, then position yourself to unblock obstacles so that nothing stands in the way of them achieving great results.

Whether you know it or not, you've probably already formed many of your own management operating principles—the guidelines you use to make decisions and get work done. These principles act like a personal value system for how you manage your work and your teams. They're guardrails for your management approach and decision-making. Knowing and understanding how they influence your work can make you a better manager, not least because you can articulate them and help others understand how you work. They'll also guide the way you build and implement your company-wide core frameworks.

Before we dive into these frameworks in the coming chapters, I want to share my own principles. I've relied on many management strategies over the course of my career, many adapted from the work of admirable managers and leaders to whom I and many others owe a great debt. Over time, I've refined the backbone of how I lead into the following principles, and I believe they form the foundation of my success as a leader and a manager:

1. Build self-awareness to build mutual awareness.
2. Say the thing you think you cannot say.
3. Distinguish between management and leadership.
4. Come back to the operating system.

If you believe in authentic leadership, as I do, you know that I can't tell you how to manage and lead in a style that is true to your preferences and behaviors. You will have your own set of principles. Nevertheless, I believe that this short list is a strong foundation. It applies to all styles of leadership and is critical to effective management.

All these principles are about one thing: building trust. If you're not self-aware, how can others trust your feedback about their own abilities and behaviors? If you're not direct with your opinions and judgments, how will people know where they stand and trust that you have their interests in mind? If you're not clear on whether you're managing to a defined goal or charting an entirely new vision as you build a company, how will your team trust that you're leading them to success? And if you don't maintain a foundation of consistency and stability, how will those around you know what to expect?

Patrick Collison, the cofounder and CEO of Stripe, and someone with whom I've had the pleasure of working for several years, recently sent me a link to a post by Ted Gioia entitled "How I Became the Honest Broker."[8] In a prior career that involved complex dealings with governments and other stakeholders, Gioia learned that the only way to make progress was to find the person whose "influence and power is built solely on a reputation for straight talk and trustworthy dealings": the honest broker who "played the long-term game." It was such a powerful realization that, in his second career as a writer and reviewer, Gioia aspired to become the honest broker for his readers. Patrick remarked that he thought I would relate, which I certainly did. In fact, I was flattered that he'd recognized my fundamental commitment to building trust. Seek to be the honest broker, for your colleagues and especially for your team.

The other tenet I believe in steadfastly is "Know thyself." It's such an old adage—a Delphic maxim, even!—that people disagree on which ancient coined the phrase. It may be counterintuitive to say that leadership, management, and company building all start with self-awareness, but I strongly believe that to be the case. Self-awareness is the most important of my four principles, so we'll begin there.

8
tedgioia.substack.com

1. Build self-awareness to build mutual awareness

Self-awareness is the key to great management. The other three operating principles are much more about functioning in the moment as a manager, but this is the one that underpins them all. By starting with yourself, you can create an environment in which everyone is self-aware—which, in turn, leads to mutual awareness among team members.

Many people think management is about other people. I think management starts with understanding what you're good at and what you need to work on. Your team won't be able to succeed if you can't describe yourself and your contributions. More importantly, you won't be able to build an effective and complementary team if you don't know what strengths you can contribute and what capabilities you lack.

Self-awareness has three components: understanding your underlying value system, identifying your innate preferences—your work style and decision-making tendencies—and being clear about your own skills and capability gaps.

Understand your values

At Google, I worked with a manager whom I'll call Eli. Eli's reports liked working for him, his teams delivered results, and he cared a lot about the company. Eli was a good manager. But we had a problem: He told his team everything. When we were planning a divisional change that would affect many teams, he informed his reports early, making other managers look uncommunicative. When we were working on a new compensation process, he told his reports and introduced uncertainty into the team's dynamic, letting his fears guide his language with announcements like "It's a mess and we don't know our compensation plan yet, so I'm totally stressed." His reports started to feel anxious about the process and rejected it before they'd had an opportunity to learn why we were putting it in place and how it might benefit them. Eli and I had a couple of difficult 1:1 sessions to discuss his behavior. In every meeting, Eli would agree with my assessment of his behavior, but as soon as he left the room he would revert to his old habits. I felt stuck.

Not long after one of these frustrating conversations, my HR partner helped me organize a manager training for my division with Stan Slap, the author of *Bury My Heart at Conference Room B*.[9] Stan led us through a session on values in which he asked all of the managers to reflect on the values that were important to us and where we thought they came from. He invited participants to come onstage, in front of hundreds of other managers, to share one of those values. Eli raised his hand.

This was the story Eli told: When he was around seven or eight, his mom fell very ill. Later, he would learn that she had breast cancer, but at the time no one in his family told him what was going on. They wanted to keep things as normal as possible. Of course, things were far from normal, and Eli noticed how much his mother was not herself, physically or emotionally. His mother's condition deteriorated, and she eventually had to go to the hospital. Eli was not allowed to visit her. One day, while his mother was in the hospital, Eli's stepdad came to pick him up from school. They drove to Eli's favorite diner and ordered pancakes. While Eli poked at his pancakes, syrup dripping down the sides, his stepdad told him that his mom had died.

Eli's value was transparency.

That story has stuck with me for a long time, particularly two lessons I took from it. First, you never know someone else's story. When you're finding a report difficult to work with, there's almost always a deeper reason for their behavior that's worth trying to understand. Second, some people don't necessarily understand why they act the way they do. If you don't understand how your actions are driven by your underlying beliefs, you'll never be able to adapt them, no matter how hard you try.

Eli knew that his lack of discretion was not only making it harder for his team to operate but also sometimes harmed the division, as with the compensation process issue. He wanted to do better for his team, but at the same time, withholding information from them felt like betraying his commitment to transparency. He and I both cared deeply about creating a supportive, stable environment for our teams, but his overemphasis on transparency was undermining that goal.

Once Eli became aware of this value and was able to share it with others, including me, we were able to talk about every situation at a meta level. We could negotiate what felt right and appropriate for him to share with his team and his division. By building self-awareness, he was able to contribute to the dynamic of mutual awareness that makes managers—and their reports, teams, and divisions—work successfully. Ultimately, Eli realized that he needed to consult his peers and his manager before he shared critical decisions, and that being thoughtful about communication was a way of caring, not withholding from those he was meant to support.

Understanding what is important to you will help you make sense of how you work, what gives you energy and what saps it, and what might trigger an outsize reaction. With those insights, you'll be able to express your values and understand when they are at odds with one another or with someone else's values. Once you do, you'll be able to use the method that Eli and I used, which is one of my favorites: a conversation about the conversation. When you "go meta," as I like to call it, you can unblock a decision or defuse a situation by saying "What I care about is X because I want to honor my value of Y, and I think you might have a different motivation." When you get frustrated, you'll be more open to the possibility that your own values are making you a blocker. Then you can develop a path forward, as Eli did. I've included an exercise in the chapter appendix on page 51 to help you get started uncovering your values.

Identify your work style preferences

Once you've started to understand your underlying values, it's time to build awareness of your personal work style and preferences. The most obvious preference is probably whether someone is an introvert or extrovert. Do you gain energy from interactions with others or from quiet reflection on your own? One of my favorite litmus tests is: Do you talk to think or think to talk? Although I'm not a heavy extrovert, I'll be the first to tell you that I talk to think, and that my best work is done in collaboration with others, not alone.

There are lots of other dimensions of preference beyond extroversion and introversion. For example, are you someone who loves to define a process, or are you someone who resists following one? Understanding your preferences will help you play to those strengths in your role. (It's no coincidence that many salespeople are extroverts, while sales ops people, who are typically more introverted, are the ones defining the processes.) More importantly, you'll learn about your potential weak points and which colleagues and team members might best complement the way you work.

Much of building this dimension of self-awareness comes down to paying attention. If you spend even just a few weeks writing down the moments when you feel energized, when you feel drained, when you feel like you're reaching new heights at your job or hitting new lows, you'll start to see patterns. If you have trouble trusting your own instincts, ask someone whose judgment you respect: When have you seen me do my best and worst work? There are also more formal ways to gain a deeper understanding of yourself and others. For example, you can find someone—a manager, coach, or mentor—who can help survey those around you and draw out observations about your preferences.

At a basic level, most work style and personality preference assessments plot you and your team on a continuum from introverted to extroverted and from task-oriented to people-oriented. (See Figure 1 on the next page; the quadrant labels are my own, adapted from assessments I've seen.)

The point of such exercises is not to be deterministic about who you are or how you work, or, worse, to stereotype people, but rather to give you and your colleagues some shared language around your expressed preferences, and to make you aware of some of the opposing poles of those leanings.

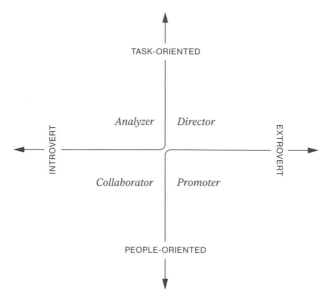

Figure 1. Work style and personality preferences.

With the caveats that it's dangerous to fall into stereotypes and that we're all unique individuals, I think of the main quadrants of all work style assessments this way:

Analyzer (introverted, task-oriented)

Analyzers are very deliberate about decisions and constantly seek data on which to base any action or reaction. They'll be rigorous and prevent you from falling into an intuitive trap that lacks data-driven support. They have trouble acting without data, though, and because they're task-oriented, they can be less good at collaborating, process building, and bringing people along with their decisions and actions.

Director (extroverted, task-oriented)

Directors have strong opinions about the "right" answer and a bias toward rapid action because they care a lot about getting to the right outcomes quickly. They're great at establishing a vision, but they want everyone to fall in line behind that vision. Often, they do the work themselves because they don't enjoy building processes, or they dictate exactly what steps need to be taken, which can be disempowering for others.

Promoter (extroverted, people-oriented)

These talented individuals are charismatic and people-oriented. They tend to have a lot of ideas and the ability to articulate an inspiring narrative. They don't like details or administration and they're usually great start-ers but not always finishers. Overall, they can see the big picture and excel at inspiring others and building relationships.

Collaborator (introverted, people-oriented)

These employees care a lot about the customer, be it an internal customer (an employee at the company) or an external one (a user of a product). Given this inclination, collaborators often build great systems to bring others along. On the flip side, people-oriented builders tend to overcomplicate things because they don't want to leave anyone out. They may create a process that everyone can agree on but that doesn't benefit the organi-zation. For example, you might end up with a process that al-lows everyone on a team to meet a job candidate, but the time in process for that candidate might be 90 days.

None of these work style preferences is objectively better or worse than another. Often, however, one might be better or worse in specific circumstances. For example, during a technical outage, you want to have systems in place that allow a small set of indi-viduals to make a lot of big decisions quickly. You may not care about getting longer-term buy-in from others because you need to take action immediately. For that, you need a director. If you're trying to build a planning process that enables you to decide what teams are going to work on for the next year, you probably want to build something that will endure and help people under-stand the importance of the work. You could do all the planning yourself with a select group of people you trust, but that would mean leaving out the people who actually have to do the work. Plus, you wouldn't be helping them develop the skills they need for future planning cycles. You need a collaborator, and probably a promoter too.

A few other assessment frameworks that follow this general pattern include DiSC (which stands for dominance, influence, steadiness, and conscientiousness),[10] as well as the well-known Myers-Briggs Type Indicator (MBTI),[11] which helps identify 16 different personality types and is based on the work of Carl Jung. My personal favorite is Insights Discovery[12] because it's more nu-anced than the MBTI yet easier to understand, and it quickly builds a strong vocabulary for certain behaviors within a team.

The Insights Discovery assessment puts you into one of four colored quadrants of a circle: red, yellow, green, or blue.

10
discprofile.com

11
themyersbriggs.com

12
insights.com

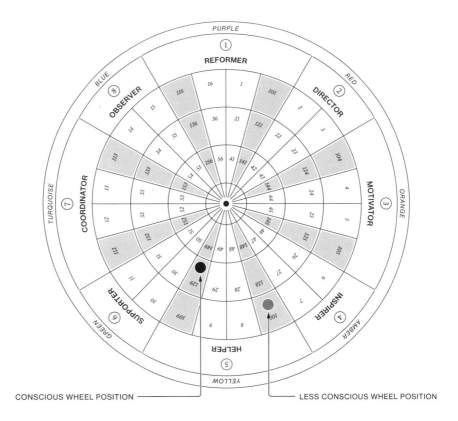

Figure 2. The Insights Discovery wheel, including an example individual result.
Adapted from the Insights Discovery wheel. The Insights Group Limited, 2021. All rights reserved.

Your placement with respect to the center of the circle depends on the strength of your preference. The results also indicate how much you dial your behaviors up or down at home versus at work. For me, the biggest insight was that my preferred style (green, near the border with yellow, in the "supporter" category) is closely followed by the opposite style on the wheel (red, or "director"), which is apparently somewhat unusual. These insights gave me the language to articulate what I think is (largely) a strength of mine: I love to get things done, but I do so via process and people, whereas other leaders who have a lot of red in their charts do so more via assigning tasks, or just doing the tasks themselves.

Analyze your skills and capabilities

Once you can articulate your core values and your work style preferences, you can get down to the more tactical version of self-awareness by asking yourself two sets of questions:

- **What can you do really well**? Which skills do you have, and which do you need to build?
- **What are your capabilities**? What are you naturally good at, and which capabilities have you acquired over time?

Skills are quite tactical: whether you can write a simple software program, use HTML, build a financial model in a spreadsheet, create a detailed marketing campaign. At a slightly higher level, they also encompass abilities, like whether you can break down a business problem and write a strategy. But they're all fairly binary: Yes, I have done this, and yes, it was effective, or no, I haven't done this, or no, it wasn't effective. Take inventory of what skills you need for your role, what you know how to do, and what you need to learn in order to identify the gaps and make a plan to fill them.

Capabilities (also called competencies) are a step above a pure skill. They're more about an innate ability to use a particular set of skills in a given situation. For example, my tactical analytical skills are not particularly strong. Although I learned how to build a financial model in business school, I wouldn't trust myself to build a good enough one to base a decision on. But my analytical capabilities are strong. I've been told that I can absorb a lot of data and opinions and quite quickly synthesize all the elements of a situation to identify the decision that needs to be made, the risks, and the potential actions to take.

Consider managing internal and external communications for a company in a crisis. This takes skill, yes, but also instincts and pattern-matching to past events, both of which allow you to handle any issue that might arise, even if it's a new one. Your skills might include project management and writing talking points for a leader. Your capabilities might include the ability to manage stakeholders, assess risk, and make sound judgments on communication strategy in high-pressure situations.

When I think about whether a capability is innate or not, I ask myself: Is doing this thing well as easy as breathing? Meaning, I've never had to think about needing to acquire that particular ability. Instead, I've been able to draw on it whenever I needed to. For example, if a large group of people needs to accomplish a task, I have no trouble identifying and listing the sequence of actions and roles required to get the work done. On the other hand, I had to acquire the ability to use various project management tools, like Gantt charts. But within those charts, the scope and sequencing of activities always came naturally to me.

Your strengths are the sum of your skills and capabilities. That's why both skills and capabilities tend to come up in conversations about strengths and weaknesses. For example, when asked about an area for development, one of my reports might say, "I want to write better emails."

When I ask why, they might answer that their team has grown to a size that requires them to have stronger communication skills. Because email is the primary method of communication within their division, they're working on that skill. But as they do that, they're also building leadership communication capabilities. Both are important, but it's the capability that really fosters growth, because it can be translated and repurposed into other forms of communication. Email is a specific skill that's useful right now, but effective communication is a much broader and more versatile capacity.

Speaking of strengths and weaknesses: The not-so-secret secret to building self-awareness is to understand that strengths can also be weaknesses. One of my most distinct memories from business school is listening to the dean of the school, Jeffrey Garten, say, "The greatest lesson you will learn here is that your biggest strength is also your biggest weakness." He added that feedback from classmates, a key feature of the program's project-based approach, would make this truth abundantly clear.

Recognizing this reality will have implications for how you build divisions and teams, run processes, and make decisions. Teams become mirrors of their managers. If you don't recognize that your strengths need to be matched by other people's strengths in other skills, you'll be bringing some real vulnerabilities to the table. I can be a forceful and effective communicator, especially when there's work to be done and we're under time pressure, but I sometimes don't stop and listen closely. Instead, I jump too quickly to action. When I'm in a team meeting or even a 1:1 and I'm presented with an urgent situation that needs a decision and an action, I now have a personal rule I try to follow: Ask a question first. This stops me from moving too quickly. It also helps build my team's confidence and strength in their own communication and problem-solving skills, especially if I've populated the team with others who are not as quick to action.

Even though it's tempting to build a team that coddles your own skills and capabilities, what you really need is a team that complements them. As a manager, it's your job to identify your team strategy, then hire a complementary team and arrange their assignments to make optimal use of each person's work preferences and strengths. For example, if you're a strong strategic thinker, you'll more easily recognize this capability in others. After all, you know what good strategic thinking looks like. You'll also be more likely to value strategic thinking since it's something you enjoy doing and talking about. Before you know it, you've hired a team full of strategists and your team meetings are consumed by discussions of two-year vision documents and big-picture brainstorming. The team is having a blast because you're all like-minded individuals and love talking about this stuff. But nothing ever gets done because no one on the team is thinking about execution.

"My father told me that it's very important to understand your strengths, but also to understand your weaknesses. When you come to understand this, it doesn't mean that you are less than you are. You have to make sure you surround yourself with people who can fill up your weaknesses. I knew this since the beginning."

—**Dominique Crenn**, owner and chef, Atelier Crenn, Michelin three-star restaurant

Your teams will be much stronger if you can build a portfolio of people with a diversity of preferences, experiences, skills, and capabilities. That's where self-awareness, followed by mutual awareness, comes in handy.

Even with a complementary team, you'll still probably need to build in some mechanisms that force you out of your comfort zone. For example, I don't enjoy doing deep reviews on spreadsheets full of data. I would greatly prefer to pick out a couple of important insights from the data quickly and spend the rest of the team meeting discussing those. But I run teams that have a lot of measurable targets, so I've had to put guardrails in place to make sure my teams meticulously review tables and data. I also elevate those around me who are obsessed with the underlying numbers (my analyzers!) by giving them airtime at meetings. I ask them to present the charts they've poured their talents into and talk about what might be driving the outcomes. That way, we spend the necessary time on these topics. Then, since I know that data deep dives are draining for me, I reward myself with a higher-level strategic discussion afterward.

The self-awareness assessment

If you're not self-aware, how would you know? Here are some telltale signs:

- You're consistently getting feedback, from various sources, that you disagree with. (This doesn't automatically mean the feedback is correct, but it does mean that how others perceive you differs from how you perceive yourself.)
- You often feel frustrated and annoyed because you don't agree with your team's direction or decisions, and it feels like your colleagues don't understand what you're trying to convey when you explain why.
- You feel drained at the end of a workday, and you can't pinpoint why.
- You can't describe what kinds of work you enjoy doing and what kinds of work you don't enjoy doing.
- You have friction with your manager, and you're both having trouble resolving it.

If you check one or more of these boxes, it's time to dig deeper into the reasons why. Many of the exercises in this book are about developing a better understanding of yourself and others. Writing a "Working with Me" document forces you to reflect on how you like to get work done. Running a career conversation with your reports helps both you and them understand the professional decisions they've made and why they made them. (There's more on self-awareness, the "Working with Me" document, and career conversations in Chapter 3.)

I strongly believe that you need deep self-awareness in order to be effective at work. You can't change *how* you work if you don't understand *why* you

"Once a mentor told me, 'Eric, you've got to look at yourself. Make sure you're looking at your strengths and weaknesses every day. You need to have a plan to become more aware of yourself every day.'

I'm still doing this. I put it in my calendar and call it '15-minute thinking and meditation.' I ask myself: If I start over today, what can I do differently? Did I make any mistakes? Can I improve tomorrow? Sometimes I write down something important. But most of the time, the thinking is enough."

—**Eric Yuan**, founder and CEO, Zoom

work the way you do. And you can't manage people and teams effectively as your company grows if you don't know yourself and what you contribute to the environment you operate in.

2. Say the thing you think you cannot say

Shortly after we started conducting quarterly business reviews (QBRs) with teams at Stripe, I sat in on one such review for a critical product area. Partway through the review, I noticed that people were talking around a significant blocker: The team was dependent on another team doing similar and related work. I stopped the QBR and said, "It feels like we're not talking about the big issue. Is there or is there not a challenge with this other team?" We spent the rest of the meeting talking through the apparent issues and made a plan for the two teams to address them. On the way out of the meeting, an engineer who'd been in attendance said to me, "Well, that was refreshing."

How often have you sat in a meeting and mused, "It really feels like there's something that isn't being talked about right now"? Or had a conversation with a report and thought, "I think they're getting upset about what I'm saying"? Or caught yourself filtering everything you say? These questions prompt a bigger one: Why don't managers say what's actually on their minds?

People often think that good management is about having a lot of filters, and for good reason. There's a lot that might feel risky to say, or that feels like a personal judgment. But be wary of over-filtering. Fine-tuning your filters and pushing yourself to name your observation in a constructive way means you'll be able to have a more honest conversation about what's going on. Then you can all start working on a solution in earnest.

In his book *Conscious Business*, Fred Kofman explains why it's so hard for us to say what we're thinking.[13] It's because every conversation has three components:

- The "it": the task being discussed
- The "we": the relationship between the people having the discussion
- The "I": your personal stance in the conversation

Each of these can add difficult unspoken dynamics to the conversation.

The "it" is about the issue at hand—for instance, how to revise a production schedule given a delay in shipping. Maybe there's disagreement about the steps different teams have taken to get to this point, or unspoken beliefs about who is at fault or responsible for the delay. The "we" concerns all the unsaid aspects of your relationship with others in the room. Do you respect each other? Do you like each other? Do you trust each other? The "I" brings up all the doubts and criticisms you may have about yourself. Am I stupid for thinking this? What will people think of me if I say this thing out loud? Do I not understand how to approach this shipping delay?

This framework is extremely helpful for understanding and working through blockers and giving air to the voices in your head. I'll add three tactics I've found useful in helping me say the things I felt I couldn't say:

Share your feelings

Because everyone has emotions, they can be a powerful management tool. Everyone understands what it feels like to be worried or overloaded. Sharing a feeling with your team can quickly contextualize the importance of your statement. If you say, "We didn't hit our targets," you haven't offered any comment on the gravity of the situation. On the other hand, if you say, "We didn't hit our targets, and I'm worried about the impact that this will have on our team and on the business," the team will immediately understand that there's a problem that needs fixing.

Be measured

Imagine how your team would react if you said, "I'm freaking out because we didn't hit our targets." The team might start to feel panicked, which would impede your ability to move necessary work forward. In the example I shared earlier in this chapter, Eli was honest about what was going on in the division and how it made him feel ("It's a mess, I'm totally stressed"), but didn't deliver the information or feelings in a measured way, which destabilized his team.

Separate the person from the idea or task

Make the distinction between who someone is and what they did. The discussion should be focused on the "it," but it can often feel like a judgment of the "we" or the "I." I once had a coach who observed that criticism and risky observations often feel oppositional—picture two people facing off against each other—when in fact it's powerful to stand next to someone and look at the same thing and make observations together. Think about the difference between saying "That presentation was terrible," prompting the other person to feel defensive about whatever role they played in it, versus saying "What did you think of the presentation? I was disappointed in aspects of it and would love to hear what you thought." Or imagine jointly discussing a piece of art. Saying "I don't like it" doesn't convey much information. It's more effective to explain why you feel that way. So rather than "The team is performing terribly," you might say, "My impression is that the team isn't communicating well right now, and I think deadlines are being missed as a result. Do you agree, or could it be something else?"

I understand why a lot of managers don't say what they think. Sometimes management can feel like a balancing act in a gymnastics competition—a high-stakes sport in which you risk not just your own failure but also that of your team and company. Take one step to the right and you've shared too much. Take one step to the left and you're unapproachable. But learning to constructively express the closest thing to your truth helps you keep your balance. It feels high-stakes because it is, but honing this ability will help you land the dismount: building trust.

That payoff—building trust—is enormous. It will strengthen your whole team. Teams where people can say what's on their minds will raise and resolve problems much more quickly. They'll also be happier, since they won't be suppressing their thoughts and feelings about their work and their environment. More importantly, being more open and direct, yet always constructive, will earn you the one-to-one trust that is critical to an effective relationship with your direct reports. There's a reason Kim Scott's book *Radical Candor*[14] made such a splash: That kind of open, caring communication is the foundation for the highest-functioning people, teams, and workplaces.

When it comes to getting better at communicating the unsaid things, practice will give you the repetitions and feedback you need. Sometimes you'll say something that will fall flat, prompting you to learn from the experience, reframe your approach, and try again next time. Once, I told someone on my team that I thought they seemed nervous in certain meetings. In response, they gave me a blank stare, followed by a defensive remark that cut off the conversation. My intention was to help this person. I wanted to explain that this perceived nervousness, real or not, was undermining their impact. The next time I brought it up, I asked them what they thought of the meeting, let them speak, and then added my own view, which was "To me, you seem a bit nervous. What do you think?" The person thought for a moment, then asked me why I thought they were nervous. I explained some of the clues, like their vocal speed and quality and their mannerisms. It was clear that they were unaware of these behaviors and how they might be affecting the way others perceived them. The conversation then turned to how the person might mitigate these patterns in future meetings, which was the conversation we needed to have so they could thrive at work.

It can be hard to make comments that might be understood as personal judgments even when they're really just reporting your own observations. I go into this in more detail in Chapter 5. Many of the templates in this book—on coaching, performance feedback, meetings, and offsites—will also give you an opportunity to practice this skill.

"Leadership is strategic, and management is more [about] implementation. Leadership is about setting direction, knowing where you want to go, convincing others to go with you, and explaining why you're going there: setting standards, setting expectations, setting tone. Management is about implementing that: getting the processes right, getting the people right, getting the teams right."

—**Zanny Minton Beddoes**, editor in chief, *The Economist*

3. Distinguish between management and leadership

As you're thinking about structuring your teams, developing your reports, and managing your own career, it's crucial to recognize the difference between being a manager and being a leader. Both are necessary for scaling a company, but they're not the same thing.

Great leaders put forth a vision and set lofty goals that inspire others to forge ahead, even when the path isn't always clear. The clarity of their vision keeps everyone focused on the big picture and sustains participation and motivation. Leaders don't have to be managers, but if they aren't, they need to know how to work with and hire managers to build the right teams to execute that vision. It often feels like leaders are asking for just a bit too much, but in the end, that's what provides motivation.

Great managers run teams that do the actual building. Management is all about human-centric execution. Great managers know how to define goals and set operational cadences, all while helping each report have a clear view of their current performance and future career aspirations. Teams with great managers have a high level of trust, experience the challenge and reward of hard work, and feel like they're making progress both as individuals and as a team. Great managers don't initially have to be great leaders, but the more senior a manager becomes, the more important it is that they also develop leadership skills. Eventually, managers need to be able to set a vision and direction for their team—and potentially make the team uncomfortable with a bit of heat—or they'll hit a ceiling in their careers.

Here's another way to think about it. I often refer to a framework in *The Practice of Adaptive Leadership* by Ronald Heifetz, Alexander Grashow, and Marty Linsky that evaluates technical versus adaptive problems.[15] Technical problems have a solution and an achievable resolution, while adaptive problems are continuously, well, adapting. They're an infinite game, if you will.[16] A technical problem might be that you consistently miss your customer service-level agreement of responding to an inquiry within two hours. An adaptive problem might be how to set product priorities in the face of evolving user needs and increasing competition. Managers are superb at solving technical problems. Tackling adaptive problems takes leadership. Once you become a great manager, you can get very comfortable. But once you become a true leader, almost every day is uncomfortable. Don't confuse the two.

Understanding the distinction between management and leadership has proved invaluable in my career. It has helped me retain high performers I might have been tempted to promote into management but who I recognized could be much more effective as leaders in non-manager roles. It has also helped me push myself and others to develop beyond technical problem management and into the adaptive leadership zone. When I take another of my

"Management has a lot to do with whether we're playing the game well, we're developing the tools, we know what the dashboard looks like, we're paying attention to the dashboard, and so on.

Leadership has a lot to do with how you set the spirit of the organization. To some degree, it could be how big the goal is and what the goal is. But usually, it's a goal that's set in a way that isn't necessarily operationalized well.

Management is how you get the mechanics of the pieces coming together. And leadership is more [about creating] a culture or energy of engagement—belief in the importance of winning. It's that 'We can do this' energy."

—**Reid Hoffman**, partner, Greylock Partners,
   cofounder and former executive chairman, LinkedIn

17

bigfive-test.com

favorite self-awareness assessment tests, the Big Five Personality Test,[17] I score as a classic great manager, high on conscientiousness and agreeableness. But great leadership often requires a person to be disagreeable and demand more. I've had to learn how to do that.

Sometimes that can be as simple as naming the need to frame the problem differently. I recently coached a talented up-and-coming product marketing leader at Stripe who kept running up against the challenge of syncing her team's work with the company's ever-changing product roadmap. We spent a whole 1:1 talking about solutions, at the end of which I observed that there would never be a one-and-done fix for the issue. Instead, she would need to continually adapt her approach and push the product team to adapt theirs. The realization that this situation called for leadership via influence and careful communication, rather than building the perfect process, freed her from seeking the perfect "management" answer. In doing so, it tilted her toward adapting how she led herself and her team to improve over time. This employee needed to show up as a leader for her team, which included very experienced people who needed her less to provide internal guidance and more to push other teams to speed up, to their mutual benefit.

Marty Linsky, one of the authors of the book *The Practice of Adaptive Leadership*, has a saying that I've repeated often to colleagues and direct reports: Leadership is disappointing people at a rate they can absorb. Leadership is ultimately about driving change, while management is about creating stability. Stability is important in a work environment, but confronting challenges and realizing new ideas require discomfort. This means that you and your teams must abandon the stable and familiar in favor of an uncertain—but exciting—new direction.

Experienced employees mostly need a leader and just a bit of a manager. If they've made it to a certain point in their careers, they're probably good at getting their work done. But they'll look to a leader to lay out the overarching vision and the milestones they should be working toward, and to pave the way for progress within the systems that operate outside of the team. The leader pushes their team to think and act differently, to welcome change, and, ultimately, to aspire to and achieve more ambitious outcomes. Less experienced employees mostly need a manager and just a bit of a leader. They'll benefit from someone who can help them think through tactics, manage their work and their day-to-day, and help them develop and operate.

4. Come back to your operating system

The bulk of this book—meaning the four chapters that follow—covers how to build a solid operating system by looking at the four core frameworks it's composed of. But it was only recently that I was able to articulate this work as an actual guiding principle. In 2018, in a string of events that feels like it could only happen in the tech industry, I was leaving a conference in Colorado when bad weather prompted a huge number of flight cancellations. I ended up problem-solving a trip home with a venture capitalist and a banker who were seated nearby, forming what we jokingly called our "escape syndicate." Our solution involved chartering a small plane (luckily for me, paid for mostly by the other syndicate members) to get back to the Bay Area. Trapped as we were for hours in the airport, and then on the flight, we traded stories. The banker, who has worked with many successful companies as they've gone public, said that he has a favorite question he asks the CEOs and leaders he gets to know: "What is your secret power?" He described one interview in which a CEO revealed that he asks every employee to submit their top ideas for the company and personally reads every submission.

I thought for a minute and realized that my secret power is this: the ability to build a repeatable operating system for every team I manage. They each have the same components: clear missions, stated goals, metrics that matter, similar meeting structures, and weekly and quarterly cadences. That means that as a leader, I can switch contexts seamlessly.

When I started managing multiple teams at Google, I felt overwhelmed by the constant context-switching. Creating a common user interface for all of them made things much easier. Just as it did for me, a common operating approach with the same core elements across all of your teams will give you a management shortcut of sorts. I later realized that a common operating system that spans an entire company, including the hiring and development of people and teams, is even more powerful.

If you're looking for a story with a little more gravitas than my airport revelation, consider the business school professor of mine who took issue with the exhortation that everyone should "think outside the box." He said, "To succeed, you actually want people thinking *inside* the box. The box *you* constructed!" I come back to that moment more often than you might imagine. Sometimes it's because I'm seeking to frame a problem for my team or my colleagues, and I know that if we can just view the fundamental factors at play in the same way, we will be able to solve it. In the context of managing my team, it reminds me that the operating system creates a foundation of consistent practices that we can all rely on, even when everything else is changing.

Your system, like mine, will be based on how you hire and develop your team and the rhythms of how you operate: quarterly goals, metrics review meetings on Mondays, team meetings on Tuesdays, weekly 1:1s, offsites for big-picture thinking, and so on. Teams and companies vary, but these fundamental approaches create stability. Don't get me wrong—there are times to break the rhythm and change the routine, but what makes doing so effective is the fact that you *have* a routine. It's like perfecting the fundamentals of figure drawing before going abstract, or learning poetic meter before writing free verse. I had another business school professor who painstakingly taught us various business frameworks, like Porter's five forces and the four Ps of marketing, then gleefully declared, "Now that you understand all of these frameworks, you can break them!"

Building self-awareness, saying the thing you think you cannot say, and knowing when you're being a manager versus being a leader are all fundamental principles of great management and building a strong team. But none of them describe how you will drive results. It's the combination of your team environment and the team's execution that produces results—and for that combination to work, you need to operate within a set of core frameworks. The principles I've outlined in this chapter create an environment of ambitious trust. The rest of this book is dedicated to the frameworks that turn the gears to produce results within that environment. As Bill Walsh eloquently explained to Steven Jamison in *The Score Takes Care of Itself*, in that kind of environment, you will not just win but *repeatedly* win.[18]

Chapter 1

Scan the QR code to access printer-friendly versions of these worksheets.

Understand Your Values
Adapted from an exercise by Stan Slap.

Here's an exercise I recommend for uncovering your values and understanding how they affect your work. This exercise is tailored to the application of your values at work, but it can apply to your personal life too.

1. Imagine yourself at 80 years old, reflecting on your career. Ask yourself: What in my work life gave me a sense of fulfillment and meaning?

2. Write down the 10 core values that are represented in your imagining of your fulfilled life (e.g., excellence, joy, balance, community, impact, learning). Check out the list of values on page 53 for examples.

3. Narrow the list down to five values.

4. Now, narrow the list down to three. If you're working with a group, discuss your three values and why you chose them.

5. Next to each value, write down the activities that give you a sense that you're working in accord with that value. For example, if your value is excellence, maybe the activity is that you never deliver a product unless you feel it is 95 percent complete.

6. Reflect on the positive outcomes of those values, then reflect on the trade-offs. For example, a positive expression of valuing excellence is that you deliver high-quality work. A trade-off is that you often miss deadlines or have trouble sacrificing quality, even when a specific situation warrants it.

You can do this exercise as a team, sharing your three key values in small groups. Individuals can then share their stories with a larger group. I've found this to be a helpful starting point for a conversation about what matters to you and how those values manifest at work. It can also be helpful to home in on three values you all share as a team, which can then become your mission.

	Value	Work activities	Positive outcomes	Trade-offs
1.				
2.				
3.				
4.				
5.				
6.				
7.				
8.				
9.				
10.				

Example values

Here's a small sampling of the values Stan Slap lists in *Bury My Heart at Conference Room B*. I recommend checking out the book for the full list of 50 values.

My value	One definition
Accomplishment	Succeeding in reaching your goals
Advancement	Progress, promotion, improvement
Adventure	Taking risks, new experiences
Affection	Love, deep friendship
Altruism	Helping those who cannot help themselves
Balance	Calm, moderation, perspective
Commitment	Dedication to cause, satisfaction in obligation
Compassion	Empathy, tolerance, and understanding of others

Self-Awareness Exercises

Articulate your values

Use the following framework to map out your personal values. (You can find a few example values on the previous page.)

Personal value	Why	Example story
Name this value. *Example:* Impact	Explain why this value matters to you. *Example:* *I am not motivated unless I believe my work matters, both immediately and in the big picture. My parents raised me to care about the world around me.*	Share an example of how this value appears in your life. *Example:* *I decided not to attend law school when I realized that the business leaders I met had more impact and influence on economic well-being and policy.*

Personal value	Why	Example story
1.		
2.		
3.		

Consider your work style preferences

Place yourself within this grid, keeping in mind the different work style types outlined on page 32. Is there a different placement for your "at-home" preferences versus your work preferences?

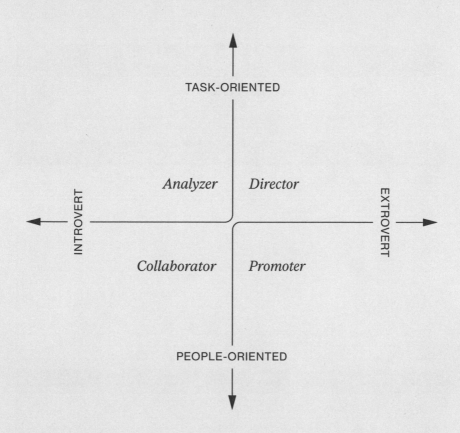

Identify your strengths

To more deeply understand your skills and capabilities, as well as any you may need to develop, start by listing your strengths: the things you're best at. Then, break them down into innate and acquired skills and capabilities (using the section on innate versus acquired skills and capabilities on page 34 as a guide).

Strength
Example: Communication

Skills	
Innate	**Acquired**
Example: Listening well and speaking clearly; fast writer	*Example*: Public speaking; speech and memo writing

Capabilities	
Innate	**Acquired**
Example: Rapid information processing and analytical abilities	*Example:* Ability to synthesize and summarize complex information in a simple way for broad distribution (e.g., marketing)

Core Framework 1

Foundations and Planning for Goals and Resources

When I started meeting with Patrick and John Collison about joining Stripe, one of the first questions I asked was "What's the company mission?" The answer surprised me: It didn't formally have one.

I firmly believe that every company's mission should be part of what I call its founding documents, which are, in turn, part of a larger planning and accountability framework within which the company exists. That framework consists of founding documents, an operating system, and an operating cadence. Think of them like the foundations, structural support beams, and mechanical components of a house.

This chapter covers how to begin building that house by establishing frameworks for setting goals, from your highest aspirations as a company to shorter-term workflows, as well as how to measure progress. It also covers resource allocation and review and accountability systems, which will be integral to your success. We'll start with founding documents and then move on to the rest.

Founding documents

Founding documents detail the plans for the entire enterprise, including the company's long-term goals and principles and your company philosophy: why and how you exist and operate. You should create your founding documents relatively early on, once you've established some traction. They become an even more important touchstone when a company grows beyond about 40 or 50 people. Once you've communicated your company's reason for being in your founding documents, you can turn your attention to building and implementing your initial company-wide operating systems.

Having strong founding documents that share why you exist and what you seek to achieve ensures that the operating systems you put in place share a common purpose, flow from your objectives, and are guided by a clear

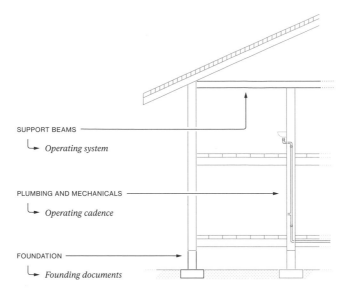

SUPPORT BEAMS
  ↳ *Operating system*

PLUMBING AND MECHANICALS
  ↳ *Operating cadence*

FOUNDATION
  ↳ *Founding documents*

Figure 3. The operating system, operating cadence, and founding documents are like the structural support beams, mechanical components, and foundations of a house.

company ethos from top to bottom, from leadership to individuals. These systems can be replicated up and down the company as it scales, and they ensure that even in times of chaos, your company's purpose and culture are beacons to guide you through. Being clear about your values also means expectations are known to all, which fosters mutual understanding and makes it easier to give feedback when someone isn't meeting expectations.

Founding documents should include a mission, long-term goals, principles (often called values), and team charters.

Mission

A mission states why you exist. Even if you try to avoid pinning it down, it will usually make itself known.

Patrick's answer to my question about Stripe's mission was not actually that it didn't have one, but that he and John, his brother and cofounder, had not formalized one that seemed to stick. But in some of the very early content on Stripe's first About page, Patrick wrote that the company wanted "to increase the GDP of the internet." Once those words were published, both employees and job candidates kept referring to that phrase as the mission. It had organically presented itself to people as the most compelling purpose for the company.

I remember one late-night phone call with Patrick in which we were going over his remarks for our annual all-company gathering. We both acknowledged that it was time to accept the mission that had been handed to us—so Stripe's mission became to increase the GDP of the internet.

"People work for people if they have a purpose. It took me a while to figure that out.

First, I saw it in the military, and I wasn't sure it would translate into the civilian world, but I discovered that it does. People don't go to church as much anymore. The thing they have is their company, so they expect more and more from those companies.

You need to spend a lot more time on values and purpose than I would have thought. Purpose is everything."

—**Charles Phillips**, managing partner, Recognize, former CEO, Infor

Missions are descriptive and aspirational. They're descriptive in that they should be uniquely specific—another organization should not be able to have the same mission. They're aspirational in that it's unlikely a mission will ever be fully achieved. Bill Gates once said, "Early on, Paul Allen and I set the goal of a computer on every desk and in every home. It was a bold idea, and a lot of people thought we were out of our minds to imagine it was possible."[19] This is exactly the type of aspiration that could be broken down into smaller, achievable milestones that a company would need to reach in order to realize that result. The same is true for Google's mission: "Organize the world's information and make it universally accessible and useful."

Every part of the stack—the team, the division, and the company—should have a mission. A team's mission should ladder up to the division's mission, and the division's mission should ladder up to the company's mission.

Here are a few examples of divisional missions that serve Stripe's company mission:

- **Design**: Define, create, and deliver all user-facing aspects of the Stripe brand and product by creating well-functioning, beautiful products and experiences that users love and are eager to recommend to others.
- **Operations**: Equip our users to build their businesses, and build the operations to support Stripe's future scale. If we do this well, we will accelerate the growth of the GDP of the internet.

And here are a few team missions within the divisional missions:

- **Logistics (*within operations*)**: Build and scale operational processes that help Stripe grow our logistics and fulfillment operations, working closely with third-party partners in the US and across the globe.
- **Foundation (*within engineering*)**: Provide usable infrastructure for Stripe to explore innovative new products while concurrently extending secure, reliable, and cost-effective mature business lines.
- **Demand (*within marketing*)**: Grow and accelerate customer acquisition and lifetime value, generating well-qualified self-service and sales leads and engaging leads with useful content through the full life cycle of their relationship with us.

Individuals can also have missions, although those missions are likely to shift quite a bit as their roles and responsibilities evolve. What's key for individuals is that they know how their work contributes to the team, then to the division, and finally to the company.

To use Microsoft as an example, one could imagine how the mission might flow from the top down (note that this is my own representation, not necessarily what Microsoft laid out internally):

"The biggest mistake I made [early on] is we did not focus on writing [down] the company's business principles. To delegate to other leaders, we need to write down our principles on hiring, on firing, on performance, on security, on many things."

—**Eric Yuan**, founder and CEO, Zoom

- **Company mission**: A computer on every desk in every home.
- **Division mission**: Build the operating system for computers.
- **Team mission**: Develop the graphical user interface (GUI) for the operator using the OS.

Long-term goals

The other thing I asked for when I started at Stripe was a list of the company's long-term goals: the bigger-picture ambitions we hoped to achieve or improve over a period of years. They weren't written down at the time, so we tackled them shortly after I joined in 2014, coming up with a simple two-page document. At the time, I thought of this document as part of a high-level three- to five-year plan. But if you read our goals today, eight years later, they're still the same. A selection:

- Grow internet-enabled commerce.
- Accelerate globalization.
- Advance the state of the art in building developer tools and infrastructure.

In a way, this small set of goals has become ingrained and bolstered the company mission. I don't think they're going to change, even in another three to five years. They provide valuable context for employees about our aspirations and reason for existence. Of course, we also have company, division, and team goals that we set both quarterly and annually. (More on that later in this chapter.) Those shorter-term goals ladder up to the long-term goals, so having that long-term ambition is a necessary precursor to setting them.

Principles

The next elements you need to codify at the highest level are your company values, which form the basis of your culture. A mission explains why your company exists. Your long-term goals outline what your company hopes to achieve. Your values, or principles, establish the culture that enables you to work toward those goals. At Stripe, we call our values "principles" because we like the connotation of a shared system of beliefs and behaviors. Whatever you call them, they should be woven through all of your company's actions, both individual and collective.

The most important thing about principles is that they feel authentic to the identity the company is developing organically. Like your company brand, they should be relevant, believable, enduring, and deliverable. They need to be a little bit aspirational, of course, but I find that too many companies make their principles so idealistic that they don't resonate with employees because they have no connection to how the company actually operates. For example, if one of your values is "We care about customers"

"Care is a company value. Meaning, we care about the community, customer, company, teammates, and ourselves. If we share the same values and culture, everything else follows."

—**Eric Yuan**, founder and CEO, Zoom

but the only understanding you have of your customers is how many you have, rather than their experience of your product, the disconnect will be obvious to everyone.

MIT professor Edgar Schein described culture as having three levels: artifacts, espoused beliefs and values, and basic underlying assumptions.[20] His well-known lily pond and iceberg images of understanding culture emphasize how artifacts are visible examples of a culture but the true culture lies beneath the surface. Principles can be tricky to articulate because you're trying to write down something that's based both on espoused beliefs, which are sometimes visible, and unconscious assumptions, which are invisible and difficult to divine. As you draft your principles, try writing down notable moments in the company's history. These might be major decisions, critical product choices, or organizational rallying moments. What was true in those moments? What belief system prevailed? Tapping into those examples is a good place to start your draft.

Don't be afraid to seek input from across your organization. At Stripe, early drafts of the principles were written by employees. They were a fascinating combination of espoused beliefs and underlying assumptions already embedded in the culture. Patrick reviewed the early work, then drafted his own version, which we then circulated within the company for comment before sharing our first official set of operating principles. We revisit and update these principles every year or two to make sure they remain authentic and relevant, but what's most important is ensuring that they are truly expressed in how we hire, reward, lead, and conduct ourselves across the company. (For a look at Stripe's latest set of operating principles, see the chapter appendix on page 111.)

SIDEBAR

—

A quick guide to Stripe's culture

This is an excerpt from a document we used to share with every interview candidate who made it to the in-person interview.

A great deal of your fulfillment at any company is determined by the extent to which the values of the people and the organization align with your own. It's hard to assess culture from the outside, and most companies are not good at describing their own nature. (How do fish describe water?) They also have incentives to say things that sound attractive rather than things that are true. We've tried to assemble this guide to Stripe with both challenges in mind. This is our best attempt to share an honest description of our culture today.

We hope you find it useful in deciding whether Stripe is the kind of place you'd like to spend your time.

We haven't won yet

People often worry that they're joining Stripe, or any nascently successful startup, too late. Have all the large problems been solved? Are there still important decisions left to be made and things to be built?

The good news: It's not too late. Many of the most important problems that Stripe will ever solve are yet to be solved. You will, within weeks of joining Stripe, work on problems that no one here has solved before. (And you'll occasionally end up working on problems that no one *anywhere* has solved before.) There are a lot of avenues that lead to trajectory-altering impact.

The bad news: Our success is far from assured. Most companies that have ever gotten to Stripe's stage have plateaued—or worse. We consider lots of things to be "broken" today, and the more successful we are, the faster things will come to break in the future. (If you've ever played a tower defense game… scaling a fast-growing startup feels a lot like that.)

Move with urgency and focus

Our users entrust us with their money, their businesses, and their livelihoods. Millions of businesses around the world—individuals, startups, and large enterprises—are open for business only if we are. When we mess up, miss a deadline, or slow down, it matters. We take that responsibility seriously.

Great Stripes bring intensity and discipline to their work. We don't care about unnecessary face time, and Stripes have a great deal of flexibility around when and where they work because they know best what is needed to get their jobs done. Many Stripes prosper here while ensuring that they have dinner with their families or friends almost every evening.

But working here will mean some late nights, some weekends, and (especially if you end up in a position of significant responsibility) paying attention to email even during off-hours. Depending on your role, you may end up in meetings with colleagues dialing in from San Francisco, Tokyo, and Paris. There is no way to schedule that meeting such that everyone attends during traditional work hours. Our business is intertwined with the global economy, so while Stripes take holidays, Stripe does not.

You will also be surrounded by exceptionally motivated, driven people. They span a diverse range of life circumstances, values, and working styles. This has the advantage of ensuring that you'll almost never be annoyed about that slacker in the next cubicle (and not just because we don't have cubicles). But it can also be stressful: If you compare yourself to others, you will almost always see someone working harder, staying longer, or being more successful.

We're not a very competitive culture in the sense that someone else does not need to lose for you to win. Your colleagues won't work to undermine you as they might in a winner-takes-all environment. However, we are a very competitive culture in the sense that if you set a high bar, you'll probably inspire someone working with you to try to push it higher. Success at Stripe means seeking out the ski slopes that are just a bit too steep.

We're moving quickly and changing regularly, and we aren't very prescriptive about most things. We expect a lot of autonomy from Stripes, both in the work they do and in how they invest in their own development. We believe in performance management and feedback, but we're not rigid in terms of career paths and box-checking. That said, don't confuse lack of top-down direction with lack of interest from the top: High performers are recognized, enabled, and rewarded. There are "conventional" forms of recognition at Stripe, like equity refreshes and bonuses. However, we get most excited about giving high-performing Stripes the room to work on the most interesting and high-impact problems.

Think rigorously

We care about being right, and it often takes reasoning from first principles to get there. Many behaviors are blindly copied and repeated far beyond their useful lives. We make a habit of trying to tease out the best version of an opposing argument. When criticized, we try to seek the truth in the accusation rather than activating our defensive shields. We invite people who many of us disagree with to come speak at Stripe, and we welcome views that don't obviously mesh with our own.

Rigor doesn't mean not-invented-here syndrome. We're interested in the world around us and think that other companies, industries, and academic fields have much to teach us. We actively hunt in other fields for inspiration and ideas that challenge our assumptions and that we could learn from.

Thinking rigorously has many natural applications to our daily work. For example, we think that the traditional way candidates are interviewed in the tech industry is suboptimal. We've invested significant effort in fixing it by introducing work sample tests, dispensing with whiteboard programming, de-emphasizing credentials, and actively working to combat unconscious bias, among other changes. But that doesn't mean we're satisfied with our current process either. We suspect that there are a lot of significant improvements still to be made.

Part of being rigorous is being judicious. Stripes have measured reactions. We engage in trying and strenuous discussions with colleagues, but we don't yell. Stripe deals with high-variance situations on a day-to-day basis, but we are thoughtful and measured in response.

–

Team charters

I recommend that teams create an additional founding document: a team charter. Team missions will follow and support the company mission and values, and they're generally one or two sentences long. (Recall the Stripe and Microsoft team missions we looked at a few pages ago.) A team charter is a longer document, maybe a page long, that should create clarity about the team's purpose. It should articulate to team members and others within the company why the team exists and what their long-term goals are.

When you grow very quickly, or when your division is large, it can be surprisingly hard to figure out who is responsible for what work, and to what end. When things get complicated, a good manager will sometimes seek to simplify the work by laying out the jobs to be done. The team charter is a summary of those jobs and what others can expect from the team, both immediately and over the long term. Open, transparent information about what each team does and is responsible for allows for a smoother path forward as teams work toward their own mission and, by extension, the company's mission.

A team mission and charter should sit somewhere discoverable, ideally on your shared intranet. (I'll talk more about Stripe's intranet, Stripe Home, later in this chapter.) Together, the mission and charter should provide a clear description of what each team does (for example, "produce data insights that help provide better outcomes for users"), explain why the work matters to the company, and share key metrics and major risks and dependencies. Bonus points for linking out to a dashboard of team metrics and goals, as well as providing a guide on the best way to contact and work with that team on the team charter page. That way, when new employees start, they can figure out whom to contact, and how, if their work requires cross-team support. See the chapter appendix on page 114 for a team charter template with some example text.

The operating system

If the founding documents are like a house's support structure, then the operating system is like a house's mechanical system. Like a mechanical system, the operating system contains various substructures that work together to make up the whole: the wiring and plumbing of your house.

An operating system is a set of norms and actions that are shared with everyone in the company. These shared systems and parameters are essential to growth and success. Keystones like an annual plan, quarterly goals, and regular communications allow everyone at the company to track progress and common priorities at the highest level. These systems can then replicate down through divisions and teams to help clarify priorities and resolve dependencies. At every level, a good operating system makes clear the desired results, how and when to communicate progress, and how to measure achievement.

Above all, a well-articulated operating system establishes a clear foundation of trust. People grow uncomfortable when they're unsure what is expected of them. This is especially true in the workplace. Folks need to know how they're expected to work together, what they're working on, and why, or they may feel like the ground is too shaky to take a single step. I remember an all-company meeting at Google where the CEO articulated this point: "Every day, you all choose where to put your time. My goal is to give you the information to make the best decision."

The operating system also represents a stable, consistent frame of reference. It serves as a touchstone when external forces inevitably affect your priorities, and it helps gird the company amid the chaos of rapid growth. Replicating the structures of the operating system at the company, division, and team levels creates a conceptual throughline, allowing people from across the company to speak the same language and removing friction from execution.

Google's use of objectives and key results (OKRs) is a famous example of a replicable structure.[21] Because they were taken seriously at the leadership level and flowed down to teams and individuals, they formed an extremely effective operating system, providing transparency around what was most important to the company and forcing the resolution of dependencies across teams. In some quarters, OKRs were delayed because Google's executive team was locked in a room hashing out the priorities. It felt a little like the papal convention, with all of us outside the room waiting for the white smoke. But I liked the delay. It meant that the company OKRs were serious and real, and that those decisions were hard. I took my team's OKRs just as seriously.

You might have encountered a company or team with a bad operating system. In these environments, there's often a lot of confusion about who is doing what, and about which goals a team is accountable for and which stakeholders they're accountable to. This anxiety is assuaged only when leaders make ownership and accountability clear and teams understand their purpose within the company. (This is also why having a team charter is so important. It can't override a bad operating system, but it does provide the basis for a good one.) Every organization, division, and team will have periods dedicated to forming their identity—I'll talk more about this in Chapter 4—but it's best to get a simple, company-wide operating system in place quickly, then continue iterating on it to refine its internal structures. Remember my sports analogy from the introduction? Don't send players onto the field with lots of equipment and no rules. People will get hurt!

The manager's role in all of this is to understand and participate in these structures at the right level. Start with the company's mission, long-term goals, and principles. Think about how you can reflect those in your own structures—your team's wiring and plumbing—especially in your team mission and how you align your team operations with the relevant operating structures. (See Table 1 on the next page for an overview.) Your job is to reinforce these elements of the company—and, if you disagree with some element, to help improve it in partnership with your own manager.

When to articulate your operating structures

Once a company can no longer fit into a single meeting room, it's time to start writing down your operating system and its component structures. Before this point—when you're still trying to find product-market fit, for example—it's too early. There's no point articulating why you exist if you're still trying to figure out whether you should exist at all! But once your organization gets to that inflection point, you should nail down your mission and founding documents, followed by your operating system. This is the time to start thinking not just about why you exist but also about who and what you need to realize that vision. How do we make decisions and prioritize? How will we know when we're successful? Considering these questions will help you build a solid foundation for both the company and teams to operate from.

We've discussed the founding documents and team charters. Now let's look at the remaining components of an operating system one by one, then cover each in more detail.

Strategic and financial planning

In 2006, I had been at Google for two years. At the time, the company was still obsessed with its search index—every site Google indexed to produce its search results—and was watching Yahoo's competing search index with concern. That same year, a Yahoo SVP named Brad Garlinghouse published the internal memo that came to be known as "The Peanut Butter Manifesto," exhorting the company to focus.[22] It was leaked externally and became required reading for just about everyone I knew in tech. The upshot is best captured in this quote: "I've heard our strategy described as spreading peanut butter across the myriad opportunities that continue to evolve in the online world. The

wsj.com

OPERATING STRUCTURES	LEADER AND MANAGER ROLES
− Mission − Long-term goals − Principles or values	• Articulate the vision (the why), the long-term objectives (the what), and the underlying principles for action and behavior (the how).
− Strategic and financial planning − Team charters − Goals − Metrics that matter	• Decide on the company strategy and, from that, the top priorities. • Set the financial plan and P&L targets for a given time period. • Determine the org structure that will best support the strategy. • Assign teams to the work that needs to be done. • Set objectives for each team. • Be clear about what you will measure and how you will report on progress.
− Ownership	• Establish work and role assignments. • Make a plan to hire or fill roles for unassigned work. • Be clear on who is accountable for what objectives and metrics. • Develop employee skills and capabilities to accomplish the work.
− Accountability mechanisms	• Establish measurement and reporting approaches. • Review progress and course-correct when goals are not being met. • Give feedback on the work and track employee development goals. • Offer rewards and recognition to reinforce positive outcomes.
− Internal communications	• Establish a consistent set of communication practices and regularly share the information that all employees and teams need to know. • Provide context for company processes and structures, and set an example by following all processes yourself.
− Operating cadence	• Align the planning cadence by which strategic priorities and financial targets are set, goals and metrics are established, and work assignments and progress are articulated, reviewed, and communicated with the company.

Table 1. Operating structures and leader and manager roles.

result: a thin layer of investment spread across everything we do, and thus we focus on nothing in particular."

What Garlinghouse was looking for was a strategy. Even in a moment of dramatic growth, a company must make choices, either about what new features to add to the core product and in what order, or about what to build to augment and extend beyond the existing growth engine. I'm fond of saying "A strategy should hurt." The trade-offs—where you invest time and resources, and where you don't—should be painful and disappointing, either internally or to your customers. There's no such thing as a strong strategy that prioritizes everything at once.

Alongside your strategy, you should conduct long-term planning, which is essentially your company strategy realized as a multiyear set of financials. At its core, this annual planning exercise entails establishing the desired outcome for company financials at the end of the year, then allocating money and

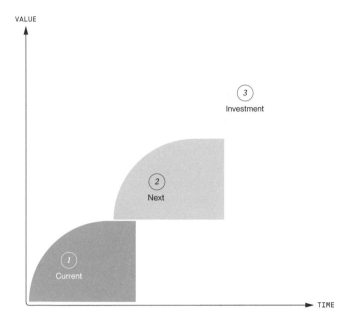

Figure 4. McKinsey's three growth horizons.

people toward initiatives and teams that will focus on hitting those goals. You must also allocate energy to the actions intended to achieve the longer-term strategic and financial outcomes, keeping the mission and long-term goals top of mind.

A lot of young companies get obsessed, rightly, with product-market fit. So at first, the strategy is simple: Keep pouring gas on the fire. Then it gets less simple, and you might find yourself in a "peanut-butter" situation. McKinsey has a famous framework of three growth horizons:[23]

- **Horizon 1**: Current source of growth
- **Horizon 2**: Next source of growth (one that's still nascent but looks promising)
- **Horizon 3**: Investment in a yet-to-be-determined third source of growth

In tech, you often need to start working on Horizons 2 and 3 very early on.

Young companies tend to resist concepts like strategy and planning, and they come by that resistance honestly—there's so much work to do, who has time for such ivory tower–like activities? If you're pre-product or pre-market fit, you need a process that allows you to adapt quickly as you're figuring out what

23

mckinsey.com

works. Your plans might focus more on the short term: "Here are some milestones we need to achieve in order to start testing and proving that people want to buy our product." But once you have product-market fit, it's time to start thinking longer-term.

A mature company is likely to have a clear picture of its intended strategy and financials over a multi-year span, as well as a good sense of which activities will allow them to reach those numbers. They can thus outline goals and plans that enable various component teams to achieve those goals.

A mid-stage company is, appropriately, somewhere in between. The trick is to find the right balance: enough structure to speed progress, but not so much that you end up overburdening teams and products that are just being established. One of my favorite learnings from Colin Bryar and Bill Carr's book *Working Backwards* was that it took Amazon quite a lot of iteration and painful company processes—the new product introduction, or NPI, seemed to be the least popular—to get to its OP1 and OP2 approaches.[24] ("OP" stands for "operating plan.") The same has been true for Stripe. Start as simply as you can, then adapt.

To strike that balance between short-term and long-term focus, I recommend developing two artifacts:

- **A financial model** of the next three or so years, plus a list of what needs to be true to achieve those numbers. Producing that list will require a set of strategic conversations and decisions. This longer-term projection may not end up being accurate, but you can revisit and revise it each year. Depending on how accurate your initial projection is, it may only require minimal revisions, or it may need a more comprehensive course correction. More mature companies do this work on a five-to-ten-year time horizon and tend to spend more time working to determine new areas for growth—McKinsey's Horizon 3—and less time iterating on the near-term plan.
- **A shorter-term plan** that answers the questions "What are we trying to get done in the next 6 months, and in the next 12?" and "What does the P & L look like by December of this year?" Teams and companies will use different systems for doing this, but the plan should be a way for a team to say, "This is where we're going long-term"—linking out to the long-term strategic themes and rough financial objectives—"and, on a quarterly basis, this is where we're focusing to move our most important metrics." Keep in mind that the financial outcomes are not the plan itself, nor are they the reason you exist as a company. But they are a critical means to create discipline and a measurement system for the company's actual work.

In order to achieve their mission, and if they're following the three-horizon structure, most companies will have a mix of more mature parts of the business—which should have clear metrics they're trying to move and short-term goals they're trying to hit—and emerging businesses or products, for which the goal may be as simple as "Launch the product and test product-market fit." Be sure to distinguish between these varying maturity levels and to plan differently for the different business stages within the company.

Resource allocation

The other part of planning is resource allocation. In simple terms, your primary resources are people and money. The art of planning is to allocate enough funds and employees to earlier-stage efforts to give them a chance to demonstrate success, while simultaneously streamlining the more mature parts of the business so that they realize operational efficiencies and demonstrate increasing profitability as early as possible, without undermining their growth.

It's somewhat easier, mathematically speaking, to track resource needs for sales and operational teams that have measurable outcomes, like new customer leads and support cases closed. I'm not going to pretend I know of a standard and trusted way to measure the ROI of engineering resources. One tactic to allocate headcount is to look at the ratio of functions—for example, 10 engineers to 1 product manager, or 1 human resource business partner to 250 employees. The downside of a ratio-based approach, however, is that other companies' benchmarks don't reflect your own company and business model. They also don't account for potential efficiency gains in ratios over time, nor for the fact that you generally want to award more resources based on impact, not on how many people are on the team. Still, you should keep ratios in mind as a gut check on where you land.

Once you allocate headcount, your gut check should also include making sure you're not starving the current cash cow, as it were. As tempting as Horizons 2 and 3 can be to pursue, your current business's most critical area—Horizon 1—invariably requires more people and money to maintain growth.

Headcount allocation comes up frequently in the conversations I have with founders. The sentiment is essentially this: "We're adding more people, but I feel like the velocity of product development and progress is slowing down. Am I being unreasonable?" With an eye toward cash burn rate, founders want to be careful about adding more people. And when they do, they want to hold those people accountable for an output commensurate with the additional people power. The slowdowns founders often observe reflect the harsh side of scale: increasing coordination and interface complexity.

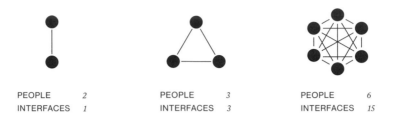

| PEOPLE | 2 | PEOPLE | 3 | PEOPLE | 6 |
| INTERFACES | 1 | INTERFACES | 3 | INTERFACES | 15 |

Figure 5. Interface complexity. The more people there are on a team, the more possible interfaces there are, increasing communication and coordination challenges.

In my advice to these founders, I describe the phases of scale I've observed that relate specifically to engineering productivity, but that ultimately represent company scale, too:

- **Phase I**: Small, scrappy developer teams work in a shared codebase, moving quickly but often taking on technical debt to ship new features or products.
- **Phase II**: Teams attempt to decouple elements of the shared codebase and build better tooling for developer productivity. This includes hiring more experienced engineers, engineering managers, and leaders.
- **Phase III**: Teams undergo a painful, complete redo of the underlying infrastructure, building a true platform or shared services architecture—and realize that the entire company, not just engineering, needs to be composed of separate units led by very experienced people. These units are more loosely coupled with respect to dependencies but tightly aligned via planning and goal setting.

It's validating for founders to hear that these phenomena are common—and even a potential sign of success. But addressing these challenges is no easy feat. You must constantly evaluate whether you've made the right investments in infrastructure, developed an optimal organizational structure, and hired the appropriate leaders, and you need to attack the root causes of slowing productivity on multiple fronts.[25]

SIDEBAR

—

Investing in developer productivity

On developer productivity, Stripe's CTO, David Singleton, wrote a compelling internal post in which he explained:

There is certainly no singular metric that works to track output comparably across engineers, environments, or projects. The way we compose our changes is relatively arbitrary. Exactly the same value for our users could be achieved in one big pull request or 20 small ones. The number of commits that someone chooses to make on the way to creating a finished PR is a matter of personal taste. Some measures that have been used historically in the industry actively encourage bad practices. For instance, trying to measure per-engineer output in terms of lines of code per day encourages complicated and verbose solutions when we all would strongly prefer simpler, more concise solutions that are easier to understand, easier to maintain, and much less likely to present reliability problems.

Still, to achieve great developer productivity, it's important that we measure our productivity to know whether we are getting better or worse over time and to target improvements in the right places. We measure both objectively, by instrumenting as much of our developer tooling as we possibly can and paying attention to the metrics generated, and subjectively, by asking engineers periodically how they feel about the productivity of our tools and our codebase.

It's also important that we invest in developer productivity—being willing to:

- Spend significant sums of money on infrastructure that makes engineering more productive
- Have a large, dedicated group of people working every day to make other engineers' lives easier

When I arrived at Stripe in 2018, I was quite struck by how coupled all of our development was. We had derived huge productivity benefits through working (largely) in a shared codebase, but many of our most critical pieces of product infrastructure were entangled in a ball of mud, which was hard to change. We mixed up reusable infrastructure with product intricacies in many places. Very few people understood enough of the codebase to make simplifying changes, and we mostly evolved these absolutely critical flows by hanging more and more logical branches and gates off of what was already there.

We've invested, since then, in various efforts that have reduced coupling in some of our core models, but we are midstream in pulling off a paradigm shift in how we build our product infrastructure and how we need to operate in building our products on top of that product infrastructure in the future. Note that this does not mean we aren't continuing to prioritize developer productivity in existing environments as we make the transition, but it makes prioritization even more important. Each service has a well-defined Stripe-facing API, which fully abstracts its internal implementation (meaning we can change it radically over time!) and underlying data. These are loosely coupled but present strong contracts in terms of the availability, latency, and throughput that other services can depend on them for.

Figure 6. A product infrastructure framework that prioritizes developer productivity.

How does this relate to developer productivity?

- This is how we maintain developer productivity as we scale. The vast majority of engineering teams have full agency over the internals of the services they build and operate without needing to consult with any others, so long as they maintain the interface they've already committed to.
- Once we have services in place for core abstractions, engineers can start to reason about how they can compose the interface that, for example, the customer service exposes to get their features working, rather than all the internal details of the implementation of the customer service that they might have to change.

This is just an excerpt from David's post. The post also discusses how to maintain a focus on security and reliability, describes our code-owner and set-piece review processes, and reflects on how to invest in efforts to improve developer workflows. David also describes Stripe's principles and behaviors for stronger development practices, and touches on benchmarks for the target percentage of engineers to devote exclusively to developer productivity (5–8 percent of all engineers), and on our own decision to exceed the benchmark in the interest of velocity.

—

Early on, it felt like Google had its own peanut-butter problem. We would submit goals and plans for team headcount, then our financial planning team would seemingly ignore those plans and add a number of people to each organization based on how many employees the organization already had. What was basically a ratio-based approach felt a little absurd, but I now understand the rationale better: The business was still unpredictable and it was hard to measure the ROI of an incremental resource, so the team simply worked off of the previous year's plan. The bigger reason to submit plans was that it made teams take a step back and think about longer-term goals and the resources needed to achieve them in the coming year. It was about building the planning-ahead muscle, reorienting around delivering on the company objectives, and measuring performance against a plan.

It's vital for companies to start building that planning muscle, and for leaders to start using objective assessment measures, so that they don't get trapped in a situation where the person most adept at arguing their case gets the most resources. Headcount planning is fraught, and leaders will tend to read into the allocations and lobby for more. Objective measures—such as revenue per head or year-over-year revenue growth for a given product or sales effort—are one tactic to lessen pressure. Another is to allocate resources on six-month cycles or to hold some headcount in a company reserve. Both tactics provide some optionality for shifting hiring toward emerging priorities and make the entire enterprise feel less like a win-lose situation once a year. They can cause challenges for recruiting, however, because the team will have a less accurate forecast against which to build a talent pipeline. Use whichever tactic will best help your company avoid being reactive only to short-term needs or internal lobbying. The overall goal is to develop a more disciplined approach to planning and resource allocation, however you achieve that.

It's also worth noting that getting more resources will be perceived as recognition or a reward. Leadership should publicly celebrate managers who are actively improving their operational efficiency, for example by coming in under budget at the end of the fiscal year or "giving back" headcount allocation.

SIDEBAR

–

Setting expectations around resource allocation

I recently met with a founder who lamented his leadership team's internal dynamics when it came time for resource allocation. A normally collaborative group would break down, and individuals would only look out for their own teams. The founder was left feeling like the sole decision-maker, and often like the "bad guy." We talked about setting more objective metrics for resource allocation, but for a company growing as quickly as his was, it was hard to set forecasts and track against benchmarks.

I suggested that he ground the conversation with his team in leadership expectations. Just as it's effective to remind people about inherent biases before making a hiring or promotion decision, it's helpful to remind people of what you expect from them as you face big decisions. In this case, I advised the founder to tell the leadership team that he expected them all to keep the big picture in mind—what was best for the company, not for their individual teams—and to collaborate to reach a final decision, work constructively across teams to find opportunities for efficiency, and, more generally, to show up as a team in order to lead the company. I emphasized that it wouldn't hurt to make those level-setting remarks every time the group faced contentious decisions.

—

After Gmail launched and Google acquired Keyhole, which became Google Earth, there was a moment of internal tension around company priorities. There was a lot of investment to be made in existing products and in international expansion for the core search and advertising business. Various teams felt like the company was becoming distracted by new projects before the main source of revenue and growth was mature enough. Then-CEO Eric Schmidt shared a simple but extremely effective framework to resolve these tensions: 70-20-10. Google would devote 70 percent of its resources to the core business, 20 percent to emerging products, and 10 percent to research and development for future products. Once he presented this framework to the company, these discussions quieted down. It was his own version of McKinsey's growth horizons, strengthened by detailed percentages and his own complement of communication tools, including straightforward emails and remarks at our all-company meeting, TGIF. It set the context for continuing to invest in new areas despite the early stage of Google's core business.

At Stripe, similar tensions emerged as we started to build new products. After many, many long meetings, we eventually landed on a tight one-page prioritization framework that amounted to: existential risks > core product (including which countries to invest in further) > new products. This was followed by a section about reserving resources for foundational company work (internal tooling, people development). It wasn't perfect, but it helped everyone calibrate their planning.

A side note related to existential risks: A key role of your leadership team should be to invest in critical work that no one else will naturally step up to prioritize. It's rare that a company's plans, incentives, and metrics structures are built to mitigate risk or stop and redo work. If you need to invest in security, pay down technical debt, or make a hard call on halting a project, you'll need a leadership voice to provide top-down instruction to do so. As a manager, be aware that there will be top-down asks from leadership and from other teams with high-priority work that you'll have to integrate into your workflow. Keep the strategy and big picture in mind, and make sure to reserve space within your own team goals for top-down company priorities and work that other teams might require to act on those priorities—even when your own resourcing plan is, sadly, getting whipsawed.

"One of my favorite books is by former Intel CEO Andy Grove, *Only the Paranoid Survive.*[26] We are very paranoid. We always think about 'What if you have 10 times more capacity or 10 times [more] usage? Can you survive? Do you have any security or reliability or performance holes?'

My number one priority as a CEO is to think about what kinds of risk factors we need to focus on. When I realized that, I told our team transparently that I had made a mistake: 'I used to only be focused on the culture, value, product. But now I think that's not right. My number one priority is to think about the risk factors.'"

—**Eric Yuan**, founder and CEO, Zoom

Annual and quarterly goals

Unlike the long-term goals I covered earlier in this chapter, annual and quarterly goals are more tactical and measurable, representing a company's output on a discrete time horizon. They serve as a contract between the accountable team and the rest of the division about the work that will be completed. For example, the Microsoft team that developed the first GUI for Microsoft Windows probably had to do so in time for a public demo in November 1983. Being ready for that demo was the goal. Progress toward goals is measured using specific metrics, which show an achieved result and the data to prove it.

Just as it's hard to set goals without clearly defined company and team missions, it's going to be hard to set good metrics (coming up next!) to measure progress if you don't have clear goals.

There are two kinds of goals: binary tasks (for example, "pilot a low-code local payment method for our checkout product") and ongoing metrics ("grow share of non-card pay-in volume by 20 percent"). And, as with your mission, it's ideal for company goals to replicate down from the division to the team to the individual. Here are some examples from Stripe, which represent both binary and ongoing goals:

Company goal: Security work. Every team should remain at up to 80 percent on the security posture dashboard, which will often require adopting new tooling and infrastructure. More broadly, we'll remain secure only if every team continues to apply rigorous paranoia to their own domain.

Division goal (*engineering*): Maintain our security baseline and make progress on the migrations to support the top three technology priority programs so that the security projects deliver the planned new invariants that we—and, by extension, our users—can rely on.

- **Binary goal**: No S0 security incidents.
- **Ongoing improvement**: Every team achieves up to 80 percent on the security posture dashboard by the end of the quarter, which requires adopting the new infrastructure.

Team goal (*admin platform*):

- **Binary goal**: 100 percent of access to Level 2 data requires an automated business justification or a two-person confirmed justification.

There are now many schools of thought on how to write goals. OKRs and SMART (specific, measurable, achievable, results-oriented, targeted) goals are two popular examples, and they're not mutually exclusive. Both strategies help you accomplish the same desired outcome: a clear, measurable objective to which you can hold people accountable.

—

Good goals

This write-up on setting good goals, which we continue to consult internally, is adapted from a public post by Michael Siliski, a former product leader at Stripe.

Having led goal-setting processes with teams of 1–500 people at all stages of product maturity, I find I get more or less the same questions and the same pushback every time. This is my answer to those questions. While you can easily find lots of tactical advice online about goal-setting processes, here I want to focus on the spirit of what we're actually trying to achieve and how to know if we've done it well. To that end, this post covers:

- Why we set goals
- What good goals look like
- Heuristics for testing your goals
- Frequently asked questions

Why we set goals

These are the goals of the goals, if you will.

- **Define success**: Goals are statements about successful end states. What are you trying to do, and how would you know if you did it? Plans are sets of activities. Executing on a plan may help you achieve a goal, but it's not the goal itself. To maximize your odds of achieving a successful outcome, start with the end in mind and work backward to the activities most likely to get you there.
- **Focus**: There are always far more things we could be doing than we have capacity for. Productive teams clearly distinguish the most important things from all of the other good ideas, and they relentlessly focus on those top priorities. This also helps ensure that all of the different parts of the team are operating in concert rather than independently working on related things.
- **Allow for autonomy**: Aligning around and committing to a shared definition of success creates accountability. Doing so without mandating specific activities allows accountability to coexist with autonomy and creativity.

What good goals look like

Remember: FOCUS(S)! Good goals are focused, concise, and comprehensible. Everyone on the team should be able to easily memorize the team's goals. This is important because the progress you make in a quarter or year is the result of thousands of independent decisions. Too many goals or too many details interfere with this. People can remember about three to five things.

- **Focus on the most important things**: Your goals should help you identify and avoid the distractions. Use plain English that is easily understandable to anyone with a passing familiarity with your team's strategy. This helps with strategic clarity, memorability, and communicability. Jargon often masks strategic gaps.
- **Objectively assessable**: Everyone on the team should have the same understanding of what success looks like and what it doesn't. Goals don't need to be quantitative, but they cannot be subjective.
- **Challenging but possible**: Your goals need to be credible. If people consider the outcome unimaginable, they'll simply ignore it and give up. Your goals should also stretch the team, inspiring and challenging people. If you ask your team to stretch, you'll often discover that they find ways to deliver more than you expect. A good rule of thumb is to shoot for about a 70 percent success rate.
- **User-oriented**: Never organize team goals by function (engineering, design, etc.). Success depends on all team functions coming together to deliver a great product, and a single set of goals helps force an alignment of efforts. Even if some goals depend more on one function than another, allow the team to flexibly organize their capabilities and creatively solve problems. Don't organize goals around the features you're delivering—thinking about your expected activities and working forward is likely to leave a large gap. Instead, focus on the customer problem you're solving and set your goals as close to the customer as possible.
- **States, not activities**: If you detail specific activities to pursue, you're removing the opportunity for teams to solve problems autonomously, creatively, and iteratively. Instead, focus on the outcome you want. How would you describe the state of the world in a success case? Define these outcomes as precisely as possible.
- **Sensitivity and specificity**: Your goals should allow for the outcomes that you would consider successful, and should rule out unsuccessful outcomes.

Heuristics for testing your goals

Assess your goals using these guidelines:

- Does your goal start with a verb ("launch," "build," "refactor," etc.)? Then you probably have an action, so reframe it to describe the outcome you want. Often, this takes the form of translating "X so that Y"

ORIGINAL GOAL	NEW GOAL
Refactor backend	Backend supports 5+ teams that are concurrently adding features
Launch v2 product	Double conversion rate via new payment integrations
Add infinite scrolling to search	X percent of search queries receive result clicks

Table 2. Refocusing your goals.

into "Y via X" (and consider if you need X in there at all). A helpful trick to figure out the proper framing is to read the goal out, ask yourself why, answer that question, then do that a couple of times until the true goal comes into focus. (See Table 2 for an example.)

- Do you have "engineering goals" and "business goals," or something similar? Stop it.
- Are your goals more than one page, more than three to five objectives, or more than three to five KRs per objective? No one will read them— let alone remember them.
- When you (or your team) look at your goals, do you wince and think, "What about X? I was really hoping to get to that this quarter"? If not, you probably haven't focused enough, and your goals are not adding value.
- Could one team member think a goal is achieved and another one completely disagree? Then your goal isn't specific enough. (By contrast, if everyone feels it's mostly successful but the assessments range from 60–80 percent done, who cares?)
- Can you imagine a scenario where the goal is achieved but you're still dissatisfied with where you ended up? Then your goal isn't specific enough, or an aspect is missing.
- Could you be successful without achieving the goal? Then your goal is overly specific, and you should rethink how to define success.

FAQs

How do you manage against the goals?

If you set good goals and have real buy-in, then the whole team should have a set of shared goals you can use as a foundation. As you talk about team performance, meetings, sprint planning, and progress, frame those conversations against the goals you set. Organize your activities around the goals, talk about them constantly, and frame the day-to-day in terms of how they will help achieve your goals. Keep them top of mind for everyone, all the time.

How do you score goals?

I usually do a lightweight mid-quarter and end-quarter review that uses green, yellow, and red color-coded scoring (representing success, mixed results, or failure). The mid-quarter review is a helpful checkpoint to refocus everyone on goals we may have gotten distracted from. The end-quarter review is mostly to help us recalibrate how aggressive we were and highlight areas where we are regularly failing to make progress. If the reviews require a lot of effort or feel like they need to be done more often, then your team probably hasn't fully internalized the goals and isn't using them to guide day-to-day activities.

What do you do if the goal changes before the time period ends?

Sometimes strategies change or we learn things that change our priorities. That's fine. Start working on the new goal immediately. Add a zero with an asterisk or something when you go to score the old one. Who cares? But if this happens to you all the time, you may be setting goals that are too specific or incorporating activity planning into the goal-setting process.

What about quantifiable measurability?

Goals generally benefit from clearly defined, measurable metrics. For example, "Median latency is under 200 milliseconds" is obviously a much better definition of success than "Latency is reduced."

However, sometimes people get hung up on enforcing quantifiability and can lose track of what really matters. It's fine for some goals to have no numbers, as long as it's clear what success looks like and it's not a subjective question. A goal like "MVP is up and running on production hardware, and multiple external companies have tested it and provided early feedback" has no numbers, but it's very concrete. The important thing is that the whole team assesses success and failure the same way. As Andy Grove said about goal assessment, the important thing is that "at the end, you can look without any argument and say, 'Did I do that, or did I not do that?' Yes. No. Simple."

What if I can't measure the thing I want to optimize?

Generally, I say use the metric in your goal anyway and try to assess it by proxy. Better than setting the wrong goal entirely. As John Tukey said, "Far better an approximate answer to the right question, which is often vague, than an exact answer to the wrong question, which can always be made precise." Plus, nothing motivates development of the right metric like using them to actually measure success across the team!

What if I have a metric but I don't know what the right target is?

Quite often, you'll agree on a good way to measure success, but you won't know exactly what a reasonable target is since you don't yet have a baseline.

Generally, I say who cares? Take a guess at a reasonable number, be honest that it's a stab in the dark, work toward it, and update your target along the way as you learn more. Better to set the goal in the right direction and not be sure exactly how far you should get than to risk going in the wrong direction.

What if you can't agree on what the goals should be?

There are any number of reasons this could be the case. Let's assume you're dealing with a reasonable set of people working together in good faith and trying to do what's best for the team. (If you aren't, it's not a goal-setting problem.) The first step is to stop arguing and try to diagnose why you're stuck. If you can figure that out, you can almost always find a good resolution.

Here are some common issues people get hung up on—work from the top down to determine where you're falling out of alignment, then work through that question while holding everything else to the side before continuing down the list:

- **Different assumptions about vision or strategy**: If we aren't aligned on what we're trying to do as a team, there's no effective way to figure out the milestones along the way.
- **Different assumptions about priorities**: If you think that we should do A first, then B, and I think we should do B first, then A, we can't align on goals.
- **Different interpretations**: Tease this out by talking through concrete scenarios and seeing if you agree on what success is and what it isn't.
- **Incomplete success statements**: If your goals don't capture something important for success, you may see people trying to pull things up a level into very broad statements. Try adding additional, very specific statements to narrow down the range of good outcomes until you're on the same page, then simplify as appropriate.
- **Different assumptions about feasibility**: If someone feels the goal is fundamentally not possible or cost-prohibitive, it's good to name this explicitly and dig into it.
- **Different assumptions about capacity**: Try expanding the time frame a bit and see if you all agree on the overall plan and are simply disagreeing about how far you should get in a specific time period.

Why "goals" and not "OKRs"?

OKRs are just goals with a particular structure. They separate the thing we're trying to do (the objective) from the concrete definition of success (the key results). I like that structural distinction—I find it helps enforce a clear definition of success—so I tend to use the OKR framework myself. As Andy Grove, the forefather of "managing by objective," framed it in *High Output Management*, OKRs separate out two key questions:[27]

- **Where do I want to go?** This answer provides the objective.
- **How will I pace myself to see if I'm getting there?** This answer provides the milestones, or key results.

—

Here are a few other thoughts on how to effectively set and use goals:

Say what percentage of goals you expect people to hit up front

Some companies and leaders like their goals to be as realistic as possible, so it's expected that 100 percent of the goals will be achieved. Other companies prefer their goals to be more aspirational, so it's expected that some of the goals—around 20–30 percent—will not be met. You can do both, but take care to specify which goals are aspirational (hit 70 percent) versus committed (hit 100 percent). Either way, always consider the dependencies required to achieve those goals.

Committed goals are a good idea if:

- There's an existential company threat, for example if a competitor has developed a better version of one of your top product features.
- Another team working on a top-priority project is blocked.
- A customer has been told a product or project will be delivered on a particular timeline.

The argument for biasing toward more aspirational goals is a simple one: Human and team behavior often lead us to anchor on and solve for a defined outcome. A more challenging goal might lead us to think differently about how to accomplish it, and thus generate fresh ideas and energy. A team might also unconsciously take the pressure off of their efforts once they hit an "achievable" goal, forestalling the possibility of carrying the work further and exceeding expectations, which might motivate the team to have more confidence in their abilities in the coming quarters. The key with more aspirational goals is to set expectations: Teams should know that hitting 70–80 percent of the goal counts as success, but that there will be great recognition and reward for exceeding those expectations. (See the chapter appendix on page 125 for guidance on helping the team write good OKRs.)

An individual's goals should include one or two personal goals

As a manager, remember that the work of the individual is both company-focused (what they'll do to contribute to the division) and individual-focused (how their work will contribute to their broader career narrative and development). Goals should reflect this. Every quarter, an individual should have at least one or two personal development goals in addition to the work output they expect to complete. That way, the team member is doing the work that's needed today but also developing abilities that allow them to grow their impact, contribute to the work the team might need to deliver tomorrow, and advance their career.

Say someone on your team can only do basic analysis, but your data is growing increasingly complex. It'll be important for that person to develop more advanced analytics skills, including how to write SQL queries to access the data from your internal systems. They might have a goal to conduct up to 30 basic analyses that quarter, as well as a goal to take a SQL class and demonstrate that they can conduct a complex analytical project by the end of the quarter. As people become more experienced, their goals might become less skill-focused and more about capabilities. Instead of "Write a detailed project plan," for example, their goal might be "Lead a complex project from plan to completion with measurable positive results."

As a manager, it's tempting to have your team focus only on what they need to get done in the quarter rather than working on more developmental goals. But just as a company can't rely on one product for revenue growth indefinitely and must invest in more speculative work on future products or revenue streams, so must teams and individuals invest in their future development. This is especially true in high-growth environments. The skills and efforts that got your work done in Q1 are not going to be the same ones required 6 or 12 months later. You must build for future scale and challenges, both in your team practices and among the individuals on your team. What's more, if part of your role is to coach and develop your people, how will you demonstrate your commitment to that aspect of your job if you don't keep people focused on their developmental goals? It's easy for a manager to say, "I'm here to coach you," but it's your actions that matter, not your words. (There's more on coaching in Chapter 5.)

The "how" is just as important as the "what"

When looking back at a particular project, quarter, or year, don't limit your review to the goals someone accomplished. Pay attention to *how* the person or team approached the work. Even if the team is hitting their goals, they might have gotten there in a more painful or less efficient way than they could have. Maybe someone needs to focus on communication and collaboration with fellow team members instead of on the quality of their output, or on how to scope a problem instead of on the technical work of solving it. Make sure you ascertain the "how" alongside the "what" and provide feedback to individuals accordingly.

You may be familiar with the concept of a Pyrrhic victory: a victory won at such a great cost that it was not worth the battle. All too often, I see the work equivalent of Pyrrhic victories. Yes, the product launched on time, but the team and the relationships therein barely survived, and people are unable to contribute quality work in the month afterward because they're exhausted and communication is brittle. One early reader of this book told me, "Performance = results × behaviors. It's multiplicative. Hitting targets while fomenting unrest and backstabbing should get you a 0, not a 95 percent [on your targets]." Your role as a manager is to make sure your team is defining goals and accomplishing them, but not at the expense of their future ability to do so. When a company is growing, it needs to have a consistent ability to get work done—sustainably—or else growth will stall.

This is very much a moment that calls for balancing management with leadership. Soliciting feedback about how the work was accomplished, recognizing folks who helped the process, and sharing feedback with individuals who hindered it will help the team fix interpersonal or procedural issues, or might prevent them from occurring or worsening. Remember to say the thing you think you cannot say: Provide direct feedback to individuals or to the team and acknowledge that a certain project was accomplished at too high a cost. That includes acknowledging your own role in that reality. Being honest and demonstrating an ability to reflect and improve will encourage mutual self-awareness, and it will help you demonstrate that leadership is not perfect, nor is it comfortable. If your team is able to stop and learn in these situations, they will be better prepared when you turn up the heat and set aspirational objectives instead of regressing to the mean or becoming dysfunctional.

Metrics that matter

Your core company metrics are another structure that can—and should—replicate down from the company level to divisions, teams, and sometimes even to individuals. Like goals, metrics can be set on both long-term and short-term horizons.

In my experience, long-term metrics tend to be lagging indicators. They represent the output of a ton of operational, short-term "input" metrics. At Stripe, we start each year with what we call company targets. These are the metrics for the year that best reflect our company priorities. Some are financial outcome metrics that reflect the work we'll do in the coming year, while others are strategic input metrics, like the number of monthly active businesses using our products. For example, we might track daily or weekly user adoption for a set of newly launched products. These are inputs to metrics that ultimately measure revenue and margin in our P&L. We also have "zero targets," meaning a measure for which the desired outcome is no incidence of the issue occurring, such as outages.

For a public company, what you report to investors is likely a version of your top metrics that matter. It should be clear which leaders, divisions, and teams are accountable for the inputs that drive those outcomes each quarter.

Some teams have less measurable outcomes, but they should still have metrics
For some teams, like benefits, human resources, or finance, it can be difficult to come up with metrics that capture the team's full added value to the division. It's obvious that you need an HR team, but it's not as obvious how to concretely measure their work. Still, it makes sense to set goals and metrics for the team. Although these might be less frequent measures of impact, using data to monitor their general progress is a good practice for team health.

For internal teams, the employee engagement survey is often the best way to measure progress, even if it's only done once or twice a year. For example, you can ask about satisfaction with the work environment and whether the benefits feel fair. For teams like legal and finance, you can work to measure inputs (usually units of time) and outputs (units of work) to calculate a return on those investments. Sometimes these teams resist measuring the time they're spending on specific tasks. But it's instructive to know, for example, that your litigation team spent 800 hours handling potential legal issues in Q3 and that the result was no negative action or settlement against the company when it might have been, say, findings that cost the company $10 million. That's about $12,500 in costs avoided per hour—which seems like a healthy ROI.

This is just to illustrate that it's worth pushing your teams to quantify their work and impact. At the company level, this will help with resourcing decisions. At the team level, knowing the quantifiable contribution of their work also helps with team morale.

SIDEBAR

–

Metrics write-up

This resource is adapted from a piece about metrics and goals written by Stripe's data science team.

Introduction
It isn't always clear how to develop and use metrics, so we've created this playbook to help you and your team(s) develop great metrics.

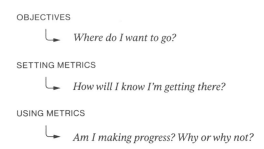

Figure 7. How to use objectives and metrics.

Metrics framework

Using the following metrics framework—see Figure 7 above—can help you manage your team effectively:

Objectives

Objectives are broad statements of prioritization, strategy, and intent. An objective should answer the question "Where do I want to go?"

Creating metrics

Metrics allow you to measure whether you're achieving your objectives. They answer the question "How will I know I'm getting there?" One objective can have one or many metrics.

Long-term metrics: mission and vision

Long-term metrics help define success against your team's mission and three-year vision. Mission metrics tend to be lagging, so they're not necessarily the metrics you monitor regularly to know if you're on track. While mission metrics move slowly over longer time horizons, you should always set milestones for long-term metrics in your annual plans.

Ideally, a team uses the same metrics for a long period of time, e.g., two to five years. Examples include payment volume, revenue, total losses, and API reliability. A team should aim for three to five charter metrics.

Short-term metrics: operating or input metrics

Short-term metrics are real-time or leading indicators that measure activities or intermediate outcomes. While they might not determine the success of your mission or three-year vision, they do inform whether you are on track for your desired outcomes. Operating metrics are often linked directly to team goals. A team should aim for three to five operating metrics.

Other metrics

Measure other results the team wants to achieve in the half. Ideally, these are continuous metrics. If you have a binary metric (e.g., ship product X), that can be a useful starting point to think of a continuous measure for that product (e.g., ship product X to 50 new users).

Once you've set your metrics, make sure you have a dashboard to review your metrics regularly.

Using metrics

Metrics can't help you if you don't use and review them regularly. Only then can they help you answer the question "Am I making progress? Why or why not?"

Metrics are imperfect, and only by reviewing them regularly do you learn how they can be improved or changed to be even more useful. Some ideas for when to review metrics:

- Have a weekly or biweekly metrics meeting.
- Discuss your metrics in a Monday morning standup or biweekly sprint planning.
- Share your metrics in biweekly email updates as a forcing function to review them.
- Hold monthly business review meetings.

–

Whatever your approach to setting metrics that matter, track your goals and define the accompanying metrics consistently across your division so that you're using the same underlying data and language to articulate what you're trying to achieve. Having shared definitions of core concepts is more critical than you might think. For example, what is a customer? Is it someone who has used your product once, or is it someone who is actively using your product? What if your product has seasonality—maybe people use it more in Q4, for example, because of the demand for holiday gifts—and about 20 percent of your customers only show up in Q4? On many consulting projects, and at both Google and Stripe, I struggled to define churn (loss of users) because some of our users churned intermittently. Ultimately, you need to agree on a company-wide definition of a term like "churn" and settle for the fact that it will never be perfect.

Hearkening back to the concept of a team's goals laddering up to the division's goals and mission—which, in turn, ladder up to the company's goals and mission—think about a company where every rung in that ladder has a different definition of a metric. There would be a lack of accountability, and potentially a great deal of friction between teams—an org leader's and a manager's worst nightmare. As you establish your operating systems, the measurement piece is often the most difficult and critical part. Getting it right may require you to work both across divisions and up and down the division to agree on core metrics and definitions. The effort is worth it—the result is that you and your team can measure success knowing that you're using the exact same measure as the rest of the company. This will build collective trust and, ideally, collective accomplishment.

Ownership

Goals and metrics should have owners who are ultimately responsible for completing the work. Assigning ownership is an important aspect of management because it requires determining whose remit, experience, capabilities, and preferences are best suited to a particular task or project. Ownership ranges from the small tasks—who's going to complete the action items from our meeting?—to who is ultimately responsible for the outcomes of a team, group, or division. In fact, each company target should have an owner or owners, who will most likely be members of the executive team. Even though a given target might have dependencies, it's important to make someone responsible for tracking progress and escalating or unblocking if progress stalls.

I remember a meeting at Stripe where we were stuck on assigning ownership for the revenue in our financial plan. The issue was that the revenue projections were dependent on new products launching, and the sales team understandably didn't want to sign up for owning a target that was so dependent on the product and engineering teams. In the end, we decided that the head of sales would be responsible for "what's on the truck" revenue—meaning revenue from currently launched products—and that we would break out a new product revenue line in our plan and hold the product team responsible for that number. It's worth surfacing and teasing these things apart, especially at the top levels of the company. That focus on clear ownership will set a model that filters down into improved execution at all levels of your division.

If you don't define ownership early in a project, division and team culture will suffer. It's easy to spot teams that don't clearly assign ownership. They're the ones that point fingers and protest with statements like "I thought the sales dev reps were delivering the leads—that's why the account execs are behind on the revenue pipeline." Or "Security is blocking us—they didn't build a ring-fenced data store for the HR data, and we can't develop people data dashboards without it." Worse still, teams that lack clear accountability risk becoming political, with folks constantly jockeying to demonstrate that they own the most important work and pointing fingers at others when work doesn't get accomplished.

It's easier to define ownership on teams that have measurable outcomes. For example, I can say that the head of North America sales is responsible for hitting the North America revenue target. For teams that must collaborate to achieve an outcome, like product and engineering, you might find yourself assigning ownership to a pair of people—risky, but possible—or being more granular about the tasks. For example: "Eve is going to write the product requirements document by the end of this week, and Tim is going to build the prototype by the end of the month."

One of the worst management mistakes you can make is to put a task out to your team—say, "We've got to build a demo for the user event by next week"—and, using what I call the "wing and a prayer" method, hope someone will step up and volunteer. Even worse is to just leave it out there, hoping someone does the work without explicitly saying so. (I go into more detail on assigning ownership in Chapter 4.)

Accountability mechanisms
Accountability mechanisms are tools that both leaders and managers should use to review progress toward their goals and missions. They apply at every level—company, team, and individual. (We'll look at all three in this section.) These mechanisms include elements like meetings to review plans and action items, metrics dashboards, and written project snippets.

The first step in implementing accountability mechanisms is to identify who is going to participate in the mechanism and the cadence. If the mechanism in question is a dashboard, who should be reviewing it? If it's snippets, how often are they submitted, and who reads them? If it's a meeting, who will attend? Decide what your mechanisms are and how often you will use them to check in on a division's or team's progress. As an example, each Sunday night ahead of our standing Monday meeting, the Stripe leadership team shares snippets of key information from the past week, priorities for the upcoming week, and progress on action items. Much of the Monday meeting agenda is derived from those snippets.

When I meet COOs from other early-stage companies, we often end up talking about quarterly business reviews (QBRs) and annual planning. Neither mechanism is easy to get right, and both need to evolve with your company. It's always a relief to commiserate with other leaders about the ongoing work of iterating on core operational foundations—but we do so while also recognizing that although these mechanisms are never perfect, the effort involved in setting them up and keeping them current is worthwhile.

QBRs are a common accountability mechanism among companies that have reached a certain level of complexity, for example more than 200 employees and many products and teams. They are both backward-looking assessments of how the team or business unit performed that quarter, including a review of key metrics, and forward-looking discussions of what the unit aims to accomplish over the next few quarters. These reviews are usually an hour to an hour and a half long. At Stripe, the division being reviewed typically shares a (roughly) five-page document or presentation for participants to review before the meeting or during a reading period at the start of the meeting.

The benefits of a quarterly review, which is more of a step back from the day-to-day, are that it:

- Keeps key stakeholders and leaders on the same page about the division's or team's focus areas and progress
- Provides an opportunity to problem-solve any persistent issues in the metrics or in accomplishing key goals
- Aligns leadership on upcoming priorities and how progress will be measured—and, if alignment is lacking, surfaces work to reset the strategy and vision
- Serves as an accountability mechanism for the unit's leader and management team

In my experience, not every division participates in QBRs or gets mentioned at a company all-hands meeting. For example, your finance team might be a key partner that supports the work that goes into the QBRs or reporting on company metrics, but it's rare that finance itself is reviewed or mentioned every quarter. That's not to say that their work isn't important! In order to keep track of progress on these types of teams, the division could create a version of the QBR mechanism at the organizational level, such as a meeting in which the finance leadership team reviews the quarterly progress of teams within the finance organization. (For more on QBRs, see the QBR guidelines and template in the chapter appendix on page 129.)

Another common company-level mechanism is a simple one: Showcase metrics and goals and report on progress at the company all-hands, whether weekly, monthly, or quarterly. Beyond a few summary emails and the all-hands meeting where you review progress toward company targets, I would argue that it's not useful to have too many company-wide review mechanisms. Maintain just a few consistently, and let divisions and teams determine the best approach for their function or area of the business.

Constantly tweaking your company mechanisms can be counterproductive, but taking stock at least once a year can help you evolve as you scale. At Stripe, we usually reset some of our meetings and accountability mechanisms in January. As we return to work, we think about what went well and what didn't in terms of how we ran and organized the company in the year prior. Then we seek feedback from others around the company so that by the end of January we can evolve our approaches for the coming year.

Team-level accountability mechanisms are likely set on annual, quarterly, monthly, and weekly cycles that reflect the company-wide cadence. Teams might not participate in or use every mechanism, and some might devise their own, but it's powerful for a company to have a few core mechanisms that are widely adopted at all levels. Having a standard set of mechanisms that are replicated throughout the company means a lower cognitive load and more aligned execution across teams.

I recommend at least these two forms of accountability mechanisms for every team:

- **Weekly team meeting**: This might be more of an update meeting, or you might use it as a forum for discussion and decision-making. Having at least one standing team meeting is critical to maintain team norms and keep everyone on the same page about priorities, progress, and action items, as well as who owns those action items. (We'll talk more about meetings in Chapter 4.)

- **Weekly team metrics review**: Use the first 15 minutes of your team meeting to review your metrics. Some managers prefer to review metrics in a report rather than in a meeting, but I think there's a great benefit to setting aside time to discuss metrics as a team. Doing so ensures that everyone is focused on the same numbers at the same time, allows you to discuss insights and trends, and signals that everyone has a stake and should be invested in measurement and hitting the numbers.

For managers, the frequency of the accountability mechanisms should correlate with how quickly your team can impact the metrics in question. That way, you can focus on actions you may need to take to make progress. For example, it makes sense to discuss support response times at a weekly team meeting: If you find that the team is missing the target, you can realistically implement changes like adding more staff, making a quick product update, or changing how much time is dedicated to responding to customers, which could affect the numbers over a seven-day period. Reviewing the metrics more often could feel demoralizing, as your decisions will take a few days to make an impact, but reviewing them less often might prevent you from identifying important trends or issues that need to be addressed.

Accountability mechanisms are not the same thing as monitoring. You'll also want to have an automated dashboard that tracks whether something out of the ordinary has happened, such as a sudden increase in support response times. Ideally, that dashboard will take measurements in real time; it might even have built-in alerts that trigger when the numbers cross certain thresholds. Many engineering teams work hard to have observability in the form of real-time dashboards and alerting to issues in the system. There, the accountability mechanism you need to put in place is to determine ahead of time who is responsible for acting on a sudden change in the dashboard and how that person should communicate the root cause and the solution to the relevant stakeholders.

Internal communications

Imagine your organization doubles in size every 12 months. That means that roughly half of today's employees were not at your company one year ago. In another year, at least three out of every four employees will not have been privy to discussions and decisions made just 24 months earlier. You need to decide how you're going to commit important information to company memory so that new members can get up to speed on important context quickly. But you also need to have a clear communications policy so that you don't create a culture divided between those who have company context and those who don't. Internal communications can become either an equalizing or a discriminating force, depending on how you approach it.

At its best, internal communication is another mechanism for building trust. It's a function that scales with your company to keep critical information accessible and useful. But at its worst, it generates internal propaganda. It should go without saying that if you need a team dedicated to convincing your employees that you have a great plan and everything is sunshine, you have a big problem. Trust is inversely proportional to hypocrisy. Good communication is about providing timely and honest information, including being willing to acknowledge mistakes. People forgive mistakes, but they lose trust when information is hidden, false, or misleading, or when leadership says something but doesn't follow through.

Part of your role as a leader and a manager is to focus on good internal communications. Your division needs to know what information will be communicated, when, and where. If team members know that every meeting will include recorded notes with decisions and next steps, they'll have much more confidence in the commitments made during the meeting. And if at a later point there's a discrepancy between how different parties remembered a discussion, you can always reference the meeting notes. Similarly, employees must feel able to access the information they need to do their jobs well, and must feel confident that accessing this knowledge doesn't depend on who you happen to know in the organization or how long you've been at the company.

When should you start investing in internal communications?

Dunbar's number—the suggested cognitive limit to the number of people someone can maintain a social relationship with—is a helpful framework for developing an internal communications strategy.[28] At around 150 people, it becomes harder to remember everyone's name, what team they're on, and what they're responsible for. Hopefully you've been documenting your internal communications practices already, but by the time your company hits 150 people, you should have an internal company website, clear communication guidelines, and policies for what information gets stored, through what channels it's communicated, and what information teams are responsible for maintaining. You should also formalize a means to deprecate out-of-date content.

Company-wide communications are one of the best ways to weave your operating principles into the company fabric. If every team is following their own playbook for certain types of communications—for example, if some organizations communicate divisional changes widely, while others do not—you're going to end up with subcultures that don't resonate with the broader company operating principles. One invaluable bulwark at Stripe is our culture of longform writing. Although many would argue that there's a bit *too* much longform content circulating within Stripe, that mode of clear documentation has, on balance, been critical to our ability to scale ideas, work, and culture quickly.

SIDEBAR
–

Stripe's writing culture

There are many internal Stripe documents describing our communication principles. This summary of why we invest in a writing culture was written by Eeke de Milliano, an early Stripe employee who led the business operations team, and later a number of product teams.

At Stripe, writing is a key part of our internal communications strategy. Discussions are written down and sent out as notes. Important company reviews require a pre-read. And "presentations" are often delivered as written memos. These documents are then stored on the company wiki so that anyone can discover them.

We've invested heavily in writing for three reasons:

- **First, writing is an equalizer**. Great documentation provides context for the people who were not in the room: another team, a colleague in a different office, or someone who has yet to join the company. The latter is particularly important for high-growth businesses. If a company doubles in headcount every year, by year three 90 percent of your team members will not have been privy to discussions from year zero. A strong writing culture levels the playing field between employees independent of location, seniority, or tenure because everyone has access to the same stories, thinking, and decisions.
- **Second, at Stripe we believe longform writing leads to higher-quality thought**. For the writer, it's much easier to spot gaps in logic when you need to string sentences together into a coherent narrative.

For the reader, it's harder to skim a write-up than, say, a visual presentation. In most cases we think that's a feature, not a bug. Longform writing forces attention to detail.

- **Finally, writing is efficient**. People who are great written communicators are, perhaps, also somewhat lazy communicators: They don't want to have to repeat themselves. When the context already exists in a document, you can spend less time getting on the same page about what happened and more time on how to move forward.

The cost of a strong writing culture is that you end up with a lot of documents. It means you have to be diligent about content management across the company. You need to differentiate between evergreen documents, work-in-progress documents, and one-time documents. You need to have a strong information discovery tool and a clear information hierarchy so that information access doesn't become information overload.

You also have to be strict about writing guidelines. Set expectations with teams regarding when they need to send out notes from a meeting and what information the notes should include. Don't just invest in writing down the big, important decisions. Document your quirks (a lexicon of company terms that explains why your company-wide meeting is called ATH, or "all the hands") and your stories (why is the llama the unofficial company mascot?).

Be clear about what "good writing" means for your company. Provide team members with a style guide and examples of great writing. Help employees become better writers by giving them feedback on their writing and by hosting writing classes.

This all takes work from leadership, teams, and individuals. And if you care about having a great writing culture, perhaps the first step is to write that down.
—

Building and assessing an internal communications program
When you're building and assessing your internal communications policy—whether for your team, the division, or the whole company—check if it meets these criteria:

- **Is it complete?** Is the information you're making accessible the information people need to do their jobs?
- **Is it accessible?** Can everyone who needs the information get access? Think about all of the different segments of your division and company, such as tenure, geography, and language.
- **Is it reliable?** Is the content accurate? Do your company-wide meetings start on time, and can people expect the same level of quality each time? Do you send weekly updates to the team consistently and at a predictable cadence?

- **Is it transparent?** Transparency doesn't mean sharing everything. It means that everyone has clarity about what will be shared, when, and with whom. For example, everyone understands that HR matters will not be shared broadly with the company. Still, it's important that employees know exactly what HR information—like salary and seniority levels, for example—is shared with which teams and individuals.

Plan to communicate important information at least three times using different mediums or channels. People tend to get desensitized to communication forums. Employees are like consumers in this way: They have different preferences around how they process information. If you want to make sure that your team is aware of the most important company metrics, for instance, you might share them at a company-wide biweekly meeting, on a company dashboard that they can access at any time, and in a company newsletter with commentary on trends.

Here are some other things to keep in mind with regard to internal communications:

Communicate more in crisis and times of change

In a crisis, the rate of company communication tends to taper off. Don't make the mistake of thinking you need all the answers before you communicate with your employees, because that will result in less communication at precisely the moment when people need to hear from you more. As I'll discuss in the section on managing through uncertainty in Chapter 4, aim to interface more with your employees during a crisis than you think you reasonably should, even if what you're sharing isn't a decision or an update. Something like a personal message or an email that shares your overall reflections can go a long way toward providing assurance that the company is taking the threat or issue seriously.

Any moment of uncertainty or change also requires more communication than you might expect, even (or especially) when you don't have all the answers. When Google bought YouTube, I was the operations leader for Google Video. You can imagine the questions and confusion that arose on my team when news of the acquisition broke. Although I didn't have a lot of insight into the future strategy, I wrote a short note to my team explaining that I thought it was a smart acquisition and one that would ultimately make us stronger. It also helped that I could say I was part of the YouTube integration team and would be able to keep everyone informed as plans for the two properties became clearer. My email showed empathy and transparency, which bought me time and trust with the team as we solidified our plans for the acquisition.

If the precipitating event or crisis is not widely known but is affecting the company—for example, the loss of a large customer—think carefully about when and how you will share the situation. In these cases, you'll usually find yourself in a Goldilocks scenario: Communicating too soon creates uncertainty and anxiety, but communicating too late stokes anger and resentment. Take the time to consult your peers and company leaders to strike an effective balance, and keep the golden rule in mind: If you were an employee who didn't have context about the event, what would you want to know and when? As a manager, take your cues from leadership and work hard to support the message.

Make company-wide meetings count

Company-wide meetings should be scheduled sparingly. When your organization is small, these meetings can be more frequent and can serve as your primary information-sharing mechanism. But as you scale, they become much less effective and probably need to happen less often. Instead, use other communication channels, like your intranet site or email. Reserve company meetings for a chance to hear from and emotionally connect with leaders and highlight critical business results and achievements. (Make sure you model what should be celebrated!) If these meetings are of poor quality, attendance and efficacy will suffer. Either invest in making these company-wide meetings great, or only hold them when you can invest the time to make them better.

Speaking of intranet sites, we call Stripe's internal site Stripe Home. It's designed to connect individuals across the company. The internal tools team, which is responsible for the tools that enable employee productivity, invested heavily in building it (among other mechanisms) to help employees better discover information. These internal mechanisms are small but critical investments in your future scale—they should not be seen as luxury items to prioritize only once you've finished working on product features.

SIDEBAR

—

Stripe Home

This description of Stripe Home is excerpted from a blog post written by Michael Schade, the head of Stripe's internal tools team at the time.[29] Not only is Home a central place that makes it easier for employees to collaborate and find information, it's also beautifully designed and engineered. Brian Krausz, a longtime Stripe engineer, and Bill Labus, one of Stripe's top designers, worked on it personally, and their commitment signaled the importance of internal collaboration and communication.

At Stripe, we've always been intentional about how we communicate, share information, and stay connected. Back when Stripe was smaller, it was easy for this to happen automatically. But by the time we hit around 150 people, it became hard to know everyone's name. So at a company hackathon, a few Stripes created People, a directory to help Stripes meet and get to really know each other.

We've since turned People into a full-fledged product called Home, weaving both how we know one another and how we share information beyond email into the same product. Used by 99 percent of Stripes in the last month, Home is the source of truth for who we are, what we're doing, and why—and a platform for enabling individuals and helping them get to know one another.

In the spirit of the original People, new Stripes are front and center on Home, along with their quick video introductions, a flipbook of existing Stripes, and a list of activities happening around the company, which range from classes we host to events for our users.

Individual Stripes collaborate—a lot. Our search system lets Stripes look across documents, people, teams, and even API models, with live filters to help narrow the corpus quickly. The search interface is completely API-driven with modular content indexers underneath, so it's easy to add new types of content to the same interface we use to find everything else.

Under the hood, Home is built on the same technology as our user-facing products (such as the dashboard) because we wanted to make it easy to move between developing user-facing and internal-facing products. This has made Home a favorite for new Stripes' spin-up projects and a popular go-to for hackathon projects.

We're still figuring out how to balance transparency with information overload, serendipity with curated content, and crisp interfaces and team boundaries with the actual human part that makes the company what it is.

–

Operating cadence

We've covered the constituent parts of a successful operating system. The operating cadence is how you, well, operationalize it. I once worked on a consulting project for DirecTV called "Operationalizing CRM," and I remember that, as I wrote those words at the top of every presentation, I found the word "operationalizing" awkward and uninspiring. Yet here I am, extolling the virtues of operationalizing your operating system!

Because humans are fundamentally creatures of habit, you'll want to create an operating cadence—the schedule or rhythm with which your company, divisions, or teams provide progress reports and make decisions—that they can follow naturally. People should be able to break with the framework if there's an emergency or another good reason to do so, but most of the time you'll want stability and predictability. If different teams set goals at different times and measure the results with different definitions of the data, chaos will reign over execution and morale will suffer.

Cadences will vary by manager, team, and individual, but they should be agreed upon up front by all of the relevant parties. They will very likely mirror the company cadence, which is often driven by milestones in the calendar year. There's no secret to designing your operating cadence—it depends on the type of team you're running and, often, on the type of business and company you're operating within. The key is to have a cadence but not get stuck in it. Often, these rhythms will require iteration, and they should be regularly revisited to keep them relevant and fresh.

Examples of operating cadences include:

- Annual planning processes
- Quarterly business reviews
- Monthly all-hands meetings
- Biweekly 1:1s
- Weekly snippets and team meetings (with metrics reviews)
- Daily standups

If you don't have a set operating cadence, observe what types of interactions and reviews are happening organically. For instance, maybe a few teams are already using a given process or communication mechanism. Figure out why they're happening and what's useful and not useful about these approaches. Once you've learned more, try testing the approach with a broader swath of the company or with the whole company for a month or a quarter, then solicit feedback. Be ready to iterate.

Within each cadence, teams and individuals will produce various kinds of reports, including written updates, automated reports, and other measures of progress. A support team, for example, might start each week by reviewing customer satisfaction, feedback, and response rates, then create a game plan to improve the numbers in the coming week. A product leadership team might review the launch calendar and share status updates on each upcoming launch. The key is to provide predictable, common, and consistent structures that serve as touchstones for every person in the division or team. Like the smaller unit of a weekly team meeting, your collective operating cadence should help people develop a shared understanding of the importance of their work, how they're going to accomplish it, what success looks like, and how to measure it. (See Figure 8 on the next page for an example of a company-wide operating cadence.)

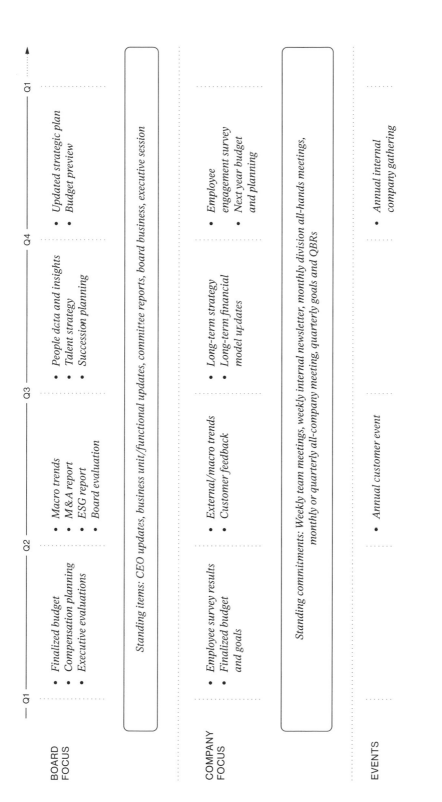

Figure 8. Example operating cadence, with board and company meetings and events.

Be sure to solicit frequent feedback on the operating system and cadence. You'll want to know:

- Does everyone know what the mission and the objectives are for the
  company, the division, and the team, as well as the work they're individually expected to do?
- Is there a clear timeline for planning and execution, and are there established measures of progress against targets?
- Are projects with dependencies aligned and agreed on across the relevant teams and leaders so ownership and priorities are clear?
- Does everyone know how you'll measure success and who is accountable for the constituent parts of the work? Do they know when plans
  or results should be delivered?
- Are there mechanisms in place to monitor progress, make decisions,
  and unblock teams?
- Are there communication structures in place to provide updates on
  goals and notify relevant teams of any changes?
- Do you recognize and celebrate success? Do you share and learn from
  mistakes? Do your internal communications reinforce the company
  values and operating approach?

I recommend designing and delegating your operating cadence to suit
the preferences and competencies of the leadership team. Only spin up
these processes once you're certain that leaders will make a dedicated effort to implement them. Ideally, there will be one owner for each key structure in the operating cadence, and all of the other leaders will agree to
honor the structure.

A colleague once observed that I managed to be "switched on" for every
review meeting, no matter how many times we'd conducted it. I think it's
generally true that strong operators are dedicated and consistent in how they
honor run-the-company structures, and that great operations are often a
matter of repetition and consistent improvement over time. Young companies tend to be filled with people who love inventing and building new things,
and therefore need to balance these tendencies by hiring or elevating leaders
who can recognize and invest in repeatable and repeated processes. You
want a mix of leaders and processes that marry creativity and invention with
operational rigor. Be clear on which leader owns which company structures,
and take care to match those structures with each leader's strengths and
abilities. The example they set will imbue the structure with cultural and exe-
cutional importance. Conversely, lack of ownership—or, worse, leadership
not adhering to company operating approaches—will undermine your ability
to build a stable architecture that grounds the day-to-day, week-to-week,

month-to-month, and year-to-year accomplishment of your mission and long-term goals.

A brief note on process

Process has become something of a pariah in modern business environments. It's known as the thing that slows people down and sucks their souls. In fact, I called this chapter "Foundations and Planning" because calling it "Your Process" might have sent readers screaming for the hills.

I often hear from founders who worry about their companies becoming "bloated" with process, meetings, check-ins, and updates. Understandably, many managers are wary of introducing too much process, and excessive meetings can become a giant drag on productivity. But having a process that guides how you run things isn't inherently bad. Bad processes cause bloat, but good processes help provide clarity, which leads to faster execution.

A few thoughts on process:

Watch out for defensive processes

In environments without clear owners and decision-makers, something starts to happen that I call defensive—or, more bluntly, cover-your-ass—process. These types of processes tend to crop up when something has gone wrong and, instead of coming up with a clear owner to avoid the mistake in the future, someone creates a process.

I remember a time at Google when the "bit flip"—the approval mechanism—to launch a new feature or product swelled from something like 3 people to over 20. It started with legal's insistence on a review, and took on more and more bloat as multiple functions wanted official notice of an impending launch. Eventually, the product managers rightly complained, and the powers that be reduced the bit flips back to a handful of people by making ownership and accountability clear. For example, the product manager was tasked with consulting legal and other impacted functions, and then it was their job to make a decision on readiness to launch based on the advice they'd received. It was no longer legal's job to defensively block launches that should have been more thoroughly vetted.

Good processes should create lightweight checks that solidify alignment and achieve a combination of speed and adherence to best practices, so that participants no longer have to divine the best way to do something. Defensive processes, on the other hand, exist because people are not aligned on who owns a particular decision, and they inevitably slow things down.

Beware of stale processes

We've all seen it happen. People ignore deadlines for requested materials. Participants start opening their laptops in meetings and don't submit updates on their work. Folks get disruptive and fall into roles: the "What about the bigger picture?" person, or the "Do we have an action item owner?" person. Just like meetings, processes can get stale and become rote. It doesn't mean the process was bad, but it may mean that the process has outgrown its purpose and it's time to revisit it. Or maybe it was a defensive process, and now that you've rooted out the source of confusion that made everyone play defense, the process can conclude.

You also don't want to change processes too quickly. You're trying to achieve the tricky balance of having a process in place for long enough to give it a real shot but not so long that bad processes will stick around and damage team productivity. Revisit your processes every six months or so. More often than that can be destabilizing, but less often will cause people to switch to autopilot and stop engaging.

Allow for experimentation
People tend to be afraid to experiment with processes because they worry that it makes them look unprofessional or indecisive. But you may not know what works best for your team until you've tried it. I'm a big fan of experimenting with systems and processes. If you do experiment with your processes, make sure to:

- State how long you're going to try the process for.
- Determine when you'll check back in to see how things are going.
- Set your evaluation criteria for whether to continue or revisit the process.

Process is not synonymous with meetings
Meetings are useful tools for doing a lot of the things you need to do to run your teams well: sharing information, having discussions, making decisions, bonding as a team. But there are many ways to get things done without meetings, depending on your team's preferences and what you're trying to achieve. One way to do this is to ask yourself: Could this meeting's objective have been achieved through a written update or by having everyone contribute to a project tracker? A good process should subtract from the number of meetings, not add more.

How to tell if something is wrong with your operating system or cadence
Pay attention to the following warning signs—they could indicate that you need to revisit your operating system or cadence:

- Goals, timelines, or accountable owners for work are unclear. In other words, you don't know which team is doing what, when.
- You feel like everything is moving too slowly.
- People are flagging problems but aren't able to suggest solutions.
- You can't find simple information on the status of the work.

- No one can tell you who the decision-maker is for a project or what the priorities are for the company or their team.
- People stop participating or showing up when asked to contribute key information or to participate in meetings.
- It's not clear which updates or meetings matter, and you hate updating the tracker or attending your own meetings.

A sound operating system running on an efficient cadence is essential to execution and lays the groundwork for great management. It's the foundation for accomplishing your work as a company builder and manager. Once it's in place, it guides and shapes all the other aspects of your company, including:

- **Hiring**: Bringing people into the organization who will carry the highest-priority work forward and set a positive company culture.
- **Team development**: Maximizing impact and efficiency through processes that help people communicate, make decisions, and collaborate, as well as measuring the impact of the team's work.
- **Feedback and improvement**: Developing and coaching employees as you collectively identify the skills necessary for organizational success, while also helping employees clarify their own development goals and career aspirations.

We'll take these elements one by one in the following chapters, starting with how to get the right people on board as your company grows.

—

Chapter 2

Scan the QR code to access printer-friendly versions of these worksheets.

Stripe's Operating Principles

These were Stripe's operating principles as of December 2021:

How we work

Users first
We have a weighty obligation to the businesses built on Stripe and the everyday people they serve. Because we're so critical to our users' success, we must keep their needs front and center in all we do.

Move with urgency and focus
A bias for action speeds our learning and delights our users. Focus on what matters most, make fast initial progress, and iterate toward the best outcome.

Be meticulous in your craft
Doing things well is in Stripe's DNA. We value craftsmanship for its own sake and are fervently committed to producing surprisingly great work.

Seek feedback
We value intellectual honesty and look for other Stripes with the expertise to refine our ideas, challenge us, and deepen our understanding across the business.

Deliver outstanding results
Stripes are high achievers with a drive to succeed. We take end-to-end accountability for seeing our work through and delivering on our commitments.

Who we are

Curious
We lead with a genuine interest in people, ideas, and the unknown. We work hard to understand other points of view and prefer investigating to being right.

Resilient
Startups are tumultuous places, and the audacity of our goals will mean occasional failure. We view setbacks as opportunities to sharpen our skills.

Humble
Stripes are humble, not arrogant or complacent, and create an inclusive environment for all. We aren't wedded to how we currently do things – lots about our current practices will turn out to be wrong.

Macro-optimistic
Stripes reject cynicism, knowing that all problems can be solved with the right

understanding and that progress is only inevitable through focused effort. We are believers in the long term.

Exothermic
Stripes generate an energy and warmth that is infectious across teams and throughout the company. We are genuinely excited about our work and about creating an exceptionally welcoming environment for all Stripes.

And leaders

Obsess over talent
The quality of the Stripes you attract and retain defines your team, so developing a keen talent radar can be your biggest competitive advantage. Be the person who reads and investigates every candidate packet. Push back when you sense that managers are making hires who are merely fine. Hold an equally high bar for performance! Create a culture of quickly addressing mishires, developing critical talent, and finding challenging work for your strongest performers.

Elevate ambitions
Know where your team is headed next year, in 4 years, and in 10 years, and develop a compelling vision for that future. Guide your team to redefine what's possible by expanding what's reasonable.

Set the pace and energy
Stripe is intense — we have broad ambitions and serious obligations to our users. Sign your team up for bold goals, articulate a plan to achieve them faster than expected, and focus on making this energizing, rewarding, and fulfilling for your teams.

Make decisions; be accountable
It's not always clear who should make a decision. Effective leaders embrace decision-making in cases of murky ownership, either making the call themselves or collaborating across the necessary teams to drive an outcome. They clearly communicate decisions and hold themselves and their teams accountable for results.

Lead with clarity and context
Translate chaos into a clear, compelling plan. Be deeply informed about what's happening across Stripe and create your team's plans in reference to the broader work.

Solve problems
Be a persistent force for progress. Our leaders must work with their teams and across Stripe to quickly and effectively solve problems — especially when they're hard.

Finally, while we continue to evolve, some of the guideposts we used to get here remain helpful. Though these aren't the focus of our core operating principles, we encourage you to also consider your work in reference to some of these "classic" Stripe slogans:

- We haven't won yet.
- Efficiency is leverage.
- Be meticulous about the foundations.
- Disagree and commit.
- Really, really, really care.
- Operate from first principles.
- Be politely relentless.

Team Charter

Mission

Example:

Provide best-in-class security to all of our users and their accounts on the dashboard. This encompasses both authentication and authorization, including dashboard roles and permissioning.

_____

_____

_____

_____

_____

_____

_____

_____

_____

_____

_____

_____

_____

_____

_____

_____

_____

_____

_____

Vision

Example:

We aim to build strong trust internally and externally in our ability to provide best-in-class security for all of our users, from enterprises to small users, while avoiding overhead for our users and support team. Account takeovers will no longer be an active problem (neither as a terrible user experience nor as a financial loss). While we won't ever be able to get them to zero, we and our customers should have full faith that when they occur (e.g., through an internal bad actor on the customer side), we did everything within creative reasonability to prevent them. We will also deliver "table-stakes" security features such that we fly through user security–related discussions with new enterprise customers.

Customers

Example:

- We're responsible for the account security of every user and account, ensuring that their accounts and the sensitive data therein remain theirs alone.
- We protect the interests of all merchant accounts by enabling them to control who in their business can access what, and by protecting them from rogue actions.

_____

_____

_____

_____

_____

_____

_____

_____

_____

_____

_____

_____

_____

_____

_____

_____

_____

_____

_____

_____

Metrics

Example:

Number of accounts that have experienced a takeover in a given month

- Measuring: User experience, risk of unhappy customer leak, support burden
- Target value: [X]

Account takeover losses

- Measuring: Direct financial loss and loss of margin due to account security issues
- Target value: [X]

Percentage of all dashboard users who have adopted two-factor authentication

- Measuring: Protection of entire user base from account takeovers
- Target value: [X]

Strategic importance

Example:

Aside from the financial benefits of reducing losses, having better account security will improve the user experience and build user trust. Strong foundations here will help prevent attacks, bad user experiences, and losses, since we will become a target if we are not world-class. A strong track record will also increase the appeal of our products to enterprise users, open up new sales conversations, and accelerate existing ones.

_____

_____

_____

_____

_____

_____

_____

_____

_____

_____

_____

_____

_____

_____

_____

_____

_____

_____

Major risks

Example:

- Team gets pulled into lower-priority work by audit or compliance activities
- Major security breach
- Major new attack vectors
- Death by a thousand cuts of one-off enterprise requests
- Tech debt

Provided interfaces

Example:

- Login code
- 2FA infrastructure
- Session infrastructure
- Login/email challenge
- Dashboard auditing models
- Account recovery/password reset flow

_____

_____

_____

_____

_____

_____

_____

_____

_____

_____

_____

_____

_____

_____

_____

_____

_____

_____

_____

_____

Dependent interfaces

Example:

- User registration UI
- Verificator (interface for SMS 2FA)
- User email system and team

_____

_____

_____

_____

_____

_____

_____

_____

_____

_____

_____

_____

_____

_____

_____

_____

_____

_____

_____

_____

_____

Organizational Foundations

To test whether you have a clear operating system, fill out the table below. How easily can you complete it for an individual report on your team, for one of your teams, and for your division? Is this information documented anywhere in your division, and is it easy to find? If you're having trouble filling out this template, imagine how your teams and reports must feel!

	Individual	Team	Division
Mission			
Objectives with owner (DRI)			
Key metrics			
Accountability mechanisms			
Operating cadence			

This information should be documented and easily accessible on your team's and division's internal homepages. On those same pages or at the top of your internal dashboard, if separate, be sure to include similar detail about your top objectives and metrics with targets for the year. (See the next template.)

Objectives and Metrics Checklist

It's worthwhile to scrutinize any documented objective for clarity and alignment with the team's or division's mission and plan to contribute to company success. You can use the following template to do so.

Objective	Metric	Baseline	Target

Are your objectives:

☐ Inspirational?

☐ Actionable by your team?

☐ Related to your team's mission and vision?

☐ Related to the company's priorities and goals?

Are the objectives SMART?

☐ Specific

☐ Measurable

☐ Achievable

☐ Results-oriented

☐ Targeted

Also check:

☐ Is the metric a leading indicator?

☐ Does it have counterweight metrics? (For example, you could increase the number of users by giving away the product for free, but you don't want to do that! So if you have a user metric, what is your counterweight revenue metric?)

☐ Is there a framework to evaluate the metric (e.g., a calculation or a query)?

☐ Does the metric have an owner?

☐ Is the metric relative, not absolute? (For example, instead of "Increase the number of users by 1,000," explain the relative growth: "Increase the number of users by 20 percent, from 5,000 to 6,000.")

☐ Does it take into account your existing user growth? (For example, you might be able to hit your revenue target just through growth from existing users, but then you haven't done anything to earn that growth.)

Writing Good OKRs

This guide was written by Stripes on our finance and tech enablement teams in collaboration with our CTO, David Singleton.

The basics

Write: Note the top-level 3–5 objectives, with 1–5 key results per objective, that you're committed to accomplishing in the quarter. Identify which are must-hit goals. (See the next section for guidance.)

Collaborate: If you partner closely with other functions or teams, get feedback and make sure you agree on the OKRs you've set.

Publish: When you're done, change "Draft" to "On track" in the document title to signal that your OKRs are published (on the company intranet or other document-sharing method) and in progress.

Guidance on ambition

Most goals should be ambitious yet attainable. This means we expect to achieve the vast majority of them over time, while also recognizing that some will be a stretch. Overall, we should expect to score in the 70–80 percent range over the quarter.

A small number of our goals (20–30 percent for any given team in a quarter) might be hard commitments. These should be marked as "must-hit," and we expect to reach 95 percent attainment or more. If these goals are trending behind, we expect to sacrifice other goals in service of hitting them.

Good OKRs start with good objectives

Best practices for good objectives

- Objectives are clearly defined goals that answer the question "Where do I want to go?"
- Objectives should be an outcome – a description of the state of the world at the end of the quarter. They should focus on the user problem you're solving.
- Objectives should be focused on the most important work. There should be no more than 3–5 of them.
- Objectives chart intent and direction – they chart outcomes.
- Objectives are long-term and often span several quarters, even years.
- Objectives nest up and down to some degree in an organization.

- Objectives should be ambitious and can be open to (some) interpretation and debate.
- Objectives can be aspirational (70 percent) or committed (100 percent). Identify which are which!
- All objectives should matter. The best objectives are inspirational.
- Objectives can be shared across teams.

Define key results

Best practices for good key results

- Key results are concrete definitions of success. Each one determines whether the objective has been achieved or not and answers the question "How will I pace myself to see if I'm on track?"
- Key results should list outcomes, not activities. There should be 1–5 key results per objective.
- Key results are measurable and binary: Either they did or didn't happen. They're not open to interpretation.
- Key results flow from a theory of a plausible causal mechanism that connects the key result with the objective and with your own work.
- Key results build a shared model of reality across teams and organizations.
- Key results should compound over time, if possible.

Common pitfalls when formulating OKRs

- Using an activity or action as an outcome.
- Having a key result that can't be measured in some way.
- Turning a roadmap directly into objectives and key results.
- Writing more than 3–5 objectives, or 1–5 key results per objective.

Iterating and Scoring

Mid-quarter scoring

At some point in the quarter, the team should get together to discuss progress to date and give it an approximate score. The easiest way to do this is a simple **green**, **yellow**, and **red** rubric accompanied by an assessment of **on track**, **off track**, or **at risk**. (If your team prefers to use percentage-based scoring, do what works best.) Items that are off track or at risk should be discussed further so that the team can find ways to redirect their energy and build in time to recover.

How to handle changes in information and priorities

If new information arises that changes an objective or key result, there should be some common practices to track and handle the changes. This could mean scoring an OKR lower or swapping it out. Do whatever makes sense for the team, but be consistent and clear. Most importantly, communicate changes to any impacted teams, and clearly document what's changed and why.

Here's some general guidance:

- If you add or drop a key result, document the decision and notify impacted teams.

- If you add an objective (e.g., due to an urgent shift in the world), document whether it resulted in deprioritizing existing work and, if so, what work was deprioritized.

- Dropping an objective should be rare. This may happen due to a change in constraints or because it truly isn't providing value to users. In these cases, it's best to stop working on it and keep it in the OKRs for scoring and discussion.

Quarterly Business Reviews (QBRs)

These QBR documents were written by Kailey Stockenbojer on the Stripe finance team in consultation with various Stripe leaders, including me.

QBR guidelines

What statements should be true after your QBR meeting

- The QBR provided clear charter (long-term) and operating (short-term) metrics, with quarterly targets looking out through the end of the year. Ask yourself: Where do we want to be in two years, and are we on track? What has to go right for us to get there? Use the metrics to comment on your trajectory.
- The QBR explained which goals we executed upon, which ones we did not, why, and how we can work together to close any gaps and get to where we planned to be (or, if plans are changing, why they're changing).
- The QBR explained how much we're investing relative to what the area is producing. Based on the results we're seeing, participants can make decisions on how much should be invested.
- Participants left with clear mutual expectations of what will be accomplished in the coming periods.
- We know what potential obstacles may come up through the end of the year.
- Leadership understands what you need to accelerate and produce outstanding results.

Delivering a stellar QBR

- **Focus on results**: We already had a plan, we took a specific action, and we can see specifically (with metrics) how execution is progressing, rather than having a winding discussion about potential plans.
- **Be candid**: The core audience is leadership. They want a candid assessment of what your team has accomplished, what it needs to do better at, and what it plans to do.
- **Be concise**: This is a six-page narrative, plus an appendix with tables and/or charts.
- **Prepare in advance**: Share the memo at least 24 hours in advance. We will also allow reading time in the meeting – the meeting will be a discussion informed by your memo.

- **Be present**: Those who join should be present in the discussion and minimize work distractions. (We recommend snoozing Slack notifications and minimizing other windows.) Even though we will consume materials digitally, we advise against linking out to supplementary materials.

Prepare for the QBR meeting

- Provide a link to your QBR document in the calendar and leadership guidebook at least 24 hours in advance of the meeting.
- If you have confidential topics to cover, add them in a separate document, set sharing settings to restricted, and add the link to the guidebook. Provide document access to your QBR attendees.
- Email the discussion materials directly to your attendees.
- Prepare an agenda of key topics you want to cover with leadership.

During the QBR meeting

- Allow time for pre-reads and announce the conclusion of pre-read time.
- Gather top-of-mind questions and topics from attendees and add them to the agenda you prepared prior to the meeting.
- If necessary, prioritize the topics to make sure you cover the most important ones first in the allotted time.
- Include metrics as a standard discussion topic.
- The QBR leader should drive the discussion based on the key topics on the agenda.
- Take comprehensive notes or arrange for someone attending the meeting to take notes. This should include action items and owners.

After the QBR meeting

- Share the notes with all QBR participants.
- Add your action items to our QBR action item tracker.
- Reflect on the quality of the QBR, including the quality of the metrics. Gather feedback from partners and leadership if it was not readily provided. What do you need to work on to have a more effective QBR? What will you change for next time?

QBR outline

Note: The suggested word count and page limits are directional, to help you stay within the six-page limit. If your content exceeds the six-page limit, the QBR leader should determine which section(s) to shorten at their discretion.

Executive summary (250 words or less)

What do you want leadership to know about your performance and strategic direction? This should be a candid assessment, not a summary of your successes.

Narrative (two pages maximum)

Write up to two pages on your team's quarterly performance and strategic direction. The narrative should speak for itself, and the "voiceover" should simply be used to focus the discussion. Your narrative should be grounded in your charter and operating metrics, including your discussion of performance against goals.

Your discussion of results should be candid. Appropriately balance your discussion based on your relative performance against your goals. If you missed your goals, the discussion should be skewed toward lowlights. (Why didn't you deliver?) If you met your goals, you should still discuss any areas that did not go well.

The narrative should discuss your quarterly results, your outlook for the remainder of the year, and longer-term strategic considerations. It's up to the leader to determine how to balance the discussion, but generally most teams should spend at least 50 percent of their discussion on strategy and outlook.

We recommend that you embed relevant visualizations of metrics in your narrative where helpful to the reader. All metrics not included in your narrative should be included in the metrics performance section of your QBR.

Example outline

We recognize that it can be useful to have examples of outlines that have helped other teams have effective discussions. You own the QBR – we encourage you to structure the narrative to best describe your team's performance and trajectory, and to only use the outline if useful.

1. **Current quarter reflection**: Explain your performance against your goals.
    1.1 Support your performance against goals with operating and charter metrics.
       1.1.1 How were metrics impacted, and how did they change over time?
       1.1.2 What did you do (or not do) to influence them?
    1.2 Discuss key ships. If you missed key ships, why?

1.3 Discuss user feedback.

    1.3.1   Document top user asks and how well you are addressing them.

    1.3.2   Document user compliments in areas where you are performing well.

1.4 Discuss overall velocity.

2. **Outlook**: Look forward to the next quarter and the next year.

   2.1 What are your top three goals in order of priority?

     2.1.1   Which metrics will your goals impact?

     2.1.2   How will user stories and pain points be impacted?

     2.1.3   Are you on track to meet these goals? If not, why?

   2.2 What keeps you up at night? (Read: What should leadership be worried about?)

3. **Other sections**: Use at your discretion, based on what is relevant for your team.

   3.1 Cross-functional asks.

   3.2 Hiring progress.

   3.3 Team morale.

Metrics performance (two pages maximum – if you have additional metrics, please put them in the appendix)

For the most part, your metrics discussion should happen in your narrative. Use this section to briefly describe changes to the metrics you use to measure your performance (changes since last QBR or anticipated changes). Include graphs. Your metrics should cover a roughly two-year time horizon (where available), not just the current period.

If you revised your metrics during planning, your charts (and/or commentary) should include both the original and revised target, where applicable.

Examples of key metrics

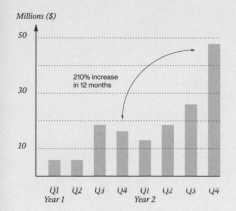

Year-over-year

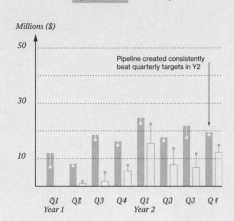

Pipeline created and deals signed

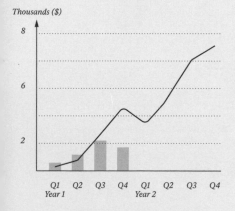

Volume: *vs. budget*

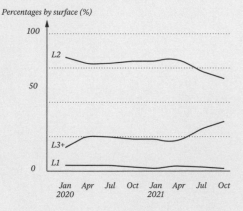

Unified web go-lives

Product P&L

Product teams: In addition to your metrics, please work with finance to include your product P&L as a table in this section.

Cross-functional focus areas

In addition to your core performance and metrics, we've defined a set of focus areas that are important to the company and require engagement from business leaders to make progress on our company objectives. Please add comments on your assessment scores (e.g., what you're doing to improve the score) and include a screenshot of the output below. Reach out to the focus area DRI with questions on the assessments.

Focus area	DRI	QX score	QY score	Comments
Reliability				
Security				
Efficiency				
Operations				
Product quality				

Progress on goals (one page maximum – if you wish to share additional goals, please put them in the appendix)

Select your top 5–10 goals and summarize them in the table on the next page. There is a strict one-page limit.

Team objective	SHIPPED	ON TRACK	OFF TRACK	AT RISK	Total
Objective 1					
Objective 2					
Objective 3					
Objective 4					
Objective 5					
Total					
% of Total					100%

Team objective	Goal	Due date	Goal state	QX score	Comments
(Optional)	(Ship and/or metric to move)				

Appendix A: Required tables

Prior QBR action items

Address the action items from your prior QBR and provide a status update on any action items you have not yet addressed.

Action item	Follow-up status/narrative	Owner

Operating expenses (for non-product teams)

If you have not included a product P&L, your finance partner can share your operating expenses budget versus actuals to include here. Product teams can optionally include this as additional detail.

Headcount

Provide your headcount by sub-team based on how your team is organized.

Sub-team				
Description				
Current headcount	Current ANS	YTD net change	Year envelope	ROY net hire capacity
Total headcount				

Top asks from users

We co-create our products with our users, internal and external. What are their highest priorities? The status should be **committed**, **partially committed**, or **not committed**.

User ask	User segment	Status	Comments

Appendix B: Additional supporting materials

Use this section at your discretion to include additional supporting materials and links. Examples might include top recent ships, top upcoming ships, additional goals, etc.

_____

_____

_____

_____

_____

_____

_____

_____

_____

_____

_____

_____

_____

_____

_____

_____

_____

_____

_____

_____

_____

_____

_____

_____

_____

_____

_____

_____

Core Framework 2

A Comprehensive Hiring Approach

If you believe talent is everything, then your hiring process should also be everything. Your goal is to find the people who will thrive and who will have the most positive impact at your company at every level. Once you've hired them, you'll need to acclimate them to the company in ways that ensure they're set up for success and can carry forth the organization's mission and culture.

One of my final interviews before joining Google was with a director who tested whether I could handle the work environment and fit with the culture. He was very open and friendly, and he got me talking comfortably. Near the end of the interview, he challenged me: "So, what's your real career ambition?" I quickly replied, "To undermine the superstructure from within." I couldn't believe I'd said that out loud! (I guess I said the thing I thought I could not say?) I think I got the job in part because I was open and honest, but also because my answer fit well with a disruptive company's mission. I was attracted to Google because I believe technology can have a positive societal impact and democratize access to opportunity. On their side, Google was looking for people who thought differently about how to build and operate products—people who could imagine a world where Google had become what it is today, almost 20 years before the fact, and then figure out how to get there.

I was interviewing for a manager role (yes, the dreaded middle management), but I soon learned that the interview process at Google was extensive and rigorous no matter the role. I think that's appropriate. A company's talent is its destiny, and when you're growing quickly, early talent will become future leaders. Among my first direct reports at Stripe was a recruiter who had previously recruited and managed operations programs for Memorial Sloan Kettering Cancer Center. She was a dynamo recruiter and, equally as exciting, a skilled communicator with great acumen for building operational processes. She's also a prime example of growing talent from within. Today, she is the head of Stripe's recruiting and people partners teams, a global organization hundreds of people strong.

Some companies mechanize hiring for most roles and conduct leadership hiring quite differently, which I think can be destructive to quality and, potentially, to trust. If you want to send a signal that bringing in talented people is critical to get right for the future of the enterprise, you need rigorous processes that reinforce that message for all levels of hiring. Although leadership hiring may be more customized in ways appropriate to the level of the hire, the fundamentals and cultural import of leader and employee hiring should be similar. If leaders seemingly waltz in, there will be suspicion of their credibility, even if they have impressive résumés.

Seek a hiring approach that balances the need to hire quickly with the need to hire the most successful person for the role rather than the most expedient one. The scariest thing you can say to an operations leader is "I want quality *and* speed."[30] They know just how hard this is to do, whereas other leaders might not realize what fulfilling this well-intended request actually involves. But when you're growing quickly, your hiring approach needs to achieve that operational nirvana. To do so, practically everyone at the company must be involved in hiring, and they must consistently prioritize the work and adhere to the operational and cultural standards you've set. The good news is that they'll be motivated to do so—these are their future colleagues, after all. Once you've set the expectations, ensure that the surrounding work and processes reinforce the goals of quality and speed while measuring and monitoring for outlying behaviors, good or bad, that affect the process.

What the industry calls "talent acquisition" is really just marketing and sales—specifically, what we call growth or performance marketing. At the highest level, you need to invest in your talent brand, lead identification, and outreach in order to direct traffic—job page views and applicants—into your "funnel." Then you need to have the means to assess lead quality and optimize conversion through the various stages of the process for the leads most likely to succeed. Many companies have built successful and repeatable sales and marketing acquisition arms, and you can do the same with the talent funnel, although admittedly with a more variable human element.

As with any strong operation, hiring starts with clarifying the organization's overarching objectives and cultural principles, followed by an outline of the process you intend to build and an overview of how you'll measure success. This process doesn't end with a candidate accepting the job but rather with a successful onboarding experience and by forging strong connections between the new hire and their manager and with the company overall. (Figure 9 on the next page offers a view of the steps involved in the hiring process, or the hiring conversion funnel.)

Throughout this chapter, you'll find information on how to navigate each step in this funnel, followed by sections on how to alter the approach when recruiting for leadership roles.

Figure 9. The hiring conversion process.

Like the adjustments you make when acquiring and converting sales leads based on the customer segment—smaller prospects might be self-serve or lower-touch, for example, while higher-volume and larger prospects might need more bespoke treatment—you'll need to make adjustments to your hiring and onboarding approaches at various stages of your company's growth and for different types of roles. It's useful to think of the unique hiring needs for different levels as a pyramid:

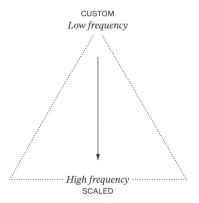

Figure 10. Unique hiring needs at different levels.

At the base, where you're hiring at volume to fill lots of open roles, much of the work and interviewing will be done by people who have already proven themselves in the role, followed by a final manager interview. Hiring at this level is generally a set process with many available interviewers. The number of people you need to do this work closely mirrors the number of people you need to hire. Instead of separate hiring committees or hiring meetings, you might even have a more uniform candidate review and approval process.

As the pyramid narrows, the process and the approach become more focused and customized to the role. For hiring at the middle of the pyramid and above, there should be a separate and set hiring team or committee that includes the same interviewers for every candidate, including key cross-functional partners. The committee will develop insights on the match between the candidate and the role. This pattern recognition should ultimately result in a committee that helps make the hiring decision with more conviction, and thus a stronger hire.

When you're hiring at the very highest level, you'll still have a hiring team, but it will take an even more bespoke approach. This team will mainly include your current executives, plus a set of individuals that you select specifically for this hiring process. (More on this in the section on leadership hiring on page 190.)

Just as you need to strike a balance when designing a planning process appropriate to your company stage, you'll need to adjust your process for hiring candidates who are not in early-career roles but are also not leadership hires: the middle of the pyramid. If this is the first person you're hiring into a new role—your first in-house lawyer, say—the process will be more tailored. But if you're hiring more support managers to add to an existing team, for example, your process can be more prescriptive, because you know what you're looking for and you generally know how to find qualified people. Over time, you'll want to gain efficiencies and build more scale into the process, but only once you've established that you can repeat it at high quality. For those top roles, you're not likely to standardize all aspects of the approach at any point.

SIDEBAR
–

The founder's role in hiring

I recently received two texts from founders asking if they should interview every candidate who is a finalist for a role at their company. If you're early in your scale—say, 100 employees or less per founder or trusted senior leader—the answer is yes. Your early hires are critical to the company's trajectory, and founders are the people best equipped to model the hiring behavior they want to see, namely a rigorous interview and a high bar for quality.

I've seen founders have the most impact in situations where the hire is just fine—those candidates who meet every qualification and pass the assessment rubric but for whom some hard-to-name concern emerges that leaves you wondering whether they have the attitude and the potential to excel.

Many interviewers will hesitate to call out amorphous concerns because they result from instinct rather than from an established question in your interview approach. Because of this, making a no-hire decision on someone who is just fine needs to be modeled. You can eventually work to build that filter into your process, but the best way to start is by demonstrating it through leadership behaviors. Be transparent about those moments when you say no to a candidate and explain why. Use them to teach others how to conduct the assessment and how to look for that indefinable thing that usually amounts to "I'm excited to work with this person, no matter the role."

If you do this well, you can teach other leaders to model the same behavior as you scale. This is what we did at Stripe. The founders set the example and taught each new leader our hiring principles and expectations. As Stripe grew, senior leaders began to take on the finalist interviewer role, and either a founder or executive team member met every finalist. This continued until Stripe had hundreds of employees. Only when the leadership team was confident that hiring managers and division leaders would proxy not just a rigorous hiring process but also the right hiring behaviors did we start to step back and concentrate our time more on the middle and top of the hiring pyramid.

—

The rest of this chapter outlines the broad steps in the hiring process:

- **Recruiting**: attracting candidates into your hiring pipeline
- **Hiring**: decision-making, from onsite to offer
- **Onboarding**: setting your new hire up to succeed

Each section will cover both employee and leadership hiring. The chapter will conclude with advice on how to close your hiring loop to improve it over time.

Hiring starts with recruiting, so we'll start there too.

Recruiting

Building market awareness for a new product can be hard. Building awareness of your company among potential talent can be equally challenging. Your company needs to actively educate candidates about its existence and seek out potential hires. Small businesses might do this via job listing sites or even Craigslist, but small yet growing technical companies will have a tough time with that approach—it's a very competitive talent market for those with technical skills, and you need to make your case to folks who have multitudes of lucrative job options. Early on, the easiest thing to do is to mine the personal networks of the founders and early employees. This approach can work initially, but it doesn't scale. It can also create a lack of diversity, because our friends tend to be just like us in terms of experience, background, and often race and gender identity.

In the early days, Stripe got creative about building its hiring pipeline. Because we built for developers, we were able to hire a few early users of the product, namely the ones who gave the most and best feedback. But soon enough, we added new tactics to our efforts to educate and differentiate. These ranged from the founders posting on Quora or Hacker News and answering questions on Internet Relay Chat to writing blog posts on the Stripe site and using Twitter to share them.

One way the early team drove traffic to Stripe and to our job postings was a competition called Capture the Flag: a series of coding challenges that created a buzz and, best of all, presented the company with participants who might be great job candidates. The initial Capture the Flag event had about 12,000 unique visitors, and 250 participants captured the flag. Three of those 250 joined Stripe directly. The event, coupled with activity in other online forums, helped Stripe start to create a strong talent brand and drive leads to the hiring process.

SIDEBAR

—

Stripe's Capture the Flag

In keeping with Stripe's strong writing culture, an early Stripe engineer and key Capture the Flag contributor, Christian Anderson, wrote about the origins of the competition for all Stripes to read and learn from. This is a lightly edited excerpt from his write-up.

Stripe's most famous community event is Capture the Flag (CTF), a programming contest that ran three times starting in 2012. We threw together the first CTF in 12 days and announced it in a blog post. We expected it to sit online in perpetuity, delighting programmers and providing our job applicants with an optional challenge. Instead, the contest was popular beyond our wildest expectations, drawing roughly 12,000 participants in the week we kept it online. Starting that week, the CTFs became an integral part of Stripe's growing reputation with our core audience (developers and those who build innovative products online). They publicly showcase our love of building, our fascination with technology, and our drive for excellence. Unsurprisingly, they have drawn many engineers to Stripe. And, in turn, these engineers have helped write the next CTF.

Stripe was an 18-person company in February 2012. Inspired by SmashTheStack's IO, a contest about identifying and exploiting security vulnerabilities, a Stripe engineer named Siddarth Chandrasekaran proposed that

Stripe write our own such challenge. He began coding on February 9. Two more engineers joined soon thereafter, and the three of them shaped the first CTF. As a participant, you needed to complete a series of six increasingly difficult levels. You moved to the next level by exploiting a vulnerability to reveal the password of the next user. The exploits included a buffer overflow for the fourth level and a timing-based side-channel attack for the fiendish sixth level.

As of the closing day, 250 people had solved every level. A couple of the winners of CTF joined us in the wake of the contest. These included one of the architects of Capture the Flag 2 (CTF2). He proposed a web security CTF as part of the ramp-up to college recruiting season. We spent three extremely intense weeks building CTF2 and launched it on August 22, 2012.[31] During those three weeks, Stripe grew from 28 to 31 people. While the core team remained small, many additional Stripes (including our first summer interns) were involved in polishing and play-testing the new CTF.

31

stripe.com/blog

CTF2 was more deliberate than CTF1 in every regard. For instance, we ran it on proper infrastructure with the expectation that we'd need to scale it. We announced CTF2 one week in advance and did some deliberate marketing ahead of the launch. And, most visibly, our designer, Ludwig Pettersson, created a beautiful CTF2 website with a *Tron* theme.

The CTF site included a leaderboard that tracked the progress of its 16,000 participants across eight levels. As with CTF1, the first few levels were deliberately accessible and the last several fiendish. It's still not uncommon, in a discussion of a new web exploit, to hear someone say, "This reminds me of the Stripe CTF!" They mean CTF2. Level 7, for instance, taught hash length extension. The authors of the famous MD5 length extension paper, Thai Duong and Juliano Rizzo, gave us a shout-out for this. They later wrote to us when they published the CRIME attack on the TLS protocol and included us in their announcement video.

After the beautiful but consuming production that was CTF2, months passed before anyone had the appetite to consider CTF3. By summer 2013, though, our collective urge to do a third CTF was building momentum. We decided that if we were going to do CTF3, it needed to address our major qualm with CTF1 and CTF2: They both optimized for breakers rather than builders. With this in mind, we decided on an ambitious new theme for CTF3: systems engineering, including distributed systems, performance, and scaling. The ambition of the theme is not surprising, given how aspirational Stripe is, but it introduced new uncertainties: We had substantial prior art for a security CTF, but none for a distributed systems CTF. If not impossible, CTF3 would be impractical. It would require us to build, run, and test arbitrary distributed systems code submitted by the participants.

One of Stripe's founding engineers and its first CTO, Greg Brockman, worked in late July and early August to validate the distributed systems idea and prototype the architecture. But the late summer and early fall of 2013 was one of Stripe's most intense times to date, and we decided to postpone the launch until January 2014 so that we could prioritize core work for the 2013 holiday season. At this point, there was a fear in everyone's minds that we'd mothball CTF3 indefinitely. However, we had come far enough to see what a great idea it was to do a distributed systems CTF, and that idea had a strength of its own. In December, Greg released two example levels internally. The company (74 people at that time) loved them. Following the holidays, a group of Stripes got together and went all in on shipping CTF3.

On the engineering side, the core team decamped to Greg's family home in North Dakota to spend a week heads-down on CTF. Mostly undeterred by the polar vortex that swept North America in January, plunging North Dakota to -10°C and grounding flights across the country, the week was prolific: We drafted five levels and preannounced CTF3 on January 15. In the week leading up to launch, fistfuls of Stripes stepped in to help. The week was a blur of all-nighters and near all-nighters, but CTF3 shipped on January 22 to enormous fanfare. We had 7,500 participants push code to us over 640,000 times. The realistic nature of the levels meant that almost every one of them had workarounds that we hadn't anticipated, but that didn't dampen the enjoyment of individual solvers. CTF3 is the one that folks have in mind when they say, "The Stripe CTF is the most fun I've had programming."

The three CTFs are a study in how to reach the developer audience, an audience that is core to the company and core to our user base (past, present, and future). When a developer tries one of our CTFs, their reaction is "Here is a company that values what I value." That's something we have to continually live up to, in our products and in our future side projects. Beyond that, the CTFs are a study in our values: For each CTF, a self-organized group of volunteers came together to build something great for the company.

–

Once you're creating traffic, you need to make sure that there's a page on your site that explains what it's like to work at the company and offers a way for candidates to browse open job descriptions. This is a big milestone, and reaching it takes work. Both company and job descriptions can be surprisingly hard to get right, especially when you're still building your product and defining various roles—that time when everyone is essentially doing every job. The key is to be as clear as you can about the work environment and the expectations at the company and in the role, but not to be overly verbose or prescriptive. You want to open the aperture wide enough to attract applicants who have the potential to succeed but not so wide that you disappoint someone who starts a role that doesn't resemble the overly high-level job posting onto which they probably projected their own aspirations. If you're not quite sure what the role will be yet, saying so will also help filter out candidates: If the ambiguity makes them uncomfortable, it's likely not the role for them. It's also critical to watch out for language about the role or expected qualifications that transmits bias about who should or should not apply. This language can be subtle and hard to identify. Luckily, there are now companies and products devoted to helping you neutralize such signals (like Textio or Grammarly) or mine data to find potentially undiscovered talent (like AdeptID).

Keep in mind that what you say early on about your company and about these first roles is the beginning of both your talent and company brand. Take as much care with these foundations as you do with your first product releases. Your first candidates and their experiences should receive the same attention and scrutiny as the first users who adopt your product.

For some time, the Stripe hiring process was managed by engineers rather than recruiters. The great part of that precedent was that it created a sense of ownership in every employee for every part of the process, and it embedded into every Stripe a desire for every new hire to succeed. The downside was that it became so celebrated that an early engineering leader posted on Quora that Stripe didn't need recruiters. When it came time to build the recruiting team, especially its leadership, that public declaration worked against my recruiting of recruiters!

I do think that inculcating that sense of ownership into every person at the company is vital, but there will also come a time when you need to hire specialists to help screen candidates and manage the candidate relationship and the hiring process. You will likely need at least one recruiter and possibly a recruiting coordinator to help with scheduling and logistics once you're past your initial team—say, 10–20 people—and you know that you will be consistently hiring. Once you're hiring multiple people a week, you should think about building a recruiting team with an experienced leader. Still, a recruiter should never be a substitute for a hiring manager, meaning the individual hiring for the role. There needs to be a tight partnership between the person responsible for the recruiting experience and the recruiting process and the person who will ultimately be accountable for the new hire's work. As you scale, it may not be clear who the manager will be for each hire, since they may not yet be assigned to a specific engineering team, for example. In that case, you need people and a process that can proxy the commitment of the hiring manager to finding the best candidate for the role. (For more on this, see the sidebar on candidate review on page 185.)

New employee recruiting

Hiring is everyone's job. At Stripe, we have extensive internal guides that outline each person's role in the recruiting and hiring process for hires below the leader level. I'm often surprised when I encounter companies where this function is a separate appendage, tacked on like a human factory that you can call up to order a new financial analyst and have one show up a month later. For scaled hiring, meaning most of your roles other than leadership, I understand why this happens: It's natural, as a company gets larger and larger, to keep specializing and sub-specializing until recruiting becomes a silo, letting individuals on a team focus on their jobs and not on interviewing. But I would caution against this tendency, because eventually people become divorced from learning how to represent the company—the culture!—and from feeling responsibilities for their colleagues' selection and success.

In order to involve a greater number of people in the hiring process and keep them engaged as you grow, particularly when it comes to high-volume hiring, you need to have both a strong process and clear commitments between the recruiting function and those who participate. It's also critical to publicly celebrate those who contribute the most, in order to send the message—repeatedly—that hiring is not a side job but a core responsibility for everyone in the company.

SIDEBAR

–

Recruiting commitments

Here's an example of some of our internal content on recruiting. This document outlines the mutual commitments between the recruiting team and the rest of Stripe so that we all meet the expectations of ourselves and of the process. All of these items link out to more detail on our intranet, Stripe Home.

Stripes' commitments to recruiting

Keep your calendar accurate.

Know the role and the interview.

Review job descriptions, capabilities, and frameworks:

- Participate in interview trainings and keep abreast of updates to interviews you frequently conduct.
- Read any prep material before the interview (particularly for roleplays or scenario-based interviews).
- Familiarize yourself with the capabilities you've been assigned to evaluate in the interview, along with any guidelines for evaluating them.

Know the routine:

- Try not to leave the candidate alone. Contact the recruiting coordinator if you're going to be late or need to leave the candidate.
- Always know who is after you and what time your interview ends. This way, we can prep the candidate for the next interview and leave time for questions.

Know the candidate:

- Review their résumé, their LinkedIn profile, and any other application materials prior to conducting the interview.
- For managers: Review written projects and feedback from earlier interview stages to understand areas that may still need to be probed.

Submit feedback on time.

Be an active participant in tropes (hiring meetings):[32]

- Read other interviewers' feedback prior to the decision (after you've submitted feedback) and come prepared to discuss points of concern or disagreement.
- Be specific and clear about FUD (fear, uncertainty, or doubt), and be sure that your FUD ties directly into one of the capabilities you were asked to assess. For example, "Candidate was dismissive toward person X and downplayed the contributions of her team when discussing past roles" is more helpful than "I have some culture FUD."
- Speak up! Hiring decisions are a chance for people to air any opinions or concerns before we decline or extend an offer. If there's ever something you don't want to share in public, feel free to contact your recruiter directly. This is much better than keeping quiet about a potential issue.

Follow up with candidates:

- Send out "excite-a-mails" upon offer extension or acceptance. This is particularly important if you've spent significant time with a candidate in an onsite interview.

- Respond to follow-up questions from candidates promptly. If you don't have the bandwidth to get back to a candidate quickly, forward the query along to recruiting or to the hiring manager.
- If a recruiter introduces you to a candidate at any stage in the process, reply to them within 48 hours.

ABR (always be recruiting)!

Recruiting's commitments to Stripes

Be respectful of Stripes' calendars.

Value referrals and referrers.

Set candidates up for success:

- Have clear job descriptions and interview frameworks scoped before beginning to interview candidates.
- Be transparent with candidates about what to expect during their interview process.
- Act as an advocate and sounding board for candidates from point of contact through rejection or offer.
- Be direct and clear about our intentions at all times, and leave candidates feeling that they were treated well, regardless of the outcome.
- Give candidates the benefit of the doubt and treat them with empathy at all stages of the process. Interviewing is hard!

Communicate clearly and often with candidates.

Shepherd candidates through their onsites.

Set hiring meetings up for success:

- Actively facilitate (in conjunction with the hiring manager) to ensure we stay on topic, move efficiently, and end on time.
- Moderate hiring discussions to ensure they are respectful and fair to the candidate.
- Discussions should be tied to particular capabilities and should primarily focus on whether or not we believe the candidate can do the job we're interviewing them for.

Communicate effectively with hiring managers and interviewers throughout the recruiting process.

Handle sensitive information carefully and privately:

- In the course of working with candidates, recruiters often learn private or sensitive information. We commit to keeping this information contained to the people who need to know it.

- Interviewers should feel comfortable coming to recruiters with private concerns about candidates, and they should know that recruiters will be discreet with this information.

Do what's right for Stripe:

- Above all, it's important to maintain our hiring bar and optimize for Stripe's long-term success. Recruiting will continue to advocate for what's best for Stripe at this moment and in the future.

—

Build insights on talent needs and candidate success

Before you open a role and start the process to fill it, be sure to study what success looks like at your company. Start by asking yourself:

- What kinds of people have we hired previously?
- Who's doing really well?
- Who's scaling at the same pace as the company? Why? What qualities and capabilities do they exhibit?
- What perspectives and experiences are we missing at the company? Where are we less diverse? What are our weak points and capability gaps?

I've attended a few events where Condoleezza Rice, the former US Secretary of State under George W. Bush, was interviewed. At one of them, she was asked how she ended up back at Stanford when she had a multitude of opportunities she could have pursued following her time in government. She answered that what she wanted most was work that allowed her to excel, to make an impact, and to pursue her passion. For her, that was in education.

I find it helpful to think about her advice as a Venn diagram with three circles: people who are good at their work, people who have a great impact on the company's progress, and people who love what they do. The ideal employee fits into all three. Make a list of all of the people at your company who fall into this bucket. What other qualities do they have in common? What questions can you ask during recruiting to suss out whether a candidate shares those qualities? Use these internal questions to hire more people who not only have the right skills but also regularly bring passion and energy to their work. Who are the people who are working hard but also clearly having a good time? They're intrinsically motivated, and it shows. In his book *Drive*, Daniel Pink argues that motivation is achieved via autonomy, mastery, and purpose.[33] I think motivation and, ultimately, a feeling of fulfillment are critical to high performance. These are the people who have the energy and space to get curious and learn.

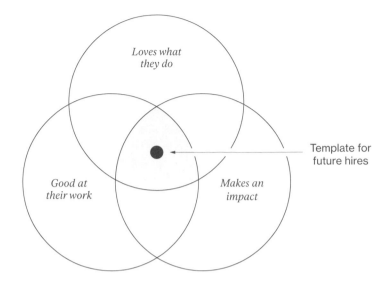

Figure 11. The ideal employee.

When I first joined Stripe, our international presence was new. We had individual country managers working as generalists to build traction wherever they were located and in whatever form was required. But as the company grew, these people needed to transition into serious team builders and managers accountable for revenue. A few of them would eventually run large divisions of their own. Some of these country managers scaled into these new roles. Others didn't, because they were great hires for the early stages of a market but didn't have the desire or the abilities to scale into the evolved version of the role.

As we brought on new country managers for further expansion, we hired candidates based on an understanding of the types of people who had already been successful in this role, but we also adapted our understanding as the role evolved. We sought people who relished the challenge of expansion to such a degree that they were willing to put in the time to learn what the company needed, constantly ask for feedback, and educate themselves about the product and their local markets. The people who will scale with your company are the ones who can anticipate what they need to learn now in order to excel at what their role will become in six months. For certain roles, that adaptation is absolutely critical.

The country leadership role at Stripe continues to shift. For more mature markets, it's less about building and more about optimizing and expanding our sales capabilities. For others, it's still about evangelism, groundwork, and early-stage sales to acquire users we can highlight to attract others. Be prepared to constantly evolve what the role requires and, as a result, to evolve your thinking about which candidates are best equipped to thrive. These candidates should demonstrate the potential to adapt with the role and, ideally, should be able to step back and ask themselves what they're missing. As you contemplate your hiring strategy, keep asking yourself: Are there experiences and skill sets that the next phase of the company will require? (There's more about this in the section on new leader recruiting on page 157.)

Open a role and help applicants self-select

Once you've decided to take the plunge and start hiring for a role, it can be tempting to make job descriptions into rosy advertisements for your company and team. Resist that urge, and instead design your job descriptions and hiring process to entice prospects who might be a good fit and discourage prospects who might not be. Set clear expectations about the role, and provide other information—like the company mission, a culture guide, and practical facts on benefits and work practices—to help the candidate better understand what it's like to work on your team and at your company. Most importantly, be transparent about the work environment. If it's fast-paced and people are expected to act independently, make that clear. Being self-aware as a company—that is, being a company made up of self-aware individuals who understand how they work best—is crucial as you grow. (Remember Operating Principle 1: Build self-awareness to build mutual awareness.) Knowing who you are allows you to hire well.

"A Quick Guide to Stripe's Culture," which I excerpted on page 66, also contains a series of questions to help candidates assess whether Stripe is a place they want to work. Each Stripe principle has a corresponding question:

We haven't won yet
- The value of Stripe (and of your equity) is not a foregone conclusion. While you'll have a hand in the outcome, are you okay with a substantial amount of risk and ambiguity?

Move with urgency and focus
- Do you want to work hard at a place that could never be described as a cushy job?
- Are you comfortable with owning your own career outcomes rather than having a clear progression of goals and milestones described to you by a single decision-maker?

Think rigorously
- When was the last time you changed your mind on a fundamental opinion you had? Do you do that frequently?
- Stripes deal with high-variance situations on a day-to-day basis but are thoughtful and measured in response. Is that what you're looking for?

Referrals

Once you're clear on what success looks like for a given role, and once you've written the job description and posted it, you'll hopefully be able to start screening candidates to enter the interview process. In addition to talent brand development, it's critical to create a strong referral process, since your existing employees likely know potential candidates. And if you've hired well, your employees' networks should be just as strong as they are.[34]

Referrals shouldn't be your only source of candidates, however. Referral processes are difficult to scale—and, as I mentioned earlier, they can undermine attempts to diversify your team. But don't underestimate how effective referrals can be. Treat those referrals well. Referrals are also a great way to gauge employee happiness and engagement, for what should be obvious reasons.

My interview at Google came about because a friend from business school introduced me to a friend of hers from college who was a manager at Google. I distinctly remember sitting next to my fiancé as we drove along one of California's winding roads, thinking that I was going to have a friendly introductory phone call. Instead, this woman grilled me for 45 minutes! By the end of the call, I realized that for my friend to refer me to this manager, she had to have strong confidence that I had both the skills and the attitude to succeed at Google. The time the manager took with me displayed a strong commitment to Google's hiring process. I often think back to the ownership she demonstrated and what it said about the company and about the importance of all employees participating in the recruiting process.

Screening processes

Your screening processes will differ based on the volume of applicants, with different people (or machine learning algorithms) conducting the initial résumé reviews. (Referrals might skip this step.) At the highest level, you're scanning résumés to check whether candidates' qualifications fit with the role qualifications you've outlined, for example a rapid trajectory or success in a similar role. Some more sought-after companies add a step to their screening process to test the applicant's commitment and to collect more data to make a hiring decision, like a coding assessment or a short written project. (I include an example of a written exercise in the chapter appendix on page 241.) But beware of creating too many hurdles while you're still building a talent brand and your pipeline.

Once a candidate looks viable, a recruiter or a hiring manager will conduct an initial phone screen to determine whether they think the person might be right for the job. If the candidate hits the mark in the phone screen, the recruiter or hiring manager will pass the candidate on to onsite interviews. Some companies have a recruiter meet the candidate and then, before the onsite stage, have a team member or manager conduct a second screen. Either way, the end of this portion of the process is an invitation for a set of formal interviews. We'll get to that stage after we look at the adjustments you'll want to make to this process when recruiting leaders, or you can flip straight to the section on the formal interviewing process on page 176.

New leader recruiting

Sometimes leadership hiring follows a core tenet of product development attributed to Henry Ford: "If I had asked people what they wanted, they would have said faster horses." When I was interviewing at Stripe, the company had just over 100 people. Patrick Collison called me with some of the feedback from the team. (We'll talk more about the importance of involving others in the hiring process later in this chapter.) A key piece of feedback was "Maybe we need her when we're 400 people, but right now, it's too early." I recall Patrick then saying "But we're going to be 400 people basically tomorrow." We both laughed, somewhat ruefully.

It was a classic example of the truism that people in your company won't tell you they need a leader. It's up to you to determine when the time is right—and if you don't, you might regret it. Growth from 100 to 400 people happens quickly if you have real traction. I sometimes call hyperscaling "riding the dragon": You need your dragon riders—your fearless leaders—before the beast takes off to still greater heights.

It can be hard to recognize exactly when you've hit one of these "I need a leader" moments, especially for founders and builders. They're usually so close to the work that they aren't aware of how many different jobs they're doing that could be done by others. I recently had a phone call with a founding CEO of a fast-growing company of 300 people. He asked me how he would know whether and when he would need more leaders, or new leaders for certain roles. I asked him to write down all of the different jobs he'd performed over the past three weeks, then think about which of those jobs only he could do as the founder and CEO, like leadership hiring, perhaps some investor conversations, establishing the culture, forming the strategic vision, and major investment decisions, either in the future product or in shoring up against potential threats. For the jobs that others could do, we talked through whether he already had someone in the role but ended up getting too involved—a sign that his current person wasn't scaling—or whether he was missing someone and was, instead, instinctively doing the work to cover the need.

It can take real effort to look at the full picture this way, and to understand when the work has grown so much in volume and complexity that it's time to bring on someone else or create a new role. It can be harder still to predict that the work is about to grow that much and that you need to hire someone immediately to do the work 6–12 months in the future. You need to pull yourself out of the day-to-day and survey what has changed in the last three to six months. Then you need to look forward in order to create a theory about what will continue to change and grow in importance such that it will need leadership.

If your company is scaling, it helps to remember that your primary goal is to work yourself out of a job. I used to have a test at Google: When my team and I got an email from a leader with a question, I would refrain from writing back immediately and wait for someone else on my team to respond. I viewed it as a failure if I was the only one who could answer the question or take action.

One particularly popular story of this kind among scaling companies is Molly Graham's description of her time working through hypergrowth at Google, Facebook, and the startup Quip, where she was COO. She draws an apt analogy to a child building a Lego creation: Even if you give the child more Legos, they'll be reluctant to share the ones they have.[35]

35
review.
firstround.com

In a hyperscale environment, it's hard to give up the things you've built and the multiple jobs you hold. But the only way for you and the company to grow is to get over that emotional response and realize that there are going to be a lot more Legos—and probably better Legos—the more you let go. Graham says, "You have to give away your job every six months." That's especially true for leaders, particularly founders and CEOs.

You also want to be constantly vigilant about gaps in capabilities—both your own and those of the company's leadership team—that are becoming critical to the future success of your company. (See the section on analyzing your skills and capabilities on page 34.) In other words, in the spirit of being self-aware, you have to know what you don't know and what you're not good at.

Being able to set ego aside and be ruthlessly critical of yourself and your division is hard. It's not just about where you have gaps today but also about what you'll need in the next three to five years. It's a fine line to walk. On the one hand, you're still fighting for survival, so it's hard to imagine that you'll need more experienced people in bigger roles. On the other hand, if you have traction, you're already starting to add complexity to your operation. Even things that work for you today, like how you fundraise as a small private company, might not be the same tomorrow, when it might require a CFO who has presided over public company financing and financial reporting processes. It's

"As CEO, I would say the number one success factor for being a good leader is being able to pick talent. That, and create followership.

But the hardest lesson I've had to learn [is that] you get to that point where it's impossible for you to be successful without trusting others to do things better. And that breakthrough is when you go beyond being a manager.

A leader has to spend their time on things no one else can do. If you're doing something that others on your team could do just as well, you're just wasting your time."

—**Lisa Wardell**, former CEO and current executive chair, Adtalem Global Education about having confidence in that potential future, but not hubris. And although it might be painful to admit you can't do it all, it's better to give the Legos away too soon rather than too late. If you don't, you risk sending your company into a death spiral.

Determine what kind of leader you need

One of my favorite stories from Google's early days is about how the founders hired Omid Kordestani. Omid was Google's 11th employee, and he built its business operations from the first employees and the first dollar in revenue to over 12,000 employees and over $20 billion in revenue. Omid showed up to meet Google's founders, Larry Page and Sergey Brin, and found himself seated at a ping-pong table. He quickly realized that they were unsure what to ask him. "You know," Omid said, "if I were interviewing someone for this role, here are the questions I might ask." And he proceeded, very gracefully, to interview himself. Unfortunately, not all candidates are like Omid, so you'll need to do the legwork to figure out the capabilities you're seeking and how to assess them.

Recruiting for a new role is tricky. If you're hiring for a new position, you probably don't know exactly what you're looking for. (That's what the experienced hire is for!) Or, even trickier, you've had someone with less experience doing part of the role, but you're not sure what the more experienced person could bring to the work and the organization. For example, what's the difference between accounting and strategic finance?

When you're in a high-growth mode, it's often the case that you don't have the capabilities you need fully in house, but you may not realize this until you've completely assessed the company's current state. Your best starting point is to build an understanding of the role and outline the experience, characteristics, and skills of a successful leadership candidate. Whether you promote from within or hire externally, you'll want to be clear on three things:

- What is the work to be done?
- What does "great" look like?
- How will we assess people against that benchmark?

Once you have the broader sketch, you'll need to think about the company's needs and trajectory to fill in the must-haves versus the nice-to-haves in your internal or external candidate's experience and abilities.

Even if you're not thinking of hiring externally—we'll cover how to determine that on page 168—talk to advisers and folks at other companies who've had success in the role, as well as to people in similar roles, to get guidance on what you should be looking for and how to assess candidates' abilities once you've built the interview pipeline. Tactically, this means connecting with companies that have reached—or, better still, reached beyond—your stage

"First, I need to understand the core of what my business is. Then, from that, I peel the layers off everything and understand where I need to be better, or where I need to hire someone who can help me fulfill those tasks. I don't know everything."

—**Dominique Crenn**, owner and chef, Atelier Crenn, Michelin three-star restaurant

and successfully filled these positions, as well as with investors, advisers, and board members, if you have them, for examples of success. Ideally, you'll talk both to people who have figured out what type of candidate they need and applied those learnings to hire a successful candidate, and to those who have successfully done the job themselves. Importantly, do not use your interview process to calibrate your understanding and expectations of a role. You will churn through potentially good candidates, and you may even damage your company's reputation in the process.

I've fielded many such requests from founders considering whether they needed a COO. They typically ask about my background, what the role meant for Stripe, and how it has evolved. They also usually want to know about the hiring process and how I made the decision to join Stripe. In the grand tradition of Silicon Valley, I make time for these conversations and seek to help others as much as I can. I hope to truly support and contribute to their efforts to research the best approach for their company.

SIDEBAR

–

My COO story

The story of how I came to be Stripe's chief operating officer is, like most of the stories we tell, likely rife with assumptions and personal interpretations. Still, I feel it's worth including here. I hope it will be instructive as you consider your own approach to hiring a COO.

As is the case with most startups, Stripe took some time to get to product-market fit and find traction with its first users. It hovered around 30–40 employees for about three years. Patrick and John were also committed to growing carefully: Stripe charged for its product from the beginning and monitored the P&L closely to avoid costs far outstripping revenue growth. Because of this caution, when users and revenue started to accelerate, Stripe was slow to invest in scaling the company. I think this happens in many companies: They've been fighting for traction for so long that they almost don't believe they've hit escape velocity. My sense is that it was at this point that Stripe's investors and advisers started pushing the founders on two fronts. First, it was time to build out the sales team. Second, the company needed to start hiring more people in all functions, and add a few new ones.

The founders began taking a series of meetings with potential heads of sales, as well as some COO types. By that I mean generalist business leaders who had depth (or, at least, enough depth) of experience in multiple functions that would be required for Stripe's next stage, including go-to-market, operations, and running company processes at scale. My first meeting with Patrick was in February 2014, when Stripe was around 70 people and starting to hire quickly. Our conversation ranged from extremely tactical management scenarios to big-picture musings on the future of economic progress. I also made it clear that I wouldn't leave Google for a head of sales role, and that I wasn't sure whether Stripe needed my experience scaling teams yet, given its size.

I didn't hear from Patrick for a few months, but he reemerged that spring to learn more about me and my experience. I think I was interesting to Stripe because I had deep customer experience, both in scaling support operations and in building and leading sales teams, but I was also extremely compelled by company building and investing in recruiting and human resources. My interest in the latter was less in the actual HR function and more in the systems and cultural markers that would need to be in place for Stripe to grow sustainably and healthily. Patrick and John saw that the combination of my experiences and interests was complementary to theirs and to Billy Alvarado's, the other executive (in addition to the general counsel) who was helping to lead the company at the time. I filled in some blank spots, but I also loved to collaborate and share responsibility, which fit with Stripe's model of decision-making. One thing I particularly appreciated about this discovery process, unlike some others I'd participated in, was that there were no default assumptions about what I would be responsible for. Instead, it was more of a mutual exploration of strengths and interests.

By that August, Stripe had over 100 employees, and Patrick and John had decided that the company needed a leader who could build and lead across multiple functions, not just sales. The role would free up bandwidth for them and for Billy and would provide experienced leadership to help the company scale. They seemed to think that I might be that person—so it was time for me to decide whether I wanted to work at Stripe. I did.

One wrinkle we faced was that Billy already had the title of COO, but he was focused on the critical financial, product, and distribution partnerships that were fueling Stripe's growth. He was also acting as CFO. During my recruiting process, Billy and I met over frozen yogurt in Palo Alto, and he was very clear that he needed to focus on partnerships (and finance, thankfully) and wanted someone to join the company who enjoyed the hiring and process-building required for scale. It says a lot about Patrick and John's hiring of Billy, and about Billy as a person, that he so willingly handed over his title and helped recruit a new COO in recognition of a new company stage and a new set of needs.

In October 2014, I officially joined Stripe as its chief of business operations—a title intended to allay suspicions that I was showing up and taking

Billy's job, which might not have sat well with employees. Then, about six months into my tenure, Patrick sent a short note to the company explaining that Billy would take on the title of chief business officer and I would become the COO. To this day, Stripe leaders are not afraid to shift our portfolios in the interest of what—and who—is best for the business at any given time. That instinct started early.

Stripe had about 160 employees when I joined, and that still seemed a bit small to require some of my skills. But I was drawn, above all, to the founders—to their ideas, ambition, and combination of EQ and IQ. I was also compelled by the rate of new users and revenue, the size of the market, the potential impact I could have given my experience, and the professional lessons I would gain as a person finally at the "head table."

In retrospect, it was a big deal for Stripe to hire an unknown quantity to take on the title of COO. The title often connotes a responsibility as the CEO's proxy and right hand, whether or not that's true in reality. Stripe mitigated that cultural risk through Patrick in particular spending countless hours getting to know my abilities, delving into how I think, and understanding whether our values aligned. I've told many folks that I'm quite complementary to both Patrick and John, yet despite our different abilities we share overlapping values and attitudes about leadership and a similar fundamental definition of what it means to be a good human. When they hired me, they placed a great deal of trust in my ability to make positive progress, and I've always been grateful for the opportunity to help lead Stripe.

–

Ideally, your outreach will validate whether you need the new leadership role. Your discussions with others should also help you create a rubric—a framework—with which you can assess potential candidates.

Here are some questions you might ask others to start to develop that rubric:

- **How is the role defined at your company? What is the person accountable for?** See if the answer matches the definition of the role you're envisioning. If it doesn't, seek to understand why not. Is it because of the business model, or is it more about the skill sets of the company's other leaders?
- **What are the most important skills or capabilities needed for success in the role?** Create a list of abilities and consider how you might test for them in your interview.
- **What was it in the person's background/your background that made them/you qualified?** You're looking for the must-haves in their

---

Do you need a COO?

When I advise founders about hiring a COO, I share a lot of the advice included in this chapter. I also push them to consider whether they really need a COO—and if so, whether it's the right time to hire one. It's not a position that many large companies have, but it's very much in vogue for growth-stage companies, and even for some in earlier stages.

The desire for a COO makes sense given the demands on the CEO, which range from customer, product, and business decisions to implementing company infrastructure and tending to company culture. But ultimately, a COO is an extra layer of management, and once companies achieve more scale and a more fully developed leadership team, that layer might not be necessary. Also, you may not yet be in a position as a company to attract the type of candidate who would be able to scale in the role for more than a year or so.

My initial role at Stripe demanded a lot of range. In addition to responsibilities across sales and operations, I was also the head of recruiting, the recruiting team manager, and a recruiter myself. Then, in time, I was the COO, with a head of people who had a head of recruiting reporting to her. Whomever you hire will have to have that ability to move up and down the "stack," or you'll need to wait until you've reached a certain scale to land the right person and position them well for impact.

One excellent concept I inherited when I joined Stripe was the idea of a business operations team: a team staffed with folks who have a mix of consulting and entrepreneurial backgrounds, who thrive on new situations and on solving problems as Stripe scales. The members of the initial "biz ops" team, as we call it, were our first salespeople, and many of them were also our first product managers. Really, they were whatever Stripe needed them to be at the time—which is a lot like the COO job. Before you hire a COO, consider building a biz ops team and hiring a head of business operations who can proxy some of the COO's responsibilities. Doing so can help you scale and figure out what you really need in a potential COO. Your business operations leader may even become your COO—I did join Stripe as chief of business operations, after all!

---

experience that earned them the position and seeing if these match your own conception of the role.

- **Can you share the biggest challenges they/you faced in their/your first year?** Note how you might help your new leader, consider whether they will face similar challenges, and figure out how you might test for the ability to overcome them at your company.
- **How do you/how does the person work with the CEO or another close collaborator/leader in the company?** Use this to clarify responsibilities and to understand how decision-making and ownership might work for those who will work most closely with the new leader.
- **Do you have any advice on finding strong candidates for this role? Are there particular companies that do this well? Do you know anyone I should talk to?** Hopefully you'll emerge with companies to research, or even names of people you might want to meet and recruit as candidates.

Another strategy is to ask one of the folks you've learned is successful in the role if they'd be willing to let you interview them as if they were a candidate. This can help you gut-check whether your vision of the role is similar to what they were assessed for. You'll start to get a feel for the answers that seem right for your own process, which will help you flesh out your rubric.

Of course, it's also a tried-and-true recruiting trick to seek outside advice and test-interview someone because you're secretly hoping to recruit them. If this is what you're doing, it's better to be honest about it. In my experience, people are happy to help, and they'll tell you whether you've got a shot at actually recruiting them. Either way, at the end of your research process you should have a spreadsheet of LinkedIn profiles of people who could be candidates for the role. All good executive recruiters start their process by amassing a set of profiles to which you can react. You'll use it to think about why these individuals may or may not be great for the role, and patterns will start to emerge that will help you create your candidate assessment rubric and refine your job description. Over time, you can add to and mark the candidates on the list and continue to hone your search.

Aside from these outside conversations, I would encourage you to build confidence in your own gut instincts about what the role requires based on first principles. Résumés and LinkedIn profiles are filled with industry and functional jargon, but if you strip it all away, you can always find an answer to the fundamental questions: What is the job to be done, and what skills and capabilities are required to do that job well?

Say the role in question will require the candidate to build a growth marketing function. That means they will need to know how to organize events, develop content, and place advertisements that drive leads for your sign-up or sales process. They will also need to test and measure what works to convert leads into customers. So you know that the role calls for someone who can design compelling programming, content, and ads, and who knows how and where to use each medium, what tools and measurement practices are required to judge effectiveness, how to work with product or engineering to refine your sign-up or onboarding process, and, ultimately, how to calculate ROI and optimize the marketing spend. Depending on your business model, some of that work might be more important than the rest. For example, if you have more of an enterprise market, finding someone familiar with events and white papers may be more important than it would be for a business that relies more on self-service channels. Remember, in this scenario the candidate also needs to know how to build a team of people who can do all that work. Knowing all this, you can add these skills and capabilities to the candidate assessment rubric. Capabilities like team building, persuasion, and analytical skill will be critical, and skills like the ability to envision and execute an effective marketing campaign will be valuable, too. Be clear in the framework about what's a must-have and what's a nice-to-have. For example: Has the person built a similar team before, and did that team produce great results? Which parts of the work have they personally done? They're going to start as a team of one, so they'll need to be able to do the most critical work either by themselves or with an agency. They may need to design and test your first set of online ads. Have they done that?

Don't forget that you know your own company better than anyone and can assess what it takes to be successful in that environment. You can add those elements into your rubric for candidate assessment. Ultimately, the rubric will become a guide for interviewers; it should point to what they're probing for and what questions they might ask, and it should tell them how to assess the candidate's answers. (See the chapter appendix on page 213 for an example rubric, and see the section on hiring on page 170 for more on interviewing.)

As the manager of a potential new leader, there's one more element to consider for your rubric: complementarity with your existing leadership team. Some companies have all leadership candidates complete work style or personality assessments. Although we haven't gone that far, Stripe did have our first CFO candidate take the Insights Discovery assessment I described in Chapter 1, which presents findings in a color wheel made up of blue, red, yellow, and green segments. I had an inkling that this hire would round out our team's color wheel, adding someone in the blue quadrant, which tends to represent more introverted, analytical, and task-oriented people. I turned out to be right, and the resulting discussion, in which we shared his results and those of the rest of the leadership team, helped build a mutual understanding of each person's preferences and showed the candidate how he could round out the group. He started the role knowing each member of the team better, and we all had a common language we could use when we needed to ensure we were bringing different perspectives to a discussion or decision.

In the end, you should emerge from this research-intensive phase with a better understanding of the role and its job description, an assessment rubric to use for candidate screening and interviews, and a list of individuals who best represent the qualities you believe you're seeking for your pipeline.

One final caution: As you develop that list of example candidates, beware of what I call the experience trap. First, know that the more experienced someone is, the better they probably are at being interviewed. (I'll cover this more in the section on interviewing leaders on page 196.) Second, look out for those who have become complacent or hit a ceiling once they've attained a certain level of experience. One reason their trajectory may have stalled is that they've become what I call a playbook thinker: They've done something once or twice and become stuck on one way to do it, unable to bring ambition and creativity into their process or adapt to a new environment. Really examine the quality of the companies they've worked for. Have they consistently sought out great companies and strong teams? That's a signal of both their judgment and their ambition. For any hire, but absolutely for leadership hires, you're seeking trajectory and momentum—but above all, you're seeking raw curiosity and signs of pure learning aptitude. Is the person ambitious and seeking new challenges, and have they demonstrated that they can overcome a challenge and deliver results? That's about desire, grit, and intelligence. Don't just test for credible experience—test for that too.

Promoting from within or hiring from outside
Once you've identified the kind of person you want for your senior or leadership role, the next question you should ask is whether you should promote from within or hire from outside.

Hiring talent from outside for senior roles is a risky business. The more senior the role, the longer and more expensive the recruiting process: Expect to be searching for at least six months for senior leaders. After all that work, only about 25–50 percent of outside hires, especially senior ones, are successful.[36] Whenever possible, start with the talent you know, develop them, and promote from within.

36
forbes.com

Unfortunately, this is not always possible. Mature organizations have the time and numbers to develop a large talent pool. It is a failure if these organizations haven't done the work to cultivate an internal successor for a critical role. (Google is now able to develop thousands of future leaders for their core divisions at any time.) But if you're not mature or not very big, you have a real dilemma: Do you promote someone internally who is not quite ready but has a lot of potential? Do you then throw them into the deep end and hope they can swim, and risk damaging their rate of success if they can't? Or do you go out into the market and risk hiring an unknown entity who may not work out?

It's also important to be honest about your company stage and whether you can attract the talent you need for the next five-plus years. If your company is quite small and early-stage, it may feel risky to candidates who are in well-compensated top positions at more stable, established companies, and you may not be able to convince them to join. The result is that you may end up hiring someone who will be a fit for a few years but not for longer. It's a difficult needle to thread: You need the person now who can help grow your company to the scale where you can attract the person you actually need. Your options boil down to bettir internally, hiring the next-few-years person and hoping they' term, or taking a ton of time seeking the five-plus-years person anu ..., you can convince them to take the risk. Depending on your context, you're likely to make different calls for different roles. The key is to zoom out and be intentional about making that call, and then to track your talent as they develop to determine whether you need to revisit the hiring decision as the company evolves.

For early-stage companies growing quickly, my experience has been that at least one-third of promotions should come from within. Fewer than this and you're not investing enough in developing existing talent. One-third should also come from outside: At an early stage, your company is unlikely to have the talent pool it needs to hire internally only. The final third is a toss-up: It depends on the company's growth rate, the organization's needs, and your ability to support and develop internal talent and recruit and onboard external leaders.

As I've mentioned, as your company gains traction, it will inevitably need to build a recruiting function. Most likely, your recruiters will be focused on the higher-volume hiring rather than on acquiring new leaders. The recruiters themselves are likely to be early in their careers and less experienced with leadership hiring. For senior roles, most earlier-stage companies rely on search firms. I've had mixed results with that path. On the one hand, good search firms can quickly produce a list of people who fit your needs, and they can even help you land the initial meetings with candidates. But they require more investment than you might imagine in order to be successful: They need to understand your company, its trajectory, what the role is, and how to position it to candidates. They also need to intimately understand your company stage, or else they won't be able to set candidate expectations effectively, whether on compensation or on the day-to-day context of what it's like to lead in that environment. Often, it's better to reach out to your own network, your board, and other advisers to collect a list of potential candidates instead of relying on a search firm whose outreach might be more likely to be ignored than your personal touch.

However, if you've already exhausted your personal networks, maybe you should turn to a search firm. In my experience, the larger, more blue-chip executive search firms are better equipped to help with classic roles, like CFOs. Roles that might be more tailored to your company's unique definition and needs might be better served by boutique firms that specialize in sales and marketing or engineering roles, for example. With or without a search firm, top leadership roles require a ton of work to recruit for. Never forget that you are ultimately the recruiter: Leadership candidates are savvy, and they know that the CEO and the rest of the leadership team are the people who will matter to their success or failure.

How to determine whether to hire from within or from outside

Once you've established the requirements and qualifications for the leadership role and have a few profiles of potential hires, go through the decision tree on the next page in order to scan your current talent pool and determine where you should hire from.

It's difficult to get the balance right between bringing in new hires and developing internal talent. Organizations can romanticize external hires and become convinced that they'll solve all their problems. The great ones do have a huge positive impact, but when those senior-level external hires don't work out, it can be very organizationally and culturally expensive. Organizations also sometimes hold on to existing talent out of a sense of loyalty and gratitude. Don't ditch the loyalty and gratitude—show people your appreciation and help them be successful in their careers—but be aware that a person's ability to take the company up to this point isn't a sure sign that they'll be able to take it even further.

I once had lunch with a very experienced recruiting leader who was at Facebook and then Pinterest as they scaled. What he said, wistfully, stuck with me: "Don't assume the folks who got you *here* will get you *there*." Be constantly vigilant in answering this question: Do I have the talent I need now and for the next two to four years for my team or company to be a success?

As you think about the continuum from scaled talent acquisition to bespoke leadership recruiting, it's also worth considering what you're seeking in a leader or senior hire, from hard skills to true capabilities, such as the ability to build and lead a team. Capabilities, especially those that are less innate, take more time to emerge and develop. Roles that will rely most on these types of abilities—often abilities that come from experience—are likely to require more custom recruiting processes. Early in a company's growth, they're also more likely to come from outside. The benefit of internal hires, however, is that you have deep knowledge of the person and their contributions. They, in turn, have deep knowledge of your product and company. Over time, some of your most valuable leaders—be they executives, managers, or individual contributors—will be long-tenured early employees. Nurture their careers and help them move across the company so they can grow and develop, as well as to embed the culture they embody into every team they work with. For external hires, you'll need a much more robust interviewing process to assess talent and make one of the most important decisions a company makes: extending a job offer.

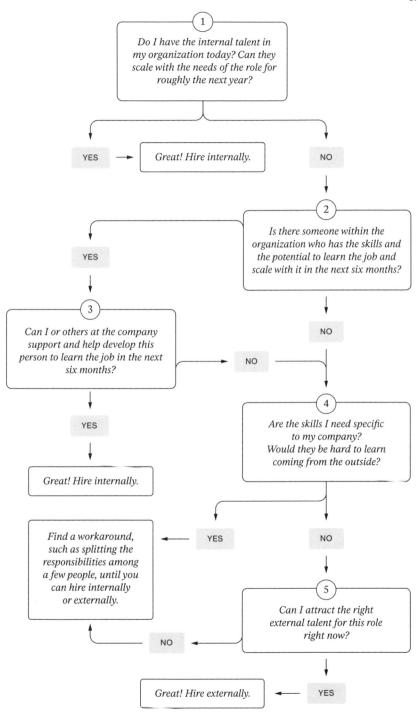

Figure 12. How to determine whether to hire from within or outside the company.

Hiring

I've interviewed thousands of people. It's not much of an exaggeration to say that in my early years at Google, most of us conducted interviews for about 40 hours a week and worked an additional 30–40 hours at night on our primary jobs.

I do think interviewing is a skill that improves with practice. It's also a skill that is best employed within a set process, with clear frameworks for assessment. By a set process, I don't mean anything elaborate, but you should have a relatively simple framework for what all interviews should focus on, a clear sense of the tactical steps a candidate will experience, and a plan for how a decision is reached on making an offer. It's also critical to prep your candidates well for their interviews. This doesn't mean telling them questions in advance but rather setting them at ease. Explain the process and how long it will take, the types of interviews they'll be doing, and what will be expected of them. For example, if it's a video interview that involves jointly looking at code, let them know to be ready to share a computer screen. It's also good to be clear about dress code (say, informal or business casual) and who they'll be meeting.

When I was in business school, I interviewed with a consulting firm focused on organizational design and human resources. The day of interviews took almost nine hours, and everyone I met picked a different section of my résumé and asked me about my work experience in minute detail for an hour. On the one hand, I was impressed by their organized concentration on getting to know me and my experience. But on the other, I wish I'd been warned that it would be a long, draining day so I could mentally prepare. From the early days at Stripe, we sent out a guide to candidates to let them know what to expect from the interview process and their onsite interviews. Candidates often shared their appreciation for this guide. In my view, a more welcoming and fairer candidate experience leads to better hires.

Once your recruiter and hiring manager screenings have created a pipeline of potential candidates—which includes efforts to solicit internal referrals and to actively source more diverse candidates if your pipeline isn't sufficiently diverse—you're ready to start onsite interviews, either in-person or virtual.

Here are some general guidelines for setting up a strong interview process—these can be applied to the initial hiring process in a young company, as well as to middle and top roles in the pyramid later on:

- Have a clear job description.
- Determine who will conduct the interviews.

- Seek to have candidates only meet a maximum of eight people in the process. Studies at Google have demonstrated diminishing returns for additional interviews. If the role is more entry-level and very well understood, this could be reduced to four or five people.
- Make sure your interviewers are trained on effective interviewing.
- Share your assessment rubric with all interviewers and assign one or two elements of the rubric to each interviewer to avoid overlap.
- For more custom or infrequently filled roles, have a kickoff meeting in which everyone gets aligned on the role, the rubric, and their part in the process.
- Potentially, have a first round of three interviews to narrow the field before you ask the entire interview panel to participate. Then, have the remaining three interviewers meet the finalists—ideally, at least three candidates—in a final round.
- Conduct a hiring committee or candidate review process to finalize your selection.
- Have the recruiter and hiring manager check the candidate's references.
- Make the offer. Hopefully, the candidate will accept—then you can set a start date and send them onboarding information!

The complexity of the process can flex up or down depending on your company stage and hiring volume. For high-volume roles, you can run a faster, higher-bandwidth process, since you'll already have a deep understanding of the role and the interviewing team will be able to pattern-match more easily. These also tend to be entry-level roles, which can have more streamlined processes—you may even be able to eventually forgo hiring committee meetings. For more bespoke roles, expect to run a heavier version of this process, since you'll hire less frequently and interviewers will need to be well versed in what you're looking for.

This is probably a good spot to mention that your choice of recruiting leader will be critical to building a whole-company process that repeatedly produces high-quality hires. Many recruiting leaders have been excellent recruiters themselves, but that doesn't necessarily mean that they are adept at building strong foundations for tooling, processes, and measurement. As with all leaders, they must be self-aware and able to hire the right people and roles—recruiting operations support, for example—to complement their abilities. In fact, it's worth putting a smart, process- and measurement-oriented person on recruiting operations as early as you can to optimize both the candidate experience and the ROI of your investment in hiring.

But even with the strongest recruiting leader and team, the success of the process ultimately relies most on the participants. That starts with fostering strong interviewing skills.

Interviewing education

It never hurts to refresh your interviewing skills, even if you've been conducting interviews for over 20 years. There are reasonably good training materials on interviewing and interviewing frameworks out in the market, such as the STAR (situation, task, action, result) method. The most effective interviewing tactic is to be consistent—meaning you should ask the same questions of every candidate, while also leaving space in the interview to probe their answers and get at their root behaviors and abilities.

The most common mistakes I see interviewers make are:

- Not using the rubric; asking different questions of different candidates, and therefore never finding a way to benchmark an excellent answer
- Not interviewing for the capabilities most needed in the role
- Assessing whether they like someone instead of whether the candidate will be successful in the role
- Overly prioritizing the right candidate experience rather than the right trajectory and aptitude to learn

The best interviews suss out how someone:

- Works with other people
- Gets quality work done themselves
- Motivates and develops themselves
- Has or can develop the expertise needed for the role
- Demonstrates leadership and resilience

It won't surprise you to hear that in every interview, I like to test whether someone is self-aware and whether they're a learner, two things that go hand in hand. The best way to test for self-awareness is to ask a candidate how their colleagues would describe them. If they only say positive things, probe what constructive feedback they've received. Then ask, "And what have you done to improve?" to check their orientation toward learning and self-improvement and to test whether they've taken the feedback to heart. While you're at it, watch for how much they use "I" or "we." Too much "I" is a flag that they may not be humble or collaborative and you should probe further. Too much "we" may obscure what role they played in the situation, which is something you'll want to clarify. I vastly prefer those who use more "we." I always learn something revealing when I ask about their specific role, usually something positive like "It was my idea, but the credit goes to the whole team." The less positive version of the answer is something like "I just did what everyone else decided."

Too often, interviews rely heavily on asking questions about a person's résumé, which is especially ineffective when assessing people early in their careers. Although I find that at least one résumé-based question is a good way

"If I interview anyone, that's the number one thing I look at: Do they really want to learn? If they want to learn, I don't care about their background anymore."

—**Eric Yuan**, founder and CEO, Zoom

to break the ice and gauge the candidate's experience, you're better off getting them thinking about what they might do in specific scenarios you present to them—or, if your approach is more résumé-based, about the specific role they played in a given situation. Good interviews include a range of questions, from situational ("How would you handle this scenario?") to behavioral ("Tell me about a challenge you overcame") to strict competency ("Describe the last Excel model you built and how you approached the design"). Sometimes behavioral questions are the hardest to come up with, so I've included a list of example interview questions in the chapter appendix on page 238.

The behavioral questions are also the best opportunity to incorporate your company values into the conversation. If one of your principles is "Put customers first," for example, you can ask the candidate to provide examples of work where they might have had to keep the customer top of mind. Don't ask about the customer-facing aspect of the work specifically—just see if they bring customers up at all. A written exercise can be another great way to put the candidate into a realistic work scenario, test how they structure their thinking and solve problems, and assess skills that are particularly relevant to the role. I've included an example written exercise in the chapter appendix on page 241.

To prevent hiring mistakes, improve outcomes, and avoid bias and an inconsistent quality of hires, your hiring processes and interviewing skills need to be well-defined and rigorously observed and measured. And don't forget about candidate experience—you're likely to reject many more candidates than you accept, and for almost every single one of them, that's the one experience they'll have of your company and what it represents. Many times, a rejected candidate has sent our Stripe recruiter a thank-you note or a gift. That's the true sign of a strong, candidate-first process. (There's more on measuring candidate experience in the section on closing your hiring loop on page 209.)

The hiring process for non-leader roles
While many aspects of leadership and non-leadership hiring are the same, a few key processes will differ based on where the role sits in the hiring pyramid. We'll start with the hiring process for non-leadership roles, then cover some of the differences when hiring new leaders.

Interviewing
You'll need to adjust your interviewing approach for scaled versus less frequently hired roles. For scaled roles, you likely have a wide swath of potential interviewers—for instance, all engineers or salespeople of a certain tenure and performance—and your interview panel members will vary depending on people's schedules. You'll also want to include a hiring manager,

or an experienced person who can proxy the role of the hiring manager if you haven't yet assigned a team for the hire.

For less frequently hired and leadership roles, I recommend having the same people interview all of the candidates. This will help with calibration and pattern recognition across potential hires, and it's more likely to result in interviewers hewing to the focus area for their specific interview, per the rubric. It's also important to have a cross-section of other people on the interview panel—not just immediate team members but also folks with a mix of seniority and functions with whom the candidate might work. For example, if you're looking for an HR partner, someone from the legal team should also be on the hiring team. If it's a finance role that partners with engineering and product, people from those teams should help evaluate the candidate.

Once your company is big enough that leadership can no longer meet every candidate, I recommend establishing a program similar to Amazon's Bar Raiser program. Described in detail in *Working Backwards*, the Bar Raiser program was created to help Amazon hire consistently stellar employees.[37] Bar Raisers are an exclusive group of interviewers who are considered good stewards of Amazon's standards and culture. One Bar Raiser is included on every interview panel. The Bar Raiser is never from the team for which they're performing the interview, and they run the equivalent of the hiring committee meeting. They can also single-handedly veto a candidate. Amazon invests heavily in training Bar Raisers to manage hiring decision conversations and to make sure interviewers are holding candidates to a consistently high and objective standard, and it's viewed as a high honor to be a Bar Raiser at Amazon. The program is a clear example of a company taking what might seem like a monumental commitment and making it a form of recognition and a signal of who best embodies the culture.

Many companies have adopted something akin to the Bar Raiser program. At Stripe, for example, we had an "Elevate" interviewer who joined interview panels for other teams. Elevate interviewers were high performers and some of our best interviewers—they tended to conduct more interviews and had honed their skills. The selection process for Elevate—and for the newer incarnation of that "culture" interview—was a combination of performance data, interview experience, and candidate assessment ability. We looked at historical feedback in our applicant tracking system, or ATS, which includes "definitely," "yes," "no," and "not sure" responses on candidates. If we didn't hire the candidate, we looked at whether the interviewer was opinionated enough to submit a "no." If we did hire the candidate, we looked at whether the interviewer's assessments of "definitely" or "yes" compared favorably with how those candidates ultimately performed as Stripes.

Stripe's offer-approval process

Early on at Stripe, we built a simple offer-approval process for new hires that's still one of my favorites. As we grew, members of the Stripe leadership team could no longer meet every candidate, but we did want to review and sign off on every offer. In order to strike this balance, we had to review the interview feedback and offer details, but we needed to do so quickly to maintain the pace of the recruiting process and meet candidate expectations.

We built a series of Slack channels for each high-level functional area—for example, business or tech roles—and added the recruiters and the leaders who would approve offers for those functions. The leaders committed to a 24-hour turnaround time for approval, and the recruiters agreed on using a consistent format to present the planned offer, including a tag to signal to the appropriate leader that there was an offer for them to review and approve. The template included the proposed job level, a link to the hiring committee summary, and all of the individual interviewer and reference feedback. The leader's role was to review the information and approve the hire or ask clarifying questions.

Often, if interview panel members held differing views on a candidate, I would probe for more details or ask whether there was a champion on the team who felt strongly about hiring the person. We would rarely veto an offer, but it happened on occasion when the interview feedback and references were lukewarm or when the panel indicated that the person was not top talent. I thought this approach would last for a year or two. But, although it's starting to show some wear, five-plus years and thousands of hires later, many teams at Stripe still use it. There are just a lot more leader approvers and recruiters in those Slack channels than there used to be!

I'll be the first to admit that designing the Elevate program and its subsequent iterations to adequately scale with Stripe has been a challenge. Not every division used Elevate interviews—see the information on candidate review as an alternative practice on page 185—and we continue to iterate on the culture interview format. But I remain convinced that a program like this is valuable for sending a message about the importance of strong hiring practices. I suspect that Amazon continues to invest time and resources into their Bar Raiser program because it has proven to be a strong means of reinforcing their culture. The questions in our Elevate interviews are similarly inclined: Do we think the candidate will act like an owner? Will the candidate be a rigorous thinker? Are they curious and a learner?

Decision-making

Before you start interviewing candidates at any sort of scale, it's critical to be clear about who ultimately makes the hire or no-hire decision. Because I'm a collaborative person and a believer in the proverbial wisdom of crowds, I don't believe that hiring managers should be the sole participants in candidate selection. I think a more effective model is a consultative process, run consistently across a division or company, that still situates the hiring manager or hiring manager equivalent as the primary decision-maker, since they're the person who is accountable for the team's results. It's also prudent to have checks and balances across the process, such as final review by a committee or executive.

One check that Stripe employed early on was to have an executive interview every candidate before a final hiring decision was made. We would push back on the interviewers and often decide not to hire. The people involved in those hiring processes learned to consider candidates more deeply, not just as someone to fill a role but also as someone we expected to grow at a fast pace with the company. Later, as the company expanded and the process had been codified, we scaled back this approach.

This progression reminded me of my first several years at Google, when the founders could no longer interview everyone themselves but would instead review every hiring packet before an offer could be extended. Over time, they delegated the packet review to divisional leaders. At Stripe, we iterated on our approach using Elevate, our offer-approval process, and, for some teams, candidate review.

Job level selection

The next decision required for an offer is where to place the candidate in terms of job level, which then determines their compensation. (See Chapter 5 for more on compensation.) Early-stage companies often haven't cemented their job levels and ladders, but putting a basic structure in place is a worthwhile investment.

A distinct memory from my first year at Stripe is when I hired a leader for our US sales team. She had worked for me previously and we had a trusting relationship—so much so that when I pushed her on getting the pieces in place to scale and measure the impact of the sales team, she pushed back and said, "You need to help me by finishing the work on the role expectations and company job level structure. How am I supposed to set expectations and compensation without that?"

Here's a quick summary of job levels:

LEVEL 1	Entry-level postgrad.
LEVEL 2	2-3 years of relevant experience.
LEVEL 3	3-4+ years of relevant experience, able to work independently.
LEVEL 4	8-10+ years of relevant experience, plus some minimum scope of role and potential impact to warrant the higher level. Could be a manager.
LEVEL 5	15+ years of relevant experience, plus some minimum scope of role to warrant the higher level. Could be a senior manager or director equivalent.
LEVEL 6+	Senior director or executive, plus some minimum scope of role to warrant the higher level.

Table 3. Job levels.

As many of my engineer friends will point out, the years of experience can be a red herring. They don't necessarily capture impact, especially for jobs like engineering, where someone with less experience could still be 10 times more productive than their peers—the much sought-after "10x engineer," in engineering parlance.

One often-used analogy, initially shared with me by a compensation consultant but also widely available on the web, uses ropes and knots instead of years of experience to explain the abilities assumed with each level. (See Table 4 on the next page.) Like the details of ropes and knots in this analogy, each function might customize their levels into a job ladder that includes high-level descriptions of the expectations at each level. However, I would caution against overworking job ladders because they can quickly turn into checklists that employees feel they can meet in order to get promoted. Remember the distinction between skills and capabilities from Chapter 1? In my experience, skills are easier to check off a list. Capabilities, such as the ability to collaborate and partner with others, are not as easy to capture, but they're often critical to success, especially as someone advances through the levels.

Once you've established the level you're hiring for and the candidate you've selected for a position, you can determine their compensation. For each level within a given function or collection of functions, you'll likely have two things: a salary band and target offer points for new hires. At Stripe, we strive to avoid the pitfalls of offer negotiation, both to avoid bias and to make the process more efficient. Instead, the recruiter and hiring manager must recommend one of two points in the salary band to offer the candidate. We do this using a compa-ratio.

A compa-ratio—see Figure 13 on page 182—divides an individual's pay rate by the midpoint of a predetermined salary range. For example, for a given level (say, Level 1) the minimum salary could be $85,000, the midpoint could be $100,000, and the maximum could be $115,000. The point on the band that you select is primarily informed by how experienced the candidate is and how much impact you expect them to have at their level. A very experienced Level 3, for example, might get a compensation offer at the higher end of the salary band rather than at the lower end. At Stripe, because these assessments of a candidate's potential impact are fallible, we also do a pay parity review every year to ensure that those in the same type of role at the same level with similar performance are paid similarly.

An entire book could be written about compensation strategies, and I wish it were. All I'll say here is that after many years of thinking about compensation levels and their externalities, I am increasingly of the belief that jobs should have set salaries, and that all compensation motivators should exist solely as bonus and equity vehicles. The set salary for a given role

	LEVEL 1 ENTRY	LEVEL 2 DEVELOPING	LEVEL 3 CAREER	LEVEL 4 ADVANCED	LEVEL 5 EXPERT	LEVEL 6 PRINCIPAL
ANALOGY	Learning about rope.	Can tie basic knots. Participates as others tie complex knots.	Ties complex knots. Calculates rope strength. Knows a lot about knots.	Understands ropemaking.	Knows more about rope than anyone else at the company.	Knows more about rope than anyone else, period.
KNOWLEDGE	Learns to use professional concepts. Applies company policies and procedures to resolve routine issues.	Developing professional expertise. Applies company policies and procedures to resolve a wide variety of issues.	Has a full understanding of their area. Resolves a wide range of issues in creative ways.	Has wide-ranging experience. Uses professional concepts and company objectives to resolve complex issues in creative and effective ways.	Has broad expertise or unique knowledge. Uses skills to contribute to the development of company objectives and principles and to achieve goals in creative and effective ways.	Expert in the field. Uses professional concepts to develop resolutions to critical issues and broad design matters.
JOB COMPLEXITY	Works on problems of limited scope. Follows standard practices and procedures. Builds stable working relationships internally.	Works on problems of moderate scope where analysis of situations or data requires review of a variety of factors. Exercises judgment within defined procedures and practices to determine appropriate action.	Works on problems of diverse scope where analysis of situations or data requires evaluation of identifiable factors. Demonstrates good judgment in selecting methods and techniques for obtaining solutions.	Works on complex issues where analysis of situations or data requires an in-depth evaluation of variable factors. Exercises judgment in selecting methods, techniques, and evaluation criteria for obtaining results	Works on significant and unique issues where analysis of situations or data requires an evaluation of intangibles. Exercises independent judgment in methods, techniques, and evaluation criteria for obtaining results.	Works on issues that impact design/selling success or address future concepts, products, or technologies.
SUPERVISION	Normally receives detailed instructions on all work.	Normally receives general instructions on routine work and detailed instructions on new projects or assignments.	Normally receives little instruction on day-to-day work and general instructions on new assignments.	Determines methods and procedures on new assignments and may coordinate activities of other personnel.	Acts independently to determine methods and procedures on new or special assignments. May supervise the activities of others.	Exercises wide latitude in determining objectives and approaches to critical assignments.

Table 4. Job levels described in terms of ropes and knots.

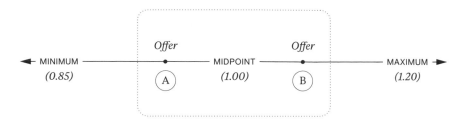

The compa-ratio

=

Pay rate
―――――――
Midpoint of predetermined salary range

Figure 13. The compa-ratio.

might change if market data changes, but otherwise you would either have to change roles or get promoted to earn a higher salary. Among other benefits, this would simplify internal transfers: If a new role has a different set salary, it's simply a reflection of the market, which makes it a neutral part of the transfer decision and not a reflection of your actual or perceived worth within the company.

It's important to remember that a company's largest expense is often compensation. That makes it a significant aspect of your annual planning process. (See Chapter 2 for more on planning.) Each year, you'll determine the number of hires for a given division and, ideally, forecast the job level of those hires so you can estimate your compensation expenses. More mature companies tend to have a lock on the exact job levels they plan to hire in a given year, whereas younger companies might list roles that can be filled with a range of experience, for example a Level 2 or a Level 3.

You'll also have a decision to make for your planners: Should they set the number of roles and specific levels they'll hire for at the start of the year, or should they hew to a budget? If you take the budget approach, the planners can then decide to hire more Level 2 employees and fewer at Level 4, for example, depending on need. I think this flexibility is generally a better approach, but the trick is to get an accurate budget for each division, which means you must correctly allocate cross-company expenses and revenue to each team, which is no easy feat. Some companies create a basic system to do this, such as allocating costs based on the number of people in a function, which is worth exploring. It's better to have people's attention focused on revenue and costs rather than "How many heads did I get?" The currency for success should be doing as much as you can with the resources you're given instead of focusing on how much your team is allocated compared to others.

Candidate selection

At Stripe, we have two core approaches to candidate selection and level assignment:

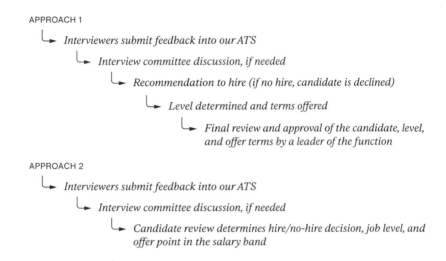

APPROACH 1
> *Interviewers submit feedback into our ATS*
>> *Interview committee discussion, if needed*
>>> *Recommendation to hire (if no hire, candidate is declined)*
>>>> *Level determined and terms offered*
>>>>> *Final review and approval of the candidate, level, and offer terms by a leader of the function*

APPROACH 2
> *Interviewers submit feedback into our ATS*
>> *Interview committee discussion, if needed*
>>> *Candidate review determines hire/no-hire decision, job level, and offer point in the salary band*

Figure 14. Stripe's core approaches to candidate selection and level assignment.

Early on, Stripe had a hiring committee discussion for every candidate. Over time, we've made the process more efficient, and now we only default to synchronous hiring committee discussions if there was disagreement about a candidate, newness in the role, or uniqueness in the position. All senior-level roles have a live hiring committee discussion, usually after the interviewers have met multiple candidates. In Approach 1, the recruiter summarizes the feedback and facilitates the discussion. If there's a hiring manager (for less scaled roles), they're tasked with consulting the committee, seeking to understand their feedback, and concluding the discussion with a recommendation to either not hire the candidate or to pursue references and, pending those, make an offer.

An important note: Stripe recruiters are assessed on their hiring volume, but this is not the primary measure of their success. The primary measure is the efficiency of our funnel—meaning conversion from one stage of the hiring process to the next—and, above all, the quality of the candidates we hire, which we strive to measure through manager surveys and performance assessments. I've told our recruiters many times that their job is to hire the best candidates who will be the most successful at Stripe, and that I expect them to be the first to call out concerning interviewer feedback or concerns with the candidate. Make sure your recruiting teams and hiring managers have the right incentives and orientation toward the big-picture goal.

Unlike companies that leave all hiring to the discretion of the hiring manager, Stripe has a more consultative process in which the hiring manager owns the decision to recommend a hire to final review but consults other interviewers in order to reach a decision. We also have a norm that anyone on the hiring committee can veto a hire. This is an extremely rare occurrence. I can only think of one instance of this happening, when a candidate's answers made an interviewer feel personally uncomfortable. But it's an important message, supported by Stripe's overall culture, that everyone taking the time to interview a candidate has a right to block the decision if they have a strong conviction against the hire.

Whether you take a candidate review approach—see the sidebar on the next page—or one in which a hiring manager partners with a recruiter to guide the process, the goals of those who steward the hiring process are to:

- **Guard the candidate experience**. Every interview process will leave the candidate with an impression of the company. You want that impression to be positive, even if the candidate isn't offered a job. (See the section on closing your hiring loop on page 209 for more about this.) If you end up hiring the candidate, the process can be as much a sales tool as it is an assessment tool. For more experienced candidates, the process should feel like a conversation and a mutual learning experience.
- **Really listen to interviewers' input**. These are, after all, the people who are likely to work most closely with the candidate and know their work best.
- **Bring the organization along**. Everyone in the organization should understand the process enough to trust the hiring decision and enthusiastically support new hires.
- **Decide based on what's best for the company, not for the team or individual**. Even if a team desperately needs to fill a position, there's never a good reason to compromise on a hire. This is easier said than done, especially when the candidate has extensive experience or was referred by someone at the company. Still, if the hiring committee has reservations, the job of both the recruiter and the hiring manager is to capture that feedback and make the right decision for the company, not for the candidate or for the referrer.

–

Candidate review

Stripe's engineering function hires at high volume, and often doesn't match an engineer to a team until after the hiring process concludes. The recruiting team and engineering leadership designed the candidate review process with these realities in mind.

Being a part of candidate review is an important role, and we take it seriously. It's been so successful that other divisions at Stripe have sought to emulate it. As with all such processes, I think its success is largely due to the consistency of the approach and the experience of the participants, who have seen a large volume of candidates and interview feedback and can pattern-match accordingly when making their decisions, while also controlling for bias.

What is candidate review?

Candidate review (CR) is a process to review interview feedback, hire and no-hire recommendations, and leveling decisions for candidates who interview for most of our engineering roles. Each CR panel includes a CR lead, CR reviewers, and CR admins, who meet multiple times per week to review feedback and approve or deny hire and no-hire recommendations and job level outcomes for all candidates who reach the onsite stage of our interview process.

Mission of candidate review

The mission of CR is to ensure that all engineering roles at Stripe are filled by extraordinarily high-caliber candidates through a consistent, efficient, and transparent decision-making framework that seeks to control for bias.

We accomplish this mission in the following ways:

- **Ensure that all engineering roles at Stripe are filled by extraordinarily high-caliber candidates**: We do this by administering a standardized interview process that tests for specific capabilities and experiences related to our ladders and levels. We then verify the outcome of that process by applying a consistent decision-making framework to each packet of interview feedback.
- **Consistency and efficiency**: We apply the CR decision-making framework consistently to all candidates for engineering roles at Stripe. Consistency in our interviews, interview rubrics, and CR process enables efficient decision-making as we develop a shared understanding of how interview performance maps to employee impact against ladder and level expectations.

- **Transparency**: We encourage bidirectional feedback to and from CR. The CR lead will, when appropriate, provide feedback to interviewers and hiring managers in the form of an email. That feedback might include, but is not limited to, interview feedback unrelated to the rubric for the interview, obvious cases of bias impacting interview feedback, use of gendered pronouns in interview feedback, or experience and goals feedback that focuses narrowly on role fit rather than broadly on fit for Stripe. A tight and transparent feedback loop helps us continuously improve as interviewers and candidate reviewers and prevents CR from feeling like a black box.
- **Bias control**: Bias is inherent to all of us, but we can seek to control for it through the consistent application of interviews and CR processes and, critically, by measuring and analyzing our results. We record all CR results along with scores for each interview rubric area to enable aggregated analyses of CR data. CR leads, recruiting managers, and tech HR meet at regular intervals to review CR outcomes in relation to important data sets, like Equal Employment Opportunity Commission self-identification, to ensure the correctness of CR decisions and to confirm that our interviews and rubrics map effectively to our ladder and level expectations.

All engineering candidates who complete an onsite interview with Stripe are submitted to candidate review and have interview feedback reviewed against our decision-making framework.

Decision-making framework
This framework provides a process to guide CR participants and hiring stakeholders to the correct hire/no-hire decision (defined as "expected to at least successfully meet expectations [SME] in their first performance review based on ladder and level expectations for the approved level") in a way that enables an equal opportunity for all candidates to demonstrate fit. CR will plan to follow the process outlined below for all candidates.

There are six distinct outcomes CR can assign to a packet after review. They are:

- Hire at suggested level
- Hire at higher level
- Hire at lower level
- No hire: hiring committee outcome overturned
- No hire: hiring committee outcome confirmed
- TBD: sent back for additional information

CR will follow these steps sequentially to determine which outcome is most appropriate for a given packet of interview feedback—you can read more about the CR decision-making framework in the chapter appendix on page 244:

1. Candidate submission
2. Interviewer scorecard review
3. Scorecard verification
4. Discussion, decision, and résumé review
5. Submit CR scorecard with CR outcome

Candidate review roles and responsibilities

CR lead: One member of each month's CR panel is responsible for ensuring that we apply the decision-making framework consistently and leading the review conversation for each packet. The CR lead also ratifies the outcome of the decision-making process, the rationale sent back to the hiring manager or recruiter, and any feedback sent to the hiring manager or interviewer. CR leads attend regularly scheduled sessions to review aggregated CR outcomes. In those sessions, the goal is to ensure that CR is being administered consistently across the rotating panels, that CR outcomes are correct, and that we are controlling for bias as much as possible, which is defined as having no statistically significant difference in outcomes by self-identified group.

CR reviewer: Responsible for reviewing interview feedback as described in the decision-making framework, engaging in a conversation about the correct hire/no-hire and level outcome, and ensuring that interview rubrics are followed and interview feedback maps directly to the rubric. CR reviewers must have a strong understanding of job ladder and level expectations, interview processes, interview questions, and assessment rubrics. In the CR meeting, they will carefully review all feedback with the following questions in mind:

- Is the ultimate hire/no-hire and level recommendation correct?
- Do the scorecards reflect the rubrics, or is the feedback subjective?
- Were the scorecard outcomes correct according to the rubric?
- Was the correct interview process followed?

CR reviewers discuss these questions along with the CR lead. CR reviewers include one member of the recruiting team.

CR admin: Owns and operates processes associated with running CR smoothly and efficiently. This includes owning the selection and spin-up process for CR reviewers and leads and ensuring the accuracy of documentation.

In CR, admins administer the process: queuing packets for review, introducing packets, and recording the CR outcome and any feedback to be delivered.

–

Checking references

If you've decided to hire a candidate, it's tempting to jump right to offering them the job. After all, you just went through a long, thoughtful process to find this candidate, and now you want to seal the deal. But that process was only a set of 30- to 45-minute interviews, and you now have a chance to collect more data. All of this is to say: Not making reference calls is a mistake.

As with the team screening, the recruiter and hiring manager can share the reference call responsibilities. If you're hiring for an entry-level role, you may only need to make one call—their summer job or internship, for example—and the recruiter is likely the one best positioned to conduct that call. The more experienced the candidate and the more high-impact the role, the more references you'll want to check. It's critical, in my view, that the hiring manager makes at least one of those calls, ideally to the candidate's current manager.

Bear in mind that the candidate provided these references. Your first thought is probably: Won't they be positively inclined? Generally, yes, but think what a signal it is if they're just lukewarm. Do not hire that person.

I also insist that those making reference calls ask—usually toward the end of the call, when the candidate's reference is comfortable—"Would you say this person is in the top 50 percent of folks you've worked with?" If they say yes, ask, "Top 20 percent? Ten percent? Five percent?" It's easy to be positive on a reference call, but 99 percent of the time, people will be honest and accurate when asked for data. If someone only says the candidate is in the top 20 percent of folks they've worked with, that's not a ringing reference.

The problem with typical feedback-seeking questions like "What's it like to work with them?," "What are their strengths and weaknesses?," "Where do they need improvement?," or "What challenges did you have managing them?" is that they can produce overly high-level answers and immediately put the reference in a position where they want to avoid sounding negative. Here are a few manager reference call questions that are more specific and behavioral:

- **Where do you see this person in three years**? Most people say five years, but that's too long. Three years gets the reference thinking about ideal shorter-term outcomes for the candidate. Focus on getting intel that will help you understand their trajectory.
- **When was the last time you didn't see eye to eye**? This should produce a specific example that shows how the candidate handles conflict.

- **What are some ways you've seen them be helpful to others?** This question will probe the candidate's collaboration and relationship-building skills. If the reference doesn't have much to say, you can dig deeper into what might be a collaboration issue. It's also a chance to push on your operating principles if you have one that focuses on prioritizing the team and the team environment.
- **Tell me about a time when you coached them on something.** This should surface a development area. More importantly, you're also likely to learn how the candidate responds to feedback.
- **How would you rate the candidate on a scale of 1–10? You can't say 7!** Another variant on asking whether they're in the top X percent. They'll likely answer with 6 (just above average) or 8 or higher (very good to excellent), which reveals a lot.
- **What's a skill you've seen them grow?** You'll get a sense of what the candidate had to work on, how they learn, and how self-directed they are.
- **What advice do you have for me as a manager to help them be successful in this role?** I always ask this question. It's an opportunity to glean final insights into their development areas and may be the beginning of your manager transition conversation if it's an internal hire. (More on this in the section on internal hires on page 194.)

Making the offer

Let's assume that the references are positive and it's time to formally make an offer. An offer letter is a critical document, and any stock plan associated with an offer is a legal agreement. Take these seriously and seek to automate generating and sending the correct documents early in your company development. Sending an offer with the wrong salary or equity amount can be trust-destroying—or worse. I know of one instance where the annual salary and four-year equity grant units were accidentally flipped. The candidate insisted on accepting the offer as it stood and left the company soon after they vested their first year of equity. (Clearly a mercenary hire, either way.) You don't send an offer letter to a candidate until after the recruiter or hiring manager has extended the offer verbally, so if anything about that offer is a surprise, your process has failed.

Recruiting processes are like extended conversations between the company—usually represented by the recruiter or hiring manager—and the candidate. Early on, seek to understand the candidate's motivation and make sure the role aligns with their career ambitions and experience. You may also talk about compensation expectations and provide high-level information on the role's compensation should they receive an offer. It's also prudent to start explaining the job ladder and, depending on the transparency of your levels—external job titles may or may not match the internal levels—discuss where they might fall on the job ladder and how that placement relates to their experience. If you don't have formal titles for many of your roles, as is the case at Stripe, it's best to make sure they understand that. This should also be clear in the job posting. Ultimately, nothing at this stage should come as a surprise; you should be sharing mutual feedback throughout the process to constantly gauge interest—and, if you think you're going to want to hire the candidate, to build that interest.

If you've done all of this well, both the company and the candidate should be excited about the offer and the close process will not be complex. Often, it's as simple as an immediate acceptance. But if there are outstanding questions on the candidate's side, your best bet is to keep up the momentum and answer them promptly. As a sales leader once told me, "Time kills all deals." The same is true for recruiting. Get the candidate's questions answered quickly, and consider offering a "sell chat" with a person who is critical to their role or even an executive in the company, depending on how important the position is to fill or how excited you are about the candidate. It's best practice for leaders, especially in high-growth environments, to keep flexibility in their calendars so they can take a 15-minute call and share their enthusiasm about the role and the candidate. The simple act of taking that time sends a message to the candidate that the company values them.

I find that in these leadership sell chats the candidate usually wants to know:

- How does the leader view the role the candidate might fill and its importance to the company?
- What are the company's medium- and long-term prospects?
- What excites the leader about the company's future?
- What might the challenges be?

Most of all, the candidate wants to be inspired by the conversation, and to feel like they're getting a good sense of what it's really like to work at the company. They also want to make sure your answers align with what they were told during the hiring process, especially about their potential role. This is why it's so critical to clearly lay out the job description and rubric: It helps you secure the best hire while also creating internal alignment.

The hiring process for leadership

To return to our hiring pyramid, leadership hires are the most bespoke part of your hiring process, no matter your company stage or size. The customizations come from many corners, from how well you understand what you're seeking in the role, and thus the precision of your rubric, to how confidential the search needs to be, either internally or for the candidate's sake. Much will translate from your core hiring process, which is what I've spent most of this chapter on. But the two aspects that will likely differ are the level of transparency and the decision-making process.

Transparency

I believe it's best to make it known internally that you're seeking to fill a leadership role. This is easy enough to do if there's no one currently in the role and no one who might believe that they're filling the role, for example if you're hiring your first CFO. But even in that case, you're hiring a new boss for whoever is doing the finance work for your company, so you'll need to prepare them for a new hire before you let everyone else know that you're looking for a CFO. It's difficult to tell someone that they're being "layered"—that is, having a new hire come in above them—and it's even harder to replace someone in an existing role. In these situations, consider your context and default toward transparency, but be very intentional about when you make the plan transparent.

In the layering scenario, you'll need to lay the groundwork with the person or people who will be most affected by the hire by providing feedback about their impact and level of experience. (See Chapter 5 for more on how to do that.) Be encouraging about their contributions but note the needs of the company that are not being met by the division, and help them start processing the need for a more experienced person. Beware of announcing a new layer too early: It can take about six months to fill a leadership role, and you might unsettle someone if they have to wait too long for some unnamed and unknown new manager to join. If possible, I recommend doing the early recruiting work—identifying what you're looking for in the role and building an initial pipeline—before you get firm about an impending transition. Then, when you have those first conversations with the people affected, you're not at a cold start but rather have a few months' jump on the process.

In a situation where you need to hire a new general counsel, for example, but you have someone in the role already, the context in which you make the process public matters even more. Although you can do some early work to identify what you need in the role and meet some highly regarded GCs, you don't want to get into conversations with potential candidates, even confidential ones, until you've talked to the person with whom you need to part ways. Ideally, you'll have coached the current person and agreed on their departure, at which point you can mutually manage a transition. (There's more on this in Chapter 5.) Perhaps during that transition, you and one or two others can start to quietly meet candidates, but you shouldn't bring anyone fully into the interview process until you've made the internal announcement about the current person's departure. Again, it's all about context, careful conversations, and intentional timelines for sharing information transparently to maintain and build trust.

On the candidate side, anyone who is in a top role at another company while also going through your process as a candidate is going to be rightly paranoid about news of their conversations with your company getting out. You and your recruiting team or search firm must operate with the utmost discretion. Although internal folks might want updates on who is interviewing for a top role, you must honor confidentiality, keep calendars private, and only provide high-level updates, for example "We have three great candidates, all from top companies we admire, and we'll share an update once we've made our selection and they've accepted the role." This can get tricky during the reference process, but it is navigable.

Decision-making

Although I am a believer in the wisdom of crowds, I think a leadership hire is a decision to be made by the CEO or a top executive rather than by a group hiring committee. If I had to boil down why, it's because of the "faster horses" phenomenon. At this level, people at other levels often don't know what kind of leadership they need. They may also fear the change brought on by a new leader. Plus, these hires can have a tremendous impact on the business and the culture, and the CEO or top executive who hires them needs to be accountable for that impact. When you're a senior company leader, I think you should be judged as much on who and how well you recruit as on any other aspect of the job. That said, even if you're the ultimate decision-maker, woe betide you if you don't run a consultative process to make your selection.

Managing the leadership hiring process

Given timeline and transparency considerations and the possibility that your decision might be perceived as some kind of coup, I encourage hiring leaders to treat the entire leadership hiring process as a change management and acceptance-building process. In some ways, it's a form of starting onboarding before you even make the hire.

I recently spoke to the founder of a successful logistics startup. She was looking to hire a new chief operating officer and had her eye on someone she thought would be great. But she expected that one of the current leaders who would report to the new COO would be resistant to the change. He was well liked by his team, so if he was against the hire it might have a cascading impact on a large part of the COO's team. What could this founder do to set her COO up for success?

This is a more common problem than you might think. Introducing new leaders to an organization is like introducing a foreign substance into the body—it's no wonder that companies anxiously try to avoid "organ rejection" of new leaders. (We'll get to hiring from within on page 194.) As with all employees, the success of the new leader ultimately begins with a hiring process adapted to the role.

The goal of the leadership hiring process is essentially the same as that of the core hiring process—it just involves wider communication as you work to get buy-in. You want to be accessible and open to feedback about the role and the hire and bring the organization along with the appropriate level of transparency and communication, yet always keep the company's needs top of mind, even if it means needing to manage change more than you anticipated.

Here are some recommended steps for building the leadership hiring process to produce the highest likelihood of gaining company buy-in for a successful, accepted leadership hire:

Screen the candidate so that at least two important people are excited about them

Leadership hires are expensive, both from a time and an organizational headspace perspective, so you want to be sure that there's enough enthusiasm for the hire before you involve others in the process. In practice, this involves a few top people—other execs, critical team members, or a board member—spending up-front time with the candidates to build confidence that they could be successful in the process before going any further.

Identify the main stakeholders affected by the leadership hire

List the primary people who should be on board and excited about this new leader. This should include the people who will be reporting directly to the new leadership hire, as well as people who would be significantly affected by the new hire and may work closely with them, for example a critical partner team or a team that will lose or gain scope as a result of the hire. That team's manager should be involved in the hiring process in some way.

It's tempting to exclude people who you think will have the most reason to be negative about the hire, since there's a risk that their feedback will be swayed by how the new hire will impact them. But remember two things at this stage. First, you as the hiring manager (depending on the role, "you" could be the CEO or another senior leader) will ultimately make the decisions. Second, these folks will have a big impact on the leader's future success at the company, so it's extra important to include them. But that doesn't mean that their feedback is the only feedback to take into account. Overall, your hiring committee is likely to include one or two other executives, two or three representatives of key stakeholders and direct reports, and one or two cross-functional partners. For critical roles, you may also have a board member meet the candidate or help sell them on the role.

Conduct an interview loop that includes key colleagues and stakeholder representatives
Send all interviewers an email before the interviews start that shares why the role is open and needs to be filled, the job description, and the key capabilities you're seeking. Include a description of the leader's background, who has met the person already, and some brief feedback, but not so much that you create bias. Make sure all interviewers know the focus of their particular interview (such as domain expertise, team management, or strategic thinking) and the rubric by which the interviewer should assess the candidate's answers.

Set up the hiring deliberation as a feedback-collection forum, not a decision-making forum
Assemble the people who interviewed the candidate for a hiring review meeting. At the start of the meeting, the hiring manager should make clear that, unlike other hiring committee processes you may have, this will be a consultative decision: The hiring committee will provide input to the hiring manager, but it is the hiring manager who will ultimately make the decision, pending references.

During the hiring committee meeting, you as the hiring manager should:

- Summarize the role, the company's needs, and what you're seeking from the hire.
- Give an overview of the candidates' backgrounds.
- Emphasize that this is a forum for gathering feedback from the interviews, which you'll use to inform your decision.
- Have the recruiter summarize the feedback submitted.
- Ask questions of the participants to understand their feedback and better inform your decision.
- Conclude the meeting by summarizing what you've heard, taking care to highlight any areas of concern that you'll need to probe with the candidate and/or their references.
- Provide an estimated timeline for making your decision. Be sure to report back to the group once a decision has been made and explain why you made that decision.

Assuming all has gone well, your final step will be to announce the hire internally. Your announcement should remind folks of the process, celebrate the person you've hired, and explain why they're right for the company and the role.

Hiring internally
If you went through the decision tree on page 171 and decided to hire from within, bringing the team along and running a considered process works the

same way, but it can be much more lightweight. The first step is to evaluate whether you have just one internal candidate or whether multiple people might step forward, even if some are a stretch for the role. If there really is just one person for the job, even after putting up an internal job posting, don't run a sham process. Instead, do the work to communicate the change—the promotion!—thoughtfully by telling those affected by the change first and then making a wider announcement. Celebrate your internal hire's success in earning their new role and help them step into it with low friction. In fact, you owe it to the person to suss out the level of friction they might encounter. If the process goes well, it will validate your choice: The surest sign that you've picked the right person internally is when the news is celebrated both in public forums and in private notes to you.

Rooting out friction is tricky to do, but one method is to consider sharing the news with a select group before announcing it to the rest of the company. For example, you could talk to a few people who would be cross-functional partners to the role and mention that you're strongly considering, say, Janelle, and see how they react. Or see how Janelle's new direct reports respond to being told that she is their new manager (keeping in mind that they may be a bit disappointed they didn't get the promotion themselves). If there's very strong pushback, it could be a sign that you've made the wrong decision. If you're certain that you've made the right call, it could signal that more change management will be needed to help Janelle succeed.

One way to reduce friction in this process is to meet with a few external candidates and make clear that you did so. I wouldn't recommend investing as heavily in recruiting as you would for a role that is solely an external hire, but those external interviews may help you validate your internal hiring decision. This approach will also demonstrate two things: that you selected the best candidate across all potential avenues, which sends a strong signal about your internal selection; and that your company has an open, inclusive process when new opportunities arise, which will build trust and faith in the candidate and in the company.

Even if you don't explore the external market, it's best practice to run an internal selection process if you have even the slightest sense that there might be more than one potential candidate. It may be more lightweight than your classic outside interview process, but this step is critical to build trust within the company. It also sends the signal that you were rigorous in your decision-making and that you value inclusive processes. In this more lightweight process, you'll want the hiring manager and maybe one or two other leaders to interview each candidate and then have a hiring committee discussion. The folks who participated in the search but were not selected may be disappointed, but they'll also appreciate the chance to be considered. You should also create a feedback loop to help them understand what they should develop in order to be considered for similar roles in the future. (See Chapter 5 for more on giving feedback.)

If you do run an internal process, be sure to keep the candidates confidential, since only one person will get the job and the others will likely want to return to their current roles without having to explain that they sought another one and didn't get it.

Finally, make sure you message the internal hire thoughtfully. Explain what you were looking for, the process you ran, and why the person you selected emerged as the right choice. That individual will need to adapt how they show up at work, especially if this was a move into management, and the more you can publicly lay the groundwork for why they were chosen and what's expected of them in their new role, the easier it will be for them to make that transition.

Interviewing

Just as the experience trap can hurt you when assembling a list of candidates, it can also lead you astray during the interview process. Experienced leaders are usually very good at interviewing—after all, they've done it for many years. Don't be swayed. Instead, make sure you have enough time to interview them and ask follow-ups to probe the depth of their knowledge. First and foremost, test their level of curiosity and their desire to learn. If you present them a scenario and they simply describe what they've done before and don't ask questions to understand your context, be wary. Seek details. Ask questions like "And what did you specifically do in that project?" Don't forget to ask if the project was successful. Look for people staying too high-level or obfuscating outcomes. You want to leave the interview thinking, "Wow, that person was on top of their shit!"

Hiring disagreements

One obvious question is: What do you—as a CEO, founder, or other senior leader acting as the hiring manager for another senior role—do if you think a leadership hire is great but the rest of the organization disagrees?

It helps to be extremely thorough with your homework. Make reference calls, and maybe have a board member or an outside adviser or two meet the candidate. Assemble all of the feedback and summarize it for those who are concerned. If everyone the person met internally is very much against the hire, you need to really understand why. They may be right. But if your homework and your gut tell you that this is the right move, sometimes you have to make the hard call to do what's best for your team or company. It's frustrating when people say, "Listen to your gut," because what does that really mean? But we all have intuition. Do your best to make your intuition concrete. Is it that the person seems to really understand the company and what it needs? Do you learn something every time you talk to them? Take care to explain your thinking, and explicitly ask for everyone's commitment and support to help the new person be successful.

I've also seen the opposite scenario: The hiring group was convinced that they'd found the right hire, but the senior leader remained unconvinced. In one case where the hiring group was right, three of the CEO's direct reports swayed him into agreeing that the candidate was who the company needed. Because those three reports had met every finalist candidate and agreed ahead of time on the rubric, they could be credible and persuasive. This is a sign that your process is working and that you have a healthy leadership team and CEO. When I've seen a hiring committee be wrong about a candidate, it's usually been because the committee included a fair number of folks who were not very experienced, either in their roles or with the type of work we were hiring for.

These are just a few examples, but I think you get the gist: The stronger your process and the more experienced and close to the work your interviewers are, the more weight you can give them when you face critical decisions as a hiring manager.

References and offers
Although all of the steps involved in extending an offer to a leader are similar to your core process, the entire enterprise will have higher stakes and take more time. References can be tricky, since the candidate won't want you to talk to anyone they currently work with—and, for the confidentiality reasons I mentioned earlier, it's generally not okay to press on this. Instead, go deep with the references they provide from previous companies, and ask them if there's anyone they really trust at their current company—maybe someone they've worked closely with in the past who can speak to their current work.

You're also going to be (rightly) tempted to seek back-channel references. These are risky. Done wrong, they undermine confidentiality. Instead, I prefer to say to the candidate, "Hey, I know some folks who've worked with you in the past. Is it okay if I reach out to them confidentially? I'll only talk to folks I know we can trust." The candidate will usually say yes, and they may want to ask who you're thinking of. Make sure the candidate can see that your goal is to get to know them and be rigorous in your process, not to seek out negative information.

With respect to the offer, if you've run a good process, the title and scope of the role will be clear, but there's likely to be negotiation on compensation. I find it best to have someone who is not the CEO or the hiring manager handle that negotiation. It may seem obvious, but one reason is so that you don't start off on the wrong foot as the person's new manager. More importantly, if you are the CEO, the candidate may assume that you can overrule any compensation framework to get them what they're asking for. Whether or not that's true—and it shouldn't be—it's not a good idea. It's better to have an experienced recruiter or a search firm, your CFO, or your compensation lead outline the executive compensation framework and explain the offer, which provides a backstop for any out-of-framework demands.

It's easy to think that once your offer has been accepted, your work is done. But in fact, that acceptance is just the precursor to the next phase of hiring. Orienting new employees, especially new leaders, to the company in their first few weeks on the job is every bit as important as coming to a mutual agreement that they should join the company.

Onboarding

Think about a time when you were new, like the first day of school or summer camp. Everything felt important, and you were on high alert for context and opportunities to learn. The same goes for new hires. The companies that simply have you show up, fill out some paperwork, get set up on your laptop, and start working are missing out on a huge opportunity to start inculcating new hires into the company and the culture.

Companies should seek to design the new-hire onboarding process in a way that feels true to the business. This should include:

- The "why" of the company, including the mission and the story behind it
- The "what" of the business, including current priorities and goals
- The "how" of company behaviors, including how people work together and the operating principles

I strongly believe that company leadership should take part in onboarding new hires, perhaps in a monthly session where leaders talk about company values and operating principles and, better still, share stories of those principles in action. Stories, not bullet points, are what really get a message across. And, of course, the entire curriculum should be thoughtfully designed to represent the fastest possible ramp to success for new hires.

At Stripe, we have a weeklong core onboarding curriculum for every new hire, no matter their level. Alongside this core curriculum, various teams, like engineering or sales, have programs that start in the first week and continue into the second. As a manager, it's important to understand what the onboarding curriculum covers, both at the company and division level, and to consider what additional content you might want to impart to your new hire during their first few weeks. You might deliver that content in your first 1:1, or you could hold a special one- to two-hour session in which you

"Often in my industry, people just get thrown onto the job. I think this is the wrong way to do it.

Training is very important, and understanding all the layers of the company is very important. If you're getting hired as a cook, it's not just about the kitchen. You need to understand how the company works, what we're doing at the farm, how we're doing things at the front of the house, how the director of operations is looking at numbers. They need an overall understanding of the company. And then the training is very important.

We also need to refresh that understanding. Because when you train someone, it's not like, 'Now you're trained.' No. You always have to be on top of it. It's a continuation of things."

—**Dominique Crenn**, owner and chef, Atelier Crenn, Michelin three-star restaurant

provide the new person (or people) context on the team and the current work and priorities—essentially, translating the company operating system to the team level so that the new hire immediately understands how their work ladders up to the overarching plan.

If the company has a sound onboarding program, all prep work should be done asynchronously before the onboarding program starts—everything from paperwork to equipment delivery and setup. Once they enter the program, new hires should emerge with:

- A sense of community with other new hires; no matter their individual seniority levels, they'll be a good informal network for one another
- An understanding of leadership's vision for the company, as well as company values or operating principles
- Deeper knowledge of the business, including a strong sense of the industry and key products
- Insight into the perspectives of users and their feedback
- Knowledge of the company operating structures and the most recent goals and priorities
- A visualization of high-level company organizational structures
- An understanding of key company processes, such as compliance procedures or what to do if an employee is contacted by the media
- A sense of where their team fits into the company's bigger picture
- An ability to find internal resources to self-educate and seek assistance

Internal mobility
Internal new hires are often overlooked in the onboarding process. Internal mobility can be a sign of good company health, but it can also be a warning about a certain manager or division. In my experience, when people change jobs, they're either running to something, running away from something, or, in the worst case, being pushed to move on because they're poor performers. The first case is obviously the preferred one, so it's important to start collecting data on your internal moves early on. For example, whenever someone changes teams, put a process in place, perhaps using internal tooling, to survey the person, their current manager, their new manager, and someone from the people team, if applicable, to ask the following questions:

- Was this move initiated by the employee or by the company?
- Is the move designed to develop the employee along their current career path, or is it a change in career direction?
- Did the person's former manager and new manager have a conversation about the transition before the move was decided?
- On a scale of 1–5, how satisfied were you/was the employee with your/their current team and manager?

- Will this move allow the employee to have a greater impact?

Over time, you can imagine what this data might signal about certain teams or managers, especially when overlaid with your employee engagement survey. Don't over-index on data showing that one or two people are unhappy with a certain team or manager, especially if the team is going through a time of great change. But if the data consistently shows a high volume of voluntary departures, you must act to understand the root causes of this "bad mobility."

In a fast-growing environment, it's often unavoidable that some people will have many different managers in fairly short time frames, whether or not they change teams. I wish this weren't true, but I've met a few folks at Google and at Stripe who have had more than six managers in one year. One way to mitigate the instability that this causes is to share best practices for manager-to-manager transitions. A thoughtful transition can minimize disruption and anxiety for the employee, ensure the new manager has the appropriate context to support the employee, and help kick-start a strong working relationship. (I've provided a short guide for healthy manager transitions in the chapter appendix on page 247.) They don't take a lot of time, and I find that the effort pays off in both trust and efficiency gains.

New hire onboarding

There's one more practice I've found to be helpful for every new hire, whether they're an internal transfer or not. Some years ago, Elad Gil interviewed me for his book *High Growth Handbook*, and I mentioned my "Working with Claire" document.[38] He surprised me by asking if he could publish it in the book alongside my interview, which I thought seemed excessive. He said, "I'm not sure you understand. This kind of detail is catnip to founders."

He was right. I won't venture to comment on catnip, but the number of people, particularly founders, who reach out to tell me that they read "Working with Claire" and it inspired them to create a similar guide is now more than I can count. I'm especially delighted when I hear that in certain companies or on certain teams everyone has such a guide. It's not just a manager tool—it's a way to accelerate relationships and is an exercise in, yes, self-awareness. (You can find my "Working with Claire" document in the chapter appendix on page 250. I've also included a "Working with Me" template on page 256 that you can use to create your own.)

One place to use your "Working with Me" guide is in the first meeting you have with a new report, which should be devoted to setting mutual expectations for how you'll work together. Plan to cover:

- **Onboarding**: Share any additional team context or information.
- **Operating approach**: Go over how you'll work together, when you'll meet, and what you'll talk about.

- **Management style**: Discuss what kind of manager you are and how your report can expect you to be involved in their work and career. Share your "Working with Me" guide and invite them to write their own if they're so inclined.
- **Communication preferences**: Talk about how you each prefer to communicate and what response times you should expect from one another. You should also align on how you'll use your 1:1 time.
- **Initial priorities**: Discuss each of your priorities with respect to the team's work and the individual's role.
- **The upcoming career conversation**: Explain that once you've worked together for a few months, you'll schedule time for a longer meeting to learn more about the person's experience, the arc of their career, and, importantly, their ambitions for the future. (See the section on career conversations on page 283 for more detail.)

Not every new hire will be ready to talk about their work preferences in that first 1:1, and they may not feel knowledgeable about their own work style. They may not have taken a work style assessment before. That's okay. Let them think about it, and suggest that they consider writing their own "Working with Me" document in the meantime. Most important is to set a tone of openness and trust by sharing some of your own experiences and preferences and encouraging them to do the same. Be sure to seek out anything they really expect or need from their manager. If you've conducted strong reference calls, you've already asked their previous manager what support you can provide. Touch lightly on these potential needs and see if there are any commitments you can make to support the person's development, for example providing more frequent coaching or sharing feedback whenever they give a presentation or lead a project.

New leader onboarding

Just as you should aim to build a core hiring approach that's similar for general and leadership hires, only adjusting it when warranted, you should seek to standardize your onboarding processes, then add some extra elements for incoming leadership hires. Onboarding is an important collective experience that should set a cultural tone for every new person in the organization. But since leadership hiring and onboarding is more fraught with rejection risk and since the impact of new leadership hires is immediately felt, either positively or negatively, it's important to invest extra effort into integrating new leaders into the company and building the support systems that will enable their success.

At Stripe, we designed a program we call the New Leader Experience, or NLE. It consists of welcome emails, a series of prescheduled meetings and pre-reads in the form of write-ups about the company and key internal documents, and a leadership assessment (the Hogan Personality Inventory[39]), plus access to a coach. We also recommend a set of first-month actions, including periodic emails to the leader's division and a 90-day 360° feedback process to provide an early view of perceived strengths and areas for improvement.

[39]

hoganassessments.com

The most important determinant of the program's success is every participant's commitment to it: not only the leader themselves but also their manager, their spin-up buddy (a Stripe term for a team member who provides onboarding support), their Stripe guide (a peer mentor who offers a safe space for any "Why do we do things this way?" or "How does this company really work?" questions), their HR partner, and their new direct reports.

SIDEBAR

–

New Leader Experience

Your new leader onboarding experience should accomplish the same objectives as the standard new-hire onboarding process, plus:

OBJECTIVE	TACTIC
Get the division excited about and accepting of the new leader.	See the onboarding process described in this chapter. **NLE:** Welcome email from the new leader's manager introducing the leader to the team, explaining why the manager is excited that the leader is joining, and what the new leader has been brought in to do. Include a personal photo (for example, including family or pets) and some personal information (like their previous job or hobbies).
Give the new leader business and company context as quickly as they can absorb it.	Core company onboarding. **NLE:** Share publicly available background reading prior to their start date, followed by an internal reading packet on their first day. Suggest key 1:1s with folks who can provide overviews of the business, the product, and their organization within the first few weeks.
Forge immediate connections with the new leader's manager, key colleagues, and stakeholders, especially fellow executives.	Schedule the most critical 1:1s for the leader's first few weeks alongside the core company onboarding process.

OBJECTIVE	TACTIC
Help the leader strike a balance between listening and learning and initial decisions and actions.	Provide both a spin-up buddy and a guide who will serve as day-to-day advisers and sounding boards during the leader's first few months.
Reinforce the leader's strengths and natural alignments with the company operating principles.	**NLE**: Hogan assessment and coaching, plus extra time with an HR partner to review observations about the team and initial feedback, followed by weekly meetings. (If you don't yet have an HR partner, the hiring manager or a peer colleague can potentially serve this role.) **90-day feedback process**: Conduct a survey or interview key stakeholders and direct reports and synthesize the feedback for the new leader.
Quickly course-correct or provide extra cover when friction arises or when the new leader takes actions or demonstrates behaviors that receive negative feedback.	Same as above. The Hogan assessment helps build self-awareness and an understanding of potential gaps, the HR partner functions as a translator and potential coach, and the feedback process provides additional input around whether course corrections are needed. Encourage the new leader to share the feedback they've received with their team and to ask for help working on their areas for growth.

Table 5. New Leader Experience objectives and tactics.

See the chapter appendix on page 257 for more details about the New Leader Experience program and a list of actions for the leader to take in their first three months.

—

One additional action to help new leaders in particularly critical roles, like members of the top executive C-level team, is to schedule a daily or every-other-day standup meeting, agile engineering-style, with their manager. It might be just 15 minutes long, but it serves as a time to quickly answer questions, capture the new leader's impressions, and align on what the division and the company might need for the future, whether it be new priorities, restructuring, or more resources. This time is especially helpful for getting the balance right on listening versus acting in the early months. The highest art of leader onboarding is equipping new leaders with the perspective to know when to switch from gathering information to taking action. When new leaders switch too quickly, they risk making poor decisions that cause lasting damage. When they switch too slowly, they risk paralyzing their division or letting problems worsen. The successful middle path is a narrow one, and the new leader's manager can be a critical sounding board during those initial months.

It's also crucial that the leader's direct reports get adequate time to collaborate with their new manager. These folks likely had to give away some

Legos and accept change, including accepting that the new leader would be taking on some of their responsibilities. The following sidebar on new leader onboarding from a direct report's perspective offers some helpful insights on the leadership onboarding process and how employees can support it.

–

New leader onboarding: a direct report's perspective

This write-up comes from a former longtime Stripe employee, Jorge Ortiz. He on-boarded many leaders to Stripe and we've had several conversations over the years about the process, as well as about how it feels to bring in your own boss, your boss's boss, or a peer with significant responsibility. This sidebar offers an adapted summary of his learnings.

Commit to their success

If you're closely involved in onboarding a new leader, it's almost certain that their presence means significant changes to your role, your responsibilities, or your experience of work.

You may have agreed or disagreed with the decision to hire the new leader. You may be enthusiastic about their arrival, full of apprehension and misgivings, or on a roller coaster between the peak of inflated expectations and the trough of disillusionment. No matter the circumstances, it is crucial that you commit to their success.

Everyone loses when a new leader fails. By definition, they have significant responsibility at your company, so their failure means a failure for your division. Users, goals, employees, and your overall trajectory will suffer. When you consider the blast radius, potential damage, time lost, and opportunity cost, the failure of a new leader is terribly expensive.

Information, quickly

A new leader needs to learn an incredible amount of information very quickly. Even a narrow part of the organization has a ton of context and complexity. A new leader is taking on responsibility for a broad part of your organization.

Ask them or discover what their most effective learning style is. Everyone learns differently. It might be reading documents, watching presentations, whiteboarding sessions, chatting 1:1, or asking lots of questions. The pace of information needs to be fast enough that they ramp up quickly but slow enough that they can digest it and ramp up effectively.

Remember that they don't know what they don't know. It's your job to help them prioritize what they need to learn and triage what they need to know now versus one month from now versus three months from now. This is a marathon, not a sprint.

First, the facts

Give your new leader data points, not judgments. If we hired them, we think they have good judgment. We believe they can come to solid conclusions and gain new insights in areas where we're currently stuck. Avoid giving them your pre-processed conclusion. Give them just the raw data points and let them make up their own minds.

Similar to giving good feedback, it takes active, conscious, mindful effort to frame information in a way that sticks to nonjudgmental, grounded facts. If they ask, or once they've had an opportunity to digest just the facts, then you can give them your own hypotheses and conclusions.

Prepare for decisions

Sometimes the new leader's responsibilities include areas you were previously responsible for. (This is common in handoff and new manager situations.) In these cases, I've found the shadow/reverse-shadow pattern to be very effective. Agree with your new leader that for the next n weeks, you will conduct those responsibilities as you've been doing, and they'll shadow everything you do in that scope and observe. For n weeks after that, the new leader will step in and conduct those responsibilities, and you'll shadow them.

You can also help your new leader by making decisions and letting them observe you (example-setting), proposing decisions and letting them approve those decisions (proactive delegation), or suggesting decisions and letting them enact those decisions (coaching). Have 1:1s at the end of every day or every other day to debrief, transfer additional context, provide reasoning, or give feedback.

Model your company values

One of the biggest changes for new leaders is understanding the company culture. One of the biggest challenges is understanding the unwritten parts of the culture.

New leaders often won't know when they're not adapting to the culture. And they face an additional hurdle: Few people will tell them. You can do a lot for your new leader by modeling behavior and hoping they pick it up. Pay particular attention to the behaviors that align less closely with your new leader's personality or instincts. Lead by example.

Give feedback, quickly and often

Your new leader likely has an impressive career trajectory, a track record of proven leadership, deep expertise in their domain, and significant self-confidence. But no matter how impressive they are, remember that you have infinitely more experience, expertise, and success at your company than they do. If there's something they need to hear, you have a responsibility to make sure they get feedback quickly, often, and from every perspective.

As with any feedback, it should come from a place of empathy. With new leaders, timeliness is particularly important. In positions of broad responsibility, even seemingly small pieces of feedback can be early indicators of much larger and more severe problems down the road. Small course corrections can prevent huge problems.

If your new leader is also your new manager, it can be tricky to deliver difficult feedback when you're just starting to build trust. In this case, it can be appropriate to give the data points to your manager's manager and let them handle delivering the feedback. If your new leader is your skip manager, you can let your manager handle delivering the feedback. If your manager and your skip manager are both new leaders (hey, it happens), find a peer of theirs with whom you've built trust.

Encourage adaptability

One of the biggest contributing factors to the success of a new leader is how well they can adapt to their new environment. New leaders are often hired based on the strength of their previous successes and experience. We expect them to bring the expertise and proven playbooks that have served them well in the past. But playbooks often depend on the assumptions and constraints that existed in a prior environment, and need to be tweaked or adapted when those change. Help your new leader adapt by showing them which assumptions or constraints might be different for them in their new environment.

Map the org

Help your new leader map out both the formal organization and the informal organization. Draw the formal org chart on a whiteboard. Explain the scope of each division, the interfaces between them, and any preexisting challenges. The informal org chart should include all of the context around the formal org chart: key decision-makers, domain experts, incentive structures, challenging situations, high performers, underperformers, and so on. Make sure to also cover forums, operating structures, operating cadences, and processes.

Loan your social capital

New leaders start with significant responsibility but little or no social capital. Achieving positive outcomes at your company will depend on some degree of social capital.

As an existing leader at your company, you've likely already built up your own social capital. You can help your new leader by loaning some to them. Some examples: Broker introductions to key people they'll be working with.

Talk up your new leader to small and large audiences ("Their experience with X is very helpful for us," "I've been impressed with how quickly they did Y"). Ask others to trust that you're ensuring some action or decision will succeed. The fastest way to build up your new leader's social capital is to set them up for early, quick wins.

Give them your capital

Sometimes your new leader's success depends not just on a loan but on a transfer of social capital.

You probably have star performers on your team. You may have recruited them, spun them up, and set them up to succeed. Working with them is a joy and a highlight of your career. If you've built a great team, they might follow you on any mission, to any corner of the world. Committing to a new leader's success might mean transferring not just the formal reporting relationship but also the special connection you have with these star team members.

Share stories and histories

With many products, technology stacks, and divisions, your company's current state can be very hard to explain or make sense of at a single moment in time. So many of your choices and outcomes have been path-dependent.

Often, the most comprehensible (and compressible) way to build a mental model of where the company is today is to understand where it started and how it got here. Telling your new leader the stories and histories of the products, technologies, and divisions that came before them can be extremely helpful for understanding why the company is where it is today.

–

Hiring mistakes

For most hiring mistakes, you won't realize the error until a few months into the person's tenure. In that case, it boils down to a performance issue. (There's more on handling performance issues in Chapter 5.) But there are cases when you realize right away—sometimes even before the person's start date—that you've made the wrong call.

It's hard to capture every potential signal, but here are some examples of actions from a candidate or new hire that might cause you to reverse your hiring decision:

- Posting confidential company information on social media
- Misrepresenting some element of their background or experience
- Treating people poorly before their start date or during onboarding
- Displaying arrogance and bad behavior toward their new team members in the first week

Basically, anything that violates your employee handbook, or any actions that show extremely poor judgment, period. For something more minor but feedback-worthy, like being consistently late to meetings, get that feedback to the person quickly and strongly. Ideally they'll improve, but watch them closely. If the issue continues, move with speed to part ways.

What do you do when you realize you've made a hiring mistake? The main thing is to do *something*. Depending on their start date and the state or country in which you're employing them, the best action is likely to rescind the person's offer or move toward a swift termination. There's no need to overexplain things internally; a short note to their team that explains the person will no longer be taking the role is fine. If you're in a jurisdiction where swift action is not as easy, look into how you might negotiate their departure. This may involve a payout, but it's better to pay and separate than to drag out a process that negatively impacts the team.

Close your hiring loop
It's almost impossible to track false negatives—people you rejected who would have been great for your company—but you can track false positives. At the micro level, when a hiring mistake happens, the hiring manager should do a quick retrospective on their process. Were there issues you should have caught in the process? Did you have the wrong desired capabilities for the role? Were there flags in the interview feedback or the references? Who conducted the interviews and reference calls? Was the onboarding thorough? Think about the role you played and how you could improve, and consider meeting with your recruiting partner to share your learnings and ask for their support to avoid similar mistakes in the future.

This individual learning is useful, but the real boon is to implement a company-wide, data-driven evaluation and methodology to improve your approach to hiring. As CEO of General Electric, Jack Welch reportedly tracked data that helped him ascertain who the best interviewers were and made sure that they trained other interviewers or were the only ones allowed to interview candidates.

The good news is that even a basic applicant tracking system, or ATS, can help you gather data to improve your process, including:

- **Time in process**: Are some roles or teams taking longer to hire? Why?
- **Funnel performance**: The recruiter equivalent of sales metrics. Are some teams hiring too few or too many folks relative to company benchmarks?
- **Interviewer stats**: Who interviews the most? What is the tenure and experience level of those interviewers? Is that appropriate for the candidates they're evaluating? Are the interviewers decisive, meaning

they indicate strong hire or no-hire choices? Are they discerning? Do they mostly recommend a hire?

Outside of your ATS, consider adding questions about the hiring process to your company engagement survey—or, if you're growing fast, implementing a short "pulse" survey to identify parts of the company where the hiring process or the environment new hires create doesn't honor your company's principles or values or your desire for an excellent talent portfolio.

Your annual or biannual engagement survey should ask employees to respond to prompts—all ranked on a scale of 1–5, from "strongly disagree" to "strongly agree"—like:

- The people on my team embody the company principles. (You can also list each principle.)
- I would recommend the company as a great place to work.
- We consistently hire excellent new team members.
- When it's clear that someone is not delivering in their role, we do something about it.

You could also get more specific with a pulse survey that you send out every month or so during times of rapid hiring and change, asking employees to rate prompts like:

- New people on my team are being onboarded quickly and effectively.
- The people we've hired on my team in the last six months meet or exceed the caliber of our current team.
- The people I work with are ambitious and hardworking.
- The people I work with are kind and selfless. They optimize for the company and for the broader team, not for themselves.
- The people in the most critical roles on my team are the right people for the job.

Most data from an ATS or company survey will give you a place to start your investigation but not a lot of detail. True insights will come from marrying data from the hiring process with people's performance once they join the company. This can be a cumbersome lift. If you can automate this data synthesis across your ATS and whatever HR information systems you use (such as Workday), plus your formal performance review approach—see Chapter 5—this will yield invaluable insights, especially as you grow. You might look at:

- **New hire performance data in the person's first 12 months versus their performance in the hiring process.** An easy thing to do is to send a quick performance survey to managers at certain milestones, such as 6 weeks, 12 weeks, or 6 months. A harder—but helpful—thing to do is to use sentiment analysis tooling to sample interview feedback (for example, positive use of the word "resilient"), in order to map qualitative interview findings with subsequent performance data and hone your interview rubric.

- **Longitudinal performance data**, mapped to interviewers' hire and no-hire recommendations.

One last note on false negatives: It might seem counterintuitive, but consider surveying the people you reject—not those from the early candidate screens, but anyone who has gone through the first interview stage or beyond. Although these results probably won't be ecstatic, they can help you improve your process for all candidates.

At Stripe, we primarily use an adjusted net promoter score (NPS) survey with a scale of 1–10, subtracting the percentage who choose 0–6 (negative to neutral) from the percentage who chose 9 or 10 (positive) to assess whether rejected candidates would still recommend applying to Stripe to others. We also seek feedback on the recruiter, the interview experience, and the overall process. Our response rate ranges from 20–30 percent of those we reject with an adjusted NPS of about 7. Recall that these interactions with your company may form a lasting impression, so treat candidates' feedback like that of any other customer: important and worth heeding, even if it's tinged with the sting of rejection.

There are moments writing this book when I've thought, "People at fast-growing companies are going to read this and think I'm crazy for believing that they can possibly devote the amount of time that much of this advice requires to the hiring process." I've had that thought myself. But if there's any chapter where the time devoted will pay off beyond your expectations, it's this one. Hiring is expensive, but talent is everything. Think of hiring as a critical and foundational experience. That foundation allows you to build a stronger house, especially if you get the leadership piece right. And once you've built it, you can start making sure that teams are working well within it.

—

Chapter 3

Scan the QR code to access printer-friendly versions of these worksheets.

Interview Framework and Rubric: Recruiting for Recruiters (L2+)

Competencies being assessed:

- Collaboration
- Conscientiousness
- Willingness to be wrong
- Intrinsic motivation
- Structured thinking
- Resilience
- Accountability

Interview process:

- Recruiter screen
- Team screen and written project (run in tandem)
- Onsite interviews
    - Collaboration and conscientiousness: 45 minutes
    - Willingness to be wrong and intrinsic motivation: 45 minutes
    - Structured thinking (hiring manager roleplay): 45 minutes
- Resilience and accountability: 45 minutes

Recruiter screen

Competencies being assessed:

- Functional expertise
- Conscientiousness
- Intrinsic motivation

Who can do this interview (including backup):

- Recruiter

Interview length: 30 minutes

Background

Example talk track:

> I'd love to hear a bit more about your background in recruiting. I'll have a few questions along the way, but I figure we could start there.

- What parts of the recruiting life cycle have you been involved with? (If not the full life cycle, are you open to it?)
- What has your volume looked like? What are your other responsibilities? (How do you prioritize?)
- How do you interact with the business? How do you approach the hiring manager relationship? (What's your partnership like with the business? How established was the process? Did you have to go in and create order from chaos?)
- What does success look like in your current role? How are you measured?
- Optional: How do you assess candidates for fit in the role you're hiring for, beyond the functional skill set?
- Optional: What's one thing you'd change about your current recruiting process? How would you go about implementing those changes?

Additional questions (if there's time):

- Is there a project or process improvement you're most proud of that you led recently?
- What has been an ambiguous, tough challenge at work, and how did you navigate it?

	Rubric		
Poor	**Good**		**Strong**
			Good answers, plus:
Life cycle: No recent (3+ years) in-house closing experience; no desire to source as part of role.	**Life cycle:** Ideally full life cycle (FLC), or candidate is at least open to FLC; has touched both closing and sourcing in their career.		**Life cycle:** Has most recently (1+ years) been FLC.
Volume: Proud of high volume and wants to continue in that space.	**Volume:** Able to articulate current volumes, speaks to numbers, and has a bias for quality over high volume.		**Volume:** Aligns with our norm (4–6 unique searches, 7-ish hires per quarter?)
Business partnership: Lack of ownership or desire to consult with the business; transactional approach to partnership.	**Business partnership:** Consultative approach, high degree of ownership, views relationship as a partnership instead of transactional.		**Business partnership:** Articulates specific examples of their partnership with the business and the importance of building or leveraging those relationships.
Success: Declines to mention metrics, expresses desire not to be measured, or focuses just on the numbers or delivery instead of the how.	**Success:** Speaks to their metrics or storytelling through data; if candidate has light exposure to data, expresses desire to dive deeper or has set up measures for themselves.		**Success:** Provides specific examples of influencing the business or process through data and evidence.
Builder mindset: Operates comfortably within the status quo; fails to express a desire or need for change.	**Builder mindset:** Highlights areas of process improvement or building they've owned or heavily influenced.		**Builder mindset:** Evidence of building aligns with similar challenges we face (scale, consistency, etc.).
Communication: Unstructured, overlong, does not pick up on interviewer cues.	**Communication:** Clear, succinct, asks clarifying questions.		**Communication:** Engaging; frames answers to add value and opinions while keeping structure and clarity.

Team screen (run in tandem with written project)

Competencies being assessed:

- Accountability
- Structured thinking

Who can do this interview (including backup):

- List relevant team members or positions

Interview length: 45 minutes

- 35–45 minutes for questions
- 5–10 for candidate to ask questions
- Ask follow-up and probing questions if you don't get a satisfactory level of depth in the first answer. If the candidate can provide more depth after prompting, this qualifies as passing the question.

Question 1:

Acknowledging that every role and candidate is different, how do you pitch your current company against competition when closing candidates?

Follow-up questions:

- If the candidate focuses only on cultural aspects: How do you represent the financial component of the offer?
- Does your pitch change when competing against a large or small company? How and why?

Rubric			
Poor	**Weak**	**Good**	**Strong**
Does not discuss value proposition at all.	Unable to describe the opportunity for their company for the space they're in.	Knows the company's growth and opportunity well (but doesn't know the space well) and can explain it in relation to competitors.	Deep understanding of the value proposition of their company and how to pitch it in relation to competitors.
Doesn't close candidates; relies entirely on a script or manager to close.	Hard selling on strengths; unwilling or unable to acknowledge weaker points or areas where the company is focused on improving.	Only talks about the positives; doesn't talk about how the candidate could impact company trajectory.	Honest and forthright about strengths and weaknesses of company value proposition; able to honestly discuss upside and risk; connects a candidate's role to company success.
	Unable to identify whether requests are unreasonable or provide alternative approaches.		Able to push back on unreasonable asks from candidates; understands that different companies have different value propositions; can steer candidates away from apples-to-apples comparisons.

Question 2:

What was your toughest recent search? Why was it so challenging, and how did you pivot and adapt along the way?

Follow-up questions:

- What did you learn from that search?
- How did you partner with your hiring managers to navigate this search? What did you own? What did they own?
- How have you applied your learnings to future situations?
- If the candidate isn't specific or keeps it high-level: Were there any specific, tactical changes you had to make? What were they, and what were the results?
- What, specifically, made this search harder than other searches? Were there any stakeholders you had to involve and get buy-in from to adapt to these changes? If so, how did you go about doing that?

Rubric			
Poor	**Weak**	**Good**	**Strong**
Unable to give an example of a tough search or challenges they faced.	Unclear why the search was difficult; they didn't make adjustments, or their suggestions were blocked; instead of adjusting, they continued with an approach that had not been successful.	Clearly identifies why the search was challenging and how they attempted to adjust their approach to solve for those challenges.	Demonstrates a sophisticated, structured recruiting process; able to creatively influence and reach decision-makers; independently drives changes in approach that yield results (like a successful hire).
Lacks creativity to design new solutions; adaptation was driven by management or stakeholder decisions.	Unable to reflect on challenges or suggestions made to unblock for current or future situations.	Able to reflect on past challenges and why changes were necessary; gathers buy-in and partners well with other team members to unblock or pivot in strategy.	Able to go very deep into the details (shows that they did the work instead of escalating to a hiring manager or manager) and think critically throughout; strategically consults other team members, hiring manager, manager, stakeholders, etc. on changes in process, and can communicate changes effectively.

Question 3:

How do you ensure that you have diverse candidate representation in your pipeline?

Follow-up questions:

- Are there any tools or strategies you use to expand your search or candidate pool?
- What tactics have you used that have worked best? What tactics have been less successful?
- When do you typically approach the topic of diversity, equity, and inclusion with your hiring partners? How do you do this?

Rubric			
Poor	**Weak**	**Good**	**Strong**
Does not have a defined approach for how they ensure diverse candidate representation, or relies on others in the organization to do this.	Understands the importance of talent branding and sourcing tactics but is unable to go into detail on methods they've used or challenges they've overcome.	Able to identify several sourcing and talent branding tactics they've used to build diverse pipelines and discuss their relative merits or challenges.	Defines what "diversity" means at a role and team level, as well as at a company level.
Unable to explain tactics or approaches used to ensure there is diverse representation in their pipeline.	Lists some tactics to expand the top-of-funnel pipeline for diverse candidate representation, but is unable to expand on approaches or their importance.	Demonstrates thoughtfulness and interest in researching and pursuing multiple approaches.	Thinks about market intel and mapping and is able to speak to approaches, data, tools, etc. they've used in the past.
No accountability in approaching the topic of diversity, equity, and inclusion with their hiring partners or peers.	Does not typically approach the topic of diversity, equity, and inclusion or diversifying pipelines with hiring partners; in specific situations where they've had to do this, they have relied heavily on their manager or other stakeholders to do so.	Understands the importance of diverse representation across the company; has many internal stakeholders involved, and takes action to approach the topic of diversity, equity, and inclusion with hiring partners when necessary.	Takes action to educate their hiring teams and partners and can give clear examples of this.
			Creates inclusive job descriptions and interview criteria.

Written project (run in tandem with team screen)

Competency being assessed:

- Written communication skills

Who can evaluate the written project:

- Recruiter and/or hiring manager, in advance of onsite

Project timeline:

- Candidates are usually given 2–3 days to submit

Context:

Request two writing samples (one internal communication and one external communication). Ideally, these are preexisting documents. However, a candidate can create something if they're no longer employed and don't have access to their company email.

- **Internal communication**: This can be a weekly or monthly update to hiring managers, a project update to stakeholders, or a shipped email. The candidate is required to remove confidential information such as names and data.

- **External communication**: Generally, this is a message to candidates. The preferred sample is interview preparation material. However, we're open to event invitations, candidate outreach, etc. We do not want to receive a template used by their team, such as a rejection email or interview availability request.

Prompt (sent via applicant tracking system)

Hi [Candidate First Name],

Thank you so much for taking the time to chat with [Team Screener] earlier! They enjoyed your conversation, and we are excited to move you forward in the process for the [Job Name] role, which includes a written project.

Since so much of what we do as recruiters is based around written work, I'd like to ask you to send along samples from each of the following categories:

- External communication to a candidate: The preferred sample is interview preparation material. However, we're open to event invitations, candidate outreach, or some other personalized candidate communication. We're not looking for templates used by your team (i.e., candidate rejection emails or interview availability requests) but rather an individual, detailed, and informative email.

- Internal communication to a hiring manager, hiring team, or stakeholders: This email can include a hiring kickoff meeting, candidate positioning, a project update (a sourcing session, an event, or another initiative would work well here), or a shipped email. Please redact confidential information such as names, contact info, and data.

We ask that this be completed within three business days, but please let me know if you need additional time. I'm happy to address questions as you have them, and please submit your work at the link below.

Thanks,

[My First Name]

Rubric			
Area	**1**	**2**	**3**
Structure	Lacks concision; is confusing; does not include a call to action or stated objectives and outcomes; shows little to no focus on partnership, strategy, or collaboration; is difficult to follow and understand.	Is concise, with a passable level of detail; states a call to action with at least one objective or outcome; focuses on partnership or results; is easy to read and flows logically.	Is concise yet detailed; has a clear call to action highlighting objectives and successful outcomes in ways relevant to the stated priorities; focuses on partnership, collaboration, scalability, or other measurable results; is easy to read and flows logically.
Grammar and syntax	Contains enough grammar, spelling, syntax, or punctuation errors to need a rewrite before presenting to a leader or candidate.	Has minor grammar, spelling, syntax, or punctuation errors; is ready to be presented to a leader or candidate with some revisions.	Has minimal to no grammar, spelling, syntax, or punctuation errors; is ready to be presented to a leader or candidate with no revisions.
Tone	Does not attempt to reflect a personable tone; fails to engage the intended audience; lacks personality or borders on unprofessional.	Attempts to reflect the right tone and engage the intended audience; lacks personality or proper tone (which may be a product of their current environment) but remains professional.	Reflects our preferred tone and engages the intended audience; is personable and conversational yet professional.

Grading

Grade the written project against all three categories and total the points to determine next steps.

7–9	Pass
5–6	Second set of eyes needed (recruiter or hiring manager)
3–4	Fail

Onsite interview 1:
Collaboration and conscientiousness

Competencies being assessed:

- Collaboration
- Conscientiousness

Who can do this interview (including backup):

- List the relevant interviewing group or team members

Interview length: 45 minutes

Question 1:

Imagine you're working with another team, and you notice that they have a process that could be improved or operationalized. Have you had an experience like this before? If so, how did you react? If not, how would you react or respond?

Follow-up questions:

Situation:

- Did you let the team know? Did you help implement a change?
- How would you communicate what could be improved with the team?
- How would you respond if the team didn't agree with your suggestions?

Action:

- What would your first step be?
- How would you tackle this kind of scenario?
- What kind of information would you need to address the scenario?
- How would you partner with the team to make relevant changes?

Result:

- How could this situation pave the way for future changes?
- What do you think the key takeaways from this situation should be?
- How would this affect your partnerships with other teams?

Rubric		
Poor	**Good**	**Strong**
Opts to do or say nothing about the process, regardless of how it could affect the other team; is able to flag potential issues and process breakdowns to management, but doesn't show initiative working with teams to unblock or make process improvements.	Gathers buy-in and partners well with other team members to unblock; demonstrates limited scope of intervention and assistance to the area of their involvement but is unable to explain the broader team and organizational impact of these changes or think about the future.	Demonstrates efficiency in their partnership with the other team; effectively prioritizes the suggested change within the broader goals of the org and works with the team to implement it; identifies whether the change is local or whether an org-wide adjustment is necessary.
Offers no clear direction on how they made their decision; lacks a data-driven approach.	Mentions the need to use data to inform decisions and shares 1–2 metrics used to measure the success of the change.	Quotes the metrics used to measure the success of the change and suggests future improvements based on the data.
		Exhibits desire to help others, regardless of whether it's a part of their core responsibilities.

Question 2:

How do you keep track of all of your different responsibilities, projects, tasks, etc.?

Follow-up questions:

Situation:

- What are some examples of the different things you're working on and prioritizing?

Action:

- How do you determine how you're going to prioritize?
- How do you communicate your prioritization to stakeholders?

Result:

- In juggling multiple to-dos, what have you learned about prioritization?
- How do you think you can improve your methods of prioritization?

Rubric		
Poor	**Good**	**Strong**
Does not consider cross-functional partners; lacks a structured approach to planning and prioritizing work; takes on work items as they arise; shows poor organization and tracking skills.	Has an organized task-management philosophy but is unable to note any ways they might improve their prioritization methods; considers cross-functional partners and how various stakeholders are involved in projects and tasks; demonstrates an ability to execute a project plan on their own.	Prioritizes work in line with org and company priorities and has a structured approach to keeping track of deliverables; has a solid tool set and approach to keeping track of and reporting on work; recognizes areas of self-improvement or provides tangible ways they can continue to develop their process for prioritizing; exhibits an ability to collaborate and work through others; defines various work streams and assigns owners; speaks to how to track progress and help unblock challenges.
Does not have a way to think through the problem systematically.	Shows a structured approach to prioritization, but does not demonstrate the ability to see the big picture when assigning priorities.	Demonstrates a holistic and thorough approach to prioritization and aligns their reasoning with the overall company priorities.

Bonus question (if time allows):

When starting a new role or starting at a new company, how do you set yourself up for success?

Follow-up questions:

Situation:

- What did you do when starting your current position?

Action:

- What are the resources you find most valuable while learning?

Result:

- What was missing from your last experience of joining a company that you now know would help you be more successful in your next role?

Rubric		
Poor	**Good**	**Strong**
Methods show little or no autonomy or self-reliance; is dependent on others.	Relies on support structures already in place but demonstrates an ability to self-start and problem-solve.	Displays autonomy, resourcefulness, and self-reliance in their methods.
When providing examples, blames others or process for poor training.	Is proactive about reaching out for support or feedback or to ask questions.	Actively seeks out additional resources that are not included in the materials provided; focuses on finding things that explain not just the what but also the why.
Is unable to provide feedback or examples of how to improve a training process.	Provides positive, thoughtful feedback that is lacking slightly in creativity or is not very actionable.	Provides clear and thoughtful feedback on how to improve their training experience; suggestions have identified clear gaps in the previous process.

Onsite interview 2:
Willingness to be wrong and intrinsic motivation

Competencies being assessed:

- Willingness to be wrong
- Intrinsic motivation

Who can do this interview (including backup):

- List relevant team members and managers

Interview length: 45 minutes

Question 1:

Tell me about a time when you used feedback from other people (e.g., users, cross-functional team members, outside experts) to strongly inform the design or solution of a project you led or helped lead.

Follow-up questions:

Situation:

- Who provided the feedback?
- What were you designing or solving?

Action:

- How did you collect the feedback?
- How did you implement the feedback or take it into account?
- How did you determine that it should inform the design or solution?

Result:

- What did you learn from the experience?
- Have you applied what you learned in other situations?

Rubric		
Poor	**Good**	**Strong**
Does not show respect for the ideas of others.	Implements feedback but does not demonstrate a robust decision-making framework for prioritizing the feedback and determining if it should inform the design or solution.	Example demonstrates how they reason clearly by prioritizing feedback with optimal impact and success.
Is unwilling to compromise their initial plan in light of new information.	Is willing to adjust their plan to incorporate feedback and new information but does so without weighing the quality of the feedback (e.g., "Hiring manager said we should do X, so I did X").	Shows an ability to distill feedback and new information and convert it into straightforward adjustments that need to be made; is able to identify stakeholders to gain diverse perspectives on changes being made and present solutions.
	Unable to share any learnings from the situation.	Shares learnings and ways they've applied them to subsequent situations.

Question 2:

What does a successful career look like to you?

Follow-up questions:

Situation:

- What motivates your career growth?
- How does this shape your career development and the opportunities you seek?

Action:

- What steps have you taken to move your career in this direction?
- How do you build goals for yourself?
- How do you hold yourself accountable for your growth and professional development?

Result:

- What have you learned from your current or past roles that has shaped your career vision?

Rubric		
Poor	**Good**	**Strong**
Career goals are shallow and uncreative and tied to trivial goals such as job title or compensation.	Sets clear career goals but cannot elaborate on the reasoning when probed further.	Describes elements of a well-rounded career that go beyond a job title.
Is unwilling to compromise their initial plan in light of new information.	With guidance from a mentor, can relay their experiences to adjust their career plan.	Can draw upon past experiences and state how they have affected their goals.
Does not demonstrate a connection between their goals and the work or learning it takes to get there.	Shows a desire to grow through their work and develop new skills in pursuit of their goals.	Has taken clear steps to get closer to their career goals.
Does not take accountability in their career growth; continuously blames external factors for driving their career path.	Takes accountability for their career development for the most part; sometimes relies on opportunities presented to them to further their career.	Demonstrates accountability in their own development; does not solely rely on others to present them with opportunities.

Onsite interview 3: Structured thinking (roleplay)

Competency being assessed:

- Structured thinking

Who can do this interview (including backup):

- List relevant hiring managers and leaders

Interview length: 45 minutes

Format of interview: Roleplay/intake meeting

Evaluation guide:

- Evaluate the candidate's structured approach to problem-solving and ability to start with an open-ended scenario, narrow down the parameters, build a solution, and measure success.
- Evaluate whether this person will be able to form strong relationships with the teams they will be recruiting for by building trust and communicating effectively.

Context:

You're opening a role on your team (use an existing role if you have one), and this is your first meeting with a new recruiter.

- Share with the candidate that you'll tackle this in three parts:
  1. Defining the scenario or role
  2. Formulating a solution
  3. Measuring success
- Include basic information: a brief description of the team (function, roles, hierarchy, etc.) and the open role (level, location, any other relevant information).
- The candidate should lead this conversation, but you can use the questions below to probe for more detail as needed. This will be a two-way conversation, so you'd like them to lean on you for guidance by asking questions, challenging assumptions, and requesting feedback.

Task:

Walk me through the recruiting process.

Section 1:

Understand and define your situation. Questions may include but are not limited to:

- What gaps will this role fill?
- Which teams will this role partner with?

- What is the team's current state? What should its future state be?
- What hiring tactics have worked well in the past (referrals, cold sourcing, events, etc.)?
- Is this a one-off role or one of many?
- What are the must-haves for the role? What are the nice-to-haves?
- What do you know about the composition of the pipeline in terms of gender, race, and other diversity characteristics?
- What assumptions does the company have about hiring velocity?
- What is your sales pitch?

Bonus: It's a great signal if they push back on your assumptions with any evidence, data, or alternate solutions.

Section 2:

Build a solution from sourcing strategy to hire. Answers may include but are not limited to:

- Pipeline strategy: Leverage information from Section 1 to inform initial strategy.
- Job description: Do they plan to call out the must-haves? Do they mention the selling points?
- Advertising and evangelism.
- Interview criteria: How does it align with Section 1?
- Team involvement: sourcing, leveraging networks, etc.

Section 3:

Measure success. Answers may include but are not limited to:

- What data or metrics will they use to ensure they're tracking against the goal?
- What expectations do they set for communicating progress and challenges?
- What is expected of the hiring manager? What should the partnership look like?
- What does success look like?
- How do they iterate their approach? (E.g., If we aren't seeing X onsites within three weeks, should we pivot?)
- How do they benchmark criteria?
- How do they manage failure?
- How will this recruiting challenge and its success or failure inform future strategy?

Rubric		
Poor	**Good**	**Strong**
Does not respond to feedback or prompting.	Takes coaching from the hiring manager well but relies on them to drive some aspects of the conversation.	Drives the conversation and leverages the hiring manager's existing knowledge base, knowing when and how to inform others.
Demonstrates scattered thinking or communication; is not able to talk through a solution in a structured way.	Has a good initial approach to tackling the problem, but is unable to adjust the approach when presented with new information or complexities.	Shows evidence of structured thinking and tackling the problem in an organized way when the hiring manager presents new data or complexities.
Does not encourage two-way engagement throughout the roleplay (i.e., runs through a list of questions and throws out a solution without checking in or gathering input).	Asks basic job-level questions but does not ask in-depth questions around the success of previous searches or how to understand more about the role, responsibilities, and context, for example.	Asks good questions to size up the situation; hits most of the points from the list of questions (it's a bonus if they think creatively outside of what's listed); questions go beyond tactical role specifics (top three skills, nice-to-haves, etc.) and demonstrate that the candidate thinks broadly about how to qualify a role.
Does not mention data or research when forming solutions or measuring success.	Mentions the importance of using qualitative and quantitative data to measure success, but does not reference or is unclear on how the data and insights would affect the search.	Takes advantage of both qualitative and quantitative data to inform process, strategy, and direction; can clearly explain why they are choosing the metrics that they plan on leveraging.
Insists on sticking rigidly to the plan they have laid out.	Is open to adjusting their plan but does not lay out a foundational plan for how to do so.	Intends to iterate or evaluate success along the way; says, "We'll check in after X onsites and adjust our approach if needed."

Onsite interview 4: Resilience and accountability

Competencies being assessed:

- Resilience
- Accountability

Who can do this interview (including backup):

- List relevant recruiting leader

Interview length: 45 minutes

Question 1:

Getting the job done may necessitate unusual persistence or dedication to results, especially when faced with obstacles or distractions. Tell me about a time when you were able to be very persistent in order to reach a goal.

Follow-up questions:

Situation:

- What were your goals?
- What were the obstacles you faced? What caused them?

Action:

- What are examples of your persistence?
- Who did you work with to achieve the results?

Result:

- Were you successful?
- What did you learn from the experience?

Rubric		
Poor	**Good**	**Strong**
Relied upon the support of others because they lost the drive or motivation to continue in their efforts.	Has been persistent in the pursuit of their goals, only requiring assistance from their manager to unblock them and achieve the desired results.	Demonstrates unwavering dedication to their goals, regardless of the size or impact of the obstacles they faced.
No clear demonstration of their persistence in pursuit of their goals; does not leverage other team members when there is a clear opportunity to do so.	Can provide examples of actions they took to move toward their goal; clearly explains why they decided to work with or without other members of the team.	Clearly explains what actions they took and what impact those actions had; can thoughtfully reflect on whether they would do the same thing if they were presented with the situation again; reasoning for working or not working with others demonstrates sound judgment.
Is unable to reflect on their experience and take away key learnings; goals were vague and not measurable in any way.	Set clear goals but was unable to adjust timelines in the face of obstacles; did not define formal success factors and only relied on qualitative feedback; is able to recognize the key learnings from their experience but is unable to explain how they would avoid these obstacles if presented with the same situation again.	Set well-defined goals from the outset, including milestones that were adjusted based on obstacles encountered; implemented a framework to measure success and leverage data; can clearly explain the lessons they have taken away from the experience and put forward suggestions on how to avoid these obstacles in the future; committed to learning and developing in the process.

Question 2:

Describe a time when you had to make a difficult decision regarding your team's priorities or strategy.

Follow-up questions:

Situation:

- What was it?
- What were the options, and how did you weigh them?
- How did you consult with others on your decision?
- How did you get data or other perspectives on your decision?
- What company values did you consider in your decision-making?

Action:

- How did you communicate your decision?
- How did you respond to skepticism or questions?
- How did you defend your decision?

Result:

- What was the end result of the decision you made?
- What data would you have wanted to help with your decision-making?

Rubric		
Poor	**Good**	**Strong**
Makes uninformed or rash decisions lacking in substantial support.	Takes a considered approach to decision-making but could have leveraged more robust data sources when making decisions.	Provides a well-rounded, informed approach to evaluating options in decision-making and uses examples of how they anchored their decision with data.
Meets opposing opinions with obstinacy or arrogance; makes the decision unilaterally, with little to no consultation with others.	Accepts the opinions of others but dismisses them when discussing how they arrived at the ultimate decision; only consults a select group of people they have existing relationships with.	Demonstrates ownership when faced with skepticism, doubt, or questions and is open to adjusting their approach when presented with questions about their strategy; consults with a wide range of people with varying opinions (or seeks out a variety of opinions), including those most affected by the decision, to solicit as much feedback as possible.
Cannot identify any company values that they took into account when making their decision, or dismisses the values themselves as non-factors.	Expresses an admiration or acknowledgment of the company values but cannot articulate how they were specifically considered in the decision-making process.	Clearly outlines how their decision-making aligns with company values and company priorities, not only their own priorities.
Unable to provide a clear explanation of the final decision; situation was left in an unclear state; cannot identify any missing data that would have aided their decision-making process.	Can provide a concise explanation of the ultimate decision reached; can identify the gaps in the data, but can't explain how to make that data a reality.	Is able to reflect on the outcome of their decision in a thoughtful way, outlining both the benefits and drawbacks for all stakeholders involved; can provide insight into the data that they would have wanted when making the decision and how, given sufficient resources, they would be able to get that data in the future; is able to explain how they would put that data to use given a similar situation and the impact it would have on their decision-making.

Sample Interview Questions

There are a lot of sample interview questions available online. Ultimately, the key is to be consistent in what you ask and be sure to ask a range of situational ("How would you handle this scenario?"), behavioral ("Tell me about a challenge you overcame"), and strict competency ("Describe the last Excel model you built and how") questions.

With thanks to Stripe's CTO, David Singleton, for many of these questions, here are a few less commonly asked questions and what you might look for in a response:

1. Working with others

Tell me about a time you worked on something that you knew you wouldn't enjoy but which was necessary for the success of your team or company.

> **Follow-up question**: How did you end up working on it? What did you accomplish? What would you do differently if you had another chance?

> **Seeking**: Does the interviewee have an eager attitude and an ability to get up to speed and execute regardless of their feelings toward the work? It's a bonus if they actively volunteer to take it on.

Tell me about the lowest-morale team you've been part of.

> **Seeking**: Did the interviewee bring levity to the group? Did they try to fix the situation? Did they run away?

When have you felt most connected to your coworkers? Tell me about a time when that connection was tested and how you adapted.

> **Seeking**: Did the interviewee demonstrate good humor and a positive and productive attitude while in the trenches with others? Were they supportive and collaborative in difficult situations? Do they value results-oriented team achievement and learning from coworkers?

2. Getting work done

What project are you most proud of? What was your contribution?

> **Seeking**: Do they seek out challenging work? Do they value navigating an unfamiliar experience? Did this project have a strong impact?

Tell me about a project where you've had to pull out all the stops to get it done.

> **Seeking**: Can they discuss the specifics of the obstacles they had to overcome and how they influenced others to do excellent work?

Tell me about a project you've led that failed. What role did you play in the project's failure? What did you learn? What would you do differently if given the chance to do it over?

> **Seeking**: Does their response demonstrate accountability, a growth mindset, an ability to self-reflect and be self-critical, resilience, learning from mistakes, and not blaming others or circumstances?

3. Personal motivation

Work can be challenging, and we know it's not the only thing on your mind. How do you approach balancing competing demands for your attention?

> **Seeking**: Are they resilient? Can they do what's necessary to maintain focus? Do they have the ability to compartmentalize and self-awareness about how to maintain focus (e.g., exercise, therapy, a flexible work schedule)? How do they seek meaning from work? When necessary, do they work with people to plan for coverage if things are getting really tough?

> **Bonus**: Do they help those around them do the same? Do they derive purpose from how their work helps others?

> **Avoid**: Do they rely primarily on colleagues to carry them through tough situations? Do they lack coping mechanisms or demonstrate a lack of self-awareness ("Nothing ever bothers me")?

What's the best example of something in your current job that you don't like?

> **Follow-up question**: How did you fix it, or have you already tried to fix it?

> **Seeking**: Are they focused primarily on fixing things instead of complaining about them?

> **Tip**: Let them explain the example, then assess its magnitude and whether it's meaningful and substantive.

What are you really excited about?

> **Seeking**: Are they passionate about anything? Are they energetic and optimistic? Would they "set the room on fire" (in a good way!)?

4. Leadership

Tell me about the best leader you've worked for.

> **Seeking**: Were they selfless, results-oriented, kind? Did they give indications of effectiveness or deliver feedback? What kind of feedback did they give?

> **Follow-up question**: What made them a great leader?

> **Tip**: Dig into the why behind the answer. It's not really important who the person specifically is, as long as the candidate can speak cogently about why this leader is the best they've worked with.

> **Follow-up question**: What are that leader's weaknesses?

> **Tip**: This is important, as it will give you a sense of what the candidate values in a leader. For example, do they value extrinsic impact, or creating a safe environment?

Tell me about a time when you personally worked super hard to get something important done quickly.

> **Follow-up question** (engineering-specific): Tell me about the worst incident you handled and how you approached it.

> **Seeking**: Are they willing to pull out all the stops and burn the midnight oil when needed? Are they willing to still "hold a pager" and do the work? Are they calm under pressure? Can they act as a prescriptive leader when needed?

Who was the best hire you ever made?

> **Tip**: This should be a specific individual. Be sure to dig into the role and the hiring process.

> **Follow-up questions**: Why exactly? What are the things that made them good for the role? What were their weaknesses? How did you convince yourself that they would be a strong performer given those qualities? How did they work out in the role? Why? What was different from what you expected?

> **Seeking**: Is the person comfortable attracting and deciding on talent? Are they effective at hiring and building teams? Are they able to develop a good hiring process and learn from mistakes?

Written Exercise Example

Asking interviewees to complete a decent, well-constructed written exercise–be sure to provide clear instructions–is an opportunity to signal that your organization's work culture values timeliness and diligence. Whether or not an interviewee returns a high-quality response to the written exercise on time will tell you a great deal about how much they value these qualities.

Product manager written exercise

This exercise should take about three hours to complete, and your output should be no more than a few pages. Treat the deliverable as a pre-read that you would send before a meeting. We'll use your response to assess written communication, product sense, data analysis, technical reasoning and scoping, critical thinking, strategic thinking, and problem-solving.

As you work through the exercise, please make reasonable assumptions. For the purposes of this exercise, all data analysis can be completed in Excel or Google Sheets, and all data definitions are provided.

Prompt:

Users love our product, but even so, they sometimes churn. This is some-thing that we take very seriously. Analyze this example churn data [link to data]. What is leading to churn? What are the most important takeaways from the data?

Imagine you're building a roadmap for improving retention: What projects and product changes would you prioritize to reduce churn? Make sure your response is specific enough to display your product sense and technical thinking.

Grading the written exercise

Attributes we're seeking:

- Written communication
- Data analysis and ability to translate data into actions
- Understanding the customer (customer sense)
- Product sense

Rubric

Score each candidate out of 12 total points: 3 each for written communication, data analysis, customer sense, and product sense. The total score should correlate to the following interview decisions:

Rubric	
Points (out of 12)	**Decision**
11–12	Strong yes
8–10	Yes
7	Judgment call
6 or below	No

Rubric			
Skill	**Poor (1 pt)**	**Good (2 pts)**	**Excellent (3 pts)**
Written communication	Hard to follow, long-winded, or sloppy.	Deliverable is easy to follow and conveys the main points. Structured, crisp, and clear.	You would feel comfortable sending this as a pre-read. Deliverable is coherently organized and well-articulated.

Rubric (continued)			
Skill	**Poor (1 pt)**	**Good (2 pts)**	**Excellent (3 pts)**
Data analysis, ability to translate data into actions	Only provides basic summary or is unable to pick a small number of cuts (e.g., presents pivot table of every view of the data without a clear approach for which slices are most impactful). Data barely informs the recommended set of actions, or actions are contradictory to the data analysis. Obvious errors in the data.	Conclusions drawn from the data are strong and accurate. Clarifies which data is most important and why it's worth actioning; parses the insights into "so-whats."	Picked a small number of important metrics to guide next steps and explained their impact on the business. Identifies why next steps clearly fix problems highlighted by the data.
Customer sense	Doesn't identify customer segments and their needs; fails to differentiate recommendations by customer segment. Dismisses particular customer segments as non-addressable (e.g., suggests that companies being acquired should not be considered).	Understands customer needs and provides concrete suggestions that vary by customer segment.	Carries customer insights and needs throughout many sections of the exercise, not just one.
Product sense	Unclear product ideas or inability to tie the product to user or business impact (e.g., recommends numerous "investigate why" steps but fails to articulate any product solutions).	Explains product gaps that need to be addressed. Makes a logical, balanced argument about why the company should consider these investments, but may lack a clear prioritization.	Provides creative, specific product ideas, highlighting users or strategy impact; clear prioritization of what is most important. Addresses something unique about their ideas (e.g., their go-to-market strategy would not just generically apply to any segment; calls out technical complexity or other risks associated with pursuing it, etc.). Recommendations are put in the context of the overall industry; discusses the implications for long-term business success.

Candidate Review: Decision-Making Framework

Because we often match an engineering hire with a team after they've gone through the hiring process, candidate review (CR) acts as both a hiring manager and an equity process. The committee reviews interview feedback, hire or no-hire recommendations, and leveling decisions for each candidate and provides final approval for the hire.

Step 1: Candidate submission

CR receives a candidate packet, submitted by the recruiter, containing the following information:

- A résumé
- A set of completed interview scorecards and a completed hiring committee scorecard
- A suggested outcome:
  - Yes for the company, no for my team (this outcome should be very rare and include a clear rationale)
  - Company hire
  - Team hire
  - No hire
- A suggested level

This packet of information is shared with each CR reviewer.

Step 2: Hiring committee scorecard and hiring manager rationale review

Hiring committee scorecard review:

- The scorecard provides an easily digestible picture of the candidate's performance, including a score (strong no, no, neutral, yes, strong yes) represented by a symbol for each interview.
- Each score should map directly to the interview rubric and therefore give a reasonably objective, high-level overview of the candidate's performance.
- CR reviews this feedback first to ground the review in the most objective measures: the standardized rubric items for each interview. CR will not review interview packets that do not include a completed hiring committee scorecard.

Hiring manager rationale review:

- This section can include some of the more subjective observations from the interviews and hiring committee. It should also help clarify how the committee reached its decision, especially in cases where the discussion led to a different outcome than CR would expect from the individually submitted objective scorecard output.

- Note: Inconsistencies are not bad, per se, but CR should be aware of instances in which the committee discussion differed from the scorecard outcomes. The scorecard should call those out early in the "hiring manager rationale" and/or "resolved FUD (fear, uncertainty, or doubt)" sections of the scorecard. Ideally, this will reduce the number of times CR sends packets back for additional information.

- In cases where the outcome is obvious, the hiring manager rationale can be as brief as "clear no hire" or "clear hire."

- In cases where the outcome is not obvious or does not reflect the objective scorecard outcomes, the hiring manager rationale is an opportunity for the hiring manager to state how they reached their conclusion.

Step 3: Scorecard verification

Once the hiring committee scorecard is reviewed, CR reviewers read through the individual interview scorecards and make sure that they:

- Reflect and are related to the rubric
- Are not based on subjective measures (subjective observations can be noted in the write-up and discussed in the trope, but the scorecard outcome should be based only on the rubric items for the interview)
- Are not too lenient or strict
- Are correct in that they reflect the rubric accurately

Step 4: Discussion, decision, and résumé review

At this point, reviewers should have a sense of:

- The expected CR outcome based on the objective interview outcomes in the hiring committee scorecard and the rubric items from the individual scorecards
- Any relevant subjective information from the individual scorecard write-ups and hiring manager rationale

The CR lead then begins a discussion to clarify any FUD or disagreement and identify whether any feedback should be provided to the hiring committee.

Finally, the group reviews the candidate's résumé to verify that the outcome makes sense and roughly aligns with the years-of-experience guidelines set forth in the engineering levels framework (a detailed framework we link to on our intranet).

Panel agrees and the CR lead selects one of the following outcomes:

- Hire at suggested level
- Hire at higher level
- Hire at lower level
- No hire: trope outcome overturned
- No hire: trope outcome confirmed
- TBD: sent back for additional information

Step 5: Submit CR scorecard with CR outcome

The CR admin submits a scorecard for the CR interview and emails any feedback to interviewers, recruiters, and hiring managers.

Interviewers, recruiters, and hiring managers are invited to provide feedback to CR via a feedback form to complete the feedback loop, leading to continual iteration and improvement.

Manager Transitions Guide

Here's a three-step guide for when a report is transitioning to another team within the company:

1. Current manager meets with the individual to preview the transition.

- Let the individual know about the transition and confirm the date of the formal move in the HR system (when their new manager will have access to their information and performance reviews).
- Give them a heads-up that you'll be scheduling a transition meeting with them and their new manager to discuss their current role and projects and their strengths and development plans.
- Make sure to answer or acknowledge any of the person's questions.

2. Current manager schedules a transition meeting.

Invite the person and their new manager to the meeting. Ensure that there's enough time to cover all of the relevant topics and to allow for all participants to ask questions.

Here's a template and agenda you can use when scheduling the meeting:

```
To: Employee
From: Current manager
Cc: New manager

Subject: Manager transition meeting

I'm looking forward to the transition meeting on [date]. The main
goal is to make sure [new manager] is well-informed by both of us
on your work scope and work in flight and has an overview of past
performance and development conversations we've had. Let's plan
to cover the following:

        · [Employee] shares current work responsibilities and
          projects or goals. I'll add any additional info that I
          think might help [new manager].
        · [Employee] shares thoughts on strengths and areas for
          development. I'll chime in on what we've discussed and
          worked on together in this regard.
        · Discussion among the three of us on how to support
          [employee's] ambitions and development areas.
```

- [Employee] provides thoughts on preferred ways of working for [new manager] to hear and for me to reinforce (or learn from!), plus any feedback for me that it might be useful for [new manager] to hear.
- We all recap any concrete next steps that emerge from the discussion.

Let me know if you have questions. I look forward to the discussion.

3. New manager follows up with any action items.

Once the transition meeting is over, the new manager should follow up with any action items, since they will be owning the relationship going forward.

Working with Claire

I first wrote a version of this document in 2010, when I was managing the global online sales and operations team at Google. I shared the draft with my executive assistant at the time, Maeve, a thoughtful Irish woman with a keen eye. I figured she'd have some sharp observations on what it was like to work with me. She read it and frowned. "You forgot the most important thing!" she said. "What? Did I leave out an important meeting?" "No," she said, "you forgot to mention that you like good craic!" It took me a moment to realize that she meant I like to have a laugh at work. ("Craic" is Irish for having a good time.)

She was right. I spend a lot of my waking hours at work, and I think those hours should be fun. I've included that note at the bottom of every version of the "Working with Claire" document since, and it really sets the tone for my working relationships. It was a good reminder that sharing what gets you up in the morning on a personal level can be as important as the mechanics of working together.

Writing this document is a good exercise in self-awareness. Feel free to use a similar structure or make it your own.

Working with Claire: An unauthorized guide

First of all, I'm really excited to be working with each of you and your teams.

Operating approach

Biweekly or weekly 1:1s

- We'll try to keep the times consistent so you can plan. I'm a big fan of a joint 1:1 document to track our agendas, actions, goals, and updates.

Weekly team meetings, as appropriate

- I view these as both update and decision-making/work-review forums. I expect people to be prepared and to participate, even though we'll have to manage video conferences and time zones.

Quarterly planning sessions

- It's my hope that we can make these happen with strong pre-work and good follow-up afterward with our teams and partners (internal or external).
- It's possible that we'll have some separate business review–type meetings, and we can work hard to keep work manageable between these and planning sessions. Stay tuned.

- Speaking of 1:1s: We'll do a career session at some point in our first few months to talk about your history, why you've made the choices you've made, what your ambitions are for the future, etc. These help me know where you are in terms of your personal development interests and ambitions with respect to longer-term plans.

- Personal goals: I believe in the two of us reviewing the top 3–5 personal goals you have each quarter or so. These are the things that you personally spend your time on, not your team plans, which I know you also spend time on. We can discuss them each quarter, then create a plan for how we can make sure you get the time, space, and support to accomplish what you need to accomplish. I do these every 3–6 months and will share mine with everyone.

Your teams

- Please add me to emails or documents that might be helpful for me to see as a way to understand the team and day-to-day work. As work is ongoing or a team member does a great job on something, forward it or link to it in our 1:1 doc. I like to see work in progress, and I'm happy to meet with folks who have done great work so they can walk me through it, at your discretion.

Finally, I look forward to personally meeting everyone on your team. Let's make sure I've done that over the next few months.

Management style

Collaborative

- I'm very collaborative, which means I like to discuss decisions and options and whiteboard big stuff in a group. I will rarely get stuck in one position or opinion, but the downside is that you won't always get a quick judgment out of me – I need to talk it through and see some ideas, data, and options. Due to this bias, I can sometimes be slow to decide, so if you need a decision quickly, make sure I know it.

Hands-off

- I'm not a micromanager, and I won't sweat your details unless I think things are off track. If I do, I'll tell you my concern, and we can work together to make sure I understand and plan how to communicate better or right the situation. That said, when I'm new to a project or team, I often get into the work alongside people so I can be a better leader. I will get involved in details and be more hands-on early in a new initiative, so just be warned about that. That way, I will know how to help if you need me later.

- I expect you are making decisions a lot without me. If you come to me, I'll usually put it back on you with "What do you want to do?" or "What should you do?" and help you decide. That said, if there is a big decision brewing, I'd love to know about it, and I'm always here to talk it out. I like to know what's going on with you and your team.

Accountable and organized

- I take action items really seriously, and I expect you to know what yours are and when they are due, and to get them done. I don't like chasing them, but I do notice when things slip. It's fine to renegotiate deadlines, but I'll be annoyed if it's the day after the deadline.

- I dislike being caught last-minute with people working hard on something that we could have gotten ahead of. Please help anticipate big work efforts, and let's get in front of them together. Similarly, I want us to be ruthless in our priorities while we are resource-constrained. I need you all sane... and me too.

Data-driven...

- I like data and dashboards so that there is one (ideally) objective way to measure progress and results, but I dislike being bogged down in data and torturing the numbers. Let's review consistent information on what really matters. The goal is to use data to get insights, but not to lull ourselves into thinking that we know what's going on or to try to find answers that might involve going with our gut.

- I also like to agree on how we do things as a group, which we can then agree to change or make exceptions to, instead of everyone inventing their own processes and frameworks.

- If we're discussing something and you know of or can imagine data that would be useful to our decision, bring it up. (See the next point: Sometimes I go into intuitive mode when I should be analyzing first.)

But intuitive?!

- I'm also intuitive about people, products, and decisions, which means that I'm happy to handle situations when I don't have a lot of facts or data. You're thinking, "Uh-oh, she's going to jump to conclusions," but I've worked hard in my career not to do that. Ultimately, I think I have a good gut instinct, but I'm not wedded to it. Your job is to get my sense of something and then argue it out with me. I love a good fight to a better outcome.

- I use my intuition a lot with respect to talent management, and I've been told I'm good at reading people. Again, I work hard not to judge or jump to conclusions, but I will put forward hypotheses about your team members. Your job is to make sure I really know the people.

- I always like to know what's going on personally with people so I can see the whole picture. I am a believer that we are whole selves, not "work selves" and "home selves," and it will help me get to know you and your team better if I know context. If something difficult is going on with someone on your team, I'd love to know and be there to support you or them.

Strategic

- I try to think about where things will end up and the straightest line to get there, but I'm pretty flexible along the way. If there is swirl, I usually think to myself, "What's the big lever here? What problem are we trying to solve? Why do we need to solve it? When do we need to solve it? What information do we need and when will we get it?" I expect you to do the same. Every day, I try to ask myself, "What's the most important thing I can do?" and do that above all else. But sometimes I get buried under email and fail.

- By the way, I am often overly generous with my time and I say yes too often. If you see this, please flag it to me. Although I love meeting with people, I sometimes don't spend enough time on the strategic stuff because I am working on other things. Help keep me honest.

User-oriented

- I put this last because I think of my key leverage as being more about scale than about individual customer work, but I'm always interested in sales status, customer issues, customer stories, and meetings with users, especially when I'm traveling.

Communication

1:1s

- Use 1:1s for items better discussed verbally and topics that can wait for our weekly check-in. Email takes a ton of time, so use it wisely.

- If we don't have a 1:1 for a while, feel free to email me or reach out.

Email

- I read fast, but I have slight carpal tunnel in my left arm. I don't love writing super long emails, nor do I think they're very productive, although watch me break this rule on occasion!

- I will read every email I get in a day, but I don't always respond—just know that I have read it. I will only respond if you ask me something directly or if I have a question. Assume I did read the email within 18 hours. If you think I owe you a response, please resend the email or ask me about it. I won't be offended.

- I love FYI emails. Send me something you saw, a customer anecdote, an article, some data, or something someone on your team did. If you write "FYI" in the subject or in the forward, I'll know it's for my information but does not require a response or urgent reading. I'll do the same for you. FYI = no response required.

- If you add me to a team email celebrating something that I somehow missed, I'll know that's the signal for me to weigh in, usually with "Yay!" Go ahead and add me to things like this, but don't overuse it, or in my experience people will start to think it's meaningless.

Chat

- If something is important, timely, or super short, feel free to ping me any time, even when my status is set to away.
- Short questions on chat are fine, but I might be inconsistent in my response times since I am often in meetings.
- If it's a long topic and not time-sensitive, maybe just wait for our 1:1.

Overall, I like more communication rather than less, and I like to know what's going on with you and your team, as that helps me do a better job for you. I don't view that as micromanagement, but if you feel like I am too much in the weeds, please tell me.

Finally, I don't believe I will create a lot of email volume, and I'll be the first to recommend that we do a quick in-person sync to resolve something instead of having a long email exchange. Or, better yet, you can be the first to recommend it, and I'll be the second.

I also like plans that are documented. I don't care if it's slides or docs or spreadsheets, but I expect detailed work has been done when needed. If you have work in progress, I'd love to be included early and often in development, but I'll generally only weigh in when asked or on final review, even if I have draft access.

More about working with me

Feedback

- I like it. I like to give it and I like to receive it, particularly when it's constructive. We're in this to get better together. We'll have an official review session every quarter, but I'll try to be timely when I observe or hear something I think you should know about. Please do the same for me. I also like to know how and what your team is feeling and thinking, and I will do skip-levels, office hours, etc. Remember, whatever I hear or see, I have your back and I'll tell you when I'm concerned. Anyone who vents to me about you is going to get my help to tell you directly.

Management and people

- I care a lot about you, your people, and everyone's development. Please make sure that we're touching base about your team and constantly building our skills as individuals and as teams, and that I know when there are superstars and challenges so that we can help people together.

Results

- Let's get good ones and know we did. Measure, measure, measure.

Humor

- Finally, I like a good laugh and to have fun with the people I work with.

Hope this was helpful, and again, I look forward to working together. You are all welcome to add to this document and make it a little more "authorized"!

Working with Me Template

My role

Describe your role and goals.

About me

Describe your personality, communication preferences, and boundaries.

Operating approach

Include how you like to work, your day-to-day cadence (including 1:1s, other recurring staff meetings, and your operating cadence), what to loop you in on, longer-term strategic and planning cadence, and how you keep a pulse on your team and meet with them.

Management style

Add a few bullet points that summarize how you manage people. Are you collaborative, hands-on, or hands-off? Explain how you make decisions and give and receive feedback, context you like to get, and any principles or North Stars you reference.

Supporting you and your team

Set expectations around how you'll discuss individuals' careers, development, and goals together, as well as check in on progress. Also, indicate how you'd like to be included on teams' work, including materials and forums.

New Leader Experience

What is the New Leader Experience (NLE)?

The NLE is a program designed to help welcome and onboard new leaders to Stripe. The program consists of welcome emails, a series of prescheduled meetings and pre-reads, a leadership assessment (the Hogan Personality Inventory), and access to a coach for six months. It also suggests a series of first-month actions and provides a 360° review process at the end of the first 90 days so the leader can receive immediate feedback.

What makes for a successful NLE?

The engagement of the team involved in the spin-up and their ongoing support is paramount. This document exists to guide those involved through a set of steps to customize the experience to the division and the situation that the new leader is joining. The hiring manager, people partner, spin-up buddy (a manager or team member assigned to help answer day-to-day questions), and guide (an expert outside of the team who provides a safe space to ask questions or discuss observations), as well as everyone the new employee meets are what make this onboarding support effective.

See the next page for an example of a Stripe leader onboarding schedule.

Who	What
When new leader accepts offer	
Recruiter	Send leadership hiring welcome/onboarding email, including: • Onboarding 101 FAQ sheet • Upcoming vacations
~2 weeks before start date	
Onboarding point person	• Confirm any unique needs for the new leader with the leadership recruiter. • Send welcome email introducing the new leader to their onboarding support team.
Hiring manager + people partner	Assign a point person to support the new leader's onboarding (could be admin support).
Onboarding point person	Populate the new leader checklist and coordinate across their onboarding support team, including the onboarding buddy, company guide, and hiring manager. (This can be asynchronous, via Slack and/or meetings.)
Onboarding point person + new leader	Schedule meetings: • **Week 1**: Manager, onboarding buddy, company guide, and people partner (weekly for four weeks). • **Weeks 2–4**: Team deep dives, new direct reports, new skip-level reports, finance business partner, recruiting partner. Also: Add to team's all-hands meeting. • **Week 4**: People-transition meetings with new direct reports and their former managers. Also: Possibly take Hogan assessment and review results. • **Weeks 5–8**: Key partners, other divisional leaders, and team immersion with people partner. Also: Add to company-wide leadership and manager forums, meet with leadership recruiter, add reminder to document first impressions and reflections. • **Week 9–onward**: Reminders to create personal development plan and "Working with Me" document, share 90-day reflections.
~1 week before start date	
Hiring manager	Send introduction/welcome email introducing the new leader to the company.

Who	What
First week (note that leader joins company-wide spin-up/onboarding sessions)	
People partner or onboarding point person	Send the leader their welcome doc, which typically includes their onboarding support team, this checklist, important 1:1s, team deep dives, suggested reading (company and division level), and suggested comms channels (e.g., Slack channels and email groups to join).
~3 months in	
People partner	Conduct 360° review interviews, synthesize findings, and discuss and identify goals for coaching.
Org dev	Complete coach-matching process.
Coach	Schedule first coaching session.

Core Framework 3

Intentional Team Development

In most of today's business environments, and especially in high-growth companies, change is inevitable. Beyond hiring and cultivating strong leaders and managers, the best way to navigate change is to invest in creating strong teams. Much of what people call "teams," however, are actually just groups of individuals parallel processing their way through work. Although those groups probably accomplish a lot, they never become a collective of people who achieve much more as a unit than they would as lone workers.

It's truly a milestone when the people you manage come together as a team and work as an integrated entity rather than as a set of individuals operating alone. The goal of this chapter is to help you reach that moment by laying the foundations for high-functioning teams.

I recently had a conversation with Tracey Franklin, Moderna's chief human resources officer, about the structures you need to put in place for a healthy company. She lamented the lack of team-focused performance tools: "Too much today is focused on the individual," she told me. "It's teams that get the work done."

I couldn't agree more. Although I could speculate as to why that's the case and discuss what a complex problem it presents for performance assessment tooling, I would instead like to share the concrete actions that I've found conducive to creating great teams. Importantly, unlike an item you strike off your to-do list, investment in teams is not something you can finish. The work is never done. Team development is more like a set of habits you cultivate over time, some performed by the manager and some by team members.

When I talk to other leaders about team development, the first concern I often hear is that there are constantly new people joining the company, which means there's an ongoing need to revamp team processes. I tend to disagree. For one thing, a new person entering the culture—the rituals—of a high-performing team will absorb that culture, as long as you help them understand the norms and the relationships between them. For another, all teams weather constant change, regardless of whether new members join, and the ability to absorb change and adapt to it is part of team development. I once had someone pitch me on hiring a "change management expert" for their team. I thought, "If we're not *all* learning how to teach and facilitate change management, we've got big problems." (In their defense, the team did a lot of work to roll out cross-company programs that required change on a large scale, but I still had a strong reaction.)

So, how do you create the environment, set the rituals, and manage constant change?

If your role or team is new, start by determining what type of group you need to realize your plans for the part of the business you're accountable for. Once you've figured that out, diagnose the current state of your team and its individual members, taking time to understand their career histories and aspirations. This will help you figure out who to delegate which tasks to, and whether you need to restructure in order to create the teams or groups you need. Then, take all that understanding and use it to help build an environment and a consistent operating approach within which the team will not just meet but exceed your aspirations.

At first, your work will be about building a common team understanding—of one another, of the type of team you want to be, and of the results you plan to achieve. This foundation can be very tactical, including elements like how you conduct meetings and make decisions. There are specific complexities to building teams that are global or a hybrid of remote and in-person, which I'll discuss later in this chapter. I'll also cover other factors that really matter to your success: working with other teams, diversity and inclusion, and team communications.

Although cultivating great teams takes consistent, dedicated work, it can have a huge payoff. I distinctly remember the first great, high-functioning team I had the privilege of managing. I'm still in touch with every single member of that team today. I don't think that's an accident. Is it too cheesy to say that great teams create team members for life?

Team structures

At an abstract level, organizational structures are ways to bring resources together in the manner that best helps you achieve your goals. When it comes to structuring teams, always start with your strategy. As you look at your plans and priorities—see Chapter 2 for more on planning—consider how best to arrange your teams to achieve both your short-term goals and your long-term strategic trajectory.

> **Words to live by**
> I'm not sure if Ted Lasso's "Believe" sign is a reference or just a locker room reality, but my first encounter with motivational quotes on the wall was in a 2006 *New York Times Magazine* article by Michael Lewis about Bill Parcells, who decorated the Dallas Cowboys' locker room with what Lewis calls "words to live by": "Blame nobody, expect nothing, do something." "Losers assemble in little groups and bitch about the coaches and the system and other players in other little groups. Winners assemble as a team." "Losing may take a little from your credibility, but quitting will destroy it." "Don't confuse routine with commitment."[40] These words to live by pop into my head on a surprisingly regular basis.

40

nytimes.com

No structure is perfect, and I'll elaborate on the various structures at your disposal later, but it's important to note up front that what you decide to emphasize in your team structure can match your strategy more or less effectively. To make this a little more concrete: If a particular product or region is critical to your growth and you have a strong leader in that division, consider how much solid-line (direct reporting) or dotted-line (indirect reporting) leverage and control, even over supportive functions, you can give that leader to speed their execution.

Remember that while your structure should match your strategy, you have a lot more structural flexibility than you might think. It's an excellent practice to preserve optionality in your team structure, since you may need to restructure to meet changing circumstances or an evolved strategy in the months or years to come. Be clear about your current approach, but, with an eye toward future change management, remind people to expect that the structure will change and that members of your team will shift portfolios as your strategy and the company evolve. In a fast-moving environment, you should reexamine divisional and team structures at least once a year. Too often can be destabilizing, but not often enough can result in a structure that no longer matches the business need or the talent.

The goal of a team is to produce the best results, and your job is ultimately to organize the team (or teams) to do so. First, let's define what we mean by a team.

Teams, working groups, and projects

Sometimes you need to form a team with a lasting mission and goals. Other times you'll want to create a task-oriented project or working group that can dissolve after the task is completed or the goal achieved. The primary difference is that a team works on a collection of persistent jobs to be done, whereas a task-oriented project or working group addresses a temporary, circumscribed action or mission to accomplish.

Too often, the terms "teams," "projects," and "working groups" are used interchangeably, to the detriment of the group's productivity. Maybe you created a working group when what you needed was a team, and as a result you did not invest in resourcing the group appropriately. Or maybe you tasked a few people with a project when you really should have created a more formal sub-team with stronger long-term accountability.

Before implementing any type of organizing construct, take a step back and ask yourself:

- What are the objectives of this group?
- What skills need to be included?
- How long will the group need to last?

The answers to these questions will help you determine which type of structure you should use and how much you need to invest in the group. Table 6 on the next page offers a guide to which structure you might want to create in order to set the right expectations for commitment and duration—and, more importantly, to align the group and your own investment in their work.

Sometimes you will be wrong, especially about the duration or type of work needed. In those cases, acknowledge the mistake and make a change. For example, move the work from a project or working group to a permanent team. If a working group needs to persist past a few months, perhaps your overall structure is wrong and that group should be its own team. If you're clear about the timeline for projects and working groups, then you should plan for a specific moment when you will assess whether the work is complete or whether the structure needs examination.

The worst thing you can do is let a temporary structure persist for too long. This causes two problems. First, you will not have invested at the right level for that structure to be successful. Second, the structure's persistence will be confusing to permanent teams, which should hold the primary scope and accountability for work that must be persistently done.

TYPE	STRUCTURE	TIME FRAME	CONSIDERATIONS & INVESTMENT	TASK OR MISSION
TEAMS	A group with a shared long-term mission	At least one year	Teams work best when they have few dependencies to get their work done. Since teams will be around for a long time, invest in lasting structures, norms, and cultures.	The team has a mission that is never complete, and the team must adapt over time to make progress.
PROJECTS	A subgroup with a shorter-term goal, but usually with the same long-term mission (e.g., members from the same team working on a project together)	A few weeks or months	Projects are natural subgroups within teams. They have a clear objective and require little setup. Sometimes projects are cross-functional, but the number of functions is limited primarily to partner teams, for example design and product.	Once the task is complete, the project should end. If it doesn't end, ask yourself whether the group is a team or sub-team with a mission instead.
WORKING GROUPS	A group with a short-term mission, usually comprised of individuals from multiple teams and functions	Less than three months	Working groups are better for work that requires cross-functional alignment. They are a collection of individuals, not a team. Working groups require some initial investment to define the objectives. Since they don't have a permanent owner, they also need a clear governance structure. It's best to identify a directly responsible individual (or DRI), define the group's scope, and outline the spin-down process for the group once the mission is accomplished or the needs are met.	Usually mission-oriented. Often the mission of a working group is to collect a cross-section of folks to study and define a problem or need. Their mission may be to recommend the path forward, and then that path becomes a set of tasks divided among the various teams represented in the working group.

Table 6. Teams, projects, and working groups.

–

Code Yellows

At Stripe, we have a structure called a Code Yellow to handle one-off threats quickly. Although Code Yellows are rare, they're a great example of how to successfully deploy a working group, usually across functions, to solve a particularly high-risk or existential threat. This adapted summary of our Code Yellow process was written by our CTO, David Singleton.

What is it?

A Code Yellow is a special operating mode intended to increase execution speed and reduce execution risk around a given project. In theory, it can be applied to achieve any aim, but we will use it most often when we must urgently address a substantial risk to our business. A group is assembled and endowed with special powers and privileges to accomplish its goal.

What does it entail?

The Code Yellow team will:

- Be shielded from other organizational obligations. This includes other projects they're staffed on, as well as things like interviews and spin-ups.
- Be resourced quickly and aggressively. Staffing will generally be cross-functional and will often entail painful trade-offs against other projects.
- Have daily standups and write up frequent situation reports (typically daily) on progress and priorities.
- Have a dedicated physical space (optional but encouraged).
- Have the power to convene the leadership team to make decisions with a 24-hour response time SLA (service-level agreement).
- Typically work longer hours than the average team, including longer hours on weekends when needed.
- Update the company on active Code Yellows at every all-hands meeting.

How long should a Code Yellow last?

Generally, a Code Yellow should last as long as is necessary to accomplish its goal. To avoid burnout, we try to limit the duration of Code Yellow projects to no more than 10 weeks. Many will be much shorter.

How can you trigger a Code Yellow?

To keep this framework from being overused, leadership team approval is required for a Code Yellow to be enacted. If someone thinks there's a project or situation that warrants this operating mode, they should speak with their manager or reach out directly to someone on the leadership team.

–

Structuring teams

At a macro level, organizations are structured either functionally or by product or business line. Teams within the organization are then oriented either horizontally or vertically:

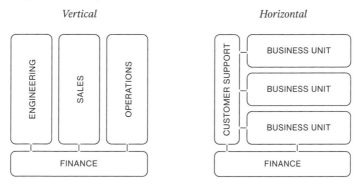

Figure 15. Examples of horizontal and vertical team structures

Earlier-stage companies tend to organize teams around functions, such as product, engineering, support, and sales, which makes sense because companies usually start with just one product. Functional structures are also useful in times of rapid growth, when team members need to concentrate on figuring out how the function works and are rapidly onboarding new people into what is often an evolving set of processes and practices.

I think of functional structures as primarily vertical. The vertical structure can translate down to the division level, and then within divisions, you might have a horizontal team embedded within the vertical ones. (See Figure 16 below.)

Examples of vertical structures include a sales team focused on the APAC (Asia-Pacific) region or a product team focused on payment methods. They're essentially teams dedicated to a particular geographical region or a

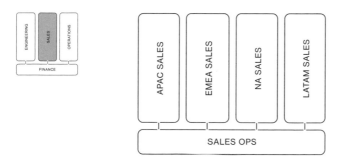

Figure 16. Examples of vertical teams within a vertical functional team structure, with support from a horizontal team.

specific product or business area. A team that cuts across all verticals in the division, like sales operations or a central analytics and data science team, is a horizontal team. For example, Stripe's support team has vertical teams that focus on specific user segments, as well as three horizontal teams that serve all user segment teams: ops platform, central ops, and analytics and insights.

Founders often ask me about forming business units once their company has multiple products. In its truest expression, a business unit has a unique product that is priced for and sold to a specific customer segment, such as small businesses or enterprises, and can operate independently, aside from the use of centralized administrative functions like finance and human resources. But in practice, the divisions are rarely that clean. Often, the same customer segment is buying more than one of your products (which is a good thing!). That means you need a structure outside of your business units that allows you to offer multiple products to the same customer from a central point of contact. And because your customers will expect a consistent support experience, you don't want to have separate support teams for each product, unless each is branded and sold independently of the parent company. In situations where you have multiple products and want to make a single leader accountable for each one's performance but also want to centralize product distribution and support, you'll often end up with a hybrid structure. In that case, you'll need to carefully design the accountability framework and consider where you place what I call the hinge. (See Figure 17 on the next page.)

As an example, you might have a hybrid structure in which a product lead or business lead is accountable for the product P&L and directly leads the product and technical teams and, perhaps, some other product-specific functions. Other functions might embed a point of contact, like a product ops person for support, into that organization. Some might even have people who are dotted-line reports into the lead, like data science. The "hinge" is the pivot point where you turn the focus from the product toward the customer.

A common hinge is a product marketing team, which has product marketers dedicated to each product. They represent customer needs and user segments and act as a bridge between the sales and product teams. Product marketers might also collaborate to develop cohesive strategies and campaigns that target a combination of products or market a solution to a specific customer segment.

If your company expands from a single product to multiple products or business lines, be prepared to constantly reevaluate your team structures to achieve the desired results. That often means moving the hinge and shifting authority and accountability toward a particular product or customer segment. Your org structure should shift accordingly.

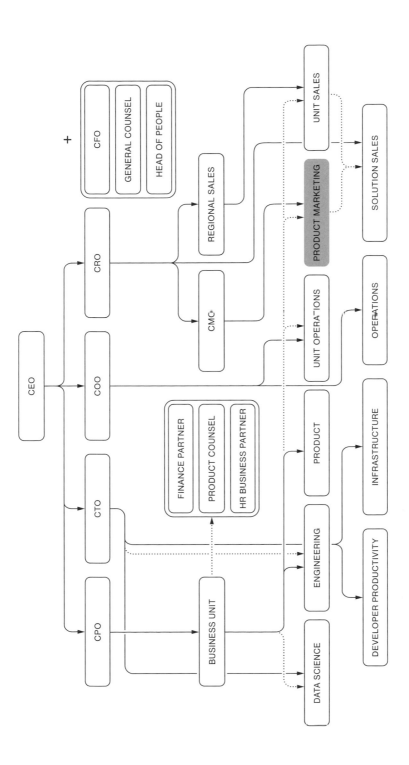

Figure 17. Example of a hybrid structure, with business units and a product marketing team as the hinge.

—

Business leads

Stripe's version of a business unit leader is called a business lead, or BL. BLs are accountable for a given area of the business, usually a discrete product or a collection of related products in a specific area, like payments. The organizational structure beneath the BL is a hybrid structure. This condensed write-up offers an overview of how the function operates at Stripe.

Introduction

To maximize our execution and decision-making capabilities, we have the business lead (BL) role: a clearly identified DRI and leader for each distinct business. The role can have multiple functions from the product development job families report directly to them and can also have clear dotted-line reports in other organizations whose contribution is critical to that particular business.

Eligibility

Teams that constitute a clearly defined business and can be evaluated on a set of easily agreed-upon metrics that are mostly extrinsic to the company and predominantly within the team's direct control (e.g., revenue for the product line, margin contributed, 30-day active users) can be organized into structures with a single multidisciplinary manager.

These groups must be explicitly approved. We expect that the primary way these groups will be created will be via the graduation of a new emerging business. Any other group that feels it represents a sensible, distinct business in which progress is actively being slowed down by the current org structure may request to be considered for this structure.

Reporting

Product development job families (engineer, engineering manager, product manager) should report directly to the BL or up through the BL, depending on the size of the organization.

Dual reporting will be likely for many roles in the business, particularly on go-to-market teams. Dual reporting means that individuals will have a primary (solid-line) and secondary (dotted-line) manager, with one of these being in the BL's org and the other being a functional lead. We will formally capture the dual reporting structure in our HR systems. In practice, this means that managers will collaborate on goal setting and performance reviews, and the individual will likely have separate 1:1s with each manager. Most dual reporting will involve dotted lines into BL orgs, including business development, data science, design, product marketing, and technical program managers.

There are two job families where dotted-line reports may go the other way, primarily because these are more generalist, flexible roles and may serve in unique capacities depending on the new business: business operations and product operations. In these cases, the individuals in these roles would have a direct manager within the BL, as well as a dotted-line manager from the functional org. There may be cases where business operations and product operations roles solid-line to the BL.

Some functions, including HR, finance, legal, and recruiting, fulfill an oversight role and will always report directly to the central function (no dotted line), but they are expected to cover the business or region.

Every role created for the business with a dotted line to the function must be agreed upon with the functional leader in that area. Functional leads are expected to support such requests unless they are clearly impractical. The people section of each area's quarterly business review (QBR) document will include a report on all of the people who work on the business: the structure, number of heads, and who is dotted in which direction.

Headcount accounting

Business leads will set a dollar-based budget (and return!) for their business each year. We expect that the investment we're making in these businesses will be presented in dollar terms at QBRs. The annual and semiannual planning cycles will be used to revisit and report on those budgets in more detail. To aid the integration of these plans with the rest of the company's headcount budgeting and planning process, finance partners will help put together a data pack for each QBR to give BLs insight into the headcount-related costs to their business.

Roles with headcount into the business that have been created outside of the BL's immediate org (i.e., in a dotted-line capacity) will be "ring fenced" for the business (not transferable to another purpose), unless otherwise agreed upon with the functional lead. BLs and their finance partners will ensure that these allocations are tracked over time and reported at QBRs, as discussed above.

Forums

Business leads are expected to operate a set of forums and processes to help keep the whole team of people who work on the business productive, whether they report in a solid line or a dotted line or not at all. BLs are welcome to mirror the company-wide forums within their orgs but are also encouraged to choose the right structures to optimize for progress in their area. In general, please strive to create the fewest, simplest, and most lightweight structures that work for the business.

Goal setting

Goals for the business, sub-teams, and individuals are expected to be set using the forums mentioned above. The business will report at QBRs on progress against those goals and planned goals for the next cycle. Dotted-line reports are expected to set their goals in the same way (i.e., most of the goals of a dotted-line report to the BL org should be about how to move the business forward).

Some job families, primarily sales, have compensation plans tied to their execution of specific goals on a quarterly basis. These job families require extra attention when there are dotted lines into a BL org. The BL (or finance partner) is expected to work closely with the relevant functional lead and functional experts (e.g., sales ops) in setting these if necessary.

Performance management

BLs will be responsible for the calibration of the individuals in their org, and for ensuring that their org accurately cross-calibrates with the rest of the company. The people org will help facilitate this by ensuring that calibration session participants cross businesses.

BLs' own performance will be assessed primarily on the results of their business and the engagement of folks working on said business. Business leads will be calibrated by the leadership team in addition to the BL's direct management group.

There is currently no BL ladder. BLs remain part of the job family they were hired into or are slotted against the best primary ladder when hired or transferred (e.g., to the product team). No matter which job family a BL happens to be a part of, they will primarily be evaluated by the business outcomes that their teams deliver for the company and our users. This will likely be defined in the team charter. BLs are also expected to be good people managers. Not fulfilling the responsibilities expected of all managers would lead to a designation of "not meeting expectations."

Note that we seek to create a cohesive product offering for our users. Therefore, there will be an ongoing expectation that BLs work across the company to ensure that our products anticipate our users' needs. We also expect each team to use our centralized infrastructure and, where it may not yet anticipate all their needs, to help the teams developing such infrastructure to understand those needs.

Integration with engineering

Given that BLs report up to different senior leaders, the engineering teams under a BL might be organizationally separate from the bulk of engineering. This includes a potential organizational separation from key platform teams, such as infrastructure or security. It is very important to the success of the BL model that we preserve a close alignment between BL engineering teams and engineering overall.

Within this context of close collaboration across all engineering teams, we aim to ensure:

- Shared culture and values across all of engineering
- Shared talent bar and recruiting and development processes
- Shared technology and best practices

We expect the greatest day-to-day challenges to occur when a BL's team needs assistance from a central infrastructure team to support the business's use case on shared technology. As the breadth of BL teams increases, many of those teams will not be a top priority for the central infrastructure teams at any given time. In order to maintain shared technology across all of engineering, the solution is for the BL's team to self-serve to a greater degree than normal, but to self-serve within the shared technical stack in a way that is compatible with the roadmap and the judgments of the central infrastructure teams.

—

As a manager, you're making micro structural choices for your own team, so it's worth tracking the macro company structure and how it's evolving. For example, how a function like design interfaces with a hybrid structure might need to change depending on where the key decisions are being made and who is ultimately accountable for product and business performance. Consider whether you work with the hybrid structure on a project-by-project basis or whether you need to embed people from your team into the hybrid organization. You may even need to establish some formal dotted lines. Remember to remind your team that these structures will evolve alongside customer and business needs and that evolution is normal and expected.

Number of reports

A high-growth environment will also require a lot of change in reporting structures. Carefully consider the number of reports you take on directly. You may decide to have all vertical and horizontal team leads report directly to you, or you may hire or promote a high performer to lead all horizontal teams. How you proceed depends on the rest of the structure you're responsible for and whether you perceive a need to add more leaders in the short term.

I'm not a fan of "I" structures—one leader with just one or two direct reports—but it's also suboptimal to have so many direct reports that you don't have bandwidth to be strategic and available for the unanticipated work that only the team leader can tackle. Continuously assess your scope, the complexity of your division's responsibilities, and company and division growth rates so that you can create a team structure that lands in the happy middle: adequately flat, but with appropriate bandwidth and space for the new leaders you're planning to hire.

Layering your team

Having too many direct reports is a common challenge for leaders. It's not easy to introduce a new layer of authority—whether they're an internal or an external hire—under you, but in a high-growth environment, it's often necessary.

To understand the role(s) you need to introduce, return to your strategy and map out the team structure best suited to accomplish your team's goals. I often start by sketching out the desired team structure on a sheet of paper or a whiteboard, with details on the remit of each role but without names attached. Then, I write out a narrative or talking points that explain why the new structure addresses the strategic need and why introducing the layer is necessary. Similar to writing a press release before you've finished a product, creating a communication plan at this stage will expose gaps in your thinking and surface potential objections people might raise.

Once you have a sound narrative to explain the change, consider who on your team is scaling to the call—meaning who has demonstrated the capacity to take on more ownership—and how their next assignment can support their development. Be sure to consider the combination of people and functions that will be best placed to work with the new leader, both for their own development and for the business. It can also be helpful to get feedback on the new structure from your HR partner and a colleague or two, especially ones who know your leadership team.

When you're ready to communicate the change, consider crafting a message to each individual who will be affected. Take care to highlight the benefits of the new structure for those who might experience no longer reporting to you as a loss. Explain why the new structure best supports the team's strategy and how the person fits into the new structure, and emphasize that you're thinking about their long-term growth and the opportunities this role will present for them. Let them know how you plan to monitor the change to ensure the new structure is accomplishing the team's strategic objectives, and remind them that further evolution is likely. You'll also want to inform them about next steps, including when you aim to finalize communications to the broader organization and when you'd like to hear back from them with any questions or feedback (ideally no more than a day or two).

A word about solid and dotted lines
The best anecdote I have about solid or dotted lines—whether someone reports directly or indirectly to a given manager—is from a time at Google when I attended a fairly large internal leadership meeting. One of the leaders, at the time the head of Google's UK business, gave a talk about his recent success growing the business. As one should, he started by describing the strategy and the team he'd assembled. When he described the team, which included direct reports but also key partner functions like finance, HR, and partnerships, he said, "Look, I was a competitive rower in university, and afterward for Great Britain. The people in your boat and the way you work together is how you win. When I make a plan, I think about who needs to be in my boat. I don't care who else they report to, I just know that I need them to be in my boat, and I treat them as such."

That stuck with me. Too often, managers are caught up in formal reporting structures when they should instead obsess about what the team that will help them win looks like, and then go about assembling that team without respect to formal reporting. This is the kind of leadership that makes the right individuals, no matter whom they report to, sign up to be in your boat.

While this change may initially be uncomfortable for some team members, being strategic about how you introduce the new layer and remaining transparent and empathetic in your communications will help folks get on board more quickly—and, ideally, will set them up to benefit from a more effective team structure. (There's more on internal and external leadership hiring in Chapter 3, and more on team restructuring and change management on page 278.)

Diagnosing team state

Once you've determined that you need to invest in a lasting team and not a more temporary structure, assess your starting point. Do you have the team you need? If not, see Chapter 3 and get to work hiring. If you do have the team, or most of it, ask yourself: How is the team doing? You should be able to answer that question at any time, but it's especially important to take stock when you start managing a new team in order to assess whether it has the structures, plan, and people it needs to deliver excellent results.

Remember Operating Principle 4 and come back to the operating system. Identify whether the team's operating system needs work—see Chapter 2—and make any needed improvements, like clarifying the mission or goals. In order to achieve those goals, you'll also need to understand the people and the team dynamics. Are the right people doing the right jobs? How happy, motivated, and fulfilled are team members with the work they're doing? Do they work well together? Are deadlines being met, and are the metrics looking good? If the answer to the question "Are you executing well and is every team member and the team overall having a positive impact?" is not a definitive "Yes!" get to the bottom of why.

To start assessing your team's state, I recommend surveying the group. The team leader, an HR partner, or an outside facilitator can send a survey to the team prior to a meeting or offsite, paying special attention to the core elements it needs to be high-functioning and any signals of dysfunction.

In his book *The Five Dysfunctions of a Team*, Patrick Lencioni lays out the five primary challenges a team might face: absence of trust, fear of conflict, lack of commitment, avoidance of accountability, and inattention to results.[41] If you find that one or more of these dysfunctions is present, have a discussion with the team about the survey results to build mutual self-awareness and determine what you might do to address any issues. This makes for a good offsite session. (See the section on team offsites on page 290.) Once you have that diagnosis and the team has made a commitment to change, your job is to model the new behaviors and hold the team accountable to the plan to move from dysfunctional to functional to—with work—highly functional.

For a high-functioning team to exceed the sum of its parts, you first need to assess whether the team as a whole is capable of achieving that state. If not, concentrate on each member individually and identify any changes you might need to make. For these assessments, I like to apply the skill-will matrix created by longtime executive coach Max Landsberg to evaluate a person's ability to accomplish a specific task:[42]

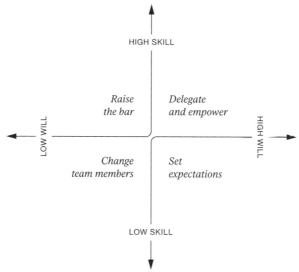

Figure 18. The skill-will matrix.

"Skill" refers to the ability to do a task, and "will" to the motivation to achieve the task. Identifying where teams and individuals are under- or over-indexing will help managers figure out what needs to change if the team is not on track.

Here's how to interpret each quadrant of the skill-will matrix:

Skill

Too little

- The team will not be able to do the work required of them.
- **Solution**: Mentor or train existing team members. If that won't be enough or doesn't work, bring on new team members who do have the skills.

Too much

- The team will lose motivation.
- **Solution**: Rethink the mission and goals of the team, requiring more and better output.

Will

Too little

- The team is unproductive.
- **Solution**: Find a way to inspire the team with a bold mission, such as expanding the team's scope from "Build the education platform for the company" to "Build the education platform for our company and our users," and see if they rise to the new remit. Use an offsite-type session to say the thing you think you cannot say and point out that you think the team may be suffering from a critical dysfunction or two. Finally, consider whether there are any individuals who are sapping the will of the whole team, and have a conversation with them or make a change to team composition.

Too much

- The team will overpromise and under-deliver.
- **Solution**: Define expectations with the team and those to whom they owe work, and help them better prioritize and scope the work. Consider whether your current talent matches the team's goals, and bolster the team's bandwidth and capabilities if it does not.

Depending on the type of business you have, some roles may fall into the lower-left quadrant of low skill–low will. Most high-growth companies can't afford to have employees in that section—and don't want to. The lower-right quadrant, low skill–high will, is common with early-career employees or folks who have made a lateral move to a new function. It's absolutely worth investing in these folks, or, better yet, having others on the team invest in them as part of their development. Build in some checkpoints to determine whether the skill is rising to meet the will.

The upper-right quadrant, high skill–high will, is basically the manager's dream. Your goal is to get everyone on your team into a position where you're able to delegate and empower people enough to achieve one of my favorite personal goals: working yourself out of a job. The upper-left quadrant of high skill–low will, on the other hand, can be one of the hardest. Your job is to get to the bottom of the lack or loss of motivation. Is it new, episodic, or persistent? Could the person be experiencing something in their personal life, or could it be that they need a new role or team? (I cover this scenario in the section on delivering feedback on page 391.)

Team changes and restructuring

Diagnosing the team is only the first step. As with most challenges, 10 percent of the work is figuring out the plan and 90 percent is executing on it and making hard choices about what you will and won't do. If you don't have the right talent or have talent issues on your team (in terms of either skill or will), you'll have a lot of work ahead of you.

Try to be smart about what work needs to happen first. Do you need to bring in new leaders and change out some talent, or do you need to develop vision and inspiration? Sometimes you need both, and in that case, you'll have to consider which order of operations will have the most impact. This is a good moment to bring out something like a trusty effort-impact matrix and think through your next steps:

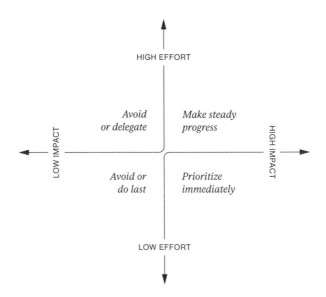

Figure 19. The effort-impact matrix.

Once you've determined the plan of action and the order of operations, make sure you manage expectations with stakeholders as you restructure the team and its composition.

Reorganizations

There are some who believe that reorganization or restructuring is always a sign of a problem. These changes can certainly be disruptive for employees, particularly those changing managers, but I would argue that needing to change the org structure can also be a sign of high growth or a strategic shift. If you're lucky enough to be in a high-growth mode, it's important to set expectations internally and normalize the fact that new organizational arrangements will be a common occurrence.

That said, there's definitely a downside to too much reorganization. The goal is to make the right call on restructuring and to do so with minimal negative impact, which this section aims to help you achieve. Use it to ascertain when it might be time to reorganize your division and how to execute the change. Whether you're the manager making the change or one of the people affected by it, it's useful to think about the principles and steps that can lead to the most successful outcomes with the least divisional thrash.

Why reorganize your team (or teams)?

If you're trying to decide whether your teams need a structural change, there are two triggers to look out for:

- **Your team structure doesn't match your strategy**. You may have a new product, or you may have recently segmented your user base and identified two priority segments to focus on in the next year. It makes sense, then, to build a new team for the new product or to orient around these new segments. This type of trigger is often why teams make structural changes at the end or beginning of a new year or new fiscal year, when companies and teams are setting new priorities and need to adjust.
- **You have a talent issue**. Perhaps a leader was fired or is leaving the company or changing roles. Their team must now be led by a different manager. Rather than tacking it on to another team, that manager may need to rethink the team's overall strategy, which may impact other teams as well. Manager changes almost always lead to some team changes, and the more senior the manager, the bigger the reverberations.

There's a third trigger I've often seen misused: an underperforming team, or a team that otherwise isn't working well together. If the reason the team is underperforming is because they're not aligned with your strategy, then you're back to the first trigger. But leaders sometimes use reorgs as an excuse to mask other failings. Ask yourself whether the issue is that the team isn't structured to execute on the strategy or whether you actually have a talent problem. If there's a talent issue, you need to dig in deeper rather than default to restructuring. You may need to bring in a new leader, change how the team works, or do more work to converge around a shared vision. (See the section on underperforming teams on page 320 for more on this, and see Chapter 5 for more on managing leadership performance issues.) You may need to change out some talent or even work on yourself to improve how you lead. Be careful not to use reorgs as a catchall solution for a team's problems.

When should you reorganize?

Before we jump into the step-by-step strategy for executing a reorganization, there are a few basic things to keep in mind:

Don't leave the ice cream on the counter for too long

One of my business school professors, Sigal Barsade, once described organizational changes to me this way: "You know when you take the ice cream out of the freezer and you leave it on the counter for a while, and then it gets all melty and when you refreeze it, it's never quite the same? That is what happens when you let an organizational change linger in limbo."

You can and should take time to consider whether a reorg is necessary and what it might look like. But be careful when you start involving others in the process, because the ice cream is now out of the freezer. Once you start including people beyond, say, your HR partner and your own manager, you have to move quickly or risk misinformation spreading while you're trying to figure out the details. Misinformation creates instability, and it can be difficult to bounce back to normal operations.

Structure versus stability

It will always feel like a reorg is coming at the wrong time. Someone just quit. A customer is threatening to churn. A product is about to launch. No matter what's happening with the business, if you're aligned on a reorg, you need to push through and sacrifice some short-term stability for longer-term effectiveness. The key is to do the reorg quickly, once people are made aware of the changes, so that they can start settling into the new normal.

That said, there are times when it makes sense to hold off on a reorg. If your company has been growing a lot and your teams have been restructuring often, you may want to delay yet another disruption to your employees' work in favor of stability. It's generally better to bite the bullet and get them through the change that's needed to get to a steadier state, but be conscious of the context and the urgency level. You might feel that the reorg you're contemplating isn't yet a steady state—perhaps there's still a missing leader you need to hire—and you might need to reorg again in a short period, so it's better to wait. It's sometimes the right call to slow down if you've turned the heat up too high, or if it might go higher still.

Is this the person you want to break your structure for?

I've made this mistake myself: You get enamored with a particular team member, and you think that they will solve all your problems. Or, worse, you have a critical person threatening to leave if they don't get more responsibility. So you restructure your teams around them. If you think about it, this is a ridiculous thing to do. If your teams believe you're optimizing for an individual rather than for the team, you'll lose their trust. And if your structure doesn't match your overall strategy, the person you've just put in charge will be set up for failure.

In a perfect world, you would never restructure around one person, but there are some exceptions. Sometimes your reorg calls for five leaders and you only have two. It's fine to bridge toward a future state with a less-than-ideal structure. But if that's the case, be transparent with the team about the interim state and where you're headed.

Sometimes you have an incredible high performer and you simply can't imagine your team or company without them. You believe you have to give them ownership of a number of teams, even if the grouping of teams doesn't make sense. You also think that because they're so good, they'll do a good job running the teams you've given them, even if the organizational logic isn't sound. More often than not, that's a false trade-off—you can find a good place for your high performer that doesn't have to come at the expense of your division, especially if you've built for optionality. Remember your horizontal and vertical opportunities. But if you are considering making an exception for a high performer, ask yourself: Is this the person you're willing to break your divisional structure for? If so, make sure you can explain why. (There's more on managing high performers in Chapter 5.)

The three phases of reorgs

A reorg involves the following three phases:

0. Decide whether you need a reorg and determine your new structure.
1. Get buy-in from the key people who need to be involved.
2. Create a communications plan and inform those affected.

Phase 0 (one month): Decide whether you need a reorg and determine your new structure

This phase should only involve a very small number of people: your manager, HR, and maybe the peers who could be affected and need to weigh in on a final structure. Examine what is triggering the reorg—a change in strategy or a change in talent—and take the time to design the new structure with that information in mind. (See the section on team structures on page 262.)

Don't include direct reports in this process just yet. The outcome of this stage should be that you have a design for the new structure with every person accounted for and that you, your manager, and your peers are on board with the change.

Phase 1 (one to two weeks): Get buy-in from the key people who need to be involved

You've set the ice cream on the counter. This is the stage where you start talking to the people who will make the change work: the relatively small group of people, usually managers, who will be changing roles, adding or decreasing scope, and managing new people.

Your first step is to share the reorg plan with each affected individual and make sure they understand the vision and the strategy. What matters is the why of the reorg, because these folks ideally need to agree with and explain the change to others. In some cases, this takes just one conversation—they see the plan and they love it. But plan to have at least two, if not three, conversations about the change. You're asking these folks to make a potentially large adjustment to how they've been working, and they'll likely need some time to reflect on it.

This conversation is obviously easier to have with someone who feels like they're coming out ahead in the new structure. For those who are not, or who feel like they're not, you'll often need to have a couple of conversations. Stay focused on the why of the change and explain how and why you feel they're best suited for the role you've asked them to play. Ideally, tie it back to the conversations you've had with the person about development and career aspirations. (More on this on the next page.) It's important to listen to their concerns empathetically but also to lay out your perspective and be firm about the decision you've made for the good of the business. There may be some as yet undecided aspects you choose to tweak, but avoid a complete rethink of the plan if someone initially overreacts. Take the time to have these conversations, and once you have agreement from all of the key parties, work on a comms plan together.

Phase 2 (one to two days): Create a communications plan and inform all of those affected

Tell the teams and people who are most impacted first—usually those who will have a new manager. Give them the courtesy of the heads-up and the chance to ask questions, but aim to announce the change to the wider group within a day of letting them know. Once you make the broad announcement, move quickly into final manager transitions and your new operating structure. Get the ice cream back in the freezer!

Again, reorganizations are not necessarily a bad thing. Needing to restructure is often a sign of dynamism, not of organizational distress. It means that your business is growing and changing rapidly. That's good news! The reason reorgs are associated with distress is because they're often poorly executed and poorly explained. Taking the time to get the reorg execution right will make your business more exciting and dynamic, not less.

Reorgs are often an opportunity for leaders and team members to take on more responsibility and step up in the new structure, so treat them as an opportunity, not a cost. Your mindset and attitude toward the change will permeate those around you. Embrace it.

(Re)building the team

Whether you've hired a new team, inherited a team, or restructured to create a new team, the bedrock of your team is the people on it. At this point, it's important to evaluate the team's skill and will and form your own impression of each person's contribution and their potential skill and will. A critical step in forming these impressions and figuring out how to best deploy the team's talent, individually and collectively, is to take time to deeply understand each team member.

Career conversations

One useful practice to understand your team members better is to schedule career conversations with them. I conduct these with each team member to learn more about their career and development goals. These conversations never fail to yield important insights about individuals' motivations and how their own aspirations may or may not fit within the team mission.

These conversations should take place after a few months of working together so that you know each other well enough to be comfortable talking about ambitions and motivations but before any sort of formal performance review has taken place. A bigger-picture discussion like this will help you get to know each other, build trust, and, ideally, inform your ability to make better decisions about what that person should focus on to achieve their career goals, whether inside or outside the team.

This is not an interview, and it's not a time to ask, "What's your five-year plan?," which causes most of us to shut down. Instead, use the career conversation to help your new report think about the decisions they've made throughout their career and why they've made them. Oftentimes, you'll start uncovering values and motivations that will be important to your interactions going forward. (Remember Operating Principle 1: Build self-awareness to build mutual awareness.) You can use these insights to discuss the person's career ambitions and what decisions might help them along that trajectory.

The career conversation serves three purposes:

- Establishing that you care about the person and their career
- Understanding the person's narrative arc—their motivations, their past choices, and their development aspirations—in a broader context than their current company or role
- Beginning to outline a longer-term career direction that you can both refer to from time to time at moments like reorgs or performance reviews, when you sense someone is feeling over- or under-challenged or you're thinking about a new role or assignment for them

I find the career conversation to be a useful reference point when observing team dynamics. It's especially helpful during performance conversations as a way to make sure we're still aligned and working toward the same long-term development goals. (I've included a starter conversation guide in the chapter appendix on page 335.) I also use it as an input when I'm deciding who to delegate work to, which I'll cover next.

Delegating

Delegating can be a tricky skill to nail, but it's a worthwhile one to cultivate. It's the key to getting your own work done, advancing your team members' development, and increasing your team's impact.

Delegating takes two forms. First is general work assignment: The team member has a job to do and needs to understand the core functions of that job. Do they understand their day-to-day responsibilities, goals, and how they will be measured and assessed? This is something you should automatically cover in 1:1s. Second is a one-off assignment that might not neatly fit into the day-to-day work but that you or someone on your team needs to accomplish.

Managers who under-delegate may model good-quality work, but they don't necessarily help teams do good-quality work. These managers will have trouble building lasting teams because they don't make a habit of letting others take on important tasks. On the other hand, managers who over-delegate are likely not close enough to the team's work, and therefore risk critical failures that result from assigning work that the team is not equipped to handle without support. Successfully delegating work should provide you and your team with more leverage, develop your people, build trust with your team, cultivate mutual reliance across your reports, and help you retain good talent. Learning to recognize the signs of over- or under-delegating will help you course-correct when work gets off track.

"To me, change is something people can adopt and accept if it's explained in a logical way at the very beginning, like the first week at the new company. At those times I have said, 'Things are going to change dramatically from what you're used to. It'll be a different pace, different compensation systems, different everything.'

And I give them the analogy of the trains in New York. Sometimes when you approach a subway station the announcer will come on and go, 'This is no longer a train to the Bronx. Now it's going to Brooklyn. You want to go to Brooklyn, stay on.'

I'm going to leave the door open for a bit, but we're changing direction now. If that direction is not for you, okay. But if you want to come with me, let's go. We're going to have a lot more accountability, a lot more transparency, and we will move a lot faster.

And the people who stay double down. I just make sure everyone knows that change is happening and why."

—**Charles Phillips**, managing partner, Recognize, former CEO, Infor

---

DRIs

Pressured by the many moving parts and tight deadlines involved in producing hardware, Apple coined the term "DRI," or directly responsible individual, to signal who would be held accountable for meeting a goal or ship date. The DRI is sometimes a team leader or executive but could just as often be a team member. Their main job is to make sure that the project has the resources it needs and that decisions are made to keep executing at speed.

Much of our work at Stripe has a complexity and a cross-functional nature derived from the intricacies of financial infrastructure and the ecosystem of players who move, regulate, and hold money around the world. We find the term DRI very useful because it's less focused on hierarchy and more on accountability. When it comes to needing a quick decision, even if the DRI is not the decision-maker, they know that their job is to get the decision made.

Similar to operating structures, the DRI role can be replicated to create interconnected project structures in which one DRI might rely on another DRI running a related but separate project. Much like a Code Yellow—see the sidebar on page 266—the most useful aspect of the term is that everyone knows what it means, and thus it affords the DRI the authority to do what's needed to meet objectives. Commonly understood terms that are specific to certain company modes or roles can be useful, provided they are well-understood (include them in onboarding!) and consistently used.

Managers who under-delegate are often also folks who might be called micromanagers. They are over-involved in everything the team does, and they demand to be included in almost all of the team's work or to review the work before it's seen by anyone outside the division.

As a leader, you're under-delegating if:

- Employees come to you with problems but rarely solutions.
- Most decisions cannot be made without you, and you become a bottleneck.
- If you're sick, traveling, or away from the team for some other reason for some time, things start falling apart.
- You feel overwhelmed by your workload and are unable to spend time on strategic work because you're firefighting day-to-day demands instead.

Managers who over-delegate are very good at making employees feel empowered and trusted, but they get too far removed from the work and don't recognize when an employee is in over their head. They may also give employees work that they're not ready for, and they don't demand high quality from their reports. I've found that people-oriented managers who care a lot about including and trusting people are at risk of over-delegating.

You're over-delegating if:

- Your team consistently produces low-quality work.
- You become aware of projects going off the rails too late.
- Your reports often tell you that they feel overwhelmed by their jobs.

- You can't say off the top of your head what critical work your team has recently completed, what work is underway, and what comes next on the priority list.
- You can't have a detailed conversation with your own manager or a peer about your teams' work and any challenges they're facing. The only time this is acceptable is when you're an executive and you have a leader under you who should be in the conversation with your peer.

Delegating is extremely inefficient initially and extremely efficient eventually. It involves more up-front work from you to develop employees' abilities so they can produce quality work at scale. This process can be especially frustrating for task-oriented personalities, so make sure to remind yourself of the long-term payoff of delegating and the benefits it affords the broader team.

When to delegate

The framework I use for delegating is similar to Jeff Bezos's Type 1 or Type 2 decisions.[43] (See Figure 20 on the next page.) It has two axes:

[43]
sec.gov

- **High impact or low impact**: Who or what might be impacted by the work? What teams does it affect? Does it have an effect on users? How many? How immediately does it affect the business? Would it change a critical company goal or metric?
- **Trapdoor outcome or adjustable outcome**: Will the work at hand lead to what I call a "trapdoor" outcome—an outcome that can't easily be reversed—or will you be able to adjust, iterate on, or change the work?

Here are a few examples of the framework in practice:

- **High impact – trapdoor outcome**: Signing a massive contractual commitment, for example a 10-year office lease for millions of dollars, or an exclusive multiyear partnership with a single provider.
- **High impact – adjustable outcome**: Publicly viewable website copy for a major launch. It can be edited, but people will see it.
- **Low impact – adjustable outcome**: Internal company content explaining the product or planning the team offsite agenda.
- **Low impact, trapdoor outcome**: An email that goes out to 50 prospects to test the messaging for a new product.

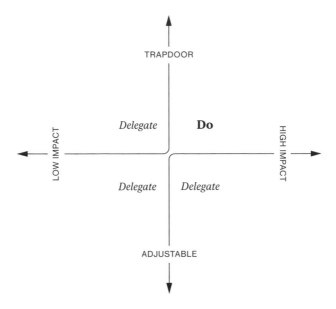

Figure 20. Delegation framework.

If the work you're doing is not in the upper-right quadrant (high impact–trapdoor outcome) and you're managing a team or teams, you should almost always delegate it. There are some exceptions, however. For example, sometimes you should delegate high-impact trapdoor decisions to help someone on your team grow. This should be a trusted high performer, and you should be clear that you expect them to keep you well-informed and closely involved in decisions or major milestones. And sometimes you should personally take on adjustable or low-impact work. There are three reasons why you might do this:

- **Modeling**: You want to show what "good" looks like. Modeling is a helpful development technique, but it needs to be paired with opportunities for your reports to practice what you've modeled. The medical school approach of "see one, do one, teach one"—model the task to your report, then delegate and have the report do the task themselves, then ask them to delegate and oversee someone else doing the task—works well here.
- **Urgent work**: Sometimes work needs to be done quickly and you haven't done enough delegating or training to give the task to someone else. If this happens, learn from it and don't let it happen again.
- **Resource constraints**: Sometimes we all have to jump in and roll up our sleeves if the team doesn't have enough people to delegate to. If this happens, take note: You're not scaling yourself or your team adequately.

How to delegate, and to whom

I like to use the skill-will matrix I introduced on page 276 for this task too. As a refresher, "skill" refers to the ability to complete a task and "will" refers to the desire to execute the task. You want to delegate more to people in the upper-right quadrant of that matrix—high skill–high will—and more selectively to those in the high will–low skill quadrant so that they can start to learn the needed skills. If there's someone on the team you're not comfortable delegating to, it's time to ask yourself why they're on the team and provide the appropriate feedback and performance management. (See Chapter 5.)

Once you've decided that a task needs to be delegated and have chosen someone to delegate it to, your final step is to get the person's agreement and help them get started. Here's a set of steps for a good delegation conversation—these could even turn into a document that you mutually review to check understanding, which is especially helpful for someone earlier in their career:

- **Bottom-line the assignment**. Describe the broader context and why the assignment is important. Set expectations and explain the goals for the work.
- **Explain why the work assignment is right for the person**. Match the project to the individual's skill set or development goals. Refer to your career conversation or quarterly goals. You might tell this person, "I'd like you to do this because you're very good at X," or "I'd like you to work on this to get you some new experience with Y."
- **Set clear deliverables**. Tell the person what you'd like the finished project to look like. This could be a spreadsheet, a written report, a detailed analysis, a set of visuals in slides, or whatever else the task calls for. Depending on the person's seniority, you may ask them to tell you what they think the finished project should look like, or you may brainstorm deliverables together.
- **Discuss timeline**. When does the project need to be completed by, and is that reasonable given their other responsibilities?
- **Get buy-in**. Take the time to ask if the project is something the person is interested in working on. If the assignment requires taking on significant work or responsibilities, this will take a couple of conversations to iron out.
- **Outline next steps**. Get them started: What first steps would you take on this project?
- **Keep track**. Agree on how you're going to stay informed on progress and when you will check back in.

Once you've cultivated your understanding of your individual team members and you've mastered effective delegation and seen some results, it's time to build a collective whole whose impact is greater than the sum of its parts.

Creating the team environment

Rituals and common practices weave the fabric of a team. They help team members build relationships, and they get people working together creatively, cooperatively, and effectively.

Offsites

Ask someone who's worked with me about my leadership style, and one of the first things they'll mention is offsites. I'm a firm believer in the power of offsites to help groups of people become real teams—ones that can solve problems, make decisions, and work through goals and strategies. Offsites are where you lay groundwork, outline common vocabulary, share working styles, and determine who you want to be as a team.

When I joined Stripe, I was pleasantly surprised to discover that the leadership team was already in the habit of having offsites. (I had found my people!) They would go off together for two or three days and use the time to step back, evaluate the business, and jointly make decisions to evolve the company and its strategy.

Before I went on one of these offsites, some of the stories I heard puzzled me. There was no planned agenda, and the team would go to great lengths to be very much *off-site*. My colleague Billy, who was the first experienced hire at Stripe, featured prominently—including as the carpool driver, since the Collisons didn't have US driver's licenses at the time. I won't get into details of the offsite persona I developed, "late-night Claire," other than to say that I'm usually early to bed, but the team soon delighted in keeping me up to see what nonsensical strategic ideas and colorful stories emerged. Plenty of bonding on all fronts, to say the least.

Why have an offsite?

Offsites generally have three objectives:

- Evolve a set of people from a work group into a team.
- Evaluate progress and determine near-term priorities and goals.
- Engender long-term strategic thinking.

Most offsites are a mix of all three.

In my experience, taking people out of their day-to-day routine has a powerful effect on their ability to focus and think differently. And it's not just about the icebreakers—if your team is geographically dispersed, planning together in the same physical location is a particularly powerful way to

"I've always been comfortable delegating. I've always had a sense that the best way to lead at any level is to surround yourself with people who really can do that job better than you can

I'm at my worst when I'm working with people in whom I don't have confidence. When that happens, you need to make changes sooner rather than later. If you don't have confidence that you can delegate to them, then you need to replace the person, not step in and do the job for them."

—**Dan Weiss**, president and CEO, Metropolitan Museum of Art

enable them to work separately. Prior to Stripe, I developed an approach to offsite design and facilitation that I felt worked for teams of all types.

As valuable as they can be, however, offsites aren't always the answer. They're not for solving talent issues—see the section on restructuring on page 278 for that—but rather for forming stronger bonds within a team that has already been designed to work well together. Before planning an offsite, assess the state of the team, and only embrace the format if you're confident that it's a wise use of your team's time, or if it's critical to determining whether you've put together the right strategy and team in the first place.

Which type of offsite is most appropriate?

Just because a group has come together in service of a goal or task doesn't necessarily mean it's a team. Building a team is conscious, active, ongoing work. It starts with an understanding of your team's development stage and a consideration of the appropriate level of investment in the group given its place in the company strategy. I recommend that more senior teams have more frequent offsites. For very senior teams, I recommend going off-site at least two or three times a year, adding new team members as they join. More junior teams should hold an offsite at least annually.

What is your team's development stage?

As it turns out, teams go through somewhat predictable stages of group development. Bruce Tuckman, one of the first researchers in this field, created a model that describes the four phases of group development: forming, storming, norming, and performing.[44] (Note that there isn't a standardized length of time a team might stay in a particular phase.) Knowing your team's development phase provides insight into how you should structure the offsite agenda to help them move forward.

44 psycnet.apa.org

As Google found with Project Aristotle, psychological safety—defined as the ability to take interpersonal risks like asking questions, offering a dissenting opinion, discussing a failure, or expressing vulnerability without fear of negative repercussions—is a central requirement for teams to progress from one phase to the next.[45] Actively work to increase and secure psychological safety in each phase of team development.

45 nytimes.com

PHASE	DESCRIPTORS	GUIDANCE
FORMING	• Goals, roles, and processes are ill-defined. • Reliance on the manager to direct. • Little psychological safety, so not much risk-taking or confrontation. • Overt politeness or agreement.	• Be more directive. • Expect and work with silence in response to questions. • Provide extra support, direction, and modeling in activities. • Actively work to build psychological safety by setting up collaborative, supportive team norms.
STORMING	• Boundaries around goals, roles, and processes are still not 100 percent clear; toe-stepping occurs. • Increased psychological safety allows conflict to emerge.	• Work toward cleaning up the goals, roles, and processes. • Frame conflict as a healthy step. Don't try to squelch it; work with it. • Help teams understand that conflict is normal and that every member is part of the team's progression.
NORMING	• Goals, roles, and processes are clearer. • The manager begins to become more consultative. • Increased commitment and collaboration. • Decision-making is cleaner.	• Celebrate getting through storming. • Continue to hone how the team gets work done. • With the team finding its stride, maintain urgency and focus on the goal.
PERFORMING	• The team is in flow. • Healthy debate and decision-making. • Smooth conflict resolution.	• Continue to button up norms. • Continue to increase the rate of challenge. • Know that this phase is not permanent; change is likely just around the corner.

Table 7. Team development phases, descriptors, and guidance.

If, for example, your team is in forming mode and has just come together, you might focus on creating clarity around the team's goals, roles, and processes. Forming is also a great time to conduct one of the work style and personality preference exercises mentioned in Chapter 1. Or, if the team is in full storming mode, perhaps spend more time on building relationships and common team identity.

Planning your offsite agenda requires you to balance the needs of the task and of the team. Focus too much on the task, and the team suffers. Focus too much on the team, and the task suffers. Neither is sustainable. As a simple rule, the more mature your team stage, the more you can focus on the tasks versus the team. (Table 8 on the next page offers some examples of task-focused versus team-focused activities.)

Plan and run your offsite

Some people enjoy meetings—and offsites—more than others. A shared offsite planning document is a helpful forcing function to ensure that you get the

TASK-FOCUSED	TEAM-FOCUSED
Setting or reviewing metrics	Getting-to-know-you work style activity, team building
Planning, setting goals, assigning DRIs	Team breakfast, lunch, dinner activity
Retrospectives on completed work product	Defining team norms
Long-term strategy discussions	Discussing team roles and accountability for key metrics

Table 8. Examples of task-focused and team-focused activities.

best, most thoughtful information from everyone on the team.[46] They also have a number of other benefits:

- **Inclusivity**: Shared docs provide a safe place for others to convey ideas without the pressure to debate in the room.
- **Anchoring effect**: By writing down your core objectives as a group and presenting them in a shared doc, you can anchor the conversation in collective goals and expectations.
- **Pre-work**: One of the more obvious reasons for a doc, pre-work creates a shared mental space for a group.

I've included a planning checklist and some templates for running off-sites in the chapter appendix on page 338. Here are a few suggestions for things you'll want to include:

Check-ins

Check-ins set an emotional rhythm for the day, which can be helpful for getting a good outcome. Ask everyone to share how they're feeling about the offsite, any reflections they have going into the day's sessions, and their objectives for the day. I recommend modeling an ideal check-in or having someone who understands the tone you're trying to set do so. It should be brief but personal and vulnerable. For example: "It's been a rough week because my mom had surgery last week. She's okay, but the recovery has been hard and I'm fitting in visits to her around work, so apologies if I seem distracted. My objective for today is to understand our top priorities. I feel like we're saying yes to too many projects, and I could use all of your help to set some boundaries." I'll never forget the check-in I forgot to model, in which the first participant shared a slightly off-color and very embarrassing story about an incident on the flight they'd taken to the offsite.

Icebreakers

Icebreakers are meant to be more personally than professionally focused. They should be a fun way to get people sharing and set the energy bar for the day. Here are some of my favorites:

- Share a personal photo that has an important meaning or represents an aspect of your personality that is important to you.
- Share your favorite book or movie or the first concert you attended. (Make sure to allow time for people to explain why and tell stories.)
- One of my first all-video offsites started with a memorable icebreaker. Each participant walked their laptop to a special object or photograph in their home and explained why that item mattered to them. Those who were less comfortable with the *MTV Cribs*–style tour were free to hold something up to the camera instead, but most of my team went the tour route. It felt like we were visiting one another's homes, in a delightful flip from going away together to staying home together.

Agenda structure

For each section of the agenda, make sure to have the following items documented in a place that the whole team can reference:

- Purpose
- Agenda
- Limit (time allocated to each item)
- Discussion notes and actions (to be completed during the offsite)

You may also ask for a notetaker for each session.

Check-outs

At the end of an offsite, I like to put everyone back in a reflective mood. This can be done with a simple one- to three-word check-out or a set of probing questions, like "What's the topic you're still left thinking about and why? Answer in 30 seconds!," "What do you think was our most important decision?," or "In one to two words, describe how you feel coming out of this offsite."

An offsite is a shared experience and a collective memory that imprints group understanding of one another and the work. This is particularly true if you hold your offsite somewhere unique: People will be able to refer to "that time we went to that funky warehouse space with bad heating" and immediately locate the moment in their memories.

Meetings

One critical team activity that doesn't usually take place in a unique location but happens very frequently is the team meeting. When you think of teams, you think of meetings, right?

Meetings can have a number of different purposes, including:

- Decision-making
- Sharing information
- Live review (of priorities, roadmaps, metrics, etc.)
- Alignment
- Problem-solving

No matter the purpose, it's easier to articulate what goes on in a great meeting than to organize and run one. Meetings take more work than most people realize. They're an important tool for execution, team building, and management, but when they're not treated as such, they become a complete energy suck. It's a good exercise to calculate how much time you and key members of your company and team spend in meetings. They are costly! And although I've been known to try to get work done as part of a meeting, they're generally not when the actual work happens.

47

youtube.com

In 2018, I gave a talk at a Khosla Ventures event on how to run an effective staff meeting.[47] I'm consistently surprised at the number of people I meet who mention it. Some even say, "I ask everyone on my team to watch it." People want to make their meetings more effective but don't always know where to start.

Running effective meetings requires investment and strong foundations. Bad meetings can expose and even create poor group dynamics: the person who's always on their laptop, the person who never talks about what's actually going on, the person who always wants to see the data before making a decision, the person who dominates, the person who shrinks. Good meetings, on the other hand, are expressions of your team at their best. Bruce Tuckman describes a state where "roles become flexible and functional, and group energy is channeled into the task."[48] Great meetings are generative, dynamic, challenging, individualistic yet collaborative, and, my favorite: decisive!

There are two components to every good meeting: the groundwork you lay up front, and the mechanics of running the meeting itself.

Groundwork

Managers often forget one very important fact when it comes to meetings: They're only as successful as the relationships between the people involved. You can't form these sorts of connections during a weekly 30-minute meeting. If you're going to have a recurring meeting with a set group of individuals, you should first invest in creating a common understanding and setting meeting norms up front. If it's not the right group for an offsite, at least have an extended kickoff meeting to proxy some of the functions of an offsite.

Building common understanding

Set out the basic stuff: who's on the team, what each person's role is, and how they prefer to work. (See the section on work styles on page 31.) If it's a new team, get on the same page about its purpose—as described in the sections on team missions and charters on page 60—and agree on team norms, such as responding in a timely fashion to requests for input on one another's work, excusing yourself from the meeting if you have to take care of something that's distracting you, and so on. Ideally you'll do this in an offsite, and actually go off-site for it.

The goal of this session is to emerge with a shared comprehension of your team members' work preferences and a mutual agreement on team norms. Ideally, you'll begin the process of understanding how people's preferences manifest when under stress and in flow, both for each team member and for the team as a whole.

Meeting roles

Once you've started laying the groundwork, it's helpful to review meeting roles. The meeting owner is often the person who called and organized the meeting, but that doesn't mean they should own all the roles. Make sure you're all clear on who will fulfill these functions:

- **DRI**: The person responsible for the meeting's success. This may be the meeting owner, or it may be the leader of a critical project the meeting will support. (See the box on DRIs on page 286.)
- **Facilitator**: This is often the DRI or the meeting owner, but it doesn't need to be. Perhaps the organizer would like to listen and observe more closely and can't do so while also facilitating. Some meetings will rotate facilitators. The goal of the facilitator is to keep the meeting on time, get through the objectives and the agenda, and capture key decisions and actions in partnership with the notetaker.
- **Notetaker**: Since it's difficult to facilitate and take notes at once, it's advisable to ask someone else to record key discussion points, decisions, and action items.

I'm a big believer in meeting notes. They create psychological safety and are an efficient source of context for anyone who needs to miss the meeting, and they're a useful way to record next steps for accountability. If there's a disagreement down the road, you can refer to the meeting notes to see what was decided. Notes can also be shared more widely if you have a transparent culture and you want to avoid too many people attending meetings just to find out what's going on.

Notes should not be a transcript of the meeting, however. The best notes are sent out after the meeting and include the top-level discussion topics, decisions made, and follow-ups or action items from the meeting, with each follow-up assigned an owner and an agreed-upon time frame for when it will be completed. The notes should also document any outstanding questions or concerns that were not covered in the meeting and that should be discussed at the next meeting or resolved prior to it.

Mutual meeting ownership

Every participant must commit to a good meeting. I sometimes find participants arrive at a meeting expecting it to be a show that the meeting owner is putting on for an audience. Instead, folks should know why they're there and what's expected of them as participants, which encourages them to own the meeting's success. You'll know your meeting participants are acting like owners if:

- Participants maintain, monitor, and correct for good meeting norms.
- Participation is broad and evenly distributed.
- Participants take on different roles in different meetings.

Here are some ways to create more meeting ownership:

- Any recurring meeting should have mutually agreed-upon meeting norms. (More on that in the section on meeting norms on the next page.) Remind the group of the norms if there are violations.
- Have clearly assigned or rotating facilitators and notetakers.
- Model ownership. Be on time, try not to reschedule the meeting, and show that you value the time and the outcomes.

If you're interested in effective meeting practices, I've found pedagogy to be a fruitful area of study. I'm the child of two educators, and I suspect that much of my unconsciously acquired management technique came from our dinner table—primarily the fact that I was not excused from the table until I'd made a robust contribution to the discussion.

Meeting purpose and structure

The next bit of groundwork is to align on the purpose of the meeting. There are many reasons to have a meeting, but any meeting becomes less useful when it tries to fulfill too many objectives at once. A meeting should only have one or two purposes: updates and priorities, for example, or alignment and decision-making. Establish the purpose with the participants so that they feel bought into what you're doing together, and use the meeting agenda to be clear about what specific topics you'll cover to serve that purpose. Use PAL as a guide:

- **Purpose**: If the purpose is alignment and decision-making, each instance of the meeting should serve that purpose, such as deciding on the features to build in the next sprint.
- **Agenda**: The agenda lists the topics that will be covered in service of that purpose.
- **Limit**: Set guidelines for how long the meeting and agenda items will take. A common meeting mistake is to try to cover too many topics in too little time, which can make the conversation too surface-level or lead to frustrating cutoffs with no resolution.

Meeting norms

Meeting norms represent the commitments you make as a group about how the meeting will run and how you agree to show up as participants. Setting expectations and norms up front means you can set the meeting back on track when it gets derailed by referencing the norm or commitment that is being violated. It's much harder to course-correct if you haven't all agreed ahead of time on what a good meeting looks like. You and your team should decide what works best for you, but I recommend the following best practices:

Figure out logistics

This includes:

- **Meeting time**: Set an optimal meeting time and agree that participants will arrive on time. Because I often lead global teams that span many time zones, I find that agreeing on the meeting time is an important step to build empathy between participants and generate buy-in. Most of my teams with participants in European and Asian time zones end up agreeing to rotate the meeting times and take excellent notes for those in the "off" time zone who might miss that week's meeting.
- **Delegation**: Decide whether someone can send a delegate if they're out of the office or have to miss a meeting.
- **Pre-reads**: Agree on whether pre-reads must be complete before the meeting or if you'll set aside 10 minutes of reading time at the start of the meeting. Be very clear about what is expected, and if you assign pre-work, hold participants accountable by asking if everyone has completed it when the meeting starts.
- **Action items**: Decide whether their status will be updated asynchronously or at the start of each meeting.

- **Electronics use**: If in person, decide whether anyone but a presenter or notetaker can have their laptop open. If folks are joining by video, decide whether laptop use will be permitted beyond video contact. Note that any phone use should be brief, ideally nonexistent. If something urgent comes up, invite the person to step out of the room and return when they can be present.

No topics are undiscussable

Benjamin Franklin reportedly once said, "Guests, like fish, begin to smell after three days." I turned this into a meeting norm with my teams. We all agree to bring out the "stinky fish"—any issues lurking beneath the surface, no matter how difficult or uncomfortable—and put them on the table, because we're going to smell them eventually. This is the meeting equivalent of Operating Principle 2: Say the thing you think you cannot say.

Be inclusive

In a great meeting, all attendees actively participate and reinforce one another's opinions, meaning they avoid interrupting one another and reference what others have said. This stands in contrast to my meeting pet peeve: when someone uses up meeting time to restate another person's idea from five minutes prior and doesn't even credit the previous speaker. The facilitator should monitor participation and gently call out when someone hasn't shared their point of view, or suggest that "we've heard a lot from Jen—does anyone else have a point of view who hasn't spoken yet?"

Disagree and commit

This principle is attributed to Andy Grove and is used by Amazon. The gist is that participants can disagree while a decision is being made, but once the decision is made, everyone commits to supporting its success.

Have a parking lot

Any participant can put ideas or questions aside to come back to later if they're not immediately relevant to the work you need to get done in the meeting. Make sure that the facilitator addresses next steps for parking lot items before the meeting ends or at the start of a subsequent one—otherwise, the parking lot will become the town dump.

Respect action items

Before a meeting closes, make sure all action items are clear and have owners and timelines. Agree as a group on how you will monitor progress on action items, and hold one another accountable for completion.

Reconfigure the meeting every three to six months

Every three to six months, audit your meetings. Are they useful? Are the right people involved? Do they achieve their purpose, and are they worth the time? Could more be accomplished asynchronously? Consider polling participants or having a neutral person do so. Depending on the results, you can:

- Refresh the meeting by resetting the norms.
- Evolve it to include different people and topics.
- Start over, given new business or company needs.

Operator mode versus creator mode

To grossly generalize, some people are operators, and some people are makers or creators. You have to balance your meetings for both kinds of people and both kinds of work. So far, I've chiefly discussed "operator mode" meetings, or what Paul Graham would call manager meetings, which tend to have clear agendas and are for decisions, updates, priorities, and alignment.[49]

[49] paulgraham.com

But you also need "creator mode" meetings. These are for brainstorming. They have much less structure and may not even result in a decision or an outcome other than having generated ideas that you may follow up on in the future. At Stripe, the early leadership team offsites I described earlier in this chapter were, I came to realize, multi-hour "creator" meetings held every four to six weeks. When I joined the first such offsite, I proceeded to over-program the agenda, the days themselves, and the follow-ups. After presiding over a check-out where I received some gentle feedback about my micromanaged programming, I realized we needed a mix of both operator and creator time.

One of my favorite moments from a subsequent meeting was an operator moment that turned into a creator moment. I had asked some specific questions about the key metrics in our balance sheet and where we hoped they'd be, and we suddenly found ourselves envisioning what the balance sheet would look like in five years' time. We began ideating on what would need to be true in order to achieve those results. It became an impromptu long-term strategy brainstorm that planted important ideas for Stripe's future.

We recently looked back at that set of projections and found that they were largely true, in no small part because we'd had an unconstrained conversation about how to realize that vision. These creative interactions are easier to engineer outside of day-to-day routines, and it's important to build them into your team time—yes, primarily through offsites. (I'll share more on leadership team meetings on page 308.)

Running the meeting

When running a meeting, there are several elements to consider beyond the participants. Broadly, you want to think through how you structure the meeting to make it engaging, accomplish its purpose, and honor your meeting norms. Here are some pointers:

Structure the meeting

Share the following, ideally ahead of the meeting:

- **Purpose**: Why are we meeting?
- **Agenda**: What topics are we discussing and why?
- **Limit**: How long are we meeting for? How long will we spend on each topic?
- **Decisions (if applicable)**: What decisions are we going to make? Who decides, or will we all make the decision?

Many people join a meeting without clarity about its intentions or goals. If there are decisions to be made, it's better to be explicit about the decision-making process rather than leave people wondering whether the meeting will result in a decision and/or who the decision-maker is.

Make it engaging

It's also crucial that everyone in the room feels free to participate fully. Follow best practices on running an inclusive meeting, including having explicit meeting norms and active facilitation. It's particularly helpful to have a facilitator who tracks participation, engages all participants, and feels empowered to move the meeting along when participants get stuck on one item or one person dominates the discussion. One way to set the right tone is to employ check-ins and check-outs.

Use check-ins and check-outs

Check-ins and check-outs are extremely simple and undervalued meeting tools, mostly because they can feel superfluous if everyone already knows one another. However, I would argue that they deepen connections between participants, and they don't need to take much time.

Check-ins

Starting the meeting with a check-in can shift the group's attention from whatever was going on before they entered the room to the meeting itself. Check-ins ensure that a meeting starts with everyone's active participation, create mutual understanding, and allow folks to share where they're at, either with respect to the topic at hand or in a more personal manner.

There are two types of check-ins you may want to use: work check-ins and personal check-ins.

Work check-ins formalize what people hope to get out of the meeting, how they're thinking about the topic at hand, and where their headspace is. The facilitator will provide a prompt and all participants will answer in an allotted amount of time, for example 30 seconds to a minute. Examples include:

- What's one thing you want to get out of this meeting?
- What context or frame of mind are you bringing to the key decision we're making today?
- What work-related assignment, priority, or challenge is top of mind for you right now?

Personal check-ins give participants an opportunity to share their state of mind. The facilitator may ask a question like "What's one work thing and one personal thing that's top of mind for you today?" If you're going to do a personal check-in, I've found that combining a work question with a personal question makes people more comfortable to give the personal update. It's astounding how even one small question can help set the tone for the rest of the meeting. Someone may share, for example, that they were up all night with their newborn and that they're going to be a bit quieter in this meeting as a result, which is helpful context for everyone to have. It also generates rapport and empathy within the group.

An example of a great check-in that's fast and covers both work and personal state is to ask everyone to rate how present they are for the meeting on a scale from 1–10, with 1 being the least present and 10 being the most present. If you have time, you can also let folks briefly elaborate on why they're a 6, say, instead of an 8.

Check-outs

Check-outs help people commit to memory what they're going to take away from the meeting. You can use the check-out to get a sense of how people experienced the meeting, to generate a commitment from your group, or to get some final contributions to the discussion. Check-out prompts include:

- What's one thing you're going to take away from this meeting?
- What's one thing you will commit to after this meeting?
- I'd love to hear everyone's final thoughts on the topic we just discussed in a few words.

My favorite check-out—probably because I tend to run out of time wrapping up meetings and capturing action items—is the one-word check-out. I ask everyone for one word about how the meeting has left them feeling or thinking. It's usually a great barometer for how the meeting went. There was a time at Google when Larry Page was fond of saying he was "uncomfortably excited," and I had to actively prevent my Google teams from answering my check-out prompt with "Uncomfortably excited!" Asking for a single word became a way for me to avoid that particular phrase.

Achieve your purpose

People are motivated by recognition and accomplishment. Cementing a good meeting can be as simple as confirming that you've achieved your purpose as you close out each topic or end the meeting. If the agenda item was to decide on three features to launch in Q2, you could close out that part of the meeting by marking the objective as "complete" in your notes and listing the three features you've decided on. This will create momentum for your next agenda item. If your meeting is focused on information-sharing or alignment, poll the group on whether they got the information they needed and whether they feel aligned on the path forward as you end your session.

Clarify the decision-making process

The purpose of many meetings is to make decisions. Sometimes these are small alignments that barely register as decisions, and sometimes they're monumental choices, like whether to acquire another company. When your meeting includes decision-making, it's helpful to be very intentional about who is making the decision and how they will decide. It's also useful to employ a decision-making framework.

There are a few different ways a decision might be made:

- **Autocratic**: One decision-maker. They may consult the team, but no matter what, they're the decider.
- **Consensus**: Everyone in the group comes to an agreement together.
- **Democratic**: The group votes on the decision and the majority wins.
- **Consultative**: The decision-maker, usually the leader, will consult the group but ultimately makes the decision.
- **Delegated**: The leader and the team agree on a delegate who will make the decision (using whatever method they choose) and agree that they will all stand behind that person's decision.

For autocratic and consultative decisions, you might choose to make the process clear by saying something like "We're making a decision today. I'm the decision-maker. I'd like to consult all of you, but I will ultimately decide."

"Ideally, you build capital with people so that they trust and respect you, and when you make a decision quickly, they know why.

There's no substitute for a thoughtful, articulate presentation of a problem and a respectful invitation to help solve it. I've done that for a long time with groups: 'I'm going to listen to you guys. I'm going to ask you for help. I'm going to share with you the information. If you don't want to be on the team, that's your business, but I'm going to make that decision anyway.'"

—**Dan Weiss**, president and CEO, Metropolitan Museum of Art

---

Decision-making and personality types

My best Myers-Briggs breakthrough was an exercise I did with my team at Google when I led global online sales and operations. We spent a session understanding one another's personality types and made a decision as a group. We mapped out the classic decision-making process on the floor in big squares: Identify the need for a decision, gather data, outline alternatives, discuss the evidence, choose a path, and take action.

As we discussed our decision, we had each person stand on the square that best represented where they were at in the decision-making process. I had two team members who would not get off the second square, gather data. The rest of us were already on the fifth or sixth square! It explained so much. After that, we were all much more aware of where each person was at in our team decision-making process and why, and we could discuss the situation at a meta level when we got blocked.

You can bring democratic or consensus-based decisions to the group by saying something like "We have a decision to make. I want to know what all of you think, and we will agree on a joint decision."

Related to decision-making, but applicable to any interaction in a meeting—or even in the hallway, for that matter—it's best practice for the most senior person in the conversation to hold their opinion until the end. If you opine first, it becomes a fraught environment for those who may disagree, unless your culture has a firmly established obligation to dissent. This also helps to check leaders' biases and egos by forcing them to listen, allowing them to integrate others' thinking prior to stating a view. There are times when it makes sense to break that default, for example when the leader wants to put forward a provocative idea to elicit a reaction. But most of the time, it's better for the leader to wait to share their opinion. This makes for a stronger decision—and a stronger culture, too.

Use a decision-making framework

Some companies and teams employ a common decision-making framework: Bain has its RAPID framework,[50] and my friend and former Google and Square leader Gokul Rajaram built a SPADE toolkit on Coda that anyone can use.[51] When I interviewed Dongping Zhao, the president of Anker, he said McKinsey's seven-step problem-solving process was the most helpful framework he'd learned in his career.[52] Each Anker employee learns the framework, which "helps bring the whole company to structured and rational problem-solving, and lowers our risk of making wrong decisions," Zhao said.

50

bain.com

51

coda.io

52

mckinsey.com

But even with a great framework, the work style composition of your team will often influence how you make decisions. I've had mixed success with decision logs, but they can be helpful to catalog your team's decision-making patterns. A decision log is a spreadsheet of every decision your team has made, including when and why it was made. The log helps cement the decision and provides information for those not on the team or not in the meeting. It's helpful to edit the log when a decision has been changed and explain why, creating context and transparency for those who might be impacted by it.

I say I've had mixed success because decision logs are most effective when they're widely adopted and rigorously kept current, neither of which is easy to accomplish without a broad and firm commitment to their use within the organization.

Honor your meeting norms

If you've achieved mutual meeting ownership, meeting participants should monitor themselves for adherence to the norms, from calling someone out for being late on an action item update to pointing out that no one is bringing up the "stinky fish." The best way to keep norms front and center is to remind people of them periodically, especially anytime there is a new participant, and to model them yourself. I've found it's particularly powerful for a meeting leader to say, "I'm going to disagree and commit," which signals that they're listening, collaborating, and willing to back another person's path forward, even if they're not sure about it.

Correct bad meeting behavior

If someone is behaving in a damaging way in meetings, I've found that the general rule of "praise publicly and criticize privately" holds, with a few amendments. First, don't confuse criticizing an idea with criticizing a person. Meetings should have healthy conflict and discussion about concepts, but they should not involve personal attacks. Second, it's fair to call out when someone is violating a meeting norm that you've agreed on up front. Note the indiscretion in a nonjudgmental way. For example, you could say, "Hey, I see you're on a laptop. No problem if you have something urgent going on, but would you mind stepping out of the room for it?"

If you'd like to correct a behavior or work style, be careful about doing that in a public way. But if you've laid the groundwork and have developed some shared group vocabulary and understanding about work styles, you can take a bit more of a risk. In our leadership meetings, for example, I might mention that someone is acting a bit "red," or directive—a work style that is task- and action-oriented but not as aware of people or process—and that perhaps we're moving to action too quickly. Correcting behavior in this way can be very valuable, but only if you've built shared trust and understanding as a team.

Otherwise, the best way to course-correct errant meeting behavior is to provide feedback outside of the room. Try to do this quickly, either by asking to talk to someone right after the meeting or by grabbing time with them before the end of the day. This doesn't need to be a long session—it could be a quick note, like "I appreciated how engaged you were on the budget decision today, but did you notice that Ted seemed disengaged?" Hopefully they'll agree, and then you can say something like "It felt to me like he was trying to contribute at the start of the meeting, but he somehow shut down. Do you think your enthusiasm might have overpowered his concerns?" Remind the person of your meeting norms and the importance of even participation across all attendees. Ideally, they'll agree to be more conscious of their behaviors in the future.

A note on leadership team meetings
The meeting cadence for your leadership team will vary based on your needs. If you're a fast-growing company, it will also evolve every three to six months. A leadership team meeting is fundamentally a staff meeting for the collection of people who run a company or division, but it differs from other staff meetings in the breadth of the discussion topics and the stakes of the decision-making. The other difference, of course, is that your top leadership team sets the model for the entire company.

Patrick Lencioni's book *The Five Dysfunctions of a Team* lays out the concept of a person's "first team": the group of individuals with whom you work most closely to accomplish goals.[53] The idea is that leaders must make a commitment to the success of their first team—the leadership team—above that of their second team, the one they directly lead. If the leadership team doesn't operate as a first team, I'd argue that the entire company is at risk of dysfunction. To build that first-team mentality, you need to dedicate time to that leadership group.

Here's a look at Stripe's leadership meeting cadence, including details about what happens at each of our regularly scheduled gatherings:

Monday morning: three hours
The purpose of this meeting is to start off the week and make sure all leaders have the right information to do their work and share with their teams. Each person shares "snippets" in a document by Sunday evening to update one another and share what's top of mind. The group then spends Monday morning reviewing metrics and the product calendar, checking in on leadership hiring, and discussing topics from the snippets or company needs that require active meeting time. (See the chapter appendix on page 341 for a leadership meeting template.)

"The less I speak the better, because the point is to solicit feedback. When we have a conversation about something controversial or something where people might feel a little inhibited, I really try to make sure I don't say anything until the end of the meeting because it shapes the conversation immediately."

—**Zanny Minton Beddoes**, editor in chief, *The Economist*

Expanding the senior leadership team

I've been asked how often Stripe adds someone to the senior leadership team. The answer is not frequently. Yet scaling companies are often adding—and should be adding—lots of new leaders, from senior to mid-level. Often, those people will ask about a spot on the executive team. Aside from the fact that they shouldn't be joining the company simply to get a top spot, it's important to be transparent with these prospective senior leaders. In our case, we explain that the senior leadership team is small and changes infrequently, although we expect it to morph over time, which it has. Meaning: A leader might end up on that team, but it's not guaranteed to happen if they accept the role they're being offered.

One thing that helped manage some of these pressures at Stripe was the development of a supplemental leadership team. New senior leaders need forums where they can learn how the company operates, get to know each other, and hear directly from the CEO or the founders. Our first step was to create a leadership team, or LT, in addition to Stripe's top leadership group, or ST (for "staff team"). The expanded group met biweekly to review metrics and discuss shared agenda items. But it was tricky to strike a balance in those meetings: We had hired more leaders in the non-technical parts of the company and fewer in tech, so the meeting wound up being more about how to run the company and less about tech and product strategy.

Eventually, it felt like LT had run its course, so we retired it. We then created what we call the operating group, which is now a large collection of many experienced leaders. The operating group has a fairly active Slack channel where leaders share information, including biweekly updates on company metrics, and a monthly meeting where leaders hear from the CEO and CFO and dig into topics of common importance.

Leaders at other companies seem relieved when I explain that we had to evolve our leadership groupings and meeting structures quite often as we scaled. There are awkward phases, to be sure, but what mattered most was to keep a tight group at the helm and not end up with 20 or 30 people in the room debating key company decisions.

Thursday afternoon: one hour

This is more of a creator meeting; it's open-ended and allows for some more personal and social time. It doesn't have a formal agenda but rather gives the group an opportunity to check in on topics that have surfaced during the week and workshop issues that one or more members are grappling with. Right before the meeting, we generate a list of topics in the team Slack channel. The meeting often starts with personal check-ins and ends early if there are no topics that can't wait until Monday.

Offsites: two full days every quarter

This is usually a trip away together, often from Thursday afternoon through midday or early afternoon on Saturday. These meetings involve some pre-work and can include a bigger-picture review of company financials and performance. When possible, we schedule the offsite soon after a board meeting, when the board and senior leadership have reviewed the business, which makes the meeting more efficient. These offsites are particularly important for taking a step back and doing more free-form brainstorming together. It's uninterrupted, big-picture strategic time. I'll be honest, though—in the early days, the team was tactically solving quite a lot, too. We also often share feedback for one another at these offsites.

The members of the Stripe leadership team are no longer all based in the same location, and as a result, the quarterly offsites have taken on even more importance. In fact, once a company gets to a certain stage, teams are rarely co-located. This makes offsites even more critical. But offsites alone won't enable distributed teams to develop successfully.

Team-building complexities

As with most skills, managing teams becomes more difficult as new variables are introduced. Managing a small team of co-located individuals is one thing, but managing distributed teams across multiple geographies requires additional skills and greater intention.

Managing distributed and remote teams

Being distributed is in the nature of a modern company. Many high growth companies have ambitions to go global, and if you already *are* global, you'll have offices and employees around the world. Larger companies have also become increasingly open to a new type of distributed work, allowing employees to work remotely from home. This was very much accelerated by the Covid-19 pandemic.

Stripe has had remote employees since its early years, so we often get asked how to support distributed teams and remote work. We haven't cracked it yet, but we've accumulated many lessons that are worth sharing about how to support distributed and remote workers.

In my experience, managing distributed teams poses three main challenges: coordination, cohesion, and participation.

Coordination

This is the most obvious challenge for distributed and remote teams. People and teams have to be more diligent about what information is documented, how decisions are made, and where discussions are held because they're operating in different physical locations and often in different time zones. Because of these coordination challenges, it's tempting to try to assign work that remote employees can accomplish independently, such as a small project for just one person, but that only isolates your team more and makes them worse at coordination.

Audit your tools and practices, as well as the projects and work assigned across your locations and remote workers, in order to:

- Put in place company norms and structures that foster asynchronous work, such as strong documentation that enables work across time zones.

- Balance the workload of distributed team members so that they have independent, "local" work but are also connected to the rest of the company or division. This will ensure that they don't feel overlooked or isolated.
- Map your processes, such as code and quality or risk reviews, to avoid team members waiting several hours for a colleague to wake up to answer a question that helps them finish their work. (See Table 9 on page 314 for more on the types of challenges remote teams face and how to address them.)

SIDEBAR

–

The challenges of collaborating across time zones

It's all too easy to ignore the cost of collaboration across time zones. To make it more concrete, here's an excerpt of an example from Stripe engineer David Doran, who is based in Dublin and is building a product with dependencies on teams in US time zones. The problem starts when he realizes he needs access to a lightweight directory access protocol (LDAP) group to commit a code change in order to address an issue he's found.

Unfortunately, the `admin-plans-readers` LDAP group is owner-approved and the owners are in the US, so I'll wait for approval overnight and come back to it tomorrow.

The next day: My request for access to join `admin-plans-readers` was approved overnight! Now I can view the merchant's manual fee plan so we can reproduce it in code.

It turns out that the fee plans weren't what I needed. What I actually need is the rate cards page, which has different owners, so I need to start the process again. That's more than three days of delay on a simple change.

This has presented two learnings on changes we need to make:

1. We have to provide a self-service interface for accessing the vast majority of systems not directly owned by the relevant team.
2. We need to develop a mechanism that preserves security and reliability properties but also allows folks in different time zones to get unblocked in the vast majority of cases where they need explicit permission or approval from another team.

–

Cohesion

Give remote work equal footing within your organization. In May 2019, Stripe launched its fifth engineering hub: remote. As David Singleton, Stripe's CTO, noted in a blog post, launching the remote hub allowed us to "situate product development closer to our customers and improve our ability to tap the 99.74 percent of talented engineers living outside the metro areas of our first four hubs" located in San Francisco, Seattle, Dublin, and Singapore.[54]

stripe.com

This statement was a valuable acknowledgment that remote employees are important team members. But out of sight is often, unfortunately, out of mind. When not everyone is working in the same place, it's easy for teams to default to siloed, independent pockets of work—or, worse, for the team members who happen to be co-located to dominate work decisions and capture the best assignments.

When your team is remote or distributed, you'll have to work harder to get people to care about one another's work and truly work together so that you're forming an actual team. The best way to achieve this is with clear, consistent communication and team operating practices that place everyone on a level playing field. (See Table 9 on the next page.) It's also about instilling strong cultural practices, meaning you need to ingrain into everyone on the team that the minute an informal in-person conversation turns into a work discussion or a team decision, it needs to move to a format that allows all relevant parties to participate, such as a Slack channel.

Participation

There are countless ways that working from another office or working remotely makes it hard for a person to fully participate in company or team practices. There are the obvious challenges, like having a harder time chiming in on a conference call or not being able to join a meeting because it's happening at midnight in your time zone. The silver lining is that because these issues are fairly obvious, teams can do a better job of accounting for them. For instance, you can designate an active moderator for the conference call or rotate meeting times for different time zones.

The less obvious ways people can't participate can be more damaging: not picking up on the dynamic in a meeting room because you're not there in person, for instance, or missing out on casual meals with colleagues. These things really matter. Beyond the obvious intentional steps to build relationships across your team, make sure you set team and meeting norms that avoid exclusionary practices. This includes creating a culture of documentation that encourages team members to record what happens in each meeting so that no one has to consult a teammate in another time zone to understand how to accomplish a task or complete a work assignment, for example.

One thing that has really helped at Stripe is that most "hallway" chats occur in Slack channels instead of in person. Some of our channels are more social—we have #cats, #dogs, and #cats-and-dogs—but most are devoted to team communication. Watch out for Slack retention rules, though—if it needs to be permanently documented, put it elsewhere.

Which of the three challenges you'll need to prioritize will depend on what kind of remote team you're managing:

TYPE OF REMOTE TEAM	PRIMARY CHALLENGE
A few remote employees on a largely centralized team	Participation. When the majority of the team is not remote, the hardest thing will be to make sure remote employees feel like equal members of the team.
A whole team that works remotely	Cohesion. This is the quintessential remote team that isn't actually a team but a group of individuals with the same manager. Invest in team building by seeing each other in person, especially early on, if possible. Spend time over Zoom on relationship building and work style understanding, not just tactical items, and be very clear about roles and accountability for every team member.
A team split across two or three different offices and some remote locations, or two teams that need to work across locations	Coordination. You see this scenario often with global offices that need to work together. Focus on making sure that teams are aware of decisions that impact them and that they feel involved in those decisions.
The whole company works remotely	The participation challenges are less pronounced in this scenario because you're all in the same boat. You're still going to have coordination and cohesion challenges, but in general everyone will be mutually attuned to following best practices.

Table 9. Types of remote teams and challenges.

The mitigations for all these challenges are the same, although some will need to be employed more firmly than others, depending on your challenge:

- **Set structures and norms for inclusive meeting practices.** Provide video links for meetings and pay attention to acoustics and sound quality. Perform active meeting facilitation and take meeting notes.
- **Level the playing field.** Create shared Slack channels for team conversations to avoid the "hallway effect" and invest in comprehensive internal documentation.
- **Make room for in-person time.** Budget for in-person gatherings at the right frequency, depending on team needs.

Set structures and norms for inclusive meeting practices

In-person interactions can, at least for a while, paper over a lot of a team's structural weaknesses. It's not the end of the world if a decision isn't well-documented, as long as everyone who needed to know the decision was in the room when it happened. But if one of your team members is in a different time zone and the decision isn't recorded, you'll create an information asymmetry and trust will erode. Make sure you're especially crisp on ownership, the operating cadence, and accountability mechanisms for remote teams, and document communication norms in more detail than you think you need to.

Level the playing field

If you're worried about participation, the most important thing you can do is to minimize practices that make a remote employee feel different. Think about a team meeting for someone who is remote versus someone who is based in the office: Someone on your team sends a meeting invite. Multiple people in the office are joining, so they include a room number on the invite but forget to include a videoconferencing link. The remote employee has to reach out to the organizer to include a link or dial-in number. Before the meeting, the office-based team members happen to sit together at lunch, and they start talking about an agenda item from the upcoming meeting. The remote employee has no idea, and now they're lacking important context before the meeting has even started. Once it begins, the remote employee has to go on mute because there's construction happening outside their home office. The office-based participants start having a discussion. It's hard for the remote employee to hear, so they sit in silence while their colleagues are debating.

There are so many ways a remote employee has a different experience from a centralized team. How much you try to level the playing field will depend on your company philosophy. Automattic, a completely distributed company, requires that everyone join conference calls from a different physical location, even if some participants happen to be in the same space. This way, no one has the experience of being the person dialing in to the conference call while others are co-located. They also get everyone together in person at least once a year, and some teams gather once per quarter. At Stripe, we ensure that every remote worker has the right hardware setup so that they can properly participate in conference calls. We also have a strong norm that any work discussion, no matter how minor or procedural, needs to happen via Slack or email so that those not physically present can follow along. Making improvements for distributed employees starts with an awareness that differences exist, and that these can turn into detrimental chasms between in-person and remote experiences.

Make room for in-person time

I've long thought it possible to build a distributed group into a strong team without a lot of in-person time. After all, look at all the global teams that operate effectively! But I haven't yet found a viable substitute for quality in-person time on a regular cadence. This is valuable for:

- **Generating spontaneous social interactions and connections**. Humans are herd animals. We have a need to connect on a level beyond the professional. You can connect on non-work topics remotely, of course, but having unplanned social interactions and developing deeper relationships is also important. You need to be able to have a laugh together, talk about personal interests, and share experiences that aren't just video meetings.
- **Getting people into a different mindset, beyond day-to-day operations**. People get comfortable with day-to-day operating rhythms pretty quickly, which is also why, if they get comfortable for too long, operating cadences become stale. Sometimes we all need to get out of our day-to-day setting to achieve a level of alignment and understanding that's hard to do in a 45- or 60-minute meeting.

For several years, I managed a group responsible for leading revenue in all of the countries Stripe operated in. The group consisted of the country and regional leads in North America, Europe, and Asia. When we first formed the group, we met in person every quarter. Usually, the leads would come to San Francisco, where we'd have two days of working offsites and at least one team social event. Those traveling to San Francisco would typically visit for a full week to meet with other people and teams as well. This time together was critical to forming both our team relationships and our strategy for growing Stripe's revenue.

In our first meeting together, we ended up listing everything we had to answer, solve, or build in order to be successful, which took up three huge whiteboards. There was a funny moment when the group got fired up about the need to build the marketing function, which was still in its infancy. I pointed out that we were struggling to answer even the current inbound sales leads, and we all ended up laughing about our poor prioritization and proverbial "good problems to have." Needless to say, it took a lot of time to work through everything on those whiteboards, but we'd laid the foundation for doing so effectively during our in-person time together.

How often should remote teams meet in person? When you're first forming a remote team, plan to meet at least once a quarter, if not more often. But once you've had a couple of solid in-person interactions, you can space them out a bit more. If you plan in person together, you can run faster and longer when you're apart. Later, you can move to meeting biannually, although if you're in growth mode and adding new members to the team, you'll want to continue to have quarterly in-person meetings for some time. Situations will arise that prevent you from gathering in person—like a global pandemic—but I still think it's a best practice to aim for, even if you have to experiment with half-day offsites held on Zoom, as we did at Stripe.

Going global

It wasn't until I led my first global team at Google that I fully internalized that being a global company isn't about doing the same work in different countries. I managed over 2,000 people in 16 offices around the world, and for the first year I traveled at least once a month. It was only then that I truly absorbed the cultural differences and strategic local needs for each business. A lot of the challenges of operating in a different time zone and handling a work schedule with major jet lag also felt much more real.

It's hard to replicate the insight you get from actually traveling for work and doing business in different countries, but I do recommend reading Geert Hofstede's work on the dimensions of national cultures.[55] It's a useful guide to understanding cultural differences and mapping your own company against the countries in which it operates. Interestingly, I've never found major differences in user needs—a marketer buying Google Ads in Indonesia wants the same thing as a marketer in Canada—but there are important differences in how you conduct aspects of your business, as Hofstede explains. There are also ecosystem variants, like whether there's a large developer

55

hi.hofstede-insights.com

community, and there are landscape factors, such as local competitors or different consumer expectations.

Make sure your team understands your company's cultural expectations and how they differ from local norms. This often comes up for sales teams with respect to the kinds of relationship-building activities clients expect. Aside from developing your own understanding, I think it's a useful team exercise to review the cultural dimensions of your business and discuss the implications for your day-to-day work, plus any guidance local teams might need to help balance their local cultural reality with the company's. My first trips to Japan and China for Google were full of lessons, predominantly in how much information was shared and business conducted late at night over drinks. Think about how you will help your teams understand prevailing behaviors without feeling like they must follow all of them when conducting business. (I don't think drinking alcohol is a sales skill requirement, for instance.)

Interestingly, when I did a cultural comparison exercise with a group of Stripe's country leads, we all realized that Stripe is not a simple mirror of American culture. That makes sense: Its founders are from Ireland. In fact, Stripe is an interesting hybrid of a few cultural dimensions. Once we realized this, we understood that it was an opportunity to build a shared global identity. It was also a chance to translate that identity into local expectations, even if they're not the norm in every culture. For example, in some cultures it's more common for outside-of-work socializing to double as a forum for doing business. At Stripe, we make sure that people are aware of this, but we also emphasize that the choice about how much to participate is theirs.

Adding remote workers

If you work at a company with global ambitions, or one that's still accommodating the shifts brought about by the pandemic, educate yourself about remote work best practices with resources from all-remote companies like Automattic[56] or GitLab.[57] Here are a few key elements to keep in mind as you add remote workers to your team:

Maturity of operating system

Remember Operating Principle 4: Come back to your operating system. If you feel fairly confident that you have a strong

56

distributed.blog

57

about.gitlab.com

operating system and cadence, as well as established norms and good sources of asynchronous information (video recordings of meetings, excellent note-taking practices, etc.), or if you're willing to invest in strengthening them, you're better positioned to add remote team members.

Role

Is this a job that requires a lot of coordination? Engineering, product, and design roles typically require more collaboration to get work done, while some roles, like legal and finance, can be done more independently. Carefully structure remote or hybrid team units so that the team can effectively manage the level of coordination needed. For example, three remote product, design, and engineering employees on a team may actually find it easier to coordinate than a team where two of those three people are co-located.

Manager support

Remote management is its own skill set. Between 2014 and 2016, Stripe had a requirement that remote employees be managed by remote managers. We felt that a remote manager would have more empathy for the remote experience and would find it easier to build the right coordination, participation, and cohesion mechanisms. We now provide more manager support and training, so non-remote managers do manage remote employees and teams, but the intention is still valuable. It takes time to build the skills to connect with a team you don't see in person, and it takes a good amount of empathy for the remote experience to design and operate the most conducive team system for those people.

Aside from empathy for the experiences of people not in the same room, managers of remote teams must develop management practices and mitigation strategies for the issues that tend to crop up with remote work. For example, managers can create and facilitate a team Slack channel and insist that meaningful side conversations be documented and sent to a team email list. Managers should also make themselves available to answer quick questions via non-in-person channels. In addition, they should be structured and consistent in how they connect with the team through 1:1s and other information-sharing tactics, like the snippets docs I mentioned in my discussion of Stripe's leadership meetings.

Experience level

At Stripe, we've found that it's easier to support remote employees who have already had experience working remotely. As we've all learned, it takes some adjustment to work well remotely, and it can be particularly hard on new graduates who are just developing their work skills and learning their jobs.

Consider the kinds of programming you can offer to bolster the remote work learning curve, especially for those with less overall experience.

A consistent theme of this book is to be very intentional with your foundations. This is especially true when you're managing a distributed company and adding remote team members. What works when everyone is together in one office will not scale when distance and time zones divide you. Consider the documentation, norms, and practices you'll need to enable folks to get their work done and to stay connected to their team and to the company, and build those in from day one. As a manager, seek to understand the different national cultures represented on your team and the particularities of the distributed and remote work experiences. Travel, try being remote yourself for a week, and adjust your team management practices accordingly. Above all, seek out feedback, including through your company engagement survey, on how productive, effective, and connected remote employees feel, and be ready to improve in response to their feedback.

Underperforming teams

Sometimes you've done everything you can to build a strong team—remote or in-person—but it's still faltering. If your teams are reviewing their goals and metrics at the right cadence, you should be able to catch that something is off track before the issue becomes too unwieldy, and you'll hopefully be able to solve the root problem. But sometimes teams don't hit their metrics or milestones for weeks running. It feels like there's always a reasonable explanation, yet you have a nagging sense that those explanations are masking a deeper issue.

How do you course-correct? Start by taking the following steps:

Investigate the root cause by asking some probing questions

You probably have a theory about what's causing the poor execution. Test your hypothesis in 1:1s with the relevant team members and see what comes to light. For example, you might observe, "There seems to be a lot of dependencies on data architecture work." If your team members confirm that that's the case, dig into why there seem to be so many dependencies, or whether the team is missing capabilities or resources that would prevent the bottleneck. You're not asking about a specific person but rather a set of work that seems perpetually behind schedule or off track.

Have an open conversation about the issue in your team meeting

Approach it from a place of curiosity, and avoid accusations. Ask the team the following questions:

- **Why do you think we're behind on our goal?** Be open to the possibility that it's the wrong goal, but don't be lenient.

- **Do these reasons feel in or out of our control?** Usually, the reasons are more in the team's control than they think, so push on this.
- **What can we do now to get back on track?** Document ideas and make sure it's clear who is accountable for the work to follow up and change course.
- **When it comes to the reasons that really are out of our control, how much impact will they have on our ability to make progress? What could we do to control those external factors?** Your team may not have considered all the angles, for example stepping in to help another team get critical work done.

If the issue is that you have the wrong goal, the next steps are fairly straightforward:

- Agree with the team that you need to adjust your goals as a result of new information.
  Make sure to clearly document the original goal, how the goal changed, and why, both with your team and with stakeholders. This is critical to maintaining credibility.
- Be transparent internally about the fact that you're resetting your goals and why you're doing it. Be particularly clear about what you learned and what you'll do differently in the future.

If the issue is your team's skill set or a collaboration issue across team members, continue to develop your hypothesis on the root cause, and seek data to build confidence that you've identified the true source of the problem. If it's an issue with an individual on the team, consult the sections on feedback in Chapter 5 for guidance. If it's a collaboration issue between two or more people, take time to meet with the individuals involved, first separately and then together. Facilitate a conversation in which each person can share nonjudgmental feedback on work style and process, and make it clear that you all need to work together to find an effective path forward. Take pains to be neutral and emphasize that the individuals need to change the dynamic for the good of the team. If you don't see a positive change, consider shifting one or both people to another team. In addition, consider whether one of the individuals involved may in fact have a performance issue in the form of poor collaboration skills—in which case, see Chapter 5 for more on feedback and performance management.

On occasion, you might think that the issue is limited to a few individuals but discover that there are actually many group dynamics contributing to what has become a fractious team environment. Don't ignore this trend. Confront it—urgently. Conduct or ask a neutral party like HR to conduct a series of interviews with team members—like a 360° review process but for a team—and have them write up a summary. Then have a critical session to discuss the team dynamics and what you will all do to address the negative trends and tendencies. Seek explicit commitments on what people will improve. Most points of friction come from a lack of mutual self-awareness—see Operating Principle 1—so return to your personality and work style assessments and spend time getting to know one another and your value systems. Give the team a vocabulary to use when working together, and make it clear that the team's dynamics matter to you and to the company's success.

In my experience, missing a goal is often due to a dependency, or many dependencies, on other teams. This is especially true as your team scope and your company grow. Perhaps your team controls one aspect of a project, but you need another team to deliver their half. Work would be much easier if everything were in your control, but that's not the reality—of work or of life. Instead, your role as a manager is to anticipate dependencies, negotiate with other teams, and work through issues when they occur, escalating to your respective leaders if needed. I often think of my work as a manager as clearing the path my team will need to travel. Anything that slows them down is on me.[58]

Working with other teams

Because some of the hardest accountability problems for a manager to navigate crop up when your team can't get their work done because they're dependent on the work of one or more other teams, it's important to de-risk those dependencies. Here's a quick guide to doing that:

- **Identify dependencies during your planning process**. For every goal, determine what work you need done by when from other teams. Discuss this work with the other teams before they finalize their own plans. Ninety percent of the time, teams are on the same page about what needs to be done. For the 10 percent of cases where teams disagree about the work, escalate to the common decision-maker for both teams. The outcome will either be that the team you're dependent on will complete the work, or that your goal will be judged not to be a company priority and you will adjust your own plans accordingly.
- **Set up a semi-regular check-in to keep your team and partner teams up to date on progress**. Check-ins can be in the form of an email, followed by a meeting if the project is getting off track.
- **Embed someone on the team**. Sometimes it's useful to have a representative from the team you're dependent on join your team meetings, and for you to send a representative to their meetings.

- **Form a working group**. In some cases, it may make sense to form a temporary working group that comprises members from the different teams. (See Table 6 on page 265 for more on the differences between working groups and teams.) You're essentially forming a mini-team that has its own shared goals and metrics for the duration of the project. Make sure the working group has a DRI who is tracking progress and holding the group accountable.

If, despite all your de-risking efforts, you still find yourself at an impasse with another team, I suggest you constructively escalate. A few retrospectives I've conducted on my biggest errors as a manager and leader uncovered my own weak spots in this area. Because I tend to be independent in how I accomplish work, relying more on my own teams than on peers, and because I'm innately collaborative and empathetic, I have more than once neglected to expose a critical dependency that was failing until it was too late.

Asking for help is not a failure. In fact, escalation paths are one of the reasons management structures exist. You don't want to be the person who has a hair-trigger escalation tendency, which will make you seem ineffective, not to mention wildly unpopular with colleagues. But you also don't want to be the one who gets your team stuck because you didn't escalate to unblock their progress. (For more on resolving dependencies, I've included a description of Stripe's unblocking process in the chapter appendix on page 343.)

Finally, in a nod to Operating Principle 3—distinguish between management and leadership—it's useful to take a look back and assess whether you had the right strategy. Often, adopting a more proactive vision will allow you to not only identify dependencies but also architect a future state that doesn't require such dependencies in the first place. This might involve a different technical architecture, a new strategy that includes a new organizational structure, or even a fresh set of priorities that negate the current path.

Managing through uncertainty

When something isn't working, everyone feels it. In these situations, I lean on a quote from author Rebecca Solnit: "Authentic hope requires clarity... and imagination."[59] Getting back on track is going to take a combination of management (clarity) and leadership (inspiration and imagination) to help the team make it through times of uncertainty or challenge.

Here's how I think about supporting teams through uncertain times:

Be transparent, to a point

When a team is experiencing uncertainty, it's rare that a manager isn't feeling it too. Some managers make the mistake of exposing too much of their own worry, which can be destabilizing for their teams. But the more common mistake I see managers making is not acknowledging the challenges head-on with their teams or pretending they've got a plan all figured out. This only serves to erode trust just when the team needs their manager most.

I try to be open and honest with my teams during times of uncertainty. This doesn't mean you must index toward negativity and pessimism—in fact, I would advise the opposite. But it's critical that you demonstrate that you have a good pulse on the team's state and that you're aware that a change is necessary, even if you don't know exactly what that change will look like yet. Try to be as objective as possible. This can be as simple as saying "I don't think we have the right people at the table to accomplish what we need to get done," or "I'm aware that the deadlines are unrealistic." You can also be transparent and say, "We don't have the details of a plan in place, and it may take us a while to get there, but I'm working on it." What's most important is that you acknowledge the situation and show empathy and a drive to improve what's not working.

Reiterate the vision

Don't forget to engage the imagination. You've placed your team on a path, and it includes a narrative about the brighter future that your work is enabling. Just because times are uncertain doesn't mean the vision is wrong or that you've lost your way. Retell the story of why you're doing the work you do and how the future will be better for it.

Move forward

Despite all of your instincts to the contrary, I recommend biasing toward action during times of uncertainty. There is a great temptation, especially when things aren't going well, to try to come up with a perfect plan or to overanalyze the situation. But trust me, you don't want to make a bigger mess! Oftentimes, the best thing you and your team can do is start moving. This may mean making small decisions and taking small- to medium-sized actions, but any action at all can be very meaningful. Communicate openly about these steps and what you're learning along the way.

Stripe's handling of the Covid-19 pandemic is a good example. As Covid infections moved beyond China, we began to discuss the implications for Stripe. Our CEO was tracking the virus closely and was most concerned about an outbreak that might impact critical teams, including our leadership team and the engineering teams responsible for Stripe's security and reliability. Although we didn't have a lot of data and had no detailed plan on how we'd proceed, we decided to start taking action to mitigate risk.

In February 2020, we shared that half of the leadership team and a few critical teams would immediately start working remotely. The danger of sharing this step was that we might imply a hierarchy of who or what was most valued at the company. But the danger in not sharing this information was that we might put the company at risk: We were still small enough that having many people get sick at once would be untenable for the business. It would also imply uncertainty, and would potentially lead employees to assume that we were not analyzing the situation—or worse, that we were not acting on what we knew. From there, we methodically communicated each decision and kept the entire company informed with emails and a resource page updated daily. Our guiding principles were to be there for our users and to prioritize the health and safety of our employees. Everyone understood our decisions and actions in the context of those objectives.

SIDEBAR

–

Reid Hoffman on managing through crisis

Although it's relevant to talk about the crisis of the pandemic, it's also useful to consider more "expected" crises (strange as it is to say). In an interview, Reid Hoffman, the cofounder and former chairman of LinkedIn, offered a great case study on how he steered the company through a major competitive threat. You can find a transcript of our conversation about leadership and management at <u>press.stripe.com/scaling-people/interviews</u>.

In May 2007, Facebook launched the Facebook Platform. The Facebook Platform gave third-party developers the ability to build applications using Facebook data. Until then, Facebook's focus was social and LinkedIn's was professional, but a platform that gave developers access to Facebook data had the potential to creep into LinkedIn territory. A number of people came to me and declared LinkedIn dead.

I wasn't so sure, but I acknowledged the possibility. "Okay," I said, "what if we were to build something on top of the Facebook Platform to test how existential the threat is to our business?" We assembled a team that would take eight weeks to build a minimum viable product, the lowest-effort product to see if there really was a competitive threat from the Facebook Platform. The team's objectives were to:

- Determine whether we could build something that was disruptive to LinkedIn on the Facebook Platform. If we found that we could, we'd accelerate development of the product so we could get there before others did.
- Understand how the Facebook Platform actually works, and whether we could learn anything useful for when LinkedIn built its own developer platform.

We assigned three different teams to sprint toward the finish line, meeting every day to discuss progress. By the end of eight weeks, we'd launched three different apps. None of them attracted more than 50 daily active users. We could have picked up a phone book and called people to get more usage than that!

Of course, the next question from the team was whether we were just incompetent. Perhaps we had become so inured to LinkedIn that we didn't understand how to build a successful app on the Facebook Platform. To test our own skills with the Facebook Platform, we pared the three teams down to one, which I ran. Our team launched an app called Bumper Stickers. Bumper Stickers allowed you to upload a sticker to your profile and slap it on other Facebook friends' profiles as well. We were the third most active app on the platform for six months straight. Bumper Stickers was not related to LinkedIn at all, and that was the point. We were pretty confident that we knew how to use the Facebook Platform, LinkedIn aside, and that there wasn't a credible threat to LinkedIn's business.

In hindsight, the launch of the Facebook Platform wasn't much of a crisis at all. But to get to that confidence, we needed to acknowledge that we didn't have all the answers, and we needed to have a plan to start getting them.

–

Diversity and inclusion

Managers play an important role in facilitating diversity, equity, inclusion, and belonging on their teams. There are many resources available on this topic, and I'm not an expert, so I'll add just a few thoughts from the perspective of a manager and a person who seeks to constantly improve as an ally, and as a woman in leadership whom others view as an example.

First, a great team and company are not only built by hiring well but also by building an environment that fosters and retains talent. I believe the work you do on diversity and inclusion is, fundamentally, work that creates a better environment for everyone. There's a good deal of compelling research on how diversity positively impacts team performance.[60] As a manager, you're responsible for the output of your team, and building a strong and diverse team that is also high-functioning is one of the most effective ways to accomplish your goals. Homogeneous teams may execute more quickly, but they don't generally push the thinking. Diverse teams get the most outsize results, although it takes time and investment to build what Harvard Business School professor and researcher Amy Edmondson calls the psychological safety to outperform.[61] Intuitively, this makes sense: The problem space that many companies are tackling is too big to hold in one set of experiences and perspectives. If you can add people with different backgrounds and opinions, and if you can draw out those perspectives on your teams, you're going to be able to take on problems more multidimensionally—but only if every person feels valued and comfortable fully participating.

I'm chiefly talking about racial and gender diversity here, but a diverse team also has less visually noticeable qualities. Socioeconomic background, education, sexual orientation, gender identity, political and religious beliefs, and where and in what circumstances a person was raised are all elements of a diverse team. When a company is growing, it's amazing how quickly team members can start cloning themselves—everyone thinks in a similar way, went to similar high schools and universities, likes the same types of extracurriculars. Why? Because they referred one another to the company. To a certain extent, this is great, since you do want great referrals. But you must watch this cycle and break it early if that's the only way you're hiring and scaling.

One of the ways I come to understand whether my team contains less visible elements of diversity is in the work we do to get to know each other, our backgrounds, and our work styles. Whether it's the career conversion I outlined earlier in this chapter or a facilitated team-building session at an offsite, I seek to create an environment where people feel comfortable sharing more about themselves. It's not something you should ever force, but it's important to ask yourself how well you know your team. As a manager, you should constantly seek to bring different perspectives and thinking into your division, facilitate open communication, and celebrate the perspectives and insights every team member offers to benefit your users—who, I'm betting, are diverse themselves—and, by proxy, your business.

Managers can exercise influence on diversity and inclusion in three areas in particular—paying attention in each to ensuring that opportunities are broadcast widely both internally and externally:

- Hiring
- Performance assessment, reward, and recognition
- Running teams

Here I'll share some brief thoughts on the role managers can play to increase diversity in each of these areas. Before you begin, I recommend educating yourself about the experiences of people who would be considered members of historically underrepresented groups in your country and your company. As someone operating in the US, for example, I've found it useful to read the Coqual publication "Being Black in Corporate America."[62]

Hiring

Assess your team portfolio. What are the backgrounds and viewpoints you're lacking? If you don't know what you don't know, ask other managers if you can join their team meetings to observe. Notice how the team dynamics might differ and what your team might be missing.

Build a hiring pipeline that exposes you to a lot of different candidates, and don't start interviewing until you have a strong, diverse pipeline. Add someone to your interviewing team who has a very different background from yours and different strengths. They may be able to recognize strengths and assess candidates that you may not find as easy to understand. Find the interviewer who complements your intuition about a candidate's strengths and challenges your assumptions.

All too often, companies rely on hiring as a panacea for fostering diversity within the organization. But many neglect the critical work of developing and retaining diverse teams once hired, particularly at the leadership level. The consulting group BCG analyzed its own industry's lack of success in this area, and its learnings are applicable beyond management consulting. The group found that among early-career consultants, all with similar GMAT scores and GPAs, those from underrepresented groups within the company failed to advance at a similar rate for two primary reasons: a weak sense of belonging and difficulty navigating professional environments.[63] With that in mind, the manager's role becomes even more important once they've built a more diverse team. The key is to run the team equitably and inclusively. After all, you can invest all you want in composing a more diverse team, but without equitable processes and an inclusive environment, the team will not be successful. It's also unlikely you will attract more diverse candidates to your company in the future.

Performance assessment, reward, and recognition

Some of the biggest mistakes I've seen with regard to having a fair system are tactical mistakes made by managers: picking someone for a project via a short process without explicit selection criteria, deciding on promotions without objective data, or adding someone to the team just because they used to work together. All of these actions have ramifications. Check yourself and run a lightweight, thoughtful process in which you clearly lay out the opportunities and incorporate performance measures into the decision-making.

In fast-moving environments, many people fill open roles or assign projects by tapping someone on the shoulder. The tendency is to fill the role with someone you know who has a skill set similar to yours. This is certainly an efficient way to hire, but it might not be the smartest—it leaves out a broad swath of people who might have raised their hands, or even those who might not have spoken up but who could have been great if you'd just looked at their performance on similar work. Create a system that makes new opportunities clear, and give people an opportunity to volunteer for a project or role on your team. If people you think should volunteer don't, talk to them to find out why, encourage them to seek out new opportunities, and help them do so.

The main goal here is to make sure all your processes feel equitable. Establish a common, agreed-upon way of evaluating the best person to promote, give a project to, or nominate for a leadership development opportunity. Have clear criteria for assessing potential candidates—see Chapter 3—and build equity checks into your people processes, like calibration for performance management and pay parity analysis for compensation. These don't need to be exhaustive audits or heavy processes: Look for straightforward but effective methods, like the medical checklists that the best hospitals use to make sure there are no errors in treatment.

Running teams

Like your company processes, the way you run your team should give people equal chances to prove themselves. Start with your team onboarding process and solicit feedback to make sure that all new team members, no matter their background, feel prepared to contribute after their first month in the role. Beyond the initial few weeks, almost any team interaction is an opportunity to be inclusive: how you collect agenda items, plan an offsite, run a meeting, or make a decision on a controversial subject. Pay attention to airtime. If someone hasn't said anything in a team meeting, give them an opportunity to share their opinion. Assume that how you manage can probably be more inclusive than it is. Ask someone you trust to observe you and suggest how you might make your day-to-day management practices more inclusive. Better yet, read the book *Unleashed* by Frances Frei and Anne Morriss.[64] It's one of the few books I've read that provides tangible frameworks and practices to build inclusion into your teams and your company.

Author David Foster Wallace's 2005 commencement speech at Kenyon College is one of the most impactful things I've read about empathy and compassion.[65] In it, he says, "The really important kind of freedom involves attention and awareness and discipline, and being able truly to care about other people and to sacrifice for them over and over in myriad petty, unsexy ways every day." It's an exhortation to resist our default beliefs and assumptions, to fight for awareness of the realities that are often hidden to us, and to be present and conscious. That is what inclusion requires.

Finally, although I am a believer in building diverse teams, understanding one another's differences, and being sensitive to the fact that we can never truly know someone else's experiences—particularly those of a person from a historically underrepresented group if you're not a member of that group—I am also a believer in teams uniting around their shared qualities and dreams. Leaders should bring in diverse team members and celebrate and understand their perspectives while also uniting the group around a common vision, with common appreciation for what is true about all of us: our shared human experience and our desire for love and respect. At the risk of sounding too optimistic, I think there's real value in creating a collective vision in a world that encourages polarization and difference. Focus on cultivating that vision.

These same principles are evident in the work of Chloé Valdary, an American writer and entrepreneur who provides social, emotional, and diversity and inclusion education.[66] Valdary developed what she calls the theory of enchantment, which has the following core tenets:

66

theoryofenchantment.com

- Treat people like human beings, not political abstractions.
- Criticize to uplift and empower, never to tear down, never to destroy.
- Root everything you do in love and compassion.

These are meaningful tenets for managers as well. Adopt these principles and create a shared vision to which all of your team members belong. Set goals, measure progress, and hold yourself and other leaders accountable not just for the diverse composition of teams but also for the team environment each manager creates. This is not for the sake of some checklist—it will make for a tighter-knit company fabric, a stronger team, and better results.

Team communication

When I think about leadership and management, I hear the voice of Sigal Barsade, the business school professor I mentioned earlier in this chapter. When she lectured on change management, she emphasized, "Communicate, communicate, and by the way, communicate."

Much of my advice for teams ultimately boils down to communication: Set expectations well, share the same information with everyone, and create an environment that facilitates an open exchange of ideas. So much of the work of a manager comes back to communication, whether 1:1 or with the team, division, or company. It's worth understanding your company's approach to internal communication so that you can layer it into your own.

As discussed in Chapter 2, internal communication is a mechanism for building trust. You reinforce this trust by sharing team meeting notes and decisions and by continuing to communicate even amid uncertainty. As you think about your team, especially if it's growing, consider mapping the formal and informal means by which team members acquire information. The more you scale, the more you need to formalize information-sharing. This is true for companies and for teams. Otherwise, there's a risk that people will acquire knowledge at different times, which can lead to a perception of politics and relationships being the only way to get anything done.

As a leader or manager, you're privy to much more information than the average employee at the company. If you neglect to key your reports into relevant information, your employees are going to be missing important context that they need to do their jobs well. I recommend including a "pass-downs" agenda item in your team meeting to share information from company leadership that's relevant for your team members to know, either for context or because it directly impacts their work. (Usually, you'll receive this from your own manager.) These pass-downs might include new information, or you might provide additional framing to company messages that have been delivered by leaders via email or at the company all-hands meeting.

Of course, you'll need to continually exercise judgment about what to share and deeply consider how to frame the information. When I sat in staff meetings with Sheryl Sandberg at Google, she would often share a piece of information and then say, "I think the right way to think about this is…" and help contextualize the decision or action that company leaders had taken. Your team will be grateful for your perspective, especially on items that might affect them, and for the chance to discuss and ask questions about important company decisions or news.

Another practice to consider is having a team snippets document that every team member completes each week. This way, you don't have to take up meeting time with updates, but everyone has information about what the rest of the team is up to and the status of important work. If you lead a larger team or division, consider a weekly or monthly cadence of updates that you share with everyone on the team. Use this time to reinforce goals and priorities, celebrate wins, discuss challenges, and ask for ideas. Above all, use it to keep the team connected to you as their leader. Don't be afraid to share personal anecdotes or photos.

Lastly, try to end every day thinking about what you need to tell other people. For my first six years at Stripe, I lived in Menlo Park and worked in the San Francisco office. The commute home, anywhere from 45–60 minutes, was a perfect time to reflect on everything I'd learned that day, consider what information the people in my division needed to have, and, when I wasn't driving, to share it out, usually via chat or email, to individuals or teams. Find the communication methods that work best for you and apply them consistently.

—

Chapter 4

Scan the QR code to access printer-friendly versions of these worksheets.

Career Conversations

Duration

60 minutes (30–45 minutes if the person just graduated from school)

Approach

Pre-conversation

1. If you're working with a new team, take a moment in one of your first team meetings to let team members know that you're planning on having a career conversation with each of them over the next few weeks, and share the context and goals of the conversation. If you're working with just one new person, you can mention the career chat in an email or an early 1:1.

    #### Script:

    Over the next few weeks, I'm going to schedule a one-off, 60-minute 1:1 with each of you to better understand your past career moves and start working with you on your future development goals. I call these chats career conversations, but they're really get-to-know-you conversations. There's no pre-work required other than being ready to talk through a bit of your life and career history. If you like, you can bring a résumé to refer to, but it's not required. These are some of my favorite conversations, and they help me understand your career narrative. I'm looking forward to them!

2. Send a reminder outlining the goals for the conversation the day before you meet. There's no need to do it earlier—otherwise, people might feel like they have to prepare more than they should.

    #### Script:

    Thanks for taking the time to walk me through a bit of your life history and career in our session tomorrow. Mostly, I want to get to know you better. In particular, I'd like to learn more about the choices you've made so far and what motivated you to make them. If you like, we can talk a bit about where you grew up, your family, and why you chose to attend the school you did. We'll focus most of the time on the learning and career steps you've taken and why. If it's useful, feel free to share or bring a copy of your résumé.

    Toward the end of the conversation, I'd love to project out five years and have you consider where you think you'll find yourself in your career. Not a title or specific role, but where you see yourself generally and what your day-to-day might look like. All of this is laying the groundwork for us to make sure that we keep the bigger picture in mind when we talk about your development. When you're facing a choice about a project or even a new role, it will likely be useful for us to reflect on your career arc and make sure whatever you choose fits with the path you've outlined. Don't worry – no one is holding anyone to any five-year career plans, but it will be a helpful reference point as we continue to work together.

Conversation

You'll want to avoid over-scripting this conversation, so I'll just share some guidelines and sample questions here.

The conversation takes a "walk me through your history" approach. The most important thing to do is actively listen, take notes that you can refer to in future conversations, and ask "why" a lot. You're trying to understand what motivates the person and why they made the choices they did, and to help them reflect on those choices. What do they think about those decisions now? How did those decisions influence their thinking? What have they not explored? What do they want to return to?

Tell me about where you grew up.

Some people launch into a fair amount of detail about their childhood, parents, parents' occupations, and schooling. Others will share one step at a time. I don't pry on family topics, but I also remain open and listen closely if people do want to share. I'm a firm believer that family life and family patterns manifest in our work selves and that it's good to be aware of them. If people are reluctant to share, I try to emphasize that I'm looking to lay out some facts on location, schooling, and early interests. I find most people don't mind sharing more.

Tell me about where you went to school.

I get the person talking about what interested them in school, why they chose their college, if applicable, and why they chose their course of study.

What did you do right after college? Why did you make that decision?

These questions help you understand why your report made the choices they did after graduating. Did they know what they wanted? If not, what were their inklings? Why did they end up choosing what they did? Where did they think they would end up? Have they ended up there? Why or why not? Post-school decisions give you insight into a person's early motivations, which they often hold on to later in life.

Tell me about your favorite job. Tell me about your least favorite job. How and why did you make the decisions you made when choosing what roles you wanted to pursue?

Focus on the roles your report has had and the choices they made within companies. I try to get a sense of their path and their choices, especially the why. I also try to get a sense of the learnings they took away from their previous roles, especially about what work they're good at and enjoy doing and what work they find harder and why. Work your way up to the present and dive in if there's an interesting or telling nugget. Really dig into their motivations in this section and see if you can both surface some patterns.

What sort of work do you see yourself doing in the future? Who are the people you'll be working with? Where will you be living?

This is the forward-looking part of the conversation, and it's much more exploratory than the first four sections. Probe on any thoughts the person has about their future, no matter how abstract.

Focus more on what their future work or role looks like and less on a particular title or position. You're trying to figure out what type of work they want to be doing (management, research, execution, leadership, communication, analytics, advanced problem-solving, consulting, etc.) and dig into what they want to get exposure to in order to get there. Eventually, this conversation can support a discussion about career development plans, but the point is to align on opportunities you should both look out for to help the person start developing those skills or opportunities. Use some of the themes from the last four sections – how they make decisions, what was important to them – to guide the discussion here.

This section ends up being useful to reference in 1:1s because people often face choices that could benefit from a refresher on their longer-term goals. (For example: Which project should I pick? What parts of my role should I try to delegate?)

Wrap-up

Recap the conversation, share any notes you took, and write down two or three development goals to keep an eye on together.

Planning and Running Your Offsite

Planning checklist

Date of offsite:

1+ month before offsite

- ☐ Set goals and objectives.
- ☐ Schedule date, time, and length.
- ☐ Start brainstorming the agenda with your team.
- ☐ Book space.

1 month before

- ☐ Order food and beverages.
- ☐ Finalize the agenda and assign each section to a DRI.
- ☐ Share rough pre-work templates with DRIs.

1 week before

- ☐ Finalize materials.
- ☐ Run through the agenda and content with DRIs.
- ☐ Send the agenda, pre-reads, and any pre-work to the team.
- ☐ Check that all meals are scheduled and confirm your headcount.
- ☐ Confirm venue setup and any materials needed with the offsite space.
- ☐ Determine how to enter the space (e.g., do you need an entrance. code, or does someone need to let you in?).
- ☐ Duplicate the session template for each planned session.
- ☐ Duplicate the icebreaker template for each planned icebreaker.

1 day before

- ☐ Send a welcome email to the team; include the venue location, how to get there, and how to enter the space, and remind the team about pre-reads and pre-work.
- ☐ Confirm details with vendors.
- ☐ Collect supplies you'll need from the office (e.g., pens, markers, sticky notes, flip charts, chargers, AV equipment).

Day of offsite

- ☐ Have your team check-in, then follow the agenda for the rest of the day.

After offsite

☐ Send notes and action items to assigned DRIs.

☐ Send a feedback form to all participants and ask them to rate the offsite.

☐ Track all action items until complete.

Day-of-offsite templates

Offsite structure

1. Offsite welcome

2. Check-in exercise

3. Icebreaker

4. Session

5. Check-out exercise

Offsite welcome email

Welcome to the [offsite name]!

To get started, I'll share a bit more context about why we've gotten this group together and how we'll be using the time. And don't worry—we've got plenty of scheduled breaks and social time.

Purpose

We're here because [explain the purpose of the offsite].

Logistics

[Ahead of the offsite, share documentation and directions and tell participants what they should bring. On the day of the offsite, share information like the Wi-Fi access code, directions to the restroom, where you'll be eating lunch, etc.]

Agenda

Session	What we'll be doing	Time	Length	Facilitator
Check-in	Share expectations for the day	9:30 a.m.	30 minutes	Cheryl Davis
Session 1	Work style assessment discussion	10 a.m.	1 hour	Bethel Musa
Break	Take a stretch	11 a.m.	15 minutes	
Session 2	Last year results retro-spective	11:15 a.m.	1 hour	Lola Aisca
Lunch	Eat!	12:15 p.m.	1 hour	
Post-lunch exercise	Big-picture brainstorm	1:15 p.m.	30 minutes	Alan Chowansky
Session 3	Decide on strategic pillars for this year (note: pre-reads required)	1:45 p.m.	1 hour	Maria Marquis
Break	Check some emails	2:45 p.m.	15 minutes	
Session 4	Finalize goals for the quarter and DRIs	3 p.m.	1 hour	Fang Li
Wrap-up and check-out	How did we do?	4 p.m.	1 hour	Cheryl Davis
Social	Social time and team-building cooking lesson	5 p.m.		Felix Marlin

Leadership Team Snippets and Updates

Please update by 10 p.m. on the Sunday night before the meeting.

Date:

Actions status: Link to action-tracking spreadsheet

Actions

- Name, action, due date

Discussion topics

- Actions (5 mins)
- User guest (10 mins)
- Metrics review: shortform (30 mins)
  - Note: Metrics review alternates weeks with launch review, in which we review upcoming launches and overall roadmap status
- Leadership recruiting weekly update (10 mins)
- Internal audit quarterly update (10 mins)
- Topic from CEO (10 mins)
- Review top goals and strategic priorities (60–120 mins)

Standing questions

- QBR reflections from the past week
- Are there any snippets to share with the wider leadership team or company-wide?
- Are there any topics discussed that anyone objects to being passed down in staff meetings?
- What decisions were made? Is there anything we should clearly communicate to the wider leadership team?

Customer issues

- Short summary of key customer issue, actions, and owner

Customer wins

- Short summary of key customer wins and contributors

Snippets

Executive team member name:

- Assigned action item updates – also in tracker
- General updates (e.g., whereabouts, travel plans, offsites)
- Potential topics for discussion and why they should be discussed
- Major company or product initiative status and learnings or customer contract negotiation status and learnings
- Top-level notes from a customer meeting or external event
- Launch, event, or PR plans in flight
- Info on top talent

Stripe's Unblocking Process

David Singleton, Stripe's CTO, created this process to help unblock a decision when individuals, groups, or teams are unable to agree on a path forward and have already tried to find a solution collaboratively.

First, try to solve locally

Stripes make thousands of decisions every day, and the vast majority are reversible or tunable. For these kinds of decisions, we should optimize for speed: Make the decision and iterate quickly.

If you find yourself involved in a disagreement over a reversible decision, ask if it really matters. If we iterate over time, will we get to an optimal endpoint either way? If so, maybe this decision isn't a big deal. Second, ask yourself if it's truly important. Can the folks who will do the majority of the work move forward on a path that any dissenters can commit to supporting, even if those who disagree might have chosen another path if they were doing the bulk of the work?

If you're making a multi-constituency decision that is important and is not easily reversed, taking some time to debate makes sense. If that doesn't quickly result in a decision, kick off the unblocking process!

Unblocking is not bad. Slow, unclear, or bad decisions are bad. For meaningful, irreversible decisions, we'd rather involve people responsible from "both sides" than hinder forward progress, move in the wrong direction, or hurt trust between teams and individuals.

We experience a real cost—both in lost productivity and in diminished happiness—when teams don't agree and can't move forward without resolving a decision. Therefore, if you find yourself in a position where you're blocked by the lack of a resolved decision, it's your duty to instigate this process. We request that once you have identified an area of misalignment, you work with your coworker(s) and commit to resolving it within five business days of kicking off the unblocking process. (In cases bound by a lack of data, the commitment is to align on how to answer within five days of the data being available.)

How to unblock

1. Document the disagreement together. This document can be extremely short. Half a page is fine. Outline:

   1.1 The problem to be solved (ideally described as the goal of the joint enterprise in the voice of the user).

   1.2 The options considered.

   1.3 The trade-offs both parties see between the options. Highlight the trade-offs that could not be resolved without further help.

2. Sometimes producing this document will result in agreement. If so, great! But if it doesn't, email it to your managers.

   2.1 If the authors report to different managers, the document should be sent to both managers.

   2.2 The managers might decide to call a meeting.

   2.3 If escalating to a single manager, the expectation is that they'll make a decision. If escalating to multiple managers, they'll hopefully decide together. But if they can't reach an agreement, they should raise the issue with their respective managers recursively (possibly adding more context to the unblocking doc) until a decision is reached (or the stack overflows).

Unblocking should be bilateral but can be unilateral

1. If one of the parties declines to unblock jointly, the other person should inform them that they'll do it alone and invite the other party once again to bring the matter "up" together.

2. If the reluctant party continues to refuse, the other may then unblock unilaterally, with the other party copied on cc.

Is this a request to unblock?

If you're raising an issue with a manager and you might then present their feedback as a decision to an individual or group that you know or suspect disagrees with your stance, that is a request to unblock. The other party should be present for the discussion.

What to do if you get a unilateral request to unblock

To support this process, all managers must refuse to listen to any argument brought to them unilaterally unless they obtain an affirmative answer to the following questions:

1. **Have you and your colleague tried to resolve this problem using constructive negotiation?** If the answer is no, please try that first.

2. **Have you tried to use the unblocking process, and have you written an unblocking document with your colleague?** If the answer is no, please do that first.

3. **Have you tried Step 2 and told your colleague that if they didn't use the unblocking process, you would bring the problem to me alone?** If the answer is no, please tell them first.

If the manager gets three yeses, they should message the missing colleague and ask them to attend. This sets a cultural norm: It's not acceptable to refuse to unblock jointly.

Example

The details of this example are fictional.

Charlie works on the widget product team and Alice works on the storage team. Charlie and Alice have different managers, Chun and Aiden, respectively. Chun and Aiden both share the same manager, Bharath.

Charlie is implementing a new set of features that require the storage of mass-market end user personally identifiable information (PII) and has received guidance from product counsel that this data should be encrypted at rest. Charlie consults with Alice to get her opinion on how to store this PII, and Alice advises that the current storage systems do not do encryption at rest. However, it's on the team's roadmap, and Charlie should wait until it's supported. Alice offers to expedite the development of this feature so it could be available for Charlie to try out in a few months' time.

Charlie says that's a problem, as the widget team wants to launch an internal alpha no later than two months from today. He proposes instead that the product team stand up a new storage system and build their own encryption at rest support. Alice thinks this is a bad idea and shares concerns about how this would be supported and maintained in the long term. Alice also thinks the amount of work it would take to build the key management system and integrate with the systems that the storage team has built around personal data deletion and compliance is being underestimated. Charlie and Alice do not reach an agreement on the best path forward.

Charlie brings up the need to build a new storage system supporting encryption at rest to his direct manager, Chun, mentioning that it will speed up development significantly. He notes that Alice was pushing for another path and that they have failed to agree on the way forward.

Chun asks Charlie if he has tried to resolve the disagreement using constructive negotiation with Alice. Because Charlie has tried that already, Chun then asks Charlie to use the escalation process described in this document.

Charlie and Alice write the following cosigned document. In writing the document, they collaboratively ask themselves, "What are we really trying to do?" and manage to frame the discussion in terms of a goal, the crux of the decision sought, and the trade-offs inherent in each path.

Fictional example document

Stripe alignment model

Authors

Alice, Storage

Charlie, Widget

Date: May 31

Goal

Deploy a widget system that meets encryption at rest needs in a timely fashion.

Decision sought

Whether to build and deploy a new storage system supporting encryption at rest in time for widget's internal trial in July.

Options considered

A. Wait for the storage team to deploy encryption at rest on their existing system, which will push the widget trial to September at the earliest.

B. Deploy a new instance of MySQL Enterprise with transparent data encryption, to be maintained by the widget team.

Trade-offs

Option A:

- Explanation of why the widget trial's July deadline is important.

- Link to docs for planned encryption at rest feature on the storage team's stack rank.

Option B:

- Explanation of how MySQL Enterprise would be deployed (mostly provided by Charlie, but Alice agrees that it captures the state accurately).

- List of the key management, maintenance, and systems integration tasks of concern (mostly provided by Alice, but Charlie and Alice agree on listing them).

Charlie and Alice jointly email the doc to both of their managers. Chun, Charlie's manager, suggests meeting in person to resolve the disagreement.

Charlie, Alice, Chun, and Aiden meet and review the document together. Both Chun and Aiden ask clarifying questions and make some live edits to the document for completeness. Ultimately, they don't agree on the best path forward after this brief discussion, so they agree to take the escalation to their manager, Bharath. (This scenario, with the mutual managers escalating to their shared manager, is expected to be an exception rather than the norm. It's detailed here for illustrative purposes.)

Chun sends the document via email to Bharath with Charlie, Alice, and Aiden on cc. Bharath reviews the document and decides that the widget team should not stand up a new storage system and Option A should be chosen. Bharath documents the rationale in reply to the escalation email. The group moves forward with this decision, and Chun and Charlie commit to following this course.

Core Framework 4

Feedback and Performance Mechanisms

Management is an iterative process. We learn as we go, and we hopefully learn from one another's examples, but it's generally hard to get it right without a lot of practice.

I find managers often fall somewhere on a continuum between the "extreme coach" and the "forgot-to coach." The extreme coach spends too much time involved in the day-to-day, providing endless feedback. The forgot-to coach is often very clear about what results they want to see but is unclear on how to help their direct reports achieve them. Most managers fall somewhere in between. In my experience, many managers wait too long to offer coaching—often until a formal performance conversation—unless the direct report specifically asks for feedback or help on work. This may be because coaching involves a certain amount of risk—you're offering judgment on someone else's work and skills.

Some executive coach coined the phrase "Feedback is a gift," and though it feels cloying to say, I do think the manager's attitude needs to be one of service. You may not be an expert in everything a person is doing, but your role is to help them be better. To do that, you need to offer service in the form of observations about what they do well and how they can improve.

One of the best manager coaches I ever had was Paul Bascobert, a partner at the consulting firm I joined out of business school. He wasn't my direct manager, but he was very involved in most of the projects I was a team member on, and he was the key partner on an engagement where I ultimately helped sell the project and led the team. Paul's original training was as an engineer, and he had a certain matter-of-fact directness that I've come to appreciate and that many engineers share. Sometimes the coaching was not so helpful: We once handed him a draft presentation we'd prepared for our client and he rifled through it, took out a pen, flipped back to the front page, and wrote, "Think harder," then handed it back to us. Not very detailed feedback—but he did set the bar high.

Paul's best coaching moment happened in the early days of the project I was leading. As you can imagine, I was more than eager to prove myself and my new team. In a practice run before we met with the client's executive sponsor, we sat with Paul and presented our proposed project scope and work streams. Well, really, *I* presented the scope and work streams. The practice session went fine, but afterward Paul asked to speak with me in his office. I was hoping for some praise on our good start or a few constructive comments about our work streams, but instead Paul asked me, "How did you think that went?"

I was puzzled. I said, "I think we're ready, right?" In response, he said, "What do you think Teresa was thinking?" Teresa (not her real name; all team members' names have been changed) was the most junior member of the project team. I was stumped. He said, "Okay, what about Mike?" Mike was the technical member of our team and was responsible for a key element of the project. Again, I was baffled. This went on for some time, with Paul asking me about each project member in turn and how I thought they had experienced the meeting. Eventually, Paul weighed in: "Teresa wanted you to acknowledge her work. And Mike would have liked to present his work stream, not you."

I'll never forget that. Paul's coaching was not about the substance of the presentation but about my failure to be the leader my team needed, to offer them recognition and a chance to share their work. How would I get this new team behind me, and how would they buy into me as their leader, if I didn't acknowledge their contributions and if I took all the best opportunities for myself?

During my entire early career in multiple organizations, I never had a formal performance review. But I learned a lot in moments like that one. I remember once, as deputy campaign manager for a gubernatorial campaign in 1998, I walked into the campaign manager's office to tell him about a big problem I'd discovered. He listened and said, sarcastically, "Wow. Has no one ever faced this problem before?" I'd come in with a problem but not done one bit of work to propose some solutions!

Some years later, my first formal performance review at Google was a revelation. I knew what my areas for development were—thanks to feedback along the way, I'd become quite attuned to what I needed to work on. But what was new to me was the attention paid to my strengths and how they were perceived. Yes, I had been given more responsibilities, even promotions, in my work in politics and consulting. But no one had ever said, "You really have talent." And sometimes, especially when the work is unending and hard, you need to have someone tell you that as part of a formal process. So here I am, advocating for both regular coaching and formal performance reviews.

Before we get to performance reviews, let's talk about informal feedback and coaching.

To some, business is already too rife with sports analogies. I get it. But I'm the daughter of a baseball coach—okay, he was a teacher who happened to coach baseball, but he identified as a coach—and I grew up watching sports. I don't necessarily love every minute and every aspect of the sports I watch, but I love watching the coach and seeing how the performance of individuals add up, sometimes, to a true team. It's one of the few places where you can be in the audience and observe what happens to people under intense pressure. I recommend paying attention in those moments.

In the Michael Lewis article about Bill Parcells I mentioned in Chapter 4, Lewis writes, "It's an elemental thing—that mysterious something in a player under pressure that either snaps or holds   and elemental things are what interest this old coach."[67] As a coach, I'm certainly getting older, and I'll never tire of trying to figure out a person's elemental thing.

Hypothesis-based coaching

One of my favorite coaching techniques is what I call intuitive coaching. Intuition gets a bad rap, I think. To some, it feels fluffy and lacking in data. The source of an intuition may be hard to pin down, but think of it this way: An intuition is just a hypothesis. You observe a few examples of a phenomenon, and you think, "I wonder if there's a pattern here." Then, like a scientist, you figure out a way to test your theory and collect more data.

Managers are often afraid to share their hypotheses with their reports because they think it means they're judging their people, which they perceive to be bad management. But good judgment is a manager's job! It's akin to making a business decision: Leaders create a strategy based on their assessment of a particular business need, then confirm whether that strategy was successful by reviewing user interviews, data, and product tests or by going to market. The same can apply to people: You observe a particular need, form a hypothesis about what might be the root cause of that need or a possible solution to it, and then you test the hypothesis, sometimes directly with the person in question.

When it comes to coaching, I think a lot of managers need to get to a point where they can feel comfortable implementing Operating Principle 2: Say the thing you think you cannot say. If you can get stronger at standing next to the person, seeing from their point of view, and offering observations and hypotheses to help them grow, that person will view you as someone invested in their success, ideally a partner. Hypothesis-based coaching is about saying the thing—making the observation—before you may feel completely ready, but doing so in such a way that the person experiences you as an ally in their journey to improve.

Sharing your hypotheses with your reports can initially feel strange, but as you start integrating this approach into your management style, you'll be able to have much more targeted performance conversations. You can then jointly explore whether the hunch you have about the root cause of a performance challenge is true. Sometimes you'll be wrong, which is in itself a data point. Oftentimes, you'll discover an insight that wasn't initially obvious to either of you but that ultimately helps your employee.

Hypothesis-based coaching also helps you act quickly rather than relying on a long process of observation and gathering data on a person's performance before coming to a conclusion. It's like deductive instead of inductive reasoning. Posit something, then start talking about it. The sooner you and your report can identify areas for improvement, the sooner you can start making changes.

The career conversation outlined in Chapter 4 is a great place to start forming hypotheses about your reports. In fact, they may volunteer some during the conversation. Once, as I probed a report's motivations for a certain career choice, they told me, "I'm always drawn to the thorniest and riskiest problems, although sometimes I get a bit too involved in solving them." That's not just a data point, it's the person's own hypothesis about a development area. File that away and bring it back up when the moment is right to coach them on how they might mitigate a tendency they want to avoid—in this case, not the part about taking on risky problems but about getting lost in trying to solve something to the detriment of bigger-picture objectives.

Intuitive coaching consists of three steps, which you may repeat a few times before getting to an insight you want to share or a firmer conclusion about a strength or development area your direct report might have:

- **Gather data**: You have more than you realize and need less than you think.
- **Form a hypothesis**: Based on your observations of your report, develop a sense of their strengths and weaknesses.
- **Test your hypothesis**: Be rigorous and vulnerable as you do this.

In the previous example, one data point is the person's opinion about their tendency to get too involved in problem-solving. The next might be your own observation that they're going too deep into the details of a particular problem space on a project. Your hypothesis might be that they lose the forest for the trees and they need to be more aware of the bigger-picture objective and willing to use the 80-20 rule: Perhaps understanding 20 percent of the root of the problem is enough to know 80 percent of what's needed to move forward. Your test might be to delegate another, similar project to the person, or, if you feel more confident—and in this case you probably should, since the person has raised the concern themselves—to have a conversation with your report about what you've observed and how you might work on mitigating their tendency to dive too deep.

Let's go into more detail about each step:

Gather data

A senior leader—let's call her Anika—recently asked me to help her with a situation she faced with one of her reports, whom we'll call Sonya. Sonya had just been promoted to managing a division, and multiple managers in her division appeared to be struggling. Anika had gathered feedback on Sonya from three of Sonya's direct reports, but she felt uncomfortable assessing whether the situation required her intervention with just three data points.

As we discussed the situation, I pointed out that Anika had a lot more data than she thought. She knew each of those three reports' roles, and she had worked with them personally. She had context on their work style, preferences, strengths, and weaknesses. She also knew the context Sonya was operating in: She was now managing managers of managers of managers! Plus, we were in the middle of a global pandemic, and as a result, Sonya's core responsibilities were ambiguous and continually changing as we revamped our plans for the year. When you're a manager who has only led companies in one mode, suddenly switching to a different mode can mean you need to take a different approach as a leader. Sonya's division wanted more clarity and direct leadership from her during a time of crisis instead of her more facilitative style, which was better suited to periods of growth and expansion.

The bigger point is this: Once Anika studied the situation—she knew the players, the division, and the broader context—she realized that she had more like 10 or 15 data points rather than three. That information was more than enough for her to form a hypothesis and start coaching.

Form a hypothesis

Based on your observations of your report, you can start to develop a sense of their strengths and weaknesses and consider any challenges you've observed that may be worth discussing.

Sometimes you'll form an early assessment of your report and how they're performing. Don't be afraid to use that as your starting hypothesis. For example, in order to help Anika, I read the peer feedback she had collected about Sonya. With our hypothesis in mind—that Sonya had been operating more as what business books might call a "peacetime" leader—a bunch of the data points started to match up. She was very good at consulting with her teams and bringing people along in decision-making processes, but her transition into a manager-of-managers role during a pandemic called for her to be more of a "wartime" leader.[68] In other words, she needed to be more precise and provide more direction. The peer feedback indicated that her teams wanted this additional clarity and increased assurance.

68

future.a16z.com

It can take a while to trust your intuition when you start practicing this kind of coaching. Sometimes you might have trouble forming a hypothesis, or you might find that the data you're collecting suggests conflicting conclusions. If that's the case, spend more time collecting data before you form a hypothesis. Over time, you'll start to get a sense of whether you need to continue collecting more data in a given situation or whether it's time to start testing your hypothesis. If most of your hypotheses are correct after three to six months of practicing this form of coaching, you can start to assume that your manager's intuition is developing nicely. If your assessments end up being wrong more often than not, you may need to spend more time in the data-gathering phase, relying more on peer feedback and results, and likely spending more time with your report.

Test your hypothesis

The best way to test your hypothesis is to share it directly with your report. When you do this, acknowledge that you're not stating a fact but presenting a theory about the way they work. You can say, "I'm testing a hypothesis. Let me know whether it feels right to you." Present the hypothesis as an observation about their behavior and the impact it has on their work, not a judgment about who they are as a person. For example, instead of telling someone, "My guess is that you're a bad communicator," which suggests some absolute truth about who they are and what they're good or bad at, it's much more effective to say, "I have a theory that you're not effectively getting important information across to the right stakeholders. For example, when we came out of that recent business review, I sensed that the CMO was unsure about your plans. Did you sense that?" And, of course, follow up with: "What might you do differently? How can I help?" Presenting your hunch as an observation or a theory explains how a report's behavior impacts the outcome of their work without passing judgment on them as a person.

It's easier to test your hypotheses when your reports have strong self-awareness—our old friend. When they hear your observation, some folks will easily be able to consider whether it aligns with what they know about themselves. Others will have more trouble making that assessment. Take note of how your reports respond to feedback, and compare their self-descriptions to your and your team's observations. If the person's self-perception is consistently misaligned with what you and others observe, you'll need to gather more data to test your hypothesis. They may have what I call a self-awareness gap, in which case you'll need to demonstrate that gap to them with a lot more detail and data. For example, if you're worried that your report isn't effectively communicating to their teams, you may want to join some of their team meetings or town halls to get more insight.

I remember the case of a very talented person who had helped build a team for the company but was ultimately not promoted to lead that team due to a self-awareness gap. This person was very strong at certain elements of their role but had a few large weak spots. They had trouble seeing and articulating the macro strategic picture and building collaborative relationships, which were big parts of the role. They received feedback about these development areas multiple times, but they didn't seem to hear the message, or didn't believe it. Because they were talented, their manager gave them a leadership opportunity to see if they could overcome their development areas and use their strengths to shine. Instead, the project was not successful. When the person received that feedback, they left the company rather than acknowledge how their refusal to work on growing their skills had contributed to the project's problems.

Remember, your job as a manager is to make the observations and provide opportunities. The report's job is to listen and decide to act. You can't force these things. In this example, the manager used a tactic I consider a best practice: Before you promote someone, have them perform some of the duties they'd have to take on in the role in order to see how they'll fare, and see if they're aware of any gaps in their abilities. Although it didn't work out in this example, it's often a strong strategy.

Giving hard feedback

Often, your intuition will tell you that you need to give your reports constructive feedback and highlight areas for improvement. Constructive feedback can feel hard to deliver because there's a risk that you'll hurt the person's feelings. To state the obvious, these types of conversations can elicit very strong emotions: shame, sadness, disappointment, fear. Framing this conversation properly will make it much easier to avoid defensive reactions and present yourself as a collaborator who is dedicated to the person's success.

Be an explorer, not a lecturer

Instead of thinking of your meeting as a hard conversation in which you're delivering bad news to a report that they must then react to, set the conversation up as a partnership: You're exploring a situation together. Now you're an explorer, not a lecturer.

This can be hard to do. After all, you're initiating this conversation because you have a hypothesis and you've gathered evidence that there's a problem to address. You also probably have some great ideas about how to solve that problem. But if you offer solutions before you both agree on the problem, there's a good chance that you'll alienate your report. Start by making sure that you're both on the same page about the issue at hand. Then, use that alignment to mutually lay the groundwork for improvement. Just as people often need to learn from their own mistakes rather than reading about other people's errors, a person is much more likely to successfully evolve their behaviors if the recognition that they need to change and the idea for how to improve come from themselves, not from an outside observer.

Your goal is to get your report to think with you about the problem and start to generate solutions. There are two methods for getting to this state: asking an open-ended question or sharing an empathetic observation. This will make it much easier to get into a curious and collaborative mindset, and it makes it much less likely that the conversation will get derailed. Framing the discussion this way also gets you to solutions faster, because both you and your report are starting from a place of trust and shared understanding instead of suspicion and differing perspectives.

Let's look at how these two methods can begin a constructive feedback conversation if, for example, you think your report did a bad job presenting at the weekly meeting or is underperforming this quarter:

Option 1: Ask an open-ended question

You might start by asking "How do you think that presentation went yesterday?" or "How do you think this quarter is going?" These are good examples of neutral, open-ended questions. Contrast these with bad examples like "Do you think that meeting could have been better yesterday?" or "Would you agree that this quarter has not been going as well as expected?"

The worst questions you can ask are completely closed questions—ones that can be answered with a yes or no response. These can get you started on the wrong foot because they signal that you've already made up your mind about how things are going—as in, "Do you think you're bad at presenting?" An open-ended question, on the other hand, begins a dialogue and invites self-reflection. It doesn't assume a particular answer but rather indicates that you're curious and hoping to explore potential answers, ideally together.

Your report may respond with acknowledgment, such as "I wish I had been more prepared" or "This wasn't my strongest quarter to date." If that's the case, you're starting from a place of shared understanding and can probe for root causes together and work through ideas for improvement. But if they respond with denial, such as "The presentation was pretty good!" or "All's well," you may want to try Option 2.

Option 2: Share an empathetic observation
Sharing an empathetic observation can start the conversation on a supportive, fact-based footing and will allow you to work on solutions together. Again, be sure to frame it as a neutral observation, not a judgment. For example, try telling your report, "I was thinking about that presentation you gave. It was so strong at the start, but I thought it could have been even more impactful at the end. What did you think?" If they ask for more information, you might say, "I noticed your talking points became less concise toward the end, for example." Or, if it's a work delivery issue, you might say, "I noticed that the last two projects you owned each missed their deadlines by two weeks. Is there something I can help with? Something I should know?"

Make the observation supportive, objective, and specific instead of emotional and generic. More emotional and generic versions might be "I feel like you've gotten a lot worse at making presentations lately," or "Things have been slipping for a while, huh?" Generalities and judgments put people back on their heels, whereas specific, empathetic observations open a dialogue.

When you share the observation, own it. Make sure the person knows that you're not trying to assume their reality; rather, you're trying to share your reality with them. Someone once said to me, "Feedback is just holding up a mirror and describing the image you see." You're not describing what the person actually looks like, just your perception of them—which may or may not be reality. Own it as such and involve your report in the conversation. Even if your report's reaction isn't "I totally agree," stating something as an observation is a neutral way to start the discussion. You're simply reflecting your experience of them, not asking them to confirm your criticism.

If going directly to an empathetic observation isn't working, try a few cycles of reverting to Option 1 and asking an open-ended question. If the person's answer is still "I think the presentation was great!" it may be time to give your own answer: "Huh. My impression was that it was not that great. For example…" It may take a few rounds before you arrive at a common understanding of the development area, but it's nearly always possible. People are more self-aware than you might expect.

That said, if the person is not self-aware and presenting additional data doesn't help close that self-awareness gap, you may need to make a change. (I cover this in more detail in the section on managing low performers on page 386.) Someone who is not self-aware is not necessarily a low performer, but it can be challenging or even impossible to coach such a person to improve and scale with their role, so they often become low performers.

Creating a culture of informal feedback

Companies often invest in their formal review processes but forget to examine their culture of informal feedback: the one-off pieces of advice or observations that people offer to help their colleagues and reports in their day-to-day work.

When I joined Stripe, there was a strong—almost too strong—culture of commenting on one another's work, and a lot of transparency on every piece of work product to enable this. When I say "too strong," I mean that a lot of the feedback was quite direct and lived in written comments and Slack messages, which could feel abrupt and intimidating for new people. With scale, both the amount of work product a person can absorb and the amount of time others have to comment on it has waned. But one practice that has persisted, which is also a form of expressing our "Users first" principle, is that before anything is sent out to a large group, the whole company, or anyone externally, we test the content with a small group for feedback. The people who do this the most are the CEO and the president: the cofounders. This sets the example for everyone, from leaders onward. It transmits the value of humility, collaboration, and respect for the time that the reader or viewer might take to absorb the content once you send it out into the world.

What Stripe does less well is bidirectional, informal feedback. We haven't cultivated a fully open culture where people frequently speak up and say something constructive without necessarily being asked. I can attribute that to fewer examples set by leaders, to our rapid growth, and to the fact that new folks lack the confidence to share feedback, or perhaps to our emphasis on generosity and kindness to one another. (Again, I think feedback is a kindness, but not everyone does.) No matter the cause, it's something for us to work on.

Companies are well served by taking the time to examine their culture of feedback. If it's found wanting, leaders are ultimately the ones who will steer any changes. That investment is worthwhile because if your company hasn't built a strong muscle for informal feedback, the formal review process can feel very destabilizing. People go into it not knowing where they stand.

To build a healthy feedback culture, model the behavior in both team meetings and 1:1s. As I mentioned earlier, "Praise publicly and criticize

"I really like it when people can disagree with each other, but you have to create the environment for it. In a business environment, you need to be brutally honest, and to be brutally honest you can't have a culture that's brutal."

—**Don Hall**, executive chairman and former CEO, Hallmark

privately" is a good rule of thumb. This largely holds true, especially for individuals, but I do make a distinction between team and individual feedback. Often, team feedback—that is, feedback about the performance of the team—should be data-driven and can be presented as an honest assessment of how things are going. Your team should come to expect that you'll tell them honestly whether you think they performed well last quarter or whether a project was executed well. Talking about that publicly, focusing on what you all learned and what the team can do differently to improve, helps build an environment of learning and open feedback.

You should also personally solicit and welcome feedback, especially when you're still setting the tone of a working relationship—when new teams are forming norms or when you're just starting to manage a new employee. For example, if you've just tried out a new meeting format, set the expectation up front that you want feedback on how the meeting went. If your team already feels comfortable sharing ideas, you could do this publicly by going around the room and asking for feedback. The team may not have fully built that norm yet, so you can also follow up privately with individuals.

Asking for feedback
Since the best way to create a culture of feedback is to ask for feedback yourself, here are some pointers on how to do that openly and often:

- **Ask on different occasions and through different forums**. Explicitly ask for feedback in 1:1s, during or after meetings, over email, and in work sessions. Phrasing the ask as a request for something you can improve makes it clear to the person that you actively want the feedback. For example, instead of asking "How do you think that meeting went?," you could ask, "What could I have done differently in that meeting?" Or, in a 1:1, instead of asking "Is there anything else on your mind?" you could ask, "What do you think I can do to make this project more successful?" Thank the person for their feedback. Don't try to explain the choices you made, or you risk appearing defensive or sending a signal that the feedback is not welcome or respected.
- **Normalize the practice of giving feedback**. If you were given feedback in private, consider mentioning this in your next team meeting. This sets a norm that giving and receiving feedback is welcome and normal.
- **Let the feedback sit**. When presented with feedback, it's tempting to problem-solve or try to explain what happened. I'm not always the best at refraining from doing this, but I've come to understand that it can sound defensive, even if you don't mean it that way. Instead, repeat the feedback to ensure you've heard the other person accurately,

"I encourage [the team] to give me feedback, good or bad, in front of others. When they see others doing it to me, they see the example. I also give them mandatory reading: *The Speed of Trust* by Stephen Covey.[69]

Nothing is personal. We want to make everything open and transparent.

Initially, some people don't feel comfortable with this model. But if you really want to improve and become more self-aware, you need it. We've adopted a lot of this from Ray Dalio's *Principles* book.[70]"

—**Eric Yuan**, founder and CEO, Zoom

then thank them for sharing it. If you do want help problem-solving, return to the topic at a later time to ask for their partnership in addressing the issue.

- **Follow up on the feedback**. At a future point, tell the person who's given you the feedback whether and how you plan to act on it. Sometimes you'll determine that the feedback is valid but you'll decide not to prioritize it. Other times you might decide that you want to dig in more. But even if you don't act on it, it's important that the person knows they were heard.

The formal review process

I'm not a believer in the recent trend of abolishing formal performance reviews in favor of "continuous feedback." Although I do believe continuous feedback—in both directions—is a hallmark of a strong employee-manager relationship, I don't think it should replace a written document. Done right, a formal written review is a summary of ongoing feedback conversations and a good place to outline development plans. If your company is growing quickly, it's also unlikely that all managers are delivering continuous feedback. The written review process will catch those cases where not enough feedback is being shared.

Alongside the written review process, you likely have a mechanism to assign employees a performance designation or rating and submit people for promotion to the next job level. If you don't, I suggest you build one. When I talk to people at companies that don't have formal performance reviews, I often find that promotion and performance rating processes are still taking place in some form, but they're happening behind the scenes—often without the knowledge of the person being "reviewed." If employees discover that this is happening out of sight, it can undermine trust. Instead, your assessment and recognition processes should be transparent, and you should guard against them becoming political and ineffective.

To build trust in the performance assessment system, people need to know how they're going to be measured, that the measurement will be considered fairly, and how results will lead to recognition and reward (additional responsibility, promotions, or compensation increases). To do this, you need:

- A talent strategy—this could be as simple as "pay for performance," i.e., performance-based compensation rewards
- Rubrics for how someone's performance will be measured—see the section on job levels and ladders on page 179
- Agreement on how to assess results against those rubrics
- A program to capture performance feedback and promotion nominations via written and numeric assessments

"The people I tend to hire and work with, we tend to be compassionately blunt with each other. Literally everyone I work with tends to feel comfortable saying 'You could have done that thing better.'

One of the earliest guys I hired to do a bunch of the management stuff at SocialNet was very frustrated that I wasn't enabling him to do the things he needed to do. His comment was 'I wouldn't hire you to run a McDonald's!' I was like, 'I wouldn't hire me to run a McDonald's, either. It would be a disaster.'

Then I asked, 'Why are you saying that?' He said, 'Well, we need to do this, this, and this, and this in the project management. And you're not enabling me to do that.' I was like, 'All right, let's talk about how we enable you to do that.'"

—**Reid Hoffman**, partner, Greylock Partners,
   cofounder and former executive chairman, LinkedIn

- A clearly communicated process for calibrating performance assessments across teams, so that individuals know there's a system in place to equalize treatment of people at the same level in the same role, and more broadly for everyone at that level across the company
- A compensation philosophy and a means for the performance and promotion processes to feed into any compensation outcomes

The manager plays a critical role in making sure the process functions as it should. If you've managed well, there are no surprises—you're merely documenting the conversations you've already had with your direct report. Ideally, if they're doing well, you're also marking a moment that results in a formal reward like a promotion, a raise, or a cash bonus. To state the obvious, you should never promise such an award before the company process has taken place—you don't know what the outcome will be! It's better to talk about it conceptually and keep coaching your report until you can officially take action. Still, these processes will hopefully culminate in a tangible moment of accomplishment for your direct report, which will be rewarding for both of you.

Minimum viable people processes
Luckily, there are increasingly good tools on the market to help manage people-related processes. Even better, the newer ones are more customizable to whatever process you design to best suit your company.

I remember one early Stripe leadership team offsite where I made the case for implementing a basic performance process. I explained that we could spend a lot of time designing something unique and custom to Stripe but that I thought our time would be better spent on product priorities and that we should instead implement a basic system as a starting point. This is a good example of when perfect can be the enemy of good. Oftentimes, seeking perfection in your performance process results in having nothing at all in place, which is far worse than having something that's just fine or good.

To me, the most fundamental elements of a strong formal review process are performance feedback, calibration, and compensation structures.

Performance feedback
Performance reviews are formal check-ins to assess how well an employee has been meeting the responsibilities outlined in their role charter and laid out at a high level in the job ladder. They can also help you identify top talent as you scale—a time when it's especially critical to understand your talent landscape, and when company leaders can no longer personally oversee every employee's work.

These reviews can be conducted on various timelines, though they're most often completed annually. They often consist of feedback from peers

"Making someone understand that they're not just a number goes a long way, in that they will give something back to you. I do that with my cooks, and I do that with my management.

You have to be able to listen. Don't just be a boss. You have to be your own leader, but they also have to lead you, sometimes. I want a director of operations who comes to me and maybe tells me that I'm wrong, or tells me, 'Chef, I think I have something that we need to think about.'"

—**Dominique Crenn**, owner and chef, Atelier Crenn, Michelin three-star restaurant

and direct reports, if the report under review is a manager, in addition to the main content: a manager's assessment of the employee's performance. Performance reviews are a good way to summarize the coaching intuitions you've shared with your reports about strengths and areas for development.

No matter your company process or timeline, I recommend managers hold performance review discussions with their reports semi-regularly—at least quarterly or biannually. As I mentioned earlier, the company process should mark the point where you formalize the feedback you've already been exchanging with your reports. This is also a moment to return to your career conversations and talk about your employees' long-term development plans.

Here's an overview of the core elements of the company process:

Peer reviews

Have the employee select three to five peers to submit brief feedback; the manager should agree that these are the best peers to provide input. Some prompts for the peer reviews:

- Share a couple sentences on how you work with this individual and how closely you work together.
- Review the relevant job ladder and share which capability you believe is a strength of your peer and how you've observed it in action.
- Share one capability from the job ladder that you think your peer might improve upon. Provide suggestions on how they might do so.
- Review our operating principles and note which one you feel your peer most embodies. Provide an example of how they embody this operating principle.

Self-assessment

Simultaneously, an employee should submit their own input, with prompts like:

- Submit a short summary of your top contributions and accomplishments over the relevant time period.
- Share a brief write-up of one capability from the job ladder that you excel at and what results you achieved using this capability.
- Share one area of development from the job ladder and ideas on how you might improve. Include thoughts on how your manager could support you and your development.

Manager review

A manager should read these two components and submit their own feedback, plus a promotion nomination, if applicable. Prompts might include:

- Submit a short summary of your employee's accomplishments over the relevant time period.
- Briefly discuss which one or two capabilities the employee used most successfully to achieve their results.
- Share at least one area for development and what ideas you have for the employee to further build their skills and abilities in this area.
- Do you wish to submit the employee for a promotion? (Yes or no.) If yes, consult the job ladder and share a short write-up on why you believe they are ready to perform well at the next level.
- Share your recommended performance designation for the employee, such as:
  - Does not meet expectations
    Partially meets expectations
  - Successfully meets expectations
  - Exceeds expectations
  - Greatly exceeds expectations

There's an argument to be made for having even fewer performance designation categories to simplify the process, such as "does not meet," "meets," and "exceeds." How you approach your performance distribution largely depends on how much you want to differentiate rewards based on performance. It may also depend on how you plan to identify top talent. If you're doing so via the performance review process, adding more performance categories provides a more nuanced view, especially as you look at individual performance designations over time. Either way, you may want to run an additional talent review process using a more comprehensive rubric for assessing performance and potential,[71] since backward-looking performance is only one component of talent identification.

The peer feedback and employee self-assessment can be submitted simultaneously. The manager review should be written after the manager has read the peer and self-assessment feedback. The manager should then submit their feedback and their promotion and performance designation recommendations into the calibration process.

A manager's advice for delivering performance reviews

This section is adapted from a note by Hannah Pritchett, a former Stripe manager. It was sent to managers in advance of a performance review cycle, and it's a nice example of peer-to-peer advice on how to approach the performance review process and lay the groundwork for a productive review conversation.

Written performance reviews are, by nature, backward-looking, but they're most productive when you use them to set the stage for a discussion about the future. I do this by spending relatively little time talking through the review and more time focused on how the person should act on the feedback in the upcoming half. Here's the order of operations that I would suggest:

Pre-meeting: Send the review to your report 24 hours in advance with a short note that asks them to take a look at the review, come prepared to discuss the feedback, and identify what they want to achieve looking forward.

During the review meeting:

- Review the feedback (10 minutes). I start by asking whether they had a chance to review the feedback and what they thought. We then discuss the feedback together. This is a good time to test your hypothesis about how they're doing and what they should work on.
- Look to the future (40 minutes). Once we've reviewed the feedback, I ask the person, "Do you feel set up for success?" Then we spend the remaining time talking through how they can approach their current work more effectively, what new projects they need to take on to practice new skills, and how I can better support them in their development. This is also a great chance for me to receive open feedback, which keeps the conversation two-way.

I use this structure to avoid arguments or justifications about what's in the review. (If you're arguing, you've already lost.) While I do answer questions about anything unclear, when someone wants to push back on a point, I acknowledge their perspective but reframe it to talk about how the next time could go differently.

By redirecting backward-looking comments to forward-looking discussion, it's more obvious that the point of a performance review is to help the person succeed going forward, so people tend to be more open to really hearing the feedback. I also enjoy these reviews more, since then they're more like a conversation than a report readout and they're more focused on career development (in tune with business needs) than just on praise and criticism.

–

Calibration

Once a company has formal performance review practices in place, it should also have a process by which groups of managers and leaders compare results across their performance assessments to seek fairness. This helps managers evaluate whether people at the same level with the same contribution and output are being assessed in the same manner, and it helps avoid situations where one manager gives someone an "exceeds expectations" and a promotion while another manager gives a person with a similar role and the same work output and effectiveness a "meets expectations." This alignment process is often called calibration, and it should serve as a check on managers who are too lenient or too tough with their designations and promotion recommendations. The key is for the company and the people team to scale this process to the right level of depth without it becoming too time-consuming or, frankly, too political. If you're growing quickly, it will need constant adaptation.

Calibration should accompany any formal performance assessment process and should therefore occur on the same timeline—usually annually, but potentially more frequently if you have biannual performance reviews. You could also allow promotion nominations to happen twice a year, even if the full 360° performance review process only occurs once a year. In that case, you might have two calibration processes: one for "off-cycle" promotions and one for the 360° process and its accompanying promotions. These processes should only take a few days to complete, and they need to occur after managers have submitted their recommendations but before their reviews, designations, and promotion decisions are final.

In a larger company, much of the calibration process can be conducted using data analysis, for example to track average designations for a given group or promotion percentages between employees of different genders or remote and non-remote employees. Leaders and HR can conduct this analysis independently and follow up with individual teams and divisions if they detect anomalies. In a small company, calibration usually consists of a roll-up process in which a leader, perhaps with an HR partner, leads different sets of managers in discussing the performance designations and promotion recommendations for related groups of employees. For example, all of the Level 4 and above managers in engineering might meet to discuss the Level 3 and below individual contributor engineers. The Level 4 managers then leave, and the Level 5 and above managers discuss the Level 4 and below individual contributors, and so on.

The calibration leader should review the data ahead of time and look for outliers (one manager who submitted higher performance designations than all the others, for example), understand the rubric, and be prepared to push on any irregularities, whether at the team or individual level. Over time, these meetings should be less about reviewing each person in detail and more about gut-checking what each designation means, plus finding individual examples so that every manager can calibrate to what, say, "meets expectations" means for a certain role and level. When the calibration is done well, all managers should leave with confidence in their designations or with action items to re-review certain individuals who may not be getting assessed similarly to others in their role.

This process can become political in some companies. I think that's because it can become a performative litany of managers discussing every person on their team and justifying their designations to an audience with a bias toward "winning" approval for their assessments. Instead, it should be educational and aimed at achieving broad alignment among managers, supported by data and a rigorous process of comparison to agree on definitions.

Here are the steps involved in a successful calibration process. Note that prior to calibration, you'll need to have established a job ladder and outlined the expectations for each level. You can then use a rubric to establish assessment criteria for meeting expectations at each level, preferably with examples.[72]

1. Managers submit a draft of their performance reviews, performance designations, and any promotion nominations.

2. This draft is turned into a packet of information, ideally generated by your performance tool, that can be consulted by the calibration group. (See the chapter appendix on page 413 for an example.)

3. Ensure that a senior leader is prepared to facilitate the calibration. This primarily involves reviewing the data ahead of time for any red flags.

4. Convene a set of managers who manage similar roles and levels. Have a facilitator from leadership and the appropriate HR partner assist and take note of decisions and follow-ups.

5. Remind the group of the types of biases that might surface as you discuss individuals' performance and promotion status. Beyond unconscious bias, be aware of availability, recency, and confirmation biases, to name just a few.[73] Understand and coach the group on how to avoid each one.

6. Examine the data and take note of which managers have low or high average designations or nominees for promotion compared to the group. Discuss whether their team is assessing folks similarly to the other teams represented in the data.

7. Discuss each level in turn, starting with your Level 1 or entry-level employees, followed by Level 2, and so on. Scope the conversation to an individual-by-individual comparison as needed to get the calibration for each designation right. Make sure you agree on what it looks like to not meet expectations and to exceed expectations for Level 1 employees across teams, then discuss any edge cases. Do the same with candidates for promotion and their track records to ensure you're promoting individuals with a similar impact and skills.

8. Once you start reviewing non-managers who are at the same level as the managers in the room (e.g., Level 4 and above), start excusing the more junior managers.

9. Throughout, make changes to the performance designations or promotion decisions and take note of action items to gather more data, such as sample work product from a particular individual whose assessment sparked debate, if needed.

10. Do a final review of the data after you've made any changes in order to check for broad parity. If there are follow-up items, report back to the group shortly afterward. For example: "We decided not to promote Brian and Sara because we found that neither of their key projects had shipped. We'll re-review next quarter."

11. Roll up all of the outcomes from the calibration sessions for senior leadership to review. The senior leadership review session can ensure that the results across functions broadly align with an expected distribution (I don't believe in forced distributions, but high n counts should result in similar distributions), and that the percentage of employees being promoted feels equitable and in line with compensation budgets.

There should also be a check at this stage for data outcomes that suggest bias, for example fewer women than men promoted in a particular function. At Stripe, we also check the assessment of our remote employees against office-based employees, to make sure there are no concerning broader trends.

The ultimate result of calibration is usually a spreadsheet or updates to your HR tool that record any changes to performance designations and promotion status. Once the calibration process is complete, managers should make any needed adjustments, then formalize the review feedback, designation, and promotion outcomes in your company's HR tool. Following that, there's usually a two-week period in which managers deliver the reviews in performance conversations with their reports. This should occur prior to the review being visible to the employee in the internal tool.

Calibration roles

As with all company people processes, the manager's role is to understand the process, be prepared, and actively participate in it. Seek to strike a balance between advocating for your team members and being objective about their performance and impact in order to achieve fair cross-company outcomes. Take note, for example, if you tend to submit performance recommendations that are too harsh (lower average designations or fewer promotion candidates) or too lenient. Use these calibration sessions to recalibrate yourself!

With respect to running the calibration sessions, it's critical that a division leader assumes the role instead of someone from HR. As the leader, you should be familiar with many of the people on your teams, and certainly with all of the key work performed by your teams. If you've prepared properly by looking at the draft data on designations and promotion nominations, you'll know where to push for more information to better align your managers' assessments.

Check your own biases. Are you only pushing for more information on the folks you know? Are you more familiar with one project than another and favoring those who worked on the one you're closer to? Above all, guard against the lowest common denominators. If you think about performance distribution as a normal curve—which it should be once your company has over 30 people—it's usually fairly obvious which team members sit in the bottom and top tails. The hardest part is figuring out the lines between the assessments. Do you have too many people successfully meeting expectations? Are some of them really just fine? Ask your managers, "Would you enthusiastically rehire this person for the role?" If not, maybe there are more folks partially meeting expectations than you thought. On the flip side, are you truly rewarding the top performers? Figure out where the line is between "successfully meets" and "exceeds expectations," and between "exceeds" and "greatly exceeds." These are where the most vigorous discussions should occur, and your role in all cases is to hold the performance bar higher and seek to reward the people who truly exceeded it.

The way to guard against a political process is to conduct good pre-work—including reviewing data sheets, manager blurbs, and rubrics—and to focus on your own efforts to be close to both your direct reports and the broader teams under them, as well as their work products. When a company has scaled, the calibration among entry-level workers can be more of a data-driven process, but the more senior the individuals, the more you'll want to understand their contributions and be the person in the room pushing back if you feel a manager has overrepresented (or underrepresented) their employee's impact. Don't ask others in the room to adjudicate when it's your role to hold the managers accountable.

Compensation

As I said in Chapter 3, an entire book could be written on compensation strategies and how they change with company strategies, talent markets, and scale. But at a minimum, you need a core compensation philosophy and some basic elements to support it.

A simple compensation philosophy might be: "Compensation should be market-competitive to help attract and retain top talent, with higher rewards for higher performance." Put even more simply: "Pay for performance." Once you've set the philosophy, decide what your fixed versus variable compensation elements will be. Salaries are generally fixed, whereas a bonus program, if you have one, is variable. Many tech companies also provide opportunities to earn additional equity beyond the new hire grant, for example through a performance-based equity refresh program.

To determine your compensation framework, you'll need to establish your job levels. (See Table 3 on page 179.) From there, you can work with an outside compensation consultant or data source (like Radford) to acquire market data that can help you set the appropriate salary bands and equity targets for new hires at each role and level. To start, you'll just need enough data to set the appropriate numbers for job offers. Ideally, you should also be able to explain to employees when you update the market data (at least annually) and whether you have a bonus or equity refresh program.

Compensation conversations

Of all the conversations you will have as a manager, the compensation conversation can be the most fraught. In my experience, people usually want to know two things about their compensation:

- Am I being treated fairly?
- Am I being recognized for my performance?

Every conversation will be different, depending on what you're communicating and who you're communicating it to, but there are a few guidelines I recommend keeping in mind as you plan these conversations:

Educate yourself

Understand the ins and outs of your compensation system. What does the company reward? How often do reviews happen? How does your company's compensation compare to market compensation? A big part of these conversations is making sure people fully understand why your company compensates people the way it does. A certain kind of employee brings up compensation incessantly. In those cases, it's especially important to share how the system works and how often compensation is reviewed. Then, when they bring it up outside of the company's established timeline, you can remind them that it's not the time to have this conversation. I try to start every compensation conversation with a review of the system and philosophy and an explanation of how compensation decisions are made.

Instill trust in your systems

Ideally, your company has a well-defined compensation philosophy. Of course, if you're still at an early stage and are growing, your compensation philosophy and system will evolve over time. Make sure to set expectations with your employees. Tell them that although your compensation structures will change and evolve, you're committed to keeping everyone up to date on those shifts. If you're concerned that your people and compensation structures are under-built or undermining trust, invest in working with leadership and your HR team, if you have one, to improve the system. Oftentimes, the system is okay but the educational materials are lacking, which you might be able to help remedy. In either case, compensation and equity misunderstandings and mistakes can permanently destroy trust, so exercise extra rigor in understanding and contributing to compensation-related outcomes for your team.

Understand the motivators

Most of the people I've managed are motivated by having a positive impact and think of financial reward primarily as an indicator of their impact. For highly motivated employees, compensation is an effective management tool to reinforce their motivation and contributions. Always use compensation as a means to reinforce strong performance rather than framing rewards as an outcome unto themselves. Where possible, point out that rewards are positive indicators of how the company views their contributions. (For all of the sales managers out there, your job is much easier because you can link measurable outcomes to compensation more easily than, say, an engineering or people operations manager can.) I've also managed the rare employee who truly was motivated by financial gain. In that case, help them contextualize the reward as an outcome for great work, not a goal that the company will define for them.

Have the conversation

Don't ignore the opportunity to use compensation as part of your management tool kit. These conversations naturally follow from formal employee processes like performance reviews. Your company should have a schedule of when compensation changes occur and when such conversations are warranted. If your employee is receiving a raise or a bonus, share the compensation news in person and use it to highlight what they're being rewarded for and to identify areas for improvement. You'll have succeeded if you can come out of that conversation having clearly communicated how the comp adjustment tracks with the employee's performance, and having gained insight into how the person thinks about their compensation. Do they feel they're being compensated fairly? Are they happy, or are they actively looking to leave?

In cases where the employee isn't receiving a compensation change, it's still important to have the conversation, perhaps in a regular 1:1. Remind them that there was a compensation review process, note that in their case there was no compensation change, and explain why. If applicable, use this as a chance to reinforce development areas and highlight ways they can increase their impact and contribution. Although it might feel tricky to foreground the fact that the person is not receiving a compensation change, it will build trust that there's a system of review in place, and in you as the manager acknowledging the outcome. In some cases, the person may simply not be eligible for an adjustment. But no matter what, the conversation may yield some insight into how they view their performance and compensation, which can support your ability to steer future conversations. (See the chapter appendix on page 416 for a guide to preparing for and holding compensation conversations.)

Comparisons

During compensation conversations, you might hear something along the lines of "So-and-so is getting paid more than me even though they're doing the same job." This is when being an expert in your company's compensation philosophy and structure comes in handy. Anything from geographical location to tenure to when market data was refreshed might account for discrepancies in employee compensation; the key is to keep the conversation focused on the employee and their performance. If they keep pushing, tell them, "I don't want to focus on someone else's comp, but if you think something is unfair, I'm happy to make sure HR looks into it." Then follow up with HR to make sure the system is working as intended and reinforce that to the employee. You can't get into details about another employee's compensation, but you've hopefully built enough trust that your team member believes your assessment.

Managing disappointment

Sometimes a person will be disappointed that they didn't get a raise, or they may feel that the raise doesn't reflect their impact on the organization. In my experience, this is usually either someone who has not heard your performance feedback or a high performer who has high expectations of rewards. If the former, use this as an opportunity to have a frank conversation about their role and performance. Consider: Is this the right role for the employee? If you've been managing well, the disappointing outcome should not be a surprise; rather, it should reinforce the messages you've been transmitting all along. If you're managing someone out or providing a lot of critical feedback, compensation conversations can be a helpful tool to make the situation feel concrete. When the person expresses disappointment, remind them that you've been providing development feedback and that they haven't had the expected level of impact in their role. Refer back to the compensation philosophy and explain that the system will not provide additional rewards if the contribution hasn't been high enough.

If the employee is performing well and has received what you would consider a meaningful compensation increase but is still disappointed, make sure that they understand the system and have perspective on how they're doing. In this case, it's useful to understand the average compensation increase across the function or company. If they're still concerned, reframe the conversation: "How can we work together to make sure that six months from now, you feel that your compensation and perceived impact on the organization are more closely aligned?"

It may be that they really want to talk about getting promoted, so focus on what that might take. If they're truly doing well, work hard to provide them with supporting details (for example, "You're receiving a larger increase than 75 percent of the company") and dig into how their expectations were improperly set. If they remain disappointed, talk about how their performance and impact are the key levers for further rewards, and probe whether they're seeking a clearer path to the next level. You can't make them any promises, but you can refer to the job ladder and be more specific about what capabilities they'll need to demonstrate in order to be promoted. Commit to working with them on this path. Then, refocus the discussion around their development opportunities and the chance to increase their impact and receive the accompanying rewards in the months to come.

Every company should have these basic people processes—performance feedback, calibration, and compensation—in place fairly early on. Once you exceed 20 or 30 employees is a good time to get started. Again, the manager's job is to understand those processes and participate effectively so that your employees are assessed and rewarded fairly—meaning appropriately for their contributions at their level—within the system you've built.

Managing high performers

Managing extraordinary employees can be both the most rewarding and the most demanding part of a manager's job. Naturally, every company hopes to hire, develop, and retain high performers. I recently met a CFO who applied the 80-20 rule to talent, maintaining that 20 percent of employees do 80 percent of the work. I'm not sure it's quite the Pareto principle,[74] but he was right that top performers pull more than their weight. What makes them top performers is often their ambition and motivation and the ensuing impact on their co-workers. It's in their nature to be demanding—mostly of themselves, but often of others, too. Managing a high performer can take more energy because they exert and demand more energy from those around them.

[74]

en.wikipedia.org

To manage high performers, you first need to understand what drives them and how they operate. (Build mutual self-awareness!) Then you can work on helping them thrive on your teams.

Pushers and pullers

High performers tend to fall into two groups, which I call pushers and pullers. Some will fall into both categories at different times.

Pushers are highly ambitious, and they're often critical. They're quick to recognize when something is broken in an organization and set high standards for themselves and those they work with. Pushers reliably use performance reviews as an opportunity to ask why they aren't getting a larger raise or being entrusted with more responsibility. They're internally motivated and don't care too much about ruffling feathers. And yes, they will push you as their manager.

Pullers are the types of high performers who will take on much more work than they should. Leaders and managers love them for projects because they know that pullers will almost always agree to work on something and deliver high-quality output. But pullers get burned out. They suffer silently and won't tell you they're unhappy until the 1:1 where they tell you they're quitting. They derive a lot of their self-worth from external validation and usually want to be liked. They have trouble saying no.

To state the obvious: You want high performers on your team. To state the less obvious: Great employees can have a disproportionately positive impact on your company, but they can also have a disproportionately negative impact on your company. Pushers can be so demanding that they refuse to help develop talent that has potential, which can demoralize others.

Pullers can become such automatic go-tos for important projects that other employees don't get a chance to develop and contribute to high-priority work, and thus feel unnoticed by leadership. The manager's challenge is to nurture the best version of each high performer but also to make sure those high performers are positively impacting the entire environment, not just their own work.

Pushers

At their best, pushers:

- Get better results from teammates and organizations.
- Model good work and motivate others.
- Have a knack for identifying top talent and attracting them to their projects or teams.
- Have a sharp radar for things that aren't working in the organization.
- Act like owners of the company and don't stop at team boundaries.

At their worst, pushers:

- Have an all-or-nothing understanding of what constitutes "good" and "bad" talent, in which a definition of "good" is reserved for a very small proportion of all-stars.
- Write off people they've placed in the "bad" talent bucket and refuse to work with or develop them.
- Inspire a feeling of distrust in others, who feel that their own work is not being acknowledged or that they're being put under unfair pressure to perform at the same level.
- Focus on bringing work into their team or organization at the expense of developing internal talent, becoming what I call empire builders.

To support pushers:

- Encourage and reward them for the high standards they set. Praise them, publicly and privately, for their work. Promote them. Give them raises.
- Work with them to identify top talent and give that talent opportunities.
- Work with them to identify areas in the organization that need attention. You may ask them to lead projects to address those areas.
- Help them develop others. If you frame this as a development area, pushers will often jump at the opportunity to get better at it. Talk to them about appreciating the strengths in others instead of just focusing on their faults.
- Highlight that in order to scale, they have to learn how to exert influence indirectly and cannot take all the work into their team. Coach them on how to delegate work and build mutual trust.

Pullers

At their best, pullers:

- Are great resources to lead high-priority projects.
- Can jump into urgent work that needs to be done well.
- Model high-quality work.
- Are a motivating force for the rest of the organization.
- Demonstrate energy and commitment and are fun to have on a team.

At their worst, pullers:

- Burn out.
- Take on work that's not the best use of their time or skills.
- Don't delegate work that could help others develop.
- Can be a demotivating force to others because they get all of the best projects.

To support pullers:

- Help them prioritize and set boundaries around their work.
- Encourage and reward them for their contributions in public and in private. Pullers will often not seek out reward but will resent the lack of acknowledgment.
- Before they take on work, encourage them to ask themselves: Am I the most qualified person to be doing this work? Is this the most important thing I can be working on? What would I have to let go of to take on this work?
- Help them find their own interests and passions rather than simply executing on the work handed to them. (See the section on career conversations on page 283.)
- Coach them on how to turn down projects.
- Assure them that turning down an invitation to work on a project doesn't mean they won't have the opportunity to work on other exciting efforts.
- Help them identify other talent that can work on projects in their stead, and focus them on delegating and developing others.

Here are some additional tactics that I've found helpful when I've managed high performers:

Anticipate when the work will become boring

Productive individuals will be the first to feel the strain of work that isn't engaging. Don't make the mistake of hoping your high performer won't notice that they're bored. If you're managing a pusher, they will tell you this in every 1:1. But if you're managing a puller, they will likely be unhappy in silence. In either case, you'll want to show your report that you're anticipating when they might outgrow their role and that you want to actively generate exciting projects for them to work on. Say the thing you think you cannot say: "I'm worried we won't have enough interesting projects for you in six months." Start jointly brainstorming work they would find exciting, and if they can't find it on your team, help them find it elsewhere. That's right: Help them find it elsewhere.

I think one reason for any success I've had as a manager is that I've always "played the person," meaning I've put their own path at the forefront, no matter the potential destination. Although I act and make decisions for the good of the organization, when it comes to individual development, I've sometimes found that the best opportunities for some of my reports were outside of our team—and, occasionally, outside of the company. As a manager, you hope that this won't come to pass, but you'd rather be the person who helped your report think through the tough decision to leave than be caught off guard by their resignation. And being honest with your employees makes it more likely that they'll come back to you. When people say leaders inspire followership, it's because great leaders help people learn, support people's success, and build trust that they will do the right thing, for the company and for their team members as individuals. Being honest about the opportunities you perceive for your people helps you become the type of leader that talented people want to follow.

Remember: There's more opportunity than you think

Looking within your own team or organization, you have more latitude to create opportunities for high performers than you might think. For example:

- **Even if your team doesn't have available management roles, you can still give someone a significant leadership role**. Remember Operating Principle 3: Distinguish between management and leadership. You can give them more strategic projects within the team, delegate team-building work to them, like hiring and planning, or have them take on important infrastructural work, like designing the technical architecture for the next level of systems scale or leading the business review process and presenting for your org.
- **Consider new organizational structures that give your employees more latitude to grow**. For example, instead of having one large team responsible for a certain project, build three smaller teams with different managers. Just don't make them too small. No "I" formations, please. In most cases, you shouldn't break your organization for an individual, but you can often have your cake and eat it too.

- **Focus on the type of work, not the title**. People can get obsessive about job titles and consequently stop thinking about the type of work they're doing. Consult your notes from the career conversation and think about the person's future aspirations. Catalog the types of experiences that might be required for the role they hope to have in five years. If your report wants a more general leadership position in the future and has been doing a lot of strategic and data work, can you give them work that is more operational or sales-oriented so that they can gain a new skill set?
- **Consider whether they should have your job**. Sometimes you've outgrown your team and your high performer has outgrown their role. This would be a good moment to consider your succession plan, or even to place yourself outside your own job in favor of someone new. I once spoke to someone who worked in a people analytics role who shared that some of the most interesting analysis she'd conducted was of top performers getting "stuck" under a boss. You want a certain amount of stability in your organization, but you also want healthy movement, especially for the folks under the boss.

Let go

If you can't find interesting opportunities for a high performer on your team, don't hold on to them for too long. Stalling a high performer will always come at the detriment of the longer-term health of your relationship with the person and your team's output. Not only will unhappy employees perform poorly but your team will also get a reputation for being a place where people can't further their careers.

Once you've reached this stage, do your best to land the high performer in another part of the organization. It will be a win for your company and a long-term win for you. If there really is no place at your company for them, open up your network, play the person, and bet on the long term. You'll have earned the high performer's loyalty and trust.

Manage for potential, not experience

A good manager spends a lot more time with their high performers than with their low performers. You've probably heard this management tip before. It's right, but it's incomplete. You should be focusing on the employees with the highest *long-term* return, not just current high performers. If you have a report who is already a clear high performer, you should help them be successful, unblock them, and coach them to be even better. But you'll have the most impact by identifying the individuals who have great potential but may lack the skills to achieve that potential. My favorite puzzle is what I call "interesting" talent: a person with a lot of upside who has an unusual mix of skills. How do you unlock the upside? Obsess about it. Maybe it's new projects, education courses, apprenticeship... Figure out what they need and the reward will be rich.

There's a certain type of person I've managed that tends to be the most creative: the person who has the off-the-wall idea or thinks about a problem from an entirely different angle than the rest of the team. These folks can sometimes feel very disruptive, but they're often the ones who engineer the breakthrough your team was seeking but couldn't find. The key is to listen to them, help them vet their ideas, then give them the freedom to pilot and test a theory.

Soon after Google launched Gmail, our support situation was a disaster. Gmail introduced a lot of new concepts for online mail at the time (threading email conversations!), and users were constantly seeking support. Often, our team wouldn't get back to them for days. Google had never tried peer-to-peer support before, but one member of my team constantly brought it up as our best bet. Finally, I asked him to find an external example and write up a way for us to test the concept. Soon enough, users were getting help immediately instead of waiting days for support. This person's idea allowed us to build a new support approach for many Google products that's still in use today.

Conduct pre-exit interviews and retros

Identify your top 10 percent of talent and your highest potential talent and interview them once a year. Ask them, "If you were going to leave, what would be the reason?" Even if you're time-constrained, having just three to five of these conversations will be very useful because you'll learn about pain points in the company pretty quickly. You'll likely gain some feedback for yourself, too. At the very least, you'll be able to directly reassure these folks that you're aware of any improvements that need to be made and you can outline plans to do so (if you have them). Even better, you can enlist them in helping to address the issues that create the most friction for their engagement and performance.

No one ever conducted a pre-exit interview with me, but there was a moment in my career when, if asked, I would have said that one particular leader in my division had soured me on my job and on the company. I took it upon myself to move to a new part of the company, but no one ever knew why. Don't miss out on that chance to learn more. Your top 10–20 percent of performers make or break your company, so spend as much time with them as you can. If you lose someone, conduct an extensive retrospective to find out why. Ask them why they're leaving but also ask their close friends or colleagues; usually they will be high performers as well. You'll learn a lot.

"Hopefully, people with important titles, like CEOs or chancellors, are leaders. But you can be a leader without a title, and I think that's the most effective leadership—when you're actually an influencer of what's happening around you. People get to leadership positions with titles because earlier in their career they were leaders without a title."

—**Sam Hawgood**, chancellor, University of California, San Francisco

Retaining top talent

The biggest mistake I've seen people make with regard to managing high performers is when a manager thinks that top talent is "good enough" and doesn't challenge them to be even better. High performers like feeling uncomfortable. They seek out the ski slopes that are slightly too steep and revel in making it to the bottom quicker than anyone else.

In terms of my own career, I think some of my success comes down to two things. The first is being good at understanding the big picture, anticipating what interesting work might emerge and moving toward that work or those companies. As Wayne Gretzky said and as many CEOs like to repeat, "Skate to where the puck is going to be, not where it has been." The second is identifying and unlocking the talents of top performers and giving them more responsibility than anyone thought possible.

As you plan projects for your team, think about who is going to work on those projects and whether they will be excited and challenged by that work. Does your team have enough projects to keep them excited for the next six months? What about for the next year? If you're working at a fast-growing company, you'll have the benefit of a fast-growing team, which hopefully means that opportunities for high performers will arise naturally.

Even at high-growth companies, though, there will be teams where the opportunities are capped. This is often the case for specialized teams, like business development. These teams usually attract talented individuals, but because they often stay small and focus on projects with consistent inputs and outputs, there aren't a lot of obvious ways to challenge the team. Get ahead of this and help your high performers think through the reality of that particular team, both the positives and the downsides. In the example of a small, strategic team like business development, the person might get to work on trajectory-changing deals, but because the team is small, they'll have less of a chance to become a people manager, at least in the near term. Say the thing you think you cannot say by talking explicitly about the trade-offs and being an honest coach for their career. Worst case, you help them move to another team where they might gain management experience more quickly. Best case, they actively choose to stay on their current team, and they know why they made that decision and what they hope to contribute and get out of it.

Telling a high performer they won't be promoted

It's very easy to promote people too quickly—after all, you want to reward them for their great work. But you need to make sure to do a gut check and ask yourself whether the person is truly performing at the next level and can sustain that performance. Everyone has development areas, and the best thing you can do for your high performer is to highlight those areas. If they're truly a high performer, they'll appreciate you for it and work all the harder to improve.

If you've decided that your top talent isn't ready for a promotion, own it. Tell them what they're still missing (refer to the coaching and feedback sections earlier in this chapter) and what needs to change for them to make it to the next level. I recently worked with an extremely talented person who, based on her own direct contributions, absolutely deserved to be promoted, but she had not yet figured out how to build and scale her team through her direct reports as opposed to through her own individual talent. I gave her this feedback during her performance review, and we spent six months strategizing about hiring, delegating, and operating her team for scaled impact. As we reached that next performance review cycle, the leadership team agreed that she was ready to be promoted. She was also ready to excel at her new level.

In some cases, you may have been giving the top performer a lot of positive feedback but haven't done the work to give them constructive feedback until the performance review cycle. This isn't ideal, but if that happens, tell them honestly, "You're doing well, but I should have given you more constructive feedback on X. It's my fault that we haven't had this conversation earlier." You're going to lose a bit of trust, but if you own up to your misstep, you should be able to rebuild the trust together.

Finally, if you're working at a high-growth company where employees are frequently promoted, make sure to continuously set expectations. The more senior someone becomes, the less often they'll be promoted, so you'll have to find different ways to recognize them beyond relying on promotions.

The steady middle

There is one school of thought that "medium" performers are just people who haven't yet shown their true abilities (or lack thereof). That can be true when the company is growing quickly and a lot of people are new, but given enough time, I believe you will see the entire normal curve of performance: high, medium, and low. Yes, a company can skew to a slightly higher-performing talent distribution, but I think you'd be hard pressed to find a company that's full of the upper tail, especially a big one.

It's easy to neglect medium performers. That's particularly unfortunate because they're often sources of stability, and many are culture carriers. Every manager should consider their team as a portfolio of talent, and each person in that talent portfolio should be assessed and either supported, coached to better performance, or moved into a more suitable role, team, or company.

Consider your team's context: Is it a fast-paced team with an ever-changing scope of work that's critical to the company's top priorities, or is it a team that must deliver similar work, consistently well, in a more predictable cycle year after year? The latter type of team might be better suited to medium performers, and those medium performers should have development plans and be recognized for their contributions. It should also be okay for people to reach a "terminal" level, meaning they might not get promoted beyond, say, Level 4. Provided they're contributing well, you should allow for that stasis, seek their feedback on how to improve the team, and take time to celebrate their consistent performance—which may look less like compensation rewards and more like verbal recognition and special assignments.

Managing low performers

Sometimes you'll notice that the one-off constructive feedback you've given a report has become a pattern. When there's a persistent gap between a report's performance and the demands and expectations of their role, you're managing a low performer.

First things first: A low performer isn't always a low performer. It's all about the context. Maybe there's a skill or will issue, or maybe they're in the wrong job. Your job is to figure that out and identify whether there's a performance issue, then either improve it or move the person out of your team or company.

Back to stating the obvious: A person with a pattern of low performance—again, within your team context; this is not a judgment on them as a person—is primarily a problem for two reasons. First, the low quality of their work and output impacts the overall quality of your team's work and output. Second, low performers are usually an enormous drag on the rest of the team and can be pernicious underminers of morale. If great management is about amplifying your team's impact and bolstering their commitment and motivation to continue to do great work, I'd argue that handling low performers is some of the most critical work you can do outside of maintaining the operating system.

By the time you've identified a low performer, your organization has already expended a big cost on recruiting, hiring, and onboarding that person, especially if they're in a senior-level role. Your goal should be to help the employee be successful at your company, or to make a decision and help them move on quickly.

What follows are some principles for managing low performers, followed by steps to help you get the employee back on track or manage their move or departure. But first, I want to raise two points to keep in mind as you're reading through this section regarding edge cases and the role of HR in this process.

Edge cases

Performance issues aren't always the result of lack of skill or will. Any number of difficult things may be happening in your employees' personal lives—the loss of a family member, financial hardship, physical or mental health issues—that could impact their performance at work.

It's tricky to provide one-size-fits-all advice here, but it's helpful to do two things in these sorts of situations. First, if you can, involve your HR team. There are, rightly, protections in place for employees who are struggling in other parts of their lives, and you should be aware of the legal and regulatory requirements to support them. Second, don't back away from feedback. With any low-performing employee, there's a gap between their performance and what the role demands. You can't lower the expectations of the role, but you can make changes to the employee's responsibilities by moving them to a part-time or less demanding role, particularly if the difficult situation is temporary.

The role of HR teams

If your company has an HR team, they will be a great resource for managing low performers. If you don't have an HR team, you likely have a lawyer or law firm on retainer. These firms can often provide materials or trainings on local legal considerations, and it's worth asking to access them. An experienced HR person will have seen many situations like yours and can help you identify areas of risk that vary by country, like potential legal exposure and regulatory requirements.

Once you've identified that one of your team members is a low performer, make sure to let your HR team know. But don't ask your HR team to do the performance management on your behalf. As the manager, you are ultimately responsible for your reports and their performance. You know their work best, and you are the leader of your team.

Now, on to the key principles for managing low performers:

No surprises

If your employee walks into a 1:1 and is surprised to learn that you're putting them on a formal performance improvement plan, you've done something wrong. By the time those bigger decisions have been made, you and the employee should have had at least two or three feedback conversations in which you've discussed their performance and, importantly, explicitly stated that their work is not meeting the expectations of the role. Done right, these conversations probably started as hypothesis-based coaching moments and turned into a more explicit sharing of concerns, for example "I'm worried you won't be able to meet your goals for this quarter."

If you haven't done this, you're starting from behind. You'll have to spend significant time getting on the same page with your report to explain the decision. They'll also no longer trust you, and it's less likely you'll be able to remediate the issue. This is why you can't hold off on giving your reports any measure of feedback, and it's why I recommend prioritizing feedback over almost any other management practice, especially for employees who seem to be missing the mark.

There are exceptions to the "no surprises" rule, like when a team member has done a one-off thing that's so egregious that it calls for immediate action. But in most cases, you're looking at a pattern of performance issues over time—but not too long a time—and you should have had ample opportunity to point out the problems. Waiting for your company's formal performance assessment process to deliver feedback to a low performer is a mistake. Provide feedback, especially on a performance issue, early and often.

Use documentation to foster clarity and trust
Document your feedback. Managers are sometimes reluctant to put their critical observations in writing, but constructive feedback is an important management tool that you shouldn't try to couch in vague language or throw in as an aside during a hallway chat. You're giving someone feedback because you want them to hear it—and if you want them to hear it, putting the observation in writing can help in a number of ways. For one thing, it reduces the chance that something gets lost in translation. For another, it can help both you and the employee uncover patterns more quickly and easily. It also helps you build trust, because you then have a written record of what was discussed and agreed on. Although this won't be necessary in the vast majority of cases, a written record of your discussions is also important if an employee decides to take legal action.

Try to provide feedback in person, ideally during a regularly scheduled 1:1, but follow up with the feedback in writing. If the feedback is one-off, document it in your 1:1 meeting document (for example, "Agenda item 2: feedback on the analysis you produced last week"). Write down the main points from the discussion, including how you're going to help the employee and what they're going to do to improve. If you're having more serious conversations about a pattern of underperformance, record your feedback and discussion in an email or a document that you send to the employee. If you're in a more serious performance situation, you should have notified HR already, and you should be sharing the documented feedback with your HR contact as well.

Show compassion

If you're an empathetic manager—and many great managers are—managing a low performer can be difficult because you acutely feel the risk of hurting a person's feelings and damaging their confidence. Managers should always manage compassionately, but compassionate management is not what many people do. Many managers think they're being compassionate by being nice when in fact they're making matters worse on all sides. In her book *Radical Candor*, Kim Scott calls this "ruinous empathy."[75] I wholeheartedly agree.

Compassionate management does not mean holding off on giving feedback because you notice the employee is already overwhelmed or prone to taking feedback badly. It also doesn't mean dropping your other work to get the person back on track. Compassionate management means providing someone with honest observations of their performance, being clear about the options an employee has to course-correct, outlining what work would be required for them to start meeting expectations, and sharing what you think is the likeliest outcome for them at your organization. It also means balancing all of this feedback with your other responsibilities. I once had a coach point out that the biggest mistake she observes managers making is spending all of their time on the problems and not enough on fueling top performers. To correct this, address the problem situations more directly and efficiently, and use your recaptured time to invest in high-potential talent.

Move deliberately

In performance management, timing is everything. Ideally, it takes no more than three months to reach a resolution for any given performance issue. In many cases, issues can be resolved in one month, depending on the employee's seniority and the context. You don't want to let issues linger, but you also want to give the person a fair chance to improve.

Another complication with waiting to address a performance issue is that the longer you wait, the more variables are introduced into the performance equation. For example, an employee often knows they're not doing well even if you haven't discussed the issue directly. They become stressed, which also impacts their performance. When you finally talk to them about the issue, they might say, "Actually, I've been experiencing extreme anxiety these past three months." Suddenly you're in a situation that involves their mental health, which completely changes your performance management conversations and likely delays the process. This could have been avoided had you worked through the process more quickly.

Phases of managing low performers

Managing low performers can feel like an up-and-down process that's difficult to track, so I've broken it down into a few phases, with a rough timeline for each. The process can be faster if the employee agrees on the issue and chooses to leave sooner. This is a key point: Having to officially fire someone is a rare occurrence. Most of the time, management of a low performer involves coaching or "managing out" an individual who independently decides to move on, at which point you mutually manage the communications and transition accompanying their role change or departure. And that's a great outcome in a low-performance situation.

The phases of managing low performers are:

Phase 0: Your one-off feedback becomes a pattern; form a hypothesis on the outcome (less than three weeks).

Phase 1: Get aligned about the performance challenge (one to three conversations, two weeks).
- Share your observations about the pattern.
- Communicate that the employee is not meeting expectations for their role.
- Document your discussion.

Phase 2: Agree on next steps (one to two conversations, one week).

Phase 3: Create an action plan (one to three months).
- **Potential outcome 1**: Follow a performance improvement plan; the employee's performance improves.
- **Potential outcome 2**: Move the employee to another team.
- **Potential outcome 3**: Employee leaves the company.

In this section, I'll outline and explore each of these phases. Where applicable, I'll also provide some language to help you frame the conversations you may have with a low-performing employee.

Phase 0: Your one-off feedback becomes a pattern; form a hypothesis on the outcome

Once you realize that your one-off feedback reflects persistent underperformance with no visible improvement, you need to start planning for a longer performance management process. If the person is a junior employee and their role is quite straightforward, this process can happen fairly quickly. If the role is complex and the person is quite experienced and senior, perhaps a manager of managers, this process is probably going to take a few months. As you think about the likely outcome, bake in a timeline and hold yourself accountable to it.

This may be counterintuitive, but it's critical to develop a hypothesis on what you think the outcome will be before you start the process. Your hypothesis might be wrong, and you should adjust it as you get more data. But I strongly believe that by having a potential outcome in mind you will facilitate a better process and series of conversations. There are three likely outcomes:

1. The employee improves and stays in the role.
2. The employee changes roles or teams.
3. The employee leaves the company.

Starting with a hypothesis about the most likely outcome will help you communicate expectations. In my experience, once you outline a performance improvement plan, employees will often ask, "Do you think I can succeed?" I would never give a flat-out no, but if warranted, I would definitely say, "I think it's going to be hard." Or you can say, "I'm worried that you won't be able to acquire the skills quickly enough to meet the requirements of your current role. I'm here to help, but I want to be honest about my concerns." In that case, the person may already agree, and then you can transition into a conversation about a potential departure or a different role. If they decide to pursue the improvement plan, they may prove you wrong (and you can adjust your hypothesis). But if they don't, you've already laid the groundwork for the next step.

Phase 1: Get aligned about the performance challenge

Once you've formed your hypothesis on the likely outcome, use a regularly scheduled 1:1 to deliver your feedback. How you deliver the feedback should be similar to one-off feedback (see the section on giving hard feedback on page 355), but with two important additions:

1. State that you are now seeing a pattern.
2. Explain that this means the employee is not meeting the expectations of the role. Ideally, you'll reference an objective source on role expectations, like a role charter, when you do this.

The latter is particularly important. You're moving from an informal coaching mode to a more formal performance assessment. This is crucial. Don't assume an employee understands that they are officially not meeting expectations until you tell them so explicitly. This can be a tricky moment, so I've outlined some ways to articulate this kind of feedback over the next few pages.

Delivering the feedback

You can start by saying something like "I've noticed that you've missed your deadline for a project three times. We talked about the need to meet deadlines in the past, and now I think this is starting to look like a bad pattern. I'm concerned that you are no longer meeting expectations for this role."

The employee will usually respond in one of two ways: with denial ("I disagree"), or with relief and a readiness to problem-solve ("I think you're right, and I need help").

Response 1: denial

If you've hired well, this should only be a small percentage (say, 10 percent) of responses. There are a few ways the conversation could proceed.

If you believe the person is misunderstanding or not grasping the situation, give them more examples of the behavior and make sure they hear that you're concerned. You can say, "I'm talking about the missed deadline last week and the one on project X a week or so before that." You might add, "It's also clear that your team is feeling a lack of delivery on promises, based on what they wrote in your peer reviews."

If they're disputing the facts, steer the discussion away from the facts and toward your perception and observation of their performance. You can say, "Even if you don't completely agree, let's talk about the perception that you miss deadlines. We need to work on that issue." Or, "I have personally observed that you miss some deadlines, and I want to focus on how that happened and what we can do to improve."

Depending on how the employee reacts, you may need to have this conversation over a few meetings. Sometimes they get upset with you, sometimes they just need some time to process, or sometimes they tell you something that shifts your perspective. If that happens, don't be afraid to pause and set up a new time to chat. When you do this, don't back away. You still believe the feedback is true, and you'll undo all your work if you don't own the feedback. You can say, "It seems like I have some observations that you don't agree with. I can see that you may need some time to process them. Why don't we pause the conversation to think about the discussion, and I can set up some more time for us in the next few days."

If you've learned something new about the employee and their situation—for example, perhaps another team missed a critical delivery date that impacted this person's deadline—and believe you might have been wrong about your initial assessment, you should end the conversation with an agreement that you're going to gather more data and will check back in. You can say, "Thank you for sharing this new information. Let me dig into this, and I'll set up some time to continue the conversation next week." Don't let this linger for longer than a week. After considering this new information, you will either still believe that this is a performance situation and restart the review process, or you'll want to debrief with the employee about why you had mistaken information or feedback about their performance.

Response 2: relief and a readiness to problem-solve

Most of the time, people will have heard your coaching and will already know that something isn't right before you have the more formal feedback conversation. This is great news because it means you agree that there's a problem that needs to be solved. You can then get into problem-solving mode by asking some or all the following questions, directly or indirectly, depending on the context and the person:

- **What do you think is going on?** The person may volunteer a personal situation that needs to be addressed or offer up an area where they need help. ("I just don't have strong enough Excel skills.") They may even share that they're unsure they're a fit for the role. You're looking for them to lay out the path, and you should continue the conversation down that path, especially if you agree with their assessment or remediation. Take advantage of the moment to probe further. You may reach an agreement that this is not the right role for them.
- **Do you like this work?** If they know that they're not succeeding in the role but aren't sure why, it's time to dig deeper. Maybe you'll get them thinking and they'll realize that the aspect of their job they like the least represents a skill they need to develop further. Or perhaps they'll realize that they don't like the role at all and should make a change.
- **Is this the right role for you?** In the vein of saying the thing you think you cannot say, sometimes it's most effective to voice this concern directly if you have it. I wouldn't start here, but if the person is struggling to talk about the positives of the role and if you're both unable to match their interests and strengths with the current role and only see gaps to be filled, it may be time to confront the main issue.

Once you've had this discussion, you will have a clearer sense of whether your hypothesis was correct and you can move on to the next steps.

Document your discussion

Make sure to document each discussion you have in this process. The best way to do this is via email because it provides an easy way for you to push information to the employee and for them to respond. Your email should state that the employee is currently not meeting the expectations of the role and outline the agreed-upon next steps, even if they're as simple as "You're going to reflect on the conversation and we'll meet again next week."

Your email can say something like:

> Thanks again for the discussion today. I wanted to send over notes from our conversation so that we have our discussion captured in one place.
>
> We discussed that your analytical skills from Projects X and Y aren't meeting the bar for your role right now. As next steps, we agreed that I'm going to send you two training videos on writing SQL queries (attached) and put you in touch with Bob, who can give you some more ideas on how to get up to speed on analytics. You're going to complete the analytical work for Project Z, which you'll share at our 1:1 next month, and we'll review how things have improved.

See the chapter appendix on page 418 for more email templates to document the performance improvement process.

Phase 2: Agree on next steps

Once you've had the conversation about performance issues, you're ideally on the same page about what's happening and have aligned on which path the process will take. For example, you might end your second feedback meeting with a joint conclusion like "We agree that I'll write up a performance improvement plan on the areas we discussed, and we'll track your progress on that plan over the next 30 days."

Even if you aren't fully aligned, you need to start moving on to discussing next steps by the third conversation. This might mean that you conclude a meeting with something like "Even though you don't completely agree that a formal performance improvement plan is needed, I'm going to write up a plan and we'll track your progress against that plan over the next 30 days."

As I mentioned earlier, there are three potential next steps:

1. Follow a performance improvement plan.
2. Move the employee to another team.
3. The employee leaves the company.

In the next section, I'll focus on the first two outcomes. The section on managing out, firing, and layoffs later in this chapter will cover situations where it's time for someone to leave the company.

Phase 3: Create an action plan

Potential outcome 1: Agree on and execute a performance improvement plan

If your initial conversation has not resulted in a quick mutual decision for the employee to depart, then a formal performance improvement plan (sometimes called a PIP) should be drafted by the manager and then agreed to by the direct report. It should include:

- The skills or behaviors that need to change and what improvements you need to see
- An end date, at which point you'll evaluate the employee's improvement
- How you're going to measure progress

Performance issues tend to be addressed by three types of fixes, and the duration of the improvement plan needs to take into account the nature of the issue:

- **Operational or tactical**: This can include improving analytical skills, meeting sales quotas, or increasing the quality and quantity of support responses. These are the easiest changes to observe or measure, but they can take time to take shape. Someone with a sales quota, for example, may need additional time to show improvement because most sales deals close by the end of a set period, usually a quarter.
- **Overall skills fit for the role**: For instance, you might need someone who is a specialist in analytical work, but the person is much more of a general athlete for the building stage. You should be able to assess within one to two months whether the person has the will and the raw characteristics to evolve into what the role requires, even if the actual skill building will take longer than that. Sometimes you need someone with those skills in the role immediately, in which case you can make the assessment even more quickly.
- **Behavioral or attitudinal**: For example, you might be managing an employee who is used to a very hierarchical structure and receiving clear instructions on their work product, but your company is more of a flat organization where people need to be self-directed. You should be able to see whether someone is able and willing to develop and operate in your company environment within two or three weeks.

The hardest part of writing the formal performance improvement plan is detailing how you're going to measure progress. For a metrics-based issue the measurement will be obvious, but otherwise you're going to have to rely on the what—work output and quality—and the how—work process, including collaboration and communication with others. Make sure you outline how you will determine output, quality, and process. This might mean seeking peer feedback from five people on the team or asking another manager who has depth in their domain to assess a piece of work. Whatever it is, try to avoid a situation where you and your employee reach the end of the performance improvement plan period and are in dispute about how to assess their progress.

Sample conversation introducing the performance improvement plan
These conversations can be difficult on both sides, so take care in preparing for them. Modify these talking points in a way that feels comfortable for you, but make sure you cover the main topics:

> As we have discussed, your current performance is not meeting the expectations of your role. In particular, your primary areas of improvement include [list areas of improvement highlighted in the PIP; provide clarification by summarizing the examples you've shared in the PIP outlining specific occasions where the person has failed to meet expectations].
>
> To help you get back on track, I've prepared a performance improvement plan. The goal of this PIP is to clearly lay out our expectations of you and to build a framework for you to meet these expectations. Your goals during the PIP period will be [list the achievements or milestones provided in the PIP].
>
> I appreciate that this is not easy to hear, but let's view this as a development opportunity. I'm committed to using this plan to help improve your performance. We'll touch base on the plan every week during our regular 1:1s and we'll spend time discussing your progress against each of these goals. Let me know if you feel you need more 1:1 time.
>
> It's definitely possible to meet the goals of the PIP. However, if you don't demonstrate that you meet the expectations of your role during the PIP, your employment may be terminated.
>
> Do you have any questions about the PIP or about this process?

See the chapter appendix on page 422 for a sample PIP template.

Once you've completed the performance improvement plan with the employee, you'll either determine that the person has performed sufficiently well and you can close out the performance plan, or you'll find that your employee hasn't grown to meet the demands of the role and you'll determine that changing roles or teams or leaving the company is necessary.

In my experience, cases where the employee has refused to believe the feedback, and thus the PIP is primarily a formal way to demonstrate the gap, will conclude with the employee exiting the company 99 percent of the time. The other case is where the employee understands the gap and is motivated to learn the necessary skills or change how they approach their work. The more tactical the skill gap, the more likely they are to be able to meet the PIP if they're sufficiently motivated. If the skill gap is more nuanced or the issue is more behavioral, it will be harder for them to succeed, but I have seen it happen. The manager's role is always to support the person through this process, but it's also important to keep an eye on the degree of difficulty, the employee's motivation level, and your hypothesis about the outcome. Sadly, I've seen too many instances where an employee squeaks by the requirements of a PIP only to find themselves in the same situation a few months later. This isn't good for the manager, the team, or the employee.

Potential outcome 2: Move roles or teams
It may be the case that you think someone is a great worker but just isn't right for their current role. As a manager, you can use hypothesis-based coaching to help identify what roles are a better fit for their skills and interests, then help the person figure out what other opportunities are available at your company and how to seek them out.

Usually, this decision comes out of the inquiry phase of your performance feedback conversation. For example, when you ask whether the employee feels their role is right for them, they may answer that they're not sure. That's a chance to take a step back and walk through their capabilities—refer to the self-awareness analysis of skills and capabilities in Chapter 1—and think about a role they might shine in. I've seen many examples of people in customer-facing roles who realize that they actually enjoy the analysis, process, and strategic aspects of the customer work more than interacting with the customers. In these cases, the employee might be better suited to sales operations than to frontline sales.

This approach can be tricky because it requires the right roles to be open, and there's a chance that you might disappoint the person. For these reasons, it should be time-bound. You might also benefit from an HR team member's counsel. If you do identify a role that might be a better fit for the employee, you'll also want to work with the recruiting team, since there should be a process for internal mobility into open roles.

Managing managers
Now that we've discussed the primary actions and key conversations for managing individuals, I want to spend a bit of time on managing managers.

Although many of the fundamentals are similar, managing managers can require a major tactical adjustment.

When I first started managing managers, I reached out to a coach and told him, stressed, that I couldn't keep track of the details of my team's work anymore. Worse, I didn't feel like I was contributing to the work in any meaningful way. My days had become walls of meetings. After some back and forth, he said, "You have to move from being a captain to a colonel." He meant that I had to make a mental shift from being in the weeds with my team's work to implementing a system that helped me stay involved enough that I could unblock and coach my teams, but not so involved that I was doing everyone's job for them. I also had to transition from managing to leading: setting the vision for our division and creating outlines with goals and measurement metrics, but not tactically solving every technical problem.

The main goal when managing managers is to be their coach, sounding board, and unblocker so that they can achieve their own goals and those of their team. For the most part, this means having 1:1s that are more about coaching than solving, and framing your own role in the process with the right mindset.

How to think about managing managers

Managers will often come to you with a management problem. Your first instinct might be to say, "Here's how you solve it." Instead, try saying "What are you going to do?" Ideally, you'll coach these managers through solving their own problems. Don't just teach them how to fish; teach them how to steer the fishing boat. Use Toyota's Five Whys method: Ask "Why?" at least five times to get to the root of the issue.[76] Most people know the answer; you just have to ask the question. If they don't, help steer them toward identifying the problem, then coach them to their own solution.

76
en.wikipedia.org

Sometimes, when someone is frustrated or I feel impatient with this process, I'll say, "Do you want me to tell you what I think the answer is, or do you want to tell me first?" This usually elicits a laugh because you're getting meta about the whole dynamic, and people appreciate you calling it out.

Individual 1:1s versus manager 1:1s

Once you start managing managers, your 1:1 time will shift from solving more technical problems ("I don't have enough time to get through my support tickets") to more adaptive ones ("I

INDIVIDUAL CONTRIBUTOR 1:1	MANAGER 1:1
· Where is my time going? · How do I solve X? · What's your feedback on this document I wrote? · What work should I prioritize?	· What is success in a year? · Are we making progress against our long-term goals? · Do we have the right systems in place? · Are my instincts right on X? · Do I have the right team and capabilities in my organization?

Table 10. Example topics discussed in individual contributor 1:1s and manager 1:1s.

think we're building the wrong product"). Table 10 above offers some examples of questions you might address in an individual contributor 1:1 versus in a manager 1:1.

In both situations, don't forget to ask how someone is doing. I generally tell folks, especially more experienced people, that the 1:1 is their time. We set up a mutual doc that we can both edit, and we track action items and link out to goals and career conversation notes. Beyond that, I ask the individual to propose each 1:1 agenda, and I only edit the doc to add in agenda item suggestions when I have them.

Whether the other person proposes it or not, 1:1s should start with two things: asking how someone is doing—checking in really matters—and agreeing on the most important item to discuss and talking about it first. This might take the whole meeting, and that's okay. Better than a rushed conversation in which someone tells you the truly heavy, important thing in the final five minutes.

Managing when you're not the expert

Once you start managing managers, you'll often encounter situations where you haven't done the day-to-day job of the team you're managing. Every healthy manager-report relationship requires that both parties feel they're getting value out of it. In cases where you aren't an expert on the functional role, your value-add will not be knowledge specific to the role but rather your availability as a thinking partner on broader skills: strategy, communication, problem-solving, management, and so on. Awareness of your own strengths is helpful here. (Operating Principle 1!) If you're particularly good at communicating hard decisions, for example, that might be something you can help your report with.

There are a lot of non-skill-related areas where you can add value. These might include:

- Introducing your report to leaders or other parts of the organization
- Helping them navigate the company to get things done
- Generating excitement around the thing they're doing

- Getting them resources
- Unblocking them
- Providing them with useful feedback by doing skip levels, observing their team, and bringing broader context into your performance management conversations

If you don't have the required expertise, your main job is to find them the help they need. Whether it's an outside mentor or a colleague of yours, make sure they get the resources they require to succeed. Be sure to set expectations up front in terms of how you expect you'll be able to provide the most value to them as a manager. You can do this through your "Working with Me" document or in an early 1:1. For example, in my "Working with Claire" document, I write:

> I expect you are making decisions a lot without me, and if you come to me, I'll usually put it back on you with "What do you want to do?" or "What should you do?" and help you decide. That said, if there is a big decision brewing, I'd love to know about it, and I'm always here to talk it out. I like to know what's going on with you and your team.

Finally, spend time on the ground. You may not have the opportunity to work your way up on the front lines before becoming a manager, but you can dedicate a few hours to doing the team's daily tasks.

I recently spent two hours with a talented individual on Stripe's risk operations team. When a business signs up for a Stripe account, Stripe performs checks to ensure that the business is legitimate and that we're able to process payments for them. Most of these checks happen automatically and via machine learning algorithms, but sometimes a human will review an account. I learned more about Stripe's risk practices in those two hours than from any number of presentations on the topic in the prior two years. You'll also get a lot of bonus points for sharing your observations with the team's manager.

A more in-depth version would be what our CEO Patrick Collison does. He calls it an "engineerication," and it's exactly what it sounds like: He blocks time on his calendar as if he's on vacation, but instead he spends three to five days acting as an engineer on a team within the company. Every time he does this, he returns energized by what he's learned—usually a lot about how to improve engineering productivity—and by how things have changed, usually for the better, since his last such foray.

Managing out, firing, and layoffs

Now we can return to Outcome 3 from the section on managing low performers. Sometimes you've implemented all of the appropriate feedback, coaching, and formal performance review processes for a low-performing report and it's clear that the person has not succeeded in improving and needs to leave the company. In some cases, you and the person may mutually realize that it's time for them to leave either before or during the performance feedback process. But sometimes it's on you to deliver the news that they've failed in their bid to improve. In either case, facilitating the departure of someone from your company takes work.

Most of the time you can manage someone out, meaning you and your report come to the conclusion that they should leave the company. When you manage someone out, you likely won't need to have a formal termination conversation. By the time you have the "you should leave" conversation, you should be confident that the employee should no longer work at the company, and ideally both you and the employee have had conversations that led to this decision organically. Other times, albeit rarely, you may need to have a formal termination conversation. Firing someone is probably one of the hardest things you will have to do as a manager, so pull in the support you need from your own manager and your HR department, if you have one, for help making the decision or to have a practice conversation, for example.

Having to fire someone is always a good reminder of how important it is to hire the right people in the first place. Still, it's an essential task of running a good organization. Barring a perfect hiring process—which I have yet to see—there will be people at your company who don't work out. Letting bad hires linger leaves organizational scars that take a surprisingly long time to heal. High performers will see that low performers aren't being managed out and will get demoralized. If your bad hire is at a senior level, they may hire others who also don't meet the bar for your organization. These hires can have a residual impact that takes years to undo.

It's crucial to fire fast but fire well. How you treat forced departures reflects on you, your team, and your company. The best outcome is for both you and the employee to agree that they should leave.

Just as it's best to chart a process for handling a low-performance situation, it's helpful to follow clear steps when you're moving someone out of the company. This shouldn't be a lengthy process—it should involve just a few clear steps that are the culmination of your feedback work:

1. Pre-work: feedback, documentation, and preparation
2. The departure conversation
3. Logistics and next steps

Pre-work: feedback, documentation, and preparation
Your pre-work for managing out a low performer consists of the performance management steps we've discussed in this chapter. It also includes ensuring that you've informed the right people and gathered any related prior information and work product.

Your preparation should involve:

- Assembling all written feedback on performance issues and, if relevant, prior performance improvement plans and results
- Familiarizing yourself with local employment laws (most countries have protected classes and discrimination laws, and some have intricate termination processes)
- Informing your manager and your HR partner, if you haven't already

The departure conversation
Managing out people in junior roles tends to be straightforward. Because the requirements of these roles are more standardized, it's easier to demonstrate when an employee hasn't been meeting those standards. And because these roles don't have many dependencies, there's often no need to discuss transition plans other than how to communicate their departure.

The more senior the employee, the lengthier and more complex the managing-out conversation tends to be. Usually, if a senior employee isn't meeting the demands of their role, it's not because they're incapable of doing so; they were likely high performers in their previous roles, or they wouldn't have a senior position at your company. In these cases, you'll need to discuss their performance issues in terms of this specific role and company. The departure of a senior leader will also have an impact on many individuals, so part of your managing-out process will need to focus on the transition plan.

Either way, having these conversations can be difficult, so I've outlined approaches you can take to both (note that these apply in markets without intricate laws with respect to employee termination):

Junior-level conversations (one to two conversations)
Start the conversation by summarizing the performance improvement plan and what you both had agreed to with regard to meeting the terms of the plan. Ask the report what they think about their progress. For instance, you can ask, "How do you think things have been going in terms of meeting the goals we discussed?"

Sometimes the employee will proactively suggest that they want to leave the company. If so, move on to discussing departure communications and logistics. Otherwise, explain that you haven't seen them make enough progress to make you feel confident that they can perform in this role. You can say something like "I haven't seen enough progress to make me confident that you can meet the demands of this role. I don't think it's going to work out here, and I want to agree on a timeline for your departure."

This is not up for discussion. You've made your decision and there's no room for negotiation. Try to move quickly from the decision—"I think it's time for you to leave this role"—to planning the person's departure. (In some countries, this also means negotiating an exit package. Either way, be firm.)

At this point, your report will likely respond in one of two ways:

- **They'll start re-litigating**. This happens less than 5 percent of the time. Sometimes they'll contest your decision or get angry at you or at the company. Continue to be kind but firm. Reiterate the reasons why you made this decision, remind them of the process you both undertook to address the concerns, and be clear that it was not successful. End by repeating your decision and some variation of "I'm sorry, but I don't see another path."
- **They'll start talking about next steps for their departure.** How much flexibility you give the person to plan their departure depends on company (and sometimes regulatory) policy. Some companies have strict guidelines around when and how people should depart. I have a preference for allowing people to control what they can still control. This will move the conversation more quickly to constructive tactics: How do you want to inform people? When will your last day be? How can I help you?

Sometimes you'll have a second conversation to hash out final departure logistics. Try to complete the conversation in two sittings. There are a few exceptions, both rare:

- Your employee hints at or outright threatens legal action. (More on this in a moment.)
- Your employee shares new information that causes you to reconsider your decision, so you need to gather additional data before continuing the discussion.

I'll say it again: Don't let the process drag out. The person being managed out will not be productive or happy at this stage, and you should help them move on so that they can join a company where they can be. The longer an underperforming employee remains on your team, the greater the damage will be to the rest of the organization.

Senior-level departure conversations

Senior employee firing tends to be a conversation that takes place over the course of a few months and most often will not involve a formal performance improvement plan. This is one of those rare manager situations where it's okay for things to be left unsaid. Half of the time, the leader will see the writing on the wall and volunteer that it may be time to leave, in which case there's no need to tell them that you were thinking of firing them anyway. This is a great outcome for both of you because the senior leader will be more willing to work with you on a smooth transition plan.

These conversations will usually involve the two of you discussing the needs of the role and whether you both think they are being met. This takes at least two or three conversations. Make sure HR is aware that you're embarking on this discussion. Ideally, you and the leader will jointly come to the conclusion that the role is not right for them. Remember, it's not about the person, it's about the gap between the role, the company's needs, and the performance you're observing.

In the event that you and the senior leader are not seeing eye to eye, you have to be firmer. Be direct and say something like "I don't see us closing the gap between what's needed and what you're delivering." At this point, you'll want to start moving to the logistics of the departure: "Let's start talking about your timing and your transition plan." Ego preservation often kicks in for the leader at this point and they'll want to start thinking about the best way to depart.

Depending on how mutual the situation is, there may or may not be some negotiation required to finalize their departure—anything from severance to medical insurance to the timing of their departure, especially if there are upcoming stock vesting dates. The less mutual it is, the more you should expect to negotiate. In this situation, the best tool at your disposal is a severance matrix, the framework your HR and employment legal teams should have developed for what might be offered for a termination departure. Refer to that framework and use it as a backstop. If the negotiation is a tricky one, it's sometimes best to involve your HR or employment legal partner, if you have one, to help run interference and enforce the matrix.

Legal considerations

An employee might threaten legal action when you attempt to manage them out. If this happens, the best thing to do is to make sure you have the right support—usually from your HR and legal teams or external counsel—to help you manage the situation. It's important that you:

- **Understand the employment laws of your country**. Seek out this information at the start of the managing-out process. Familiarize yourself with basic employment law, discrimination law, and protected classes.

"I had to act quickly, but in a very respectful way. It doesn't mean that if it doesn't work out with someone that they're bad people. I'm very human this way, but I also have to put my foot down. It's like 'No. That's not working out. This is not the vision. This is not how we treat people, and this is not how we run a business.'"

—**Dominique Crenn**, owner and chef, Atelier Crenn, Michelin three-star restaurant

- **Look out for words like "retaliation" or "discrimination."** If these come up in the conversation with your employee, the best thing to do is generally to pause the conversation. Let the employee know that this is not the conversation you were expecting to have and that it probably makes sense to continue it with the right people in the room. Include your HR and legal teams in future conversations or let them take the next steps without you.

Gross misconduct and layoffs

There are two other types of termination conversations: firing for gross misconduct and layoffs. Although it's less common for a manager to handle these conversations, it's helpful to be prepared to understand them should they arise.

Firing for gross misconduct

If someone has clearly violated your company's code of conduct, the termination conversation is usually straightforward, although it might come after an internal investigation and thus occur some days after the incident was observed, discovered, or reported. I recommend having one conversation in which you explain that the person has violated the code of conduct and lay out the terms of departure. Because these sorts of violations are severe, I recommend that you plan for the employee to leave the same day.

In the case of an investigation, you might notify the person that there has been an accusation that they violated the code of conduct and that there will be an investigation to interview them and anyone who was involved or who might have witnessed the violation. Let them know that you will inform them of the conclusion of the investigation within, say, 24 hours. Try to make the waiting time short. If it's determined that they did not violate the code of conduct or if the investigation is inconclusive, then you likely need to have a feedback conversation about the perception that they committed a violation and what they might do differently in the future. And yes, this means you need to have a code of conduct.

Layoffs

Since layoffs are often accompanied by broader changes to the organization—see the section on managing through uncertainty on page 323—there's generally an overarching communication and change management plan you should follow. A layoff is not a firing; it's a role elimination due to restructuring, and it must meet those standards. This plan is best directed by the company's HR and legal teams, or outside consultants if you don't have in-house HR and legal support. The communications should be tightly managed.

When something bad happens to an employee

I once opened Slack to find a message from a woman I work with: "My dad didn't wake up today." Six words was all it took to convey that someone's life had completely changed.

Horrible things happen, and every tragedy is unique. But there are, generally, three types of tough situations you may find yourself handling as a manager:

A one-time event (e.g., death of a family member or friend, miscarriage, severe injury, divorce, lawsuit)

Hopefully you've put in the work—through your 1:1s, expectation-setting, and working together—to develop a relationship where your report trusts you enough to share with you. In these situations, being able to relate to your reports really matters. First and foremost, be empathetic and express an appropriate reaction. Then ask the person what they need and how they want to be supported. Finally, figure out what resources you can get them and how you and the team can help take over their work so that they have the time to figure things out. Don't ask about timelines or work handover immediately. Usually, folks will let you know how much time they think they need and how to transition their work after a few days.

An ongoing hardship (e.g., mental illness, a sick family member, a failing relationship, substance abuse)

These situations are often trickier to manage because the employee may not be telling you what's going on with them. It's your job to be an observer of the people you work with and track their behavior. If you think something is wrong, check in with the person and use some of the tips from the sections on coaching and feedback. Don't invade someone's privacy; instead, share an observation. Sometimes it helps to share that you've observed a change in their behavior and you wonder whether it's because of an external factor. You could say, "I've noticed that it seems like you're struggling with getting to work on time for your first meeting. Is that true, and can I help in some way?" Or "I've noticed that you seem a little down and distracted. I don't want to pry into anything private, but I'm worried that something may be going on outside of work that is impacting your work. Can I help?"

Nine times out of ten, the person is just waiting for you to notice, and they do want to talk about it. Other times they might deny what's going on. In those cases, you'll have to decide how severe you think the issue is. For example, extremely out-of-character behavior might indicate a mental health issue, and you'll need to decide whether to involve your HR team.

Balance your empathy with the demands of the business. If someone needs to take time off work, help them get the right resources, but also let them know how you're going to get the work done while they're gone (which may mean hiring someone to fill in).

An employee's experience has legal ramifications (e.g., sexual harassment, discrimination)

This is not mutually exclusive to these other two points. Make sure you know your legal obligations to the company. For example, in California, if an employee comes to you reporting sexual harassment, you must make that report known by law. I've had employees start to disclose something to me and say, "I want to tell you about something that happened, but you can't tell anyone." I've had to stop them and explain, "I may or may not be able to commit to that," then remind them of my obligations and make other company resources known (an anonymous reporting tool, for example, or HR). This last point is also very important: Whenever an employee comes to you and alleges any kind of workplace abuse, you should ensure that the employee has access to the right resources to address this problem.

No matter the situation, don't compartmentalize and go on with your day if something is really off. Stop, trust your intuition, and seek help. The worst mistake is to fail to act in these situations.

That said, make sure not to be alarmist, and keep information confidential. You shouldn't recount individual stories that include personal details to other managers. Instead, contact HR or any external advisers on human resources and legal matters your company has, and find the best resources you can offer. Occasionally, it may make sense to share the situation with your own manager, but do so with respect to confidentiality and don't over-disclose. These scenarios are probably as good a time as any to apply the golden rule: Treat others as you would like to be treated. Be human.

By way of example, I once had an employee in a critical role who didn't show up to work. No notice, no appearances for a few days. I started to get very worried that something had happened to them, and I had to explain their absence to the team and to the peer teams we worked with. One peer was the person responsible for a key project this employee worked on, and thus was their dotted-line manager. When I explained that the employee had not shown up to work for a few days with no notice, the other manager shook his head and said, "When you get into management, no one tells you that sometimes people go missing." It really put things into perspective.

Ultimately, HR helped me work with our security team to conduct a wellness check at their home. The employee was not there, but we were able to contact their family and determine that the employee was handling a very difficult mental health issue. In this case, HR, my manager, and I decided that it was best that this person didn't return to work, and the employee agreed. I

"I think the best lesson I can give is: If you want to be a leader, ask yourself why. What are the rewards?

The real reason you should want to do this is because it gives you the ability to have an impact that enriches and improves the lives of others. I saw that early on. That's why I wanted to hire and support really strong people. If you can do that and you have enough self-confidence to be in a room full of people who might be smarter than you, then you can lift an institution."

—**Dan Weiss**, president and CEO, Metropolitan Museum of Art

then had to explain to the person's team and coworkers that they were leaving the company for personal reasons and that some team members would need to take over some of this person's responsibilities in the short term. I remember thinking that I thought I'd seen a lot as a people manager, but clearly not everything. Hard things happen.

Some final thoughts on management

Rereading this chapter, part of me wondered whether it might be off-putting to aspiring managers. Great management takes a lot of work, and leadership is another job on top of that. What I haven't made explicit in the preceding pages is how rewarding it is.

During my move from Google to Stripe, I was packing up some personal items from my desk when I came upon an envelope. It was full of handwritten notes from the people I'd managed over the years. I thought about recycling it, but I just couldn't. This was the purest expression of my work.

Management touches people. If it's successful, it affects their lives and trajectories for the good. My parents are both teachers, and as is typical, I resisted following their path. Yet here I am, doing something very akin to teaching, with a similar potential for personal reward through its impact on others. You never know when all the time you've put in to help someone be their best will pay off—but when it does, months or even years later, it can mean everything. Maybe to them, but definitely to you.

—

Chapter 5

Scan the QR code to access printer-friendly versions of these worksheets.

Performance Review Template

This template is meant to help managers create an outline for a written performance review. It will also help them prepare for calibration conversations. Consider including links to guidance on job ladder expectations and how to set performance designations for managers to consult.

Name:

Current level:

Start date in role:

How long they were here during the review period:
(Note whether the review period was less than a half-year and consider any time on leave.)

Proposed designation:

Proposed promotion (yes or no):

In one sentence, why did you not choose a higher designation?
(N/A for "greatly exceeds")

In one sentence, why did you not choose a lower designation?
(N/A for "does not meet")

In one sentence, summarize the takeaway you want to deliver to this person with this half's designation and review:
(You should communicate this to the person during their review.)

Impact

Using the template questions below, describe the 2–3 projects or areas where the person had the most impact this half. Keep in mind that company-building work, including mentorship, recruiting, and diversity, equity, and inclusion, should be included here if they made significant contributions.

Area for impact 1: Describe briefly here.

Name/description of project/area, including relevant context (e.g., size of project, level of difficulty, etc.).

- What was the duration of their contribution?
- Who were the key collaborators or stakeholders?
- What was their role and expectation for impact in this area?
- What was the resulting impact, and were expectations met?
  If not, why not? Include relevant metrics if possible.

414

Area for impact 2: Describe briefly here.

Name/description of project/area, including relevant context (e.g., size of project, level of difficulty, etc.).

- What was the duration of their contribution?
- Who were the key collaborators or stakeholders?
- What was their role and expectation for impact in this area?
- What was the resulting impact, and were expectations met? If not, why not? Include relevant metrics if possible.

Area for impact 3: Describe briefly here.

Name/description of project/area, including relevant context (e.g., size of project, level of difficulty, etc.).

- What was the duration of their contribution?
- Who were the key collaborators or stakeholders?
- What was their role and expectation for impact in this area?
- What was the resulting impact, and were expectations met? If not, why not? Include relevant metrics if possible.

Strengths

Describe which 1–2 strengths this person demonstrated during the review period and provide an approximate designation for that strength relative to their current level. In identifying strengths, consider, but don't feel limited to, the core capabilities of the role.

For each strength, provide a short summary referencing 1–2 supporting examples. If the person is a people manager, consider the manager ladder and principles in your assessment.

Strength 1: Describe briefly here.
- Approximate designation (partially meets, successfully meets, etc.) for this strength
- Summary, including 1–2 examples

Strength 2: Describe briefly here.
- Approximate designation for this strength
- Summary, including 1–2 examples

Development areas

Describe which 1–2 development areas this person demonstrated during the review period and provide an approximate designation for that development area relative to their current level. If a person did well overall, development areas may be all "successfully" or even "exceeds" or "greatly exceeds"; if they did not, they may be "partially" or "does not meet" relative to their current level. In identifying development areas, consider, but don't feel limited to, the core capabilities of the role.

For each development area, provide a short summary referencing 1–2 supporting examples. If the person is a people manager, consider the manager ladder and manager principles in your assessment.

Development area 1: Describe briefly here.

- Approximate designation for this development area
- Summary, including 1–2 examples
- Ideas for how to improve

Development area 2: Describe briefly here.

- Approximate designation for this development area
- Summary, including 1–2 examples
- Ideas for how to improve

Promotion proposal: yes or no

If no:

- When might they be ready to uplevel (H1, H2, or later)?
- Briefly, what do they need to do for promotion in the future or, for higher levels, to grow in their career?

If yes:

- How long has the person been demonstrating next-level capabilities and behaviors?
- Provide 1–2 examples of how this person has been demonstrating next-level capabilities and behaviors.
- In 1–2 sentences, what is the primary area for development at the next level? (This is not meant to prevent upleveling but to proactively identify next steps in the person's career development.)

Compensation Conversations Preparation and Guide

Compensation conversations link pay to performance and influence individuals' sense of trust and fairness. They are among the most critical discussions a manager has. The purpose of this document is to help you prepare, especially for what may be tougher conversations.

Timeline and resources

Outline your company timeline and link to any important resources, such as fact pages about your compensation program and manager education guides.

Preparation

Be sure you understand and can explain the compensation philosophy.

Prepare at the individual level:

- Think through each person's story, including their current career stage, date of last uplevel, and the size of their last salary increase.
- Try to gauge what the person may be expecting based on this data and anticipate how any compensation changes may align with or disappoint those expectations.

Be prepared to own the message:

- Be ready to move flexibly with the conversation. This may include a blend of teaching, active listening, congratulating, or working through a tough message.
- If the person received a promotion or increase: Celebrate! Recognize the person and reinforce the impact and behaviors they've demonstrated. However, do not set the expectation that they will receive the same total increase moving forward.
- If a misalignment of expectations arises: Be ready for a reaction. Money affects people personally, so it can be an emotional subject. Own the results, even if the message is difficult or disappointing. Empathize and listen, but be careful not to apologize or make promises about a future outcome you can't guarantee. Consider tying the outcome to performance or another rationale, as needed.
- Other tips: Remember to communicate even if there is no change in compensation. If you don't know the answer to a question, say that and offer to circle back once you've gathered more information.

Outline of a compensation discussion

Check for understanding:

- Ask the person if they've reviewed and understand our philosophy. If the answer is no, take a moment to explain it to them and refer them to resources.
- Answer any questions they have. If you're not sure of the answer, commit to coming back with an answer at a later date.

Describe the outcome of the process:

- Remind them of their current compensation.
- Share or affirm their base salary for the coming year. If there has been an increase, celebrate it! Point to the critical work the person delivered and talk about their positive trajectory. Highlight the areas for further development you're working on together. If there is no change, refer back to the program design and, if appropriate, tie the compensation outcomes to performance and the development areas you're working on together.
- Share their target bonus for the coming year. If there's a change, highlight it.

Open it up for discussion:

- Create space for questions.
- Move with the conversation (congratulations, working through concerns, etc.).
- Reinforce that you value their contributions to the company and the team.

Performance Improvement Documentation Templates

Initial documentation of feedback after meeting

(1:1 and/or performance review of "partially meets expectations")

[Name],

I wanted to recap what we discussed [yesterday/over the past few weeks] in our [1:1/performance review].

We talked about you not currently meeting the expectations for [area of development]. You have [summarize performance relative to expectation]. A few examples that we discussed related to these areas were:

- [Example of not meeting expectations: the situation, the observable behaviors, and the impact they had]
- [Additional example of not meeting expectations]

In order to improve on the areas identified above and bring your performance in line with the company's expectations of you, you will need to work on:

- [Performance expectation expressed as an actionable next step]
- [Additional performance expectation expressed as an actionable next step]

If you focus your effort on these areas, I think you can quickly make the necessary improvements. We'll start checking in on these goals weekly for the next [X] weeks, to make sure you're continuing to improve in these areas.

As your manager, I'm here to support you—please let me know how I can help. My goal is to see you get back on track and succeed in your role here!

Progress update

[Name],

I'm following up to summarize what we discussed in our 1:1 yesterday with regard to the areas of improvement to get you back on track.

[Restate performance expectation from initial feedback.]

You have [describe performance relative to expectation and provide progress assessment]. Specifically, a few examples that demonstrate progress are:

- [Example related to progress: the situation, the observable behaviors, and they impact they had]
- [Additional example related to progress]

You should continue [doing X] and also [examples of what else they can do].

[Restate performance expectation from initial feedback.]

As we discussed, [area of development] still needs to improve.

- [Example of what behavior needs to change: the situation, the observable behaviors, and the impact they had]
- [Additional example of what behavior needs to change]

Please note again that [area of improvement] is a part of your core role, and it is critical that you demonstrate this in order to meet expectations of [ladder and level].

For both of these areas of development, we'll continue to check in over the next few weeks.

Employee getting back on track

[Name],

Over the past [time period], we have talked about you improving your performance in [area of development]. You have [summarize performance relative to expectation]. A few recent examples related to these areas were:

- [Example of meeting expectations: the situation, the observable behaviors, and the impact they had]
- [Additional example of meeting expectations]

You have been demonstrating good progress, and I can confirm that you are meeting performance expectations for your role and level. I expect you to sustain this performance, and we'll continue to monitor these areas in our 1:1s.

It's great to see you're back on track!

Insufficient progress (after a reasonable period)

[Name],

Over the past [time period], we have talked about you not currently meeting the expectations for [area of development]. You have [summarize performance relative to expectation and the impact]. A few recent examples related to these areas were:

- [Example of not meeting expectations: the situation, the observable behaviors, and the impact they had]

- [Additional example of not meeting expectations]

I recognize that you have been putting in some additional effort. However, I am concerned that these examples are further indication that the feedback we've been discussing for the last several weeks has not been addressed.

At our next 1:1, I think we should realistically discuss whether you are going to be able to meet performance expectations for [ladder and level]. I know this is difficult to hear, but I want to make sure that you understand the situation.

Performance Improvement Plan Template

Note: This template may need to be adapted for different geographical jurisdictions.

A performance improvement plan (PIP) is a signed, standalone document that outlines clear performance expectations for a person, identifying areas in need of development and setting deadlines to measure success. The duration of a PIP should provide a reasonable amount of time to fairly assess a person's performance against set metrics (typically four to six weeks). By the end of a PIP, the person is either successfully meeting performance expectations for their role and level or is likely transitioning out.

A PIP should not be the first time a person receives performance feedback. You should have already had several documented conversations identifying areas needing development, including providing examples of the person's performance gaps and offering support to empower them to meet expectations.

Performance improvement plan

Name:

Manager:

Date:

As we have previously discussed, and as outlined below, your performance has not met expectations for your role and level. The goal of this performance improvement plan is to identify areas for development and provide you with the opportunity to improve your performance. We want you to have the tools and resources you need to perform at your best and succeed.

Role expectations

You are expected to know, understand, and meet the performance standards of your role. As a [role], we expect you to [main goal of role and impact]. In order to achieve this, the following duties are an imperative part of your success:

- [Include 3–5 points summarizing key expectations for the role based on job description, level, and ladder. These should specifically relate to areas in need of improvement.]

Areas for improvement

Although you meet some of the skills and abilities of your role, there are specific areas where you are not consistently meeting expectations.

Specifically, the following areas require immediate improvement:

Area of improvement 1
- Description of expected standard and how this standard relates to the company; consider operating principles
- Description of gap or deficiency in relation to expectation (where is the person falling short?) and what the impact is on the project or team
- Examples: Share specific, demonstrable examples of where the employee has not met the expectation, including dates

Area of improvement 2
- Description of expected standard
- Description of gap or deficiency
- Examples

Area of improvement 3
- Description of expected standard
- Description of gap or deficiency
- Examples

Improvement goals and targets

To help you form an action plan to improve your performance in the areas listed above, I've created specific goals and targets that I expect you to meet during the course of this PIP. In order to pass this PIP, you must accomplish the following goals:

Area of improvement 1

- Goal and time frame: What do you want to see the person accomplish and when? What does success look like?

- Deliverable: What is the expectation for improvement? How will the person demonstrate that they have accomplished this goal?

Area of improvement 2

- Goal and time frame

- Deliverable

Area of improvement 3

- Goal and time frame

- Deliverable

Milestones

In the PIP period, I expect you to complete the following projects within the deadlines provided:

- [Project 1] by [deadline]

- [Project 2] by [deadline]

- [Project 3] by [deadline]

Resources

We are committed to helping you achieve these improvement goals and targets, meet expectations, and pass this PIP.

I am available to help you prioritize and remove or navigate any blockers that you encounter during the PIP. Please note that while there are a variety of resources available to you, you are expected to take initiative and demonstrate self-direction when pursuing the goals set out in this PIP.

If you feel that you need additional support or training in a particular area during the PIP, please raise this with me so that we can discuss the best way forward. I encourage you to take advantage of educational resources such as [insert relevant links] to build your skill set. Please also feel free to reach out to your HR partner, [name], if you need additional support or guidance.

Progress checks and evaluation
We will meet every week to discuss your progress against the PIP. Please keep notes and records of your accomplishments and any blockers so that we can discuss them.

We will evaluate your success in the PIP in [X] weeks, at the conclusion of this PIP on [date]. Please note, however, that I may terminate the PIP at any time prior to its conclusion. The fact that you have entered into a PIP for [X] weeks in no way guarantees employment for that period of time. This PIP does not change the at-will nature of your employment, meaning that you or the company may terminate your employment at any time for any reason, with or without notice.

Given the duration and seriousness of your performance deficiencies, failure to successfully meet the expectations outlined in this PIP may result in termination of your employment. If you successfully complete the PIP, please note that you must maintain this level of performance moving forward, and further underperformance may result in termination of your employment without a further PIP.

Summary

This performance improvement plan is an important time for you to focus on your areas for development and demonstrate that you are able to meet all of the performance expectations for your role. I am committed to being clear in my feedback and guidance to you in order to provide you with the best opportunity for success at this company. Please feel free to reach out to me at any time with questions you have about the process.

I have read this performance improvement plan, discussed it with my manager, and understand the information and expectations it includes.

_____

Employee signature

_____

Manager signature

Managing Out Checklist

☐ Provide feedback on performance issues.

☐ Document the feedback.

☐ If relevant, run a formal performance improvement process.

☐ Familiarize yourself with local employment regulations.

☐ Inform your manager and your HR partner, if you have one.

☐ Hold the coaching-out conversation with your report.

☐ Agree on the timeline for leaving and the communication plan.

☐ Announce the departure to your team or organization and any transition plan details if their role requires immediate coverage.

Conclusion

You

This book started with an essential operating principle: the imperative to build self-awareness. As it comes to an end, I'd like to revisit that principle from a different perspective.

Company building and management—everything I've put into Chapters 1 through 5—are centered on others. All of the systems, principles, and structures I've described are designed to bring the people around you together in service of your company's mission. That is as it should be. But none of these tactics can be employed to their greatest effect, or at full power, when you yourself are not strong. Although your team can sometimes carry you, if you're not working at your highest level, they will struggle to do so too. In order to successfully use everything I've included in this book, you need to manage yourself, your energy, and your career. You also need to take time to foster your relationships with your managers, colleagues, and company leaders, especially founders.

I'm often asked about how I've done these things myself over the last few decades at high-growth companies. So I'd like to leave you with a few thoughts, in hopes that they'll help you figure out your own methods for showing up to work every day with inspiration and energy for the important work of company building and managing.

Manage your time and energy

The more senior you become, the more creative reality gets at finding ways to beat you up every day. You will have days—sometimes many in a row—when your highest performer is threatening to quit, a top customer has just informed you that they're moving to a competitor, you're leading a company-wide meeting the next day and haven't had time to prepare, and the cross-functional project you kicked off last week is already going off the rails. Many people don't have the psychological strength and resilience to keep going. In *The Hard Thing About Hard Things*, Ben Horowitz calls this "the struggle," when "nothing is easy and nothing feels right."[77]

To make it all work, you have to learn how to manage your time and energy. First, diagnose what gives and takes your energy. The easiest way to do this is to map out your good and bad days and track what activities add to and detract from your energy. An easy tactic is to keep check marks on your calendar of good days and bad days. After a month, look at all the good days and all the bad days, and then the good weeks and bad weeks, and see what trends jump out. When I did this exercise, I found that the weeks when I had more than one work event that kept me from having dinner with my kids and getting them to bed were bad weeks. I then resolved to restrict my work-related late nights to once a week—a personal guideline that I occasionally break, but not often. Your goal is to study what combination of time spent on which activities creates your best performance, then determine where you need to set boundaries to preserve your strongest self.

Figure out which tasks are easy and which tasks are hard for you
I keep a list of daily and weekly priorities that ladder up to my quarterly goals. Every month, I review my to-dos from the past four weeks. Sometimes there are tasks that remain incomplete week after week. These tend to fall into two main categories:

- **Tasks that I'm unsure how to get done or that I'm not best suited to do**. These are the tasks I should have gotten help on. I should have either immediately delegated the work or asked someone to help me work through it.
- **Tasks that don't fit into my normal way of operating**. These are the tasks that require a full day of deep thinking, which my typical meeting-filled schedule is not set up for. I need to change my schedule to complete these tasks.

Once you understand the kinds of work that energize and demotivate you, you can employ tactics to help you get through your day. I've outlined the key tactics I use to get through mine here:

Delegate
Almost everything on your plate is a growth opportunity for your team. Check out the section on delegating on page 284 for a more detailed explanation of how to delegate your work.

Give yourself permission to set boundaries
Only you know what boundaries you need to set. No one else will protect them for you. For example, I only started to exercise regularly when I decided that exercise was part of my job to be the best possible leader I could be.

Know when you're most productive
I get my best work done in the morning, so I try to keep my schedule clear—sometimes successfully—for deeper thinking during those hours.

Learn to disappoint people with your time
A request from a report—review a document, provide feedback on a meeting or input on some work—will almost always feel urgent. But managers often spend too much time on the "urgent" but less important work. There will be times when you have to tell someone that you can only get back to them by the end of the week rather than the end of the day. When people ask me to review materials, I request that they give me a deadline that isn't tomorrow, and I block time in my calendar to review the work before the end of the day they need the feedback.

A lot of meetings with leaders happen because someone needs you to stop and pay attention to something that would take 10 or 15 minutes for you to do asynchronously—but you don't, so you end up in a meeting. Try to break this cycle.

Compartmentalize
Management is about cultivating the psychological strength to compartmentalize. A difficult 1:1 or a bad meeting can throw off your whole day if you're not able to put it to the side. Sometimes you don't personally like the person you're managing. That's okay. Just make sure not to schedule all the hard stuff in one day. If you need to, give yourself transition time to take a deep breath and reset. Think about the people and activities that give you energy boosts and place them strategically in your calendar. A quick walk outside or a walking 1:1 can change an entire day.

Reframe how you think about your strengths and weaknesses
In Chapter 1, I recounted how Jeffrey Garten, then dean of the Yale School of Management, explained to every new student that their biggest strength may also be their biggest weakness. Every time someone compliments a strength of yours, think about the flip side that might be a weakness. One of mine is that I'm quite strong at operating independently, but that leads me to fall into two traps. The first is that I see work that needs to be done, add it to my plate, then become resentful of colleagues who are not helping, somehow expecting them to be mind readers. The second is that I rarely seek input from peers, even when I'm not the person best suited to a task. Being aware of the flip-side weakness should make you even more effective at using your strength. In my case, communicating when I think help is needed, including for myself, and being more intentional about who takes on which tasks, means I can play more to my strengths.

There are also times when you can only feel your weaknesses and get discouraged. When that happens, take a moment to reframe the situation. In a high-growth company, everything is moving so fast that you don't get a chance to stand still and take stock—so much so that you might make mistakes that were avoidable if you'd just had more time. But the good news is that in that environment, even pretty bad screwups have less impact because they're quickly forgotten. Change is such a constant that the entire situation is likely to evolve in a short amount of time. If you're beating yourself up particularly hard for a mistake, remember that everyone will move on quickly. Dust yourself off and be glad that you're in a fast-moving environment. Put the moment in perspective, reframe your thinking, and move on.

Focus on the important and urgent work

When you feel overwhelmed, or just when you're planning your week or day, one simple framework is a classic: the Eisenhower matrix of important–not important and urgent–not urgent. Go over your to-do list or whatever you feel you need to accomplish and categorize the items as either important or not important and urgent or not urgent. Then start prioritizing. Make sure you make time to get both the important–urgent and important–not urgent work done. The latter often falls to the wayside, but believe me, it will come back to haunt you.

Ask for help

Ask for help when you need it. There was a moment at Google when I had taken on multiple teams and was also put in charge of integrating the operations at the newly acquired YouTube. I ended up running that operations team in addition to my increasingly complex Google responsibilities. My daughter was just a year old, so I was also still adjusting to being a new parent. I remember a 1:1 with my manager around that time in which I asked for his help prioritizing everything on my plate. I ended up crying. Mortifying as it was—and by the way, 1:1s do involve crying sometimes, so don't be mortified if it happens—it was only then, talking it out with him, that I realized how overwhelmed I was and that I needed help. We quickly realized that I needed to recruit a full-time leader for YouTube, and we brainstormed internal candidates, one of whom eventually took the role.

There's also a funny element to this story. At the time, Google had a performance rating system with a top score of five. On a few occasions after this incident, I'd be chatting with fellow managers and they'd mention that they thought the top rating was purely aspirational, that no one ever actually got a five. I'd laugh sheepishly and talk about the quarter when I had a complete breakdown in my manager's office and got a five. Let's hope having a meltdown wasn't in the rating criteria!

"All good leaders have to be self-aware. If you're not able to learn from your experience and your mistakes—and we all make mistakes, all the time—and if you're not able to evolve as a result of that kind of feedback, you're not going to become a better leader.

There is a world of information and knowledge around you that you need to be receptive to. If you're not a good listener, then it's hard to imagine how you can be a good leader. Having said that, I'm much more comfortable offering this kind of perspective to you now than 20 years ago, when I had just started a new leadership job and I didn't even know what the hell the job was. I just tried to keep up."

—**Dan Weiss**, president and CEO, Metropolitan Museum of Art

Foster relationships

The reason the expressions "It's a marathon, not a sprint" and "If you want to go fast, go alone. If you want to go far, go together" are so often repeated is because they're true. You need to pace yourself, and you need to have someone to run with.

When I think about some of the hardest moments building Google and then Stripe, I think back to the many meetings, dinners, and occasional late nights when the stress turned into laughter. I treasure the friendships I carry from those experiences. You'll meet people you can reach out to at any moment for the rest of your life, and I guarantee they will be there to help. These friendships come from all corners: your manager, your colleagues, your team, even your boss's boss. Take the time to make those connections, ask for help, and share the load.

I'll say it again: Ask for help. Management is not just about building a complementary team but also about having the mutual self-awareness to look at your entire orbit and seek out those with different strengths. You can't go far together unless you're not just self-aware but also confident enough to be vulnerable and seek others' assistance.

Working well with your own manager

Leverage goes two ways. Your manager should get leverage from you, and you should get leverage from them. Your manager can help unblock your team, advocate for more resources, provide the necessary context to do your job well, work with you to identify priorities, and hopefully help you develop. You'll be a better manager if you can successfully "manage up," by which I mean being able to work with your manager to get the best results for your team and for the company. I don't mean being political, which is how the term "managing up" seems to be used more of late. Help your own manager be their best, and never surprise them with late news of challenges hitting your team or poor results.

The good news is that if you're reading this, you're likely a manager yourself, and you probably already have an idea of what makes a report great to work with. Think about the things you appreciate as a manager. Your manager probably won't be that different! Get to know each other personally. If your manager could use some feedback, provide it constructively and suggest ways the two of you might work more effectively together. It's in both of your interests to jointly succeed.

Working with other managers

Speaking of managing up, it's equally important to manage sideways. Your colleagues are critical to you and your team's success, and part of your role is to understand where you and your team sit within your organization's larger

"As a manager, you have a certain skill, which is how you were promoted to be the leader. But now you need different skill sets to lead people.

It's also important to have the broader context of your role. Ron Williams, the former CEO of Aetna, talks about the 'two and two,' which is knowing the people and job roles two levels below and two levels above you. He says, 'Don't just look at your own job. Think: How does your job work into the whole system? Think about the incentive for the person two levels up and two levels down. What's driving them? Is it aligned? If not, then get it aligned.'

Understanding the whole organization and process around you will help ensure you are aligned with your organization's mission."

—**Charles Phillips**, founder and managing partner, Recognize, former CEO, Infor ecosystem. For people to work together well, the whole must produce something greater than the sum of its parts. How does that happen? By forging formal and informal connections.

Although running into someone in an actual (or virtual) hallway helps, you also need to actively identify and cultivate relationships that you can draw on to succeed even as you're helping the other person do the same. Share information about your team's mission and goals with key partners and stakeholders, and seek out those you need to work with, especially those who might create or prevent obstacles. Remember that other leaders are great resources, both as sounding boards for handling tough situations—there's nothing better than practicing a hard 1:1 with another manager—and as sources of information about what matters and how to flourish in the organization. It's easy to neglect those relationships when you're too focused on your day job.

I suggest taking two actions:

- **Map your team's partners and stakeholders, and either hold 1:1s with them or sit in on meetings with key individuals or teams.** Share your team's objectives and discuss how you can best work together.

- **Identify leaders you admire within your company or even at other companies.** Ask them to coffee or lunch to get to know each other and compare notes on management practices and the work of your respective teams and companies. Some of these connections might become folks you can call on to test out ideas or seek advice in difficult situations.

I find these relationships also grow out of working together on a shared project for your team or company. Working with your own manager to make sure you're making connections and getting integrated with organizations outside of your immediate area of focus is also time well spent.

To return to my favorite habit of stating the obvious: Be a good peer. Honor your commitments, listen thoughtfully, and help others. Share information you think might be helpful. If you have an issue with a fellow manager or with their team, make sure they hear it from you, and then work together to resolve the issue before it escalates.

Working with founders

Founders have their jobs because they had a vision that turned into a business. Senior managers have their jobs because they made management their business. (That doesn't necessarily mean that they're good managers, but it does mean that they've likely been doing it for a while.) Founders did not train to be managers, at least not initially. And first-time founders may never

"The more you can put yourself in the shoes of other parts of the system that you're interacting with, the better. Especially if you can do it before there's a reason to. If you could better understand both the personality of the person that you're going to be dealing with and their stresses and strains, that's very helpful.

People who have that natural curiosity and that natural willingness to learn about things that are directly critical to getting your own job done—that's a trait I've seen in many leaders."

—**Sam Hawgood**, chancellor, University of California, San Francisco have seen a company operate at a size larger than their company is at that very moment.

This means that if you're coming from a place of management experience, you can provide invaluable insight into what might be around the corner simply by having worked at other companies that are larger than the one you're at right now. It also often means that the founders will question how you operate. Things that you've assumed are static components of management can be completely rethought. Founders are coming from a place of first principles, and you'll be coming from a place of experience. You can both learn a lot from each other.

Your relationship will also involve friction by design. If you're a leader, you've likely been brought in because you have some relevant experience and because you can help the company do things differently as it scales. Your challenge is to figure out what rate of change the organization and the founders can and should absorb and how you should work together to determine those changes. Here are some principles I've found helpful to do that:

Check the fruit

A senior leader at Box once told me about his experience when he first joined the company. He had a lot of ideas about how he wanted to change things, but he met with a lot of resistance. The company simply wasn't ready. He explained to me how he changed his mindset: "I would think of my ideas as pieces of fruit that weren't yet ripe. I'd put my pieces of fruit in a bag on the counter and wait for them to ripen. Every once in a while, I would take a 'fruit idea' out of the bag and test whether it was ready. Usually, the test was easy— there was an issue and we needed a solution, or the founder heard the idea and was suddenly on board. Sometimes the founder would come to the conclusion independently and bring the idea up himself. If I took the fruit out of the bag, squeezed it, and the organization still didn't feel quite ready for it, I'd put it back in the bag to ripen for another day."

Prepare for a lot of ideas to stay in the bag forever. But it's often better to wait for an organization to be ready for an idea than to push something through that the company will reject.

Build the Camry, not the Escalade

Sometimes you still want to make a change even if the founders don't think the fruit is ready. (That is, after all, part of your job.) When this happens, a lot of people make the mistake of trying to build a Cadillac Escalade when they should really be trying to build a Toyota Camry, or maybe even a bicycle. Ask yourself what the most lightweight change is that you can make, then grow from there.

In my first year at Stripe, I told Patrick Collison that I thought we needed an LMS and a CMS. He cocked his head quizzically: "What is an LMS and a CMS?" I struggled to give him a compelling answer. I could explain that an LMS is a learning management system and a CMS is a content management system, but that wasn't what Patrick wanted to know. He wanted to know why we needed such things, and why we should make a heavy investment in those platforms at that moment.

My first mistake was to use acronyms instead of explaining what we really needed: one central, easy-to-update place to house all of our training content, and one central, easy-to-update system to store and publish updates to critical internal and external company content. My second mistake was to propose the Escalade instead of the Camry. Instead of suggesting we use brand-new tools, I should have started by suggesting that we try to collate all of our content using the tools we already felt comfortable with—at the time, Stripe was using a document editor called Hackpad—and see what worked and what didn't. That's what we ended up doing. We did end up moving to another tool (and then another) a few years later, when it became clear that we needed something more robust.

As a general rule, suggest changes as a pilot. Be clear about what you're changing, how you'll assess success, and when you'll determine whether to make the change permanent.

Understand what matters

Just as you should understand your reports' values, you should work to understand your founders' values, too. Better yet, ask them to write down the company values if they haven't already. (This could get you started on your founding documents, as discussed in Chapter 2.) In particular, ask them to articulate the trade-offs they're willing to make. For example, your founders may have a value of shipping extremely polished products. Ask them what they're willing to give up for this level of quality. Are they willing to push back a launch deadline? Are they okay with losing a large potential customer to do so? Offsites are really good forums to get on the same page with your values, but you can ask the founders in 1:1s as well.

Consider your career

Sometimes great leaders spend so much time thinking about achieving business success or paving their direct reports' career paths that they neglect their own. No one knows what's inside your head, heart, and gut the way you do, and your number one job is to be your own career coach. I'm always surprised when someone is waiting for their manager or some other exogenous force to tap them on the shoulder with an opportunity or an idea for their career. It's great when someone else has ideas or advice, but you're the person who should be the expert on what's best for you. For me, this has meant periodically taking a step back and assessing whether I was learning the things I wanted to learn and having the kind of impact I wanted to have.

The funny thing about careers is that they often make sense in hindsight but rarely feel coherent in the present. Mine was no different, even though I can now look back and easily identify the big decisions I made to get to where I am and draw a throughline between those experiences. Some felt monumental at the time, like joining Stripe. Others felt small and ended up being quite important, like going from the consumer side of Google to its B2B arm. I find I'm jealous of people who have an early-life revelation about their career path: those folks who know from early on that they want to be a doctor or a professor or a designer and chart a course toward their goal. The rest of us—I'd hazard to say the majority of us—are going to wind our way toward a career path in what often feels like a bad game of Chutes and Ladders, taking one step up and sliding down three, or maybe going sideways.

So, how do you chart a career course? You won't be surprised to hear that my main advice is to build self-awareness. Much like how you manage your energy, it's critical to track which potential jobs and capabilities come naturally to you and which ones sap your motivation. You're seeking the combination of your own aptitude, innate or acquired, and your motivators and passions. For example, I'm quite good at fundraising, which is important for work in politics and nonprofits (and startups!), but I don't particularly enjoy it. I wouldn't seek out a position where it might comprise more than 50 percent of the role, which is often the case for senior roles in academia, nonprofits, or cultural institutions. Building this type of self-awareness is a form of pace layering for yourself: You need to track your day-to-day energy but also your higher-level, longer-term energy curves.

I recommend keeping a personal document, starting fairly early in your career, in which you note various roles you've tried and seek to answer the following questions:

- Were you good at it? How do you know that? If you weren't good at it, why not?
- Did you enjoy it? Why or why not?
- What did it reveal about the type of work you do or don't want to do?
- Where did you have clear gaps in abilities?
- What skills did you need to acquire? Was that easy or hard to do?
- Were you interested in the work? Did you want to keep going and learn more?

You get the idea. These can be short entries and bullets that summarize learnings. Even if you only keep a few bullet points for each position, consider how powerful it will be to look back on this document every 6, 12, or 18 months to see what you're learning. If you're hoping to become a leader, this document can help you identify your complements so that you can hire to augment your own preferences and abilities.

The biggest trap I've seen people fall into is getting stuck either chasing someone else's version of success or in a role that doesn't prioritize their strengths or make them feel fulfilled. As a side note, I'm conscious as I write this that it's an incredible privilege to be in a financial position to make these choices. Stay conscious of your opportunities, be humble, and, if you are so lucky, consider using some of your own time to help others who may not have these choices.

To avoid getting stuck, I use a 5-year and a 6-, 12-, and 18-month approach. First, I envision the next five years. I never think, "I want this title." Instead, I try to envision the shape of what I might want to be doing five years from now. Let's say you want to be a COO, which is one of the most amorphous career paths of all. In this exercise, you'd basically ask yourself, "Am I on track to be a COO or a general manager responsible for multiple functions in the next five years?" If not, you need to understand why and consider whether you're on the right path or need to change something in order to get on the right path. If I feel like I'm roughly on the right path, I shorten the time increments and ask myself:

Every 6 months: Does this feel like the right role to learn what I want to learn in the next 6–12 months? Am I clear on how I will acquire that knowledge and from whom? If not, I start tacking toward where I think I need to be.

Every 12 months: Should I be making changes or seeking changes to my role to augment my learning and stay on my five-year path? If so, how do I make that known to my manager or to leaders who mentor or sponsor me? How do I demonstrate additional aptitude via new projects or added responsibilities?

One thing I like to have for the coming 12 months is two or three potential directions my role might take or alternate roles I might move into depending on the course of my company and my own ambitions. For example, I imagine that if I stay the course, I might end up managing managers or adding an adjacent team to my remit. If I toggle to a new path, I might work on a new area of the business and learn a new functional skill. In either case, I need to be growing in roughly the time frame I'm picturing based on the organization's growth and my manager's feedback on my progress. Again, make sure you have the self-awareness to check whether your ambitions match your demonstrated impact. The more impact you have, the more you earn the right to have those ambitions.

Every 18 months: Is my five-year aspiration right? This is where you consult your personal document. What have you learned in the last 12–18 months about your skills, your energy, and your motivators? At one point when I was at Google, I was interviewed for a blog about women in leadership and found myself saying that I imagined I'd eventually end up as the CMO of a midsize company. At the time, it wasn't a far-fetched potential career path, but now I look back and I have to laugh. How wrong I was! Eventually I realized that this was not where the next five years should lead me, mostly based on my own motivators and demonstrated abilities. So I moved away from an advertising, sales, and marketing focus to acquire skills leading additional functions, like product management.

Above all, don't follow others' career aspirations and paths. Devise your own and hew to it, no matter the prevailing wisdom at the time. In order to do this, you need to become more and more comfortable keeping your own counsel. Line up your head, your heart, and your gut to guide your career in a way no one else can or will.

Company building and managing people are both tremendously hard but tremendously rewarding. Understand your energy, your abilities, and the constraints and guidelines you need to place around yourself and your work to maintain strength and stability. If you're not feeling stable, take stock and consider new tactics. Delegate, reframe your thinking, ask for help. As you gain personal strength and the ability to compartmentalize, be the manager your own manager looks to for leverage. Be the type of colleague others aspire to be like. If your foundation is strong and you're charting your career instead of letting it happen to you, you can be all of these things. When you feel less strong or out of control, marshal your resources and return to your starting point: you.

At the start of this book, I shared that I hoped it would be a resource people return to in certain moments, when they face a challenge or when they have a new opportunity to build and lead. When a player struggles, a coach will usually say, "Get back to the fundamentals." To me, this book is about fundamentals. They're not innovative. Some are very tactical, and they all require you to do the work. But hopefully I've presented a set of ideas that can speed you on the path to confidence, to self-awareness, to saying the thing you cannot say—and even, I hope, to building your own operating system. Beyond that, my hope is that you take away something—maybe even a few

"The first level [of your career] is hard skills, the second level is soft skills, and the third level is the most challenging level: how you show up emotionally, how you keep being a champion and make everything possible. Sometimes [you] have to suspend disbelief and lie to yourself to keep on doing it."

—**Dongping Zhao**, president, Anker Innovations

things—that will make your current and future endeavors more successful, not just for you but for all the people who build alongside you.

As my inability to throw away that envelope of thank-you notes attests, I'm more grateful than I can express to have had the kinds of relationships with companies and teams that are born of working together to create something new out of nothing. I know how much these experiences have shaped me. This book is a way for me to form those same kinds of connections with more founders and managers than I'd ever have a chance to otherwise. Here's to all of you, and all that you will build.

Endnotes

1.	Holacracy, https://www.holacracy.org.

2.	Paul Morris Fitts and Michael I. Posner, *Human Performance* (Westport: Greenwood Press, 1979), 11–15, 18.

3.	Nina Keith and Karl Anders Ericsson, "A Deliberate Practice Account of Typing Proficiency in Everyday Typists," *Journal of Experimental Psychology: Applied* 13, no. 3 (2007): 135–145, https://doi.apa.org/doiLanding?doi=10.1037%2F1076-898X.13.3.135.

4.	Joshua Foer, *Moonwalking with Einstein: The Art and Science of Remembering Everything* (New York: Penguin Books, 2021), 172.

5.	Bradley W. Young et al., "K. Anders Ericsson, Deliberate Practice, and Sport: Contributions, Collaborations, and Controversies," *Journal of Expertise* 4, no. 2 (2021): 2573–2773, https://journalofexpertise.org/articles/volume4_issue2/JoE_4_2_Young_etal.pdf.

6.	Colin Bryar and Bill Carr, *Working Backwards: Insights, Stories, and Secrets from Inside Amazon* (New York: St. Martin's Press, 2021).

7.	Garson Kanin, *Remembering Mr. Maugham* (New York: Atheneum, 1966), 45.

8.	Ted Gioia, "How I Became the Honest Broker," The Honest Broker, May 26, 2021, https://tedgioia.substack.com/p/how-i-became-the-honest-broker.

9.	Stan Slap, *Bury My Heart at Conference Room B: The Unbeatable Impact of Truly Committed Managers* (New York: Portfolio Penguin, 2010).

10.	"What Is DiSC?" DiSC Profile, https://www.discprofile.com/what-is-disc.

11.	The Myers-Briggs Company, https://www.themyersbriggs.com.

12.	"Insights Discovery," Insights, https://www.insights.com/us/products/insights-discovery.

13.	Fred Kofman, *Conscious Business: How to Build Value Through Values* (Louisville: Sounds True, 2014), 10–12, 136–138.

14.	Kim Scott, *Radical Candor: Be a Kick-Ass Boss without Losing Your Humanity* (New York: St. Martin's Press, 2019), 32–33.

15.	Ronald Heifetz et al., *The Practice of Adaptive Leadership: Tools and Tactics for Changing Your Organization and the World* (Boston: Harvard Business Press, 2009), 19–23.

16.	Simon Sinek, *The Infinite Game* (London: Portfolio Penguin, 2019).

17.	Big Five Personality Test, https://bigfive-test.com.

18.	Bill Walsh, Steve Jamison, and Craig Walsh, *The Score Takes Care of Itself: My Philosophy of Leadership* (New York: Portfolio Penguin, 2009).

19.	Nick Statt, "Microsoft at 40: Read Bill Gates' Anniversary Email to Employees," CNET, April 3, 2015, https://www.cnet.com/tech/tech-industry/microsoft-at-40-read-bill-gates-anniversary-email-to-employees/.

20. Edgar H. Schein and Peter Schein, *Organizational Culture and Leadership* (Hoboken: Wiley, 2017), 17–27.

21. Andrew S. Grove, *High Output Management* (New York: Knopf Doubleday, 2015), 110–114.

22. Brad Garlinghouse, "Yahoo Memo: The 'Peanut Butter Manifesto,'" *Wall Street Journal*, November 18, 2006, https://www.wsj.com/articles/SB116379821933826657.

23. "Enduring Ideas: The Three Horizons of Growth," *McKinsey Quarterly*, December 1, 2009, https://www.mckinsey.com/business-functions/strategy-and-corporate-finance/our-insights/enduring-ideas-the-three-horizons-of-growth.

24. Bryar and Carr, *Working Backwards*, 17–21, 61–65.

25. For more on how scale slows companies down and how to combat the phenomenon with good strategy and loosely coupled, tightly aligned execution, I recommend reading a post by Stripe's corporate strategy leader, Alex Komoroske, called "Coordination Headwind: How Organizations Are Like Slime Molds," https://komoroske.com/slime-mold.

26. Andrew S. Grove, *Only the Paranoid Survive* (New York: Currency Doubleday, 1996).

27. Grove, *High Output Management*, 110–114.

28. Robin I. M. Dunbar, *How Many Friends Does One Person Need?: Dunbar's Number and Other Evolutionary Quirks* (London: Faber and Faber, 2011), 4.

29. Michael Schade, "Stripe Home," Stripe Blog, April 19, 2018, https://stripe.com/blog/stripe-home.

30. Frances Frei and Anne Morriss, *Uncommon Service: How to Win by Putting Customers at the Core of Your Business* (Boston: Harvard Business Review Press, 2012), 29.

31. Greg Brockman, "Capture the Flag 2.0," Stripe Blog, August 22, 2012, https://stripe.com/blog/capture-the-flag-20.

32. Fun fact: Stripe's hiring committee meetings are called "tropes." As far as I can tell, it's because early Stripes decided any form of "meeting" should be avoided.

33. Daniel H. Pink, *Drive: The Surprising Truth About What Motivates Us* (New York: Penguin, 2011).

34. Carlin Flora, *Friendfluence: The Surprising Ways Friends Make Us Who We Are* (New York: Doubleday, 2013), 122–126.

35. "'Give Away Your Legos' and Other Commandments for Scaling Startups," First Round Review, https://review.firstround.com/give-away-your-legos-and-other-commandments-for-scaling-startups.

36. Mike Ettore, "Why Most New Executives Fail—And Four Things Companies Can Do About It," *Forbes*, March 13, 2020, https://www.forbes.com/sites/forbescoachescouncil/2020/03/13/why-most-new-executives-fail-and-four-things-companies-can-do-about-it/.

37. Bryar and Carr, *Working Backwards*, 34–36.

38. Elad Gil, *High Growth Handbook: Scaling Startups from 10 to 10,000 People* (San Francisco: Stripe Press, 2018), 52–57.

39. "Hogan Personality Inventory," Hogan, https://www.hoganassessments.com/assessment/hogan-personality-inventory/.

40. Michael Lewis, "What Keeps Bill Parcells Awake at Night," *New York Times Magazine*, October 29, 2006, https://www.nytimes.com/2006/10/29/sports/playmagazine/what-keeps-bill-parcells-awake-at-night.html.

41. Patrick Lencioni, *The Five Dysfunctions of a Team: A Leadership Fable* (San Francisco: Jossey-Bass, 2012).

42. Max Landsberg, *The Tools of Leadership: Vision, Inspiration, Momentum* (London: Profile Books, 2011), 51–55.

43. Jeff Bezos, "Amazon.com 1997 Letter to Shareholders," US Securities and Exchange Commission, https://www.sec.gov/Archives/edgar/data/1018724/0001193125165309-10/d168744dex991.htm.

44. Bruce W. Tuckman, "Developmental Sequence in Small Groups," *Psychological Bulletin* 63, no. 6 (1965): 384–399, https://doi.org/10.1037/h0022100.

45. Charles Duhigg, "What Google Learned from Its Quest to Build the Perfect Team," *New York Times Magazine*, February 25, 2016, https://www.nytimes.com/2016/02/28/magazine/what-google-learned-from-its-quest-to-build-the-perfect-team.html.

46. Claire Hughes Johnson, "Claire's Offsite Toolkit," Coda, https://coda.io/@clairehughesjohnson/claires-offsite-toolkit.

47. Khosla Ventures, "Running an Effective Staff Meeting | Claire Hughes Johnson," YouTube Video, 26:41, July 21, 2018, https://www.youtube.com/watch?v=GIiaF-W874q8.

48. Tuckman, "Developmental Sequence in Small Groups," 396.

49. Paul Graham, "Maker's Schedule, Manager's Schedule," PaulGraham.com, July 2009, http://www.paulgraham.com/makersschedule.html.

50. "Rapid: Bain's Tool to Clarify Decision Accountability," Bain, August 11, 2011, https://www.bain.com/insights/rapid-tool-to-clarify-decision-accountability.

51. Gokul Rajaram, "Gokul's S.P.A.D.E. Toolkit: How to Implement Square's Famous Decision-Making Framework," Coda, https://coda.io/@gokulrajaram/gokuls-spade-toolkit.

52. "How to Master the Seven-Step Problem-Solving Process," McKinsey & Company, September 13, 2019, https://www.mckinsey.com/business-functions/strategy-and-corporate-finance/our-insights/how-to-master-the-seven-step-problem-solving-process.

53. Lencioni, *Five Dysfunctions*, 135.

54. David Singleton, "Stripe's Fifth Engineering Hub Is Remote," Stripe Blog, May 2, 2019, https://stripe.com/blog/remote-hub.

55. Geert Hofstede, "National Culture," Hofstede Insights, https://hi.hofstede-insights.com/national-culture.

56. Matt Mullenweg, *The Distributed Podcast*, https://distributed.blog.

57. "The Remote Playbook," GitLab, https://about.gitlab.com/company/culture/all-remote.

58. Harvard Business School professor Frances Frei once shared with me this (paraphrased) observation from Carol Dweck, who is best known for her work on developing a growth mindset: "There are two types of parenting, and one is right. You can either prepare the path for the child or prepare the child for the path." (The correct answer: Prepare the child for the path.) As a manager, I think you need to pay attention to both dimensions: Sometimes your role is to prepare the path for your team, but above all, you must prepare your team for the path.

59. Rebecca Solnit, *Hope in the Dark: Untold Histories, Wild Possibilities* (Chicago: Haymarket Books, 2016), 20.

60. For example, Sundiatu Dixon-Fyle et al., "Diversity Wins: How Inclusion Matters," McKinsey & Company, May 19, 2020, https://www.mckinsey.com/featured-insights/diversity-and-inclusion/diversity-wins-how-inclusion-matters.

61. Amy C. Edmondson, *The Fearless Organization: Creating Psychological Safety in the Workplace for Learning, Innovation, and Growth* (Hoboken: Wiley, 2018).

62. "Key Findings: Being Black in Corporate America: An Intersectional Exploration." Coqual, 2019, https://coqual.org/wp-content/uploads/2020/09/CoqualBeingBlackinCorporateAmerica090720-1.pdf.

63. Justin Dean et al., "The Real Reason Diversity Is Lacking at the Top," BCG, November 19, 2020, https://www.bcg.com/publications/2020/why-is-diversity-lacking-at-top-of-corporations.

64. Frances Frei and Anne Morriss, *Unleashed: The Unapologetic Leader's Guide to Empowering Everyone Around You* (Boston: Harvard Business Review Press, 2020).

65. David Foster Wallace, *This Is Water: Some Thoughts, Delivered on a Significant Occasion, About Living a Compassionate Life* (London: Little, Brown, 2009).

66. Chloé Valdary, "Activist to Artist," The Theory of Enchantment, https://theoryofenchantmcnt.com/about.

67. Lewis, "Bill Parcells."

68. Ben Horowitz, "Peacetime CEO/Wartime CEO," Future, April 14, 2011, https://future.a16z.com/peacetime-ceo-wartime-ceo/.

69. Stephen M. R. Covey and Rebecca R. Merrill, *The Speed of Trust: The One Thing That Changes Everything* (New York: Free Press, 2006).

70. Ray Dalio, *Principles* (New York: Simon & Schuster, 2017).

71. Such as Sigma Assessment Systems' 9-Box Grid, https://www.sigmaassessmentsystems.com/9-box-grid/.

72. One Stripe engineer recently let me know that she found our initial engineering job ladder disempowering. Her feedback was that the ladder should focus on outcomes rather than a list of skills or inputs. For example, an L3 engineer should be able to scope a project, coordinate among peers, and drive an improvement to the product and the underlying code independently, from start to finish. I wholeheartedly agreed with her criticism. In a company filled with motivated individuals who specialize in problem-solving, avoid being too prescriptive with your expectations, and use your performance guidance to motivate people and teams to accomplish high-impact outcomes, not tick boxes on a checklist. Stripe's job ladders continue to evolve based on comments like the one this engineer shared with me.

73. Culture Amp's "10 Performance Review Biases and How to Avoid Them" is a helpful resource, https://www.cultureamp.com/blog/performance-review-bias.

74. "Pareto Principle," Wikipedia, last modified January 21, 2022, https://en.wikipedia.org/wiki/Pareto_principle.

75. Scott, *Radical Candor*, 32–33.

76. "Five Whys," Wikipedia, last modified February 2, 2022, https://en.wikipedia.org/wiki/Five_whys.

77. Ben Horowitz, *The Hard Thing About Hard Things: Building a Business When There Are No Easy Answers* (New York: Harper Business, 2014), 63.

Bibliography

Bryar, Colin, and Bill Carr. *Working Backwards: Insights, Stories and Secrets from Inside Amazon*. New York: St. Martin's Press, 2021.

Covey, Stephen M. R., and Rebecca R. Merrill. *The Speed of Trust: The One Thing That Changes Everything*. New York: Free Press, 2006.

Dalio, Ray. *Principles*. New York: Simon & Schuster, 2017.

Dunbar, Robin I. M. *How Many Friends Does One Person Need?: Dunbar's Number and Other Evolutionary Quirks*. London: Faber and Faber, 2011.

Foer, Joshua. *Moonwalking with Einstein: The Art and Science of Remembering Everything*. New York: Penguin Books, 2021.

Fitts, Paul Morris, and Michael I. Posner. *Human Performance*. Wesport: Greenwood Press, 1979.

Flora, Carlin. *Friendfluence: The Surprising Ways Friends Make Us Who We Are*. New York: Doubleday, 2013.

Frei, Frances, and Anne Morriss. *Uncommon Service: How to Win by Putting Customers at the Core of Your Business*. Boston: Harvard Business Review Press, 2012.

Frei, Frances, and Anne Morriss. *Unleashed: The Unapologetic Leader's Guide to Empowering Everyone Around You*. Boston: Harvard Business Review Press, 2020.

Gil, Elad. *High Growth Handbook: Scaling Startups from 10 to 10,000 People*. San Francisco: Stripe Press, 2018.

Grove, Andrew S. *High Output Management*. New York: Knopf Doubleday 2015.

Grove, Andrew S. *Only the Paranoid Survive: How to Exploit the Crisis Points that Challenge Every Company and Career*. New York: Currency Doubleday, 1996.

Heifetz, Ronald, Alexander Grashow, and Marty Linsky. *The Practice of Adaptive Leadership: Tools and Tactics for Changing Your Organization and the World*. Boston: Harvard Business Press, 2009.

Hofstede, Geert. *Culture's Consequences: Comparing Values, Behaviors, Institutions and Organizations Across Nations*. New York: SAGE Publications, 2001.

Horowitz, Ben. *The Hard Thing About Hard Things: Building a Business When There Are No Easy Answers*. New York: Harper Business, 2014.

Kanin, Garson. *Remembering Mr. Maugham*. New York: Atheneum, 1966.

Kofman, Fred. *Conscious Business: How to Build Value Through Values*. Louisville: Sounds True, 2014.

Landsberg, Max. *The Tools of Leadership: Vision, Inspiration, Momentum*. London: Profile Books, 2011.

Lencioni, Patrick. *The Five Dysfunctions of a Team: A Leadership Fable*. San Francisco: Jossey-Bass, 2012.

Pink, Daniel H. *Drive: The Surprising Truth About What Motivates Us.* New York: Penguin, 2011.

Schein, Edgar H., and Peter Schein. *Organizational Culture and Leadership.* Hoboken: Wiley, 2017.

Scott, Kim. *Radical Candor: Be a Kick-Ass Boss Without Losing Your Humanity.* New York: St. Martin's Press, 2019.

Sinek, Simon. *The Infinite Game.* London: Portfolio Penguin, 2019.

Slap, Stan. *Bury My Heart at Conference Room B: The Unbeatable Impact of Truly Committed Managers.* New York: Portfolio Penguin, 2010.

Solnit, Rebecca. *Hope in the Dark: Untold Histories, Wild Possibilities.* Chicago: Haymarket Books, 2016.

Walsh, Bill, Steve Jamison, and Craig Walsh. *The Score Takes Care of Itself: My Philosophy of Leadership.* New York: Portfolio Penguin, 2009.

Acknowledgments

My first trip to Ireland for Stripe found me at a small press event outside the Money20/20 conference in Dublin. As I started to introduce myself, one very Irish journalist called out, "You're the lady! You're the lady with the lads!"

It's not enough to simply acknowledge Patrick and John Collison. There's the trust they placed in me when I joined them at Stripe, not to mention their endless curiosity, their incisive and open minds, and their insistent desire to collaborate on company building. So much of what drives Stripe is about access. Access to economic infrastructure, yes, but even more so to knowledge. Patrick pushed for this book to exist because he couldn't find a similar tactical guide that would have helped him as a founder. John has returned from many a dinner with Stripe users saying, "They just wanted to talk about scaling. They wanted to talk to Claire." Then he'd encourage me to document my learnings. I wouldn't call myself an expert on leadership, management, or organizational behavior, but Patrick and John made me realize that my hands-on experience has value. They didn't just tell me that it mattered—they showed me.

Although the idea for this book sits squarely with Patrick and John, it would not exist without Eeke de Milliano or Melanie Rehak. Eeke was a member of the business operations team when I joined Stripe and one of the people whom I've most benefited from managing and mentoring. After she left Stripe and before she joined Retool, where she's now head of product, Eeke took this book on as a project—interviewing me, transcribing our notes and my interviews with leaders, and polishing them into a first draft that propelled me to think that I could actually make this book happen. She truly coauthored that first draft, and I'm grateful for it.

Then, just as Eeke moved on, I met Melanie. Melanie is the author of *Girl Sleuth: Nancy Drew and the Women Who Created Her*, and she made time to become my partner on the subsequent drafts and final version of this book. She helped me identify gaps and restructure the content—yes, this book went through a few reorgs!—and was my primary editor and occasional coauthor when I got stuck. It's not an overstatement to say that Melanie became an important friend, both to me and to this book. We joke that one of the few bright spots of the pandemic was finding each other. Without a doubt we will someday meet in person, and maybe we'll even convince our respective teenage children to join us (fat chance).

I'd also like to thank my early readers, among them a collection of people who've worked closely with me in the past and whom I admire for their management and leadership. Much gratitude to David, Stephen, Tiffany, and Vicki. Also, to a set of folks whom I don't know as well but who spent some of their very precious time as company founders reading the earliest content. Thanks to Adam, Christina, Jason, Mackenzie, and Saji for being a test audience, whether you knew it or not.

The great leaders I interviewed, some of whom I knew but most of whom received a cold outreach or a warm introduction, showed a generosity I will never take for granted. One my most significant sources of energy during this project was the time I spent interviewing Charles, Dan, Dominique, Don, Dongping, Katie, Lisa, Reid, Rick, Sam, and Zanny. Thank you all.

Much of this book is an amalgamation of my learnings from every single person I've worked with, especially those in my immediate teams. I hope you all know who you are. To all of you I want to say that any accomplishments attributed to me wouldn't have occurred without each of you, nor would they have mattered. I'm grateful to have had the chance to work together.

Scaling People is also informed by my professors at the Yale School of Management, especially Sigal Barsade and Sharon Oster—both of whom we tragically lost in 2022—as well as David Cromwell, Jeffrey Sonnenfeld, and Victor Vroom, plus every leadership development training I've attended, the coaches who have followed up with me on said trainings, and the reading I've done on organizational behavior and company building, whether in school or via blog posts or tweets by people I admire. All this is to say I'm sure I haven't credited enough people for the ideas and concepts in the book. I only wish the power of my memory was equal to the power of all that you taught me.

I expect that what people will most appreciate in *Scaling People* is the tactical content: the sidebars, examples, and templates. Countless current and former Stripes—yes, we call employees Stripes, and they come in all stripes—contributed to what I think is the best of the book. Although a few of these folks are named, there are many others who collaborated and commented to create the work you see. Some of the templates are current, while in other cases Stripe has since evolved new practices, as all companies should as they grow. Whether what a person created is still used today or was used at some critical point in Stripe's growth, what's important is that all of that work was so important at the time. It's a reminder that company building is not done by some exogenous force. It's the work of many, many individuals who, brick by brick—or doc by doc, as it were—build the foundation upon which so many others stand. All of those individuals at Stripe, and at similar companies, are often unnamed and unsung and deserve celebration.

This book would also not exist without Angelina, Maeve, and Leslie. All three of these amazing women took a turn at keeping me and our teams organized and sane amid the maelstrom that is high-growth company leadership. They also took on "Cheshire," which was the code name for my book project, and, in the face of countless pressures and my own distraction, they never let it disappear.

I can't say enough about the tremendous dedication of the Stripe Press team and many members of the Stripe communications team. Thanks most of all to Sasha for believing in this project and for shepherding the book, and me, through many phases of development. To Kate and Emma for their encouragement and optimism, and to Rebecca for seeing this project over the finish line with an amazing amount of attention to detail and care for the end product. Speaking of the end product, I'm grateful to the amazingly talented folks on the Stripe Press design team—Josh, Kevin, Travis, and Tyler most of all—and to Tammy for the creative work to help *Scaling People* find its audience.

There are many friends and family members to thank for their encouragement. Among them are the actual writers in my family, my brother Evan and his wife, Adelle, as well as my mother, Mary Joe Hughes. When I was an unruly teenager, my mother once said, in profound exasperation, "You are the book I never wrote." Luckily, our relationship and her ability to publish have thrived since then. Now working on her second book, Mary Joe Hughes is a dear friend and cheerleader to so many people in her life, including me. Although I'm tempted to name many of my friends just because they mean so much to me, I must give special mention to Courtney, who makes my mom's cheerleading pale in comparison. And Courtney brought me to Stella, who epitomizes the ethos of sound mind, sound body—but more the reverse.

My children, Chloe and Miles, keep me both proud and humble. Chloe once watched me give a talk at a Yale School of Management orientation where I was asked the inevitable question about balancing career and family. I pointed out that you need to pick the right partner above all, but that everything, *everything*, is about being aware and intentional about trade-offs. I said that when it comes to my kids' lives, I try very hard to be there when it matters. Many months later, Chloe, aged 12, wrote me a note that read, "I really loved watching you give your speech. I thought it was really informative, but not boring. It was also funny. My favorite story was the one about the mom who told you that you were always at the important stuff, because it was so true. You're always there when it counts." Yes, I kept that note, too.

Jesse is the partner who never questioned that I could write such a book and dutifully reminded me that I was allegedly doing so. His support has been unwavering during every single step of my career and our life together. He is the stable center for me and for our family.

Finally, I want to acknowledge every single founder and operator I've met over the years. No matter the business model, geography, or company stage, builders share a combination of steadfast resolve and openness to learning that creates a common bond. I recently met the COO of a 30-person company who talked about admiring my career from afar. I'm honored, but it's all of you whom *I* admire.

Index

About the Author

Claire Hughes Johnson currently serves as a corporate officer and adviser for Stripe, a global technology company that builds economic infrastructure for the internet. She previously served as Stripe's chief operating officer from 2014 to 2021, helping the company grow from fewer than 200 employees to more than 7,000. At various times she led business operations, sales, marketing, customer support, risk, real estate, and all of the people functions, including recruiting and HR.

Prior to Stripe, Claire spent 10 years at Google leading various business teams, including overseeing aspects of Gmail, Google Apps, and consumer operations, as well as serving as a vice president for AdWords, Google Offers, and Google's self-driving car project. She serves on the boards of the renewable energy company Ameresco, the multi-platform publication *The Atlantic*, the autonomous vehicle company Aurora Innovation, and the customer software company HubSpot. She is also a trustee and the current board president of Milton Academy.

Claire holds a bachelor's degree from Brown University and an MBA from Yale University. She lives outside of Boston with her husband, two children, and two neurotic dachshunds.

Stripe
Press